A Parent's
and Student-Athlete's
Guide to ATHLETIC
SCHOLARSHIPS

Getting Money Without Being Taken for a **(Full)** Ride

DION WHEELER

CONTEMPORARY BOOKS

Library of Congress Cataloging-in-Publication Data

Wheeler, Dion.
    A parent's and student-athlete's guide to athletic scholarships : getting money without being taken for a (full) ride / by Dion Wheeler.
      p.   cm.
    ISBN 0-8092-2443-7
    1. College sports—Scholarships, fellowships, etc.—United States.
2. Universities and colleges—United States—Directories.   I. Title.
GV351.W47   2000
796'.079'73—dc21   99-89752
                                                     CIP

Cover design by Jennifer Locke
Interior design by Precision Graphics

Published by Contemporary Books
A division of The McGraw-Hill Companies
4255 West Touhy Avenue, Lincolnwood (Chicago), Illinois 60712-1975 U.S.A.
Printed in the United States of America
International Standard Book Number: 0-8092-2443-7
4 5 6 7 8 9 10   DSH/DSH   0 1 0 9 8 7 6 5

CONTENTS

PREFACE

This book is designed to help your son or daughter become a successfully recruited high school student-athlete. It is constructed to provide you and your children the tools, devices, and strategies to give your youngster the best opportunity to continue an athletic career in college and to receive financial aid based on his or her athletic ability. For the purposes of this book, the term *financial aid* will include scholarships, grants, low-interest loans, or any combination of the above. In short, *A Parent's and Student-Athlete's Guide to Athletic Scholarships* is intended to give a prospect an advantage over other equally qualified student-athletes who dream of college athletics and a scholarship based on athletic ability.

For the past nine years, I have been and continue coaching at an NCAA member university. One of the primary responsibilities in my position is recruiting high school student-athletes.

I was a coach at three high schools in two midwestern states over a 14-year period. Much of this time was spent working with college recruiters, as well as the parents and prospects of those who were being recruited. I have two grown children who were both successfully recruited: one by a Division I state university and the other by a Division III private college. One was an all-American and the other's career was cut short by injury.

I empathize with the positions that all the parties involved find themselves in and know intimately what each one is going through during all phases of the recruiting process, especially the crucial and fragile negotiating prior to an offer of athletic or other financial aid and a roster position.

I owned a college prospect recruiting service. My clients were academically and athletically qualified student-athletes wanting expert help in becoming professionally exposed to college coaches. I designed and distributed individual profiles of clients to coaches at virtually every college in the country. I contacted and often negotiated with coaches and recruiters on behalf of my clients. I have produced and/or edited nearly 100 videotape profiles for my clients. My recruiting service had a 94 percent success rate for my student-athlete clients who were offered roster positions and significant financial aid packages. Most have completed their college careers and have received their degrees. Many others are still in college, continuing their athletic careers and matriculating toward their degrees.

You are about to use the insider knowledge I accumulated, sometimes painfully, over many years of experience as the parent of recruited student-athletes, a high school coach, and a college coach and recruiter, as well as the owner and operator of a college prospect recruiting service.

Effectively using the information found in this book will require discipline, courage, and persistence (fundamental traits of successful athletes). If you closely follow the suggestions of this guide and are in fact qualified athletically and academically to compete in college both in the classroom and in your sport, you can look forward to being successfully recruited and receiving significant financial aid for athletic ability.

Throughout this book, you will find statements that give you the facts: the *truth*. These truisms are hard-edged, often not what you want to hear. Why? Because they will force you to clearly recognize that a journey toward your athletic and academic dreams will not be convenient or easy. *The truth is that if it were easy everyone would do it!*

Essential Companion Guide

To be able to follow the suggestions in this guide, you must obtain an essential companion guide, the NCAA *Guide for the College-Bound Student-Athlete*. You can get a free copy from your guidance counselor or your athletic director. If a copy is not obtainable, only then call the NCAA and request a copy.

The NCAA number is (800) 638-3731. The Internet Web address is www.ncaa.org. Also let the organization know that a copy is unavailable at your high school.

RECRUITING AND FINANCIAL AID

While there is no intention to provide you with a course on comparative recruiting philosophies of different colleges, some discussion of why colleges recruit is necessary. You need some information about the basics of recruiting philosophy in order to understand why and how the suggestions made in this guide can help you achieve your athletic and academic goals.

Colleges offer athletic financial aid and other types of financial aid for many reasons, some more obvious than others. Many big-time Division I programs offer "full-ride" athletic scholarships for the most obvious reason: money! They sign and enroll blue-chip student-athletes so that they can have powerful, winning programs. Generally, powerful, winning programs in Division I football and basketball generate substantial revenue for their institutions.

Most other colleges want to have winning programs, too; but they have additional reasons for recruiting student-athletes and offering financial aid based on athletic ability. Even though coaches may be from programs that are not so powerful, they, too, must recruit as hard and as smart as they can. Often these coaches must recruit with additional burdens:

- Institution's financial aid award packaging formula
- Recruiting objectives of the coach
- Combined recruiting and enrollment philosophy of the institution for which they coach

Colleges Operate Like Businesses

Most institutions use the awarding of financial aid as a tool to encourage potential students to enroll there. Financial aid is a powerful marketing tool used to remain or become competitive in the bidding war among colleges for worthy students.

Fundamentally, here's how it works: each institution creates a budget (which, by the way, few colleges publish) that is required to deliver the level of educational services desired by the institution's administrators. The institution's administration calculates how much money is required to deliver the desired educational services, while at the same time keeping the college financially solvent. Generally, college administrators fashion tuition policies to accomplish those two interwoven objectives.

The money required to keep the college operating on a sound financial basis comes from a number of different sources. In addition to other sources of funding, the most important source of funds related to the mission of this guide is tuition, fees, room, board, and other expenses charged to students enrolled in any college.

Most institutions calculate non-student funding resources (i.e., endowment, state funds, billable use of facilities, donations) available as income to the institution in the fiscal year. The amount of non-student funding is subtracted from the budget. The remainder of the income required by the budget must be generated from the tuition, fees, and other related charges from the college's student body.

Generally, figures are calculated that define the number of students required to enroll and what enrollment will cost each student. The calculation of the number of students multiplied by the cost per student is structured to allow the institution to remain financially stable. For a number of reasons, some understandable, others not so understandable, many colleges announce inflated costs for attending the college for that year. The final, inflated cost published by the institution is called the *sticker price*—somewhat analogous to a new-car sticker price.

The largest group of colleges that discount the sticker price are private colleges with substantial sticker prices. Less expensive private colleges provide less (financial aid) discounted tuition. Often state colleges and universities have their tuition levels written into law. This type of restriction fundamentally disallows the college from using the flexibility accorded to the director of financial aid to use professional judgment in order to discount the sticker price.

However, state taxes keep state colleges' tuition lower than most private schools and therefore constitute invisible tuition discounts. According to a College Board survey done during the 1996–97 school year, more than 65 percent of private college students were paying less than $12,000 a year in tuition. So don't allow yourself to be intimidated by the sticker prices.

In a January 6, 1997, *U.S. News & World Report* article recommending methods for cutting the costs of college education, it stated, "And 'pretend' is the operative word. There just aren't enough people with enough money. . . ." Nowadays, after acceptance letters go out, a season of what the article describes as "souk like" haggling and price cutting begins. The actual college cost of a private-college education is at least *30 percent less* than the sticker price.

Apparently, the institution's administrators hope to attract as many students who will pay the full tuition (known as "full freight" students) and other costs as possible. Those students will then not only be paying the cost of their education, they also provide additional funds to cushion the cost of enrolling students who administrators decide shouldn't have to pay or can't afford to pay the full tuition and fees. The more "full freight" students a college can enroll, the more financial aid flexibility the institution has, thus enabling it to provide financial aid relief to those "can't pay" and/or "shouldn't have to pay" students.

It would take three chapters to explain the convoluted and tortured reasons why some students, especially the "shouldn't have to pay" category of students, are provided relief from full tuition and fees. Very generally though, discounts are provided because of: *merit* (pretend and real), *academic* potential or achievement, *athletic* ability, *special circumstances* (to be determined by the financial aid director's "professional judgment"), *ethnicity*, *family relationships*, and *need*!

Each college can, and normally does, create a financial aid awarding formula that uses its own unique mix of available federal, state, and its own institutional funds. This formula is calculated to meet the dual and concurrent requirements of delivering the institution's intended level of educational services to its students while maintaining financial solvency.

An important component in receiving sufficient funds necessary to accomplish the two interwoven service and solvency goals is financial aid provided by government programs, both state and federal, to students with proven need according to the department of education's computers. Usually, *need* is determined by applying a formula to the financial information that a student provides on the *Free Application for Federal Student Aid (FAFSA)*. Based on the formula, needy students can be awarded financial aid in the form of grants, work-study payments, and loans.

All states provide financial aid to needy students, usually in addition to federal aid. And if the financial aid director wants you to have a larger discount because the college wants you (in your case for your athletic ability), in his or her *professional judgment* you just might be needier than first evaluated.

The truth is that when colleges talk about money, need can mean many things. It's important to remember that all federal and state *need*-based financial aid is based on the formula used in the FAFSA. Need does not mean poverty status. The FAFSA forms are available after January 1. Get the form from your high school guidance counselor.

Generally, state and federal funds are awarded to the enrolling student, but paid directly to the college. Some colleges offer their own grants or awards to students. Institutional grants are based on a college's own unique formula, called *institutional methodology*, for awarding financial aid. This money comes directly from the institution's own financial aid budget and not from the state or federal government.

A Word About Student Loans

If you are a prospect for a Division II or III program, it is likely that your financial aid package will include a subsidized student loan. There are two different types of subsidized loans: Stafford and Perkins. Whether you agree or not, student loans are considered financial aid. You borrow money that you don't plan to begin repaying for at least four years.

When you borrow money, you have to at least pay interest on the amount you've borrowed. You, the borrower, don't have to pay interest on the money as long as you are a student in good standing. However, the interest is being paid—by the federal government. It is willing to risk paying interest on $2,625 (the freshman year maximum) for the next four years to give you an opportunity to attend college and play your chosen sport. The government also risks non-payment by the student-athlete because it guarantees the loan. When you begin repayment, the government continues to subsidize the interest rate on your loan, keeping it well below market rates.

Obviously, a grant (money given to you that you don't have to repay) is a better deal than a loan. But it is probable that a loan will be part of a financial aid package. Loans are good deals, which is why last year students borrowed over $27 billion in subsidized loans.

Loan Update

Starting in 1998, up to $1,000 of interest can be deducted on student loans that pay for college expenses: tuition, fees, books, room and board. And the good news gets better! The deduction increases to $1,500 in 1999, $2,000 in 2000 and $2,500 in 2001. And still more good news—if you choose to work for a charitable organization or some types of governmental bodies, you could have your loan forgiven with no tax consequences! Who said that Congress isn't interested in helping Americans with the spiraling costs of higher education?

Many student-athletes, competing in all three National Collegiate Athletic Association (NCAA) divisions, are receiving some federal and/or state financial aid. Moreover, many students are awarded institutional financial aid, in addition to federal and state aid. A student-athlete's total financial aid package is often a combination of a number of different financial aid components.

Financial aid to students with proven athletic ability is generally awarded in four ways:

1. "Full ride" athletic scholarships—Division I and II
2. Partial athletic scholarships—Division I and II
3. Combination financial aid awards including partial athletic scholarship—Division I and II
4. Combination financial aid not to include athletic scholarship—Division III

Note: NCAA Rule 15 requires that Division III colleges are obliged to tell you that they do not offer athletic scholarships. (Later in the book you will learn more about this assertion.)

PREPARING FOR COLLEGE AND THE FUTURE

2

The future is where you will spend the rest of your life! Do you wish to be in control of your future so that you get from it what you want and deserve? Is your answer yes? If it is, you must grasp this fact: it is highly unlikely that you will get what you want from the future unless you know what it is that you want. Before reading another word, close this book and consider what kind of future you want for yourself. The more specific you are as to what you want to own, what experiences you would like to enjoy, what accomplishments you wish to achieve, what career and/or occupational goals you have, the more valuable this imaging activity is. As you discover each element, item, or aspect of your desired future, *write it down*! Take the time to do it now!

Notes:

Welcome back. You have completed discovering your future—great! If you were traveling to a destination to which you had never been, you certainly must know you'd be a fool to try to get there without a map or directions, right? Your most important destination is your future.

Is it smart to journey somewhere without a clue about how to get there or how you'll know when you've actually arrived at your destination? You know the answer. *The truth is that if you don't know where you're going, you'll probably end up somewhere else.* If you haven't done the imaging activity, demonstrate some discipline, go back and *do it now!*

You have one more activity to accomplish before we move on to the issue that caused you to purchase this book. You have identified the fundamental elements of a future you wish for yourself. For each element, you must identify in writing what you know you must achieve, acquire, and do, as well as what you are prepared to do, acquire, and achieve to secure the future you have described. *The truth is that there is no worthwhile goal that can be achieved without effort, discipline, and sacrifice.*

Review the elements of your desired future. Now focus on the goal of becoming successfully recruited.

You are about to begin the process of turning this most important goal from a fantasy, a dream, into reality. Complete the following steps:

1. State your exact goal.
    State your goal clearly and precisely. Do this in order to visualize your exact goal.

2. State the date.
    Indicate the future date by which the goal will be accomplished. Use the month and year. Specifically targeting the exact date for the accomplishment of your goal helps you avoid procrastination. (You know, putting things off!)

3. Determine what you will sacrifice.
    What will you personally sacrifice to achieve your goal? *The truth is the more you want, the more you must be willing to sacrifice.* Be sure you understand what it is that must be sacrificed and what you will sacrifice. If what you intend to sacrifice is less than what you know is required to achieve your goal, it is highly unlikely you will achieve it.

4. State your plan of action.

The great Olympic sprinter, Michael Johnson, tells of his father always asking him, "How do you plan to do that?" whenever he told his dad that he wanted to get something or achieve something. He credits the discipline of planning essential for developing his determination to sacrifice as he prepared for achieving Olympic immortality.

Is your plan worth the discipline and sacrifice it takes to commit it to paper? By writing your plan, you have created something tangible upon which your thoughts and ideas are recorded. You can then refer to the plan on a regular basis.

Writing your action plan organizes your goal-oriented direction and activities, makes them more understandable, more real, and therefore more doable. Referring to the plan as you move toward your goal provides you with the information you need to make any mid-course corrections that may be required.

You must constantly reinforce your visual image, your desire, and your belief, or your plan will wither and die. You will experience almost immediate results if you read your plan daily.

This goal-planning strategy works not only for achieving successful recruitment, it works for achieving any important goal you might have.

Sample Goal

1. I want to be on a college swimming team and receive a large financial aid award.
2. I will be successfully recruited by April 2002.
3. I will make successful recruitment my priority. If I must miss time with friends or must choose between other things or activities and pursuing my goal, I will pursue my goal. I will devote 100 percent of the time and effort necessary to achieve my goal.
4. I will:
   - Create an irresistible profile.
   - Send profiles and cover letters to 50 college swimming coaches in NCAA Division II and III.
   - Organize a communications log and file folder holder.
   - Respond immediately to every request for information from any coach until I know I don't want to attend that college.

- Prepare for phone and personal discussions of opportunities with college coaches.
- Visit at least three colleges.
- Gain acceptance into at least two colleges.
- Negotiate with the coach for the best financial aid package at the school of my choice.
- Use *A Parent's and Student-Athlete's Guide to Athletic Scholarships* suggestions and process.

I know it won't be easy, but I can and will use the discipline and make the sacrifices required to accomplish my goal!

The truth is that if anything is easy, everyone will be doing it:

- It's easy to be lazy.
- It's easy to let others take care of you.
- It's easy to whine about how tough life is.
- It's easy to not try something challenging and therefore avoid disappointment.
- It's easy to blame your disappointment on others.
- It's easy to blame others for your lack of accomplishment.
- It's easy to blame circumstances for a lack of achievement.

It's important to remember as you proceed toward the future that the only place that cheese is free is in a mousetrap.

Do the goal-setting activity now!

YOUR EDUCATION AND ATHLETICS

3

Hopefully, acquiring a good education is one of the goals you listed in the previous activity. While the goal of this book is to help you be successfully recruited by a college coach and receive financial aid for your athletic ability, its mission is to help you obtain the best possible education.

The truth is that you will do much more important things in your life than compete in athletic contests. That means the academic portion of your collegiate work is *more* important to your preparation for future success and fulfillment than your athletic activities.

You may be one of the many young athletes who dreams of a career in professional sports. You may have been told by others that nature has wired you up well enough that if you work hard you could in fact become a professional athlete.

While many young American athletes dream of careers in professional tennis, golf, softball, soccer, and track and field, most student-athletes who dream wish to be professional baseball, football, or basketball players.

The truth is:

- On average, fewer than 225 rookies earn a position on a professional football team in any one year.
- More than 250,000 seniors will play high school football in that same year.
- A professional football player can expect to average a pro career of 3.5 years.

- Professional football players sometimes end their careers financially broke, live on average fewer than 60 years, and have many
more personal problems than the general public.

Basketball has equally disturbing statistics:

- More than 150,000 high school seniors play basketball each year.
- About 70 rookies make pro teams each year.

Do the Math!

While basketball players appear to live longer, their personal problems seem to be even greater than football players.

I'm not advocating that young athletes not aspire to be professional athletes; it's a worthy goal. But *the truth is that your future
success will be determined more by what you achieve in the classroom* than in any sport.

Certainly, your athletic preparation and performance are important.
You will not be recruited unless the recruiter-coach feels that you can
contribute to the success of his or her program. So, for the rest of your
high school career, you must seriously and with the greatest amount of
discipline prepare yourself for college competition, both in the classroom and in your sport. Your academic credentials will be just as
important to your successful recruitment as your athletic credentials.

NCAA Bylaw 14.3

The academic requirements to be eligible as a freshman continue to
become tougher. To be eligible at a Division I or II institution, you
must complete, with a 2.0 average, a core (required) curriculum of at
least 13 academic units, or full-year courses, that must present the
following units:

- Four in English
- Two in social studies
- Two in math, including algebra and geometry
- Two in science (at least one lab course, if a lab course is offered
at your high school)
- Two or more in any of the above or in foreign language, com-
puter science, philosophy, or nondoctrinal religion
- One more from among English, math, and natural or physical
science

To be eligible for Division I competition, you must earn a grade point average (GPA) of 2.5 on a 4.0 scale. You must earn at a national testing site on a national testing date a minimum combined score of 820 on the Scholastic Assessment Test (SAT) or a minimum total score of 68 on the subtests of the American College Testing (ACT) Assessment; or earn down to a lower 2.0 GPA on a 4.0 scale and score a higher minimum combined score of 1010 on the SAT or minimum total score of 86 on the subtests on the ACT.

The NCAA has developed a sliding scale in order to accommodate variations in GPA in combination with either the SAT or ACT scores you might achieve. The sliding scale can be located in your NCAA *Guide for the College-Bound Student-Athlete.*

Division II schools have no sliding scale. To be eligible at D-II institutions, you must earn a 2.0 GPA on a 4.0 scale in the core curriculum and either a combined score of 850 on the SAT or a composite of 68 on the ACT. Because Division III schools must claim they don't award financial aid based on athletic ability, they aren't bound by the constraints of Bylaw 14.3. Check all eligibility information against your NCAA *Guide for the College-Bound Student-Athlete.* It is essential to discuss your transcript and core courses with your high school counselor to be certain that you have met all the NCAA Bylaw 14.3 requirements.

Even though the NCAA Clearing House is relatively new, it is demonstrating a tough attitude about student-athletes meeting the core curriculum requirements. This information should make it clear that if you don't take your academic preparation as seriously as your athletic preparation, you are most certainly jeopardizing your dream.

As was mentioned previously, if your dream is to simply tolerate college athletics as a short, unwanted stopover before becoming a professional athlete, you are making a colossal error! Research indicates that high school student-athletes who maintain this dream-poisoning attitude often don't even graduate from high school, much less become either college athletes or professional athletes.

By using the exposure strategies and techniques found in this book, you will generate massive, national exposure or minimal, regional exposure—whichever you want. *The truth is you will have a large, even unfair advantage over the many other qualified prospects who have the same dream as you.*

The advantage will mean nothing if you don't demonstrate to college coaches that you are constantly developing and improving, both academically and athletically. If you delude yourself into thinking that the exposure you receive from using what you learn in this book will be all that is required for you to be successfully recruited, you are in for a huge disappointment.

While exposure is the only strategy that accomplishes successful recruitment, coaches won't recruit student-athletes who they suspect may have a difficult time staying eligible or who fail to demonstrate continuing improvement in their sport.

The best way to avoid problems is to be the finest student and dedicated athlete you know how to be. You must: *study, hustle, think, practice, believe in, and discipline yourself and compete as hard as possible.*

Another valuable exposure technique is enrolling in top-level summer camps in your sport. Be sure college coaches are either running the camp or are teaching at the camp. *Camps provide instant exposure.* By making these commitments, you can reach the dream of playing your sport on the collegiate level and receive financial aid from the college for which you compete.

The truth is that the future is never inherited; it is created! Create your future now! In your future is where you will spend the rest of your life.

Unfortunately, many prospects want the recruiting process to be easy. They are uncomfortable with, some even hostile to, the expectation that they must perform in the classroom, sacrifice during practices, and execute on the field of competition. They don't want to make disciplined choices for themselves that may interfere with having fun and hanging out with friends. They refuse to let their sport or their education interfere with their social life. If this describes you, you must reorder your priorities.

The truth is that you will spend the rest of your life as an adult. Doesn't it make sense to be well prepared for the rest of your life, your future?

If it was easy, everyone would be recruited! It's not! And few are! So be prepared to be tough on yourself. Almost everyone owns a will to win. Everyone has heart during the last 10 meters of the race! Too many athletes call upon their will to win only at the instant of competition. Winners have the *will to prepare* to compete!

If anyone tells you the recruiting process will be easy, they are mistaken. As you will discover, it is fundamentally unfair. You'll also learn that every effort you make will generate substantial benefits.

You now have an opportunity to do what few young people do: take control of your future. If you hold tightly to your dream and follow the suggestions in this guide, you can obtain what you want.

CONSTRUCTING THE PROFILE

4

The most useful exposure tool is the personal profile. A properly created profile can generate tremendous interest in you as a student-athlete. As you will learn, a thoughtful and well-constructed profile will create many benefits for you. A sloppy profile filled with hot air and information that is useless to recruiters or coaches will be promptly discarded.

The guiding principle to building an effective profile is simple to understand and often difficult to do. Be truthful!

You and your parents have a lot at stake concerning your college education. The emotional intensity generated by the considerations of money and pride can (and too often does) cause people to inflate the accomplishments of the prospect. Student-athletes, parents, and high school coaches must overcome the understandable urge to over-sell the potential, achievements, statistics, and coachability of a prospect. However, some selling should take place in your cover letter, which will be covered in the next chapter.

Recruiters and coaches have experienced many snow jobs and are alert for them. Most coaches, if they, in any way, shape, form, or manner, sense that you are trying to deceive them, will check the accuracy of the information you have provided.

The truth is that lying on the profile will most certainly destroy your chances to be successfully recruited.

Your profile should contain the following information:

Name

Address

Phone number (include area code)

High school

Enrollment

Conference

Coach's name

High school phone number

Date of birth

Height/weight

40 time (depending on the sport)

Bench press (depending on the sport)

Squat (depending on the sport)

Vertical jump (depending on the sport)

NCAA Clearing House PIN (to be covered later)

FAFSA/student aid report (SAR)/Expected Family Contribution (EFC) number (to be covered later)

Academic statistics: graduation date, SAT/ACT score(s), intended major or undecided, NCAA core course GPA, class rank, current courses, significant academic honors (honor roll; National Honor Society; school, local, regional, or national awards; avoid Who's Who)

Athletic statistics: all customary statistics (see following list) for the most recent season related to the sport for which you wish to be recruited and other significant athletic awards and honors

Coach's evaluation

Customary Athletic Statistics by Sport

Your profile should include the following statistical information pertaining to your sport:

Basketball:

- Assists
- Field goal percentage—2 point/3 point

- Free throw percentage
- Rebounds
- Steals

Baseball:

- Batting average
- Earned run average (ERA) (pitchers)
- Extra base hits
- Fielding average
- Throwing speed (pitchers)
- Runs batted in (RBIS)
- Stolen bases
- Win/loss record (pitchers)

Cross country:

- Distances and times
- Places—conference, invitational, regional, state

Diving:

- Dives, degree of difficulty, best score
- Places—conference, invitational, regional, state

Football:

- Attempts and completions
- Assists and tackles
- Field goals—attempts and goals, longest, average
- Fumbles recovered
- Interceptions
- Kickoffs—attempts, longest, average
- Punt returns—attempts, longest, average
- Punts—attempts, longest, average
- Receptions—number, total yards, average yards, touchdowns
- Sacks
- Tackles—solo
- Yards rushing—attempts, average, total yards

Golf:

- Average score—9- and 18-hole
- Medalist number
- Places—conference, invitational, regional, state

Gymnastics:

- Event—scores: average and best
- Places—conference, invitational, regional, state

Soccer:

- Assists
- Blocked shots
- Goals

Softball:

- Batting average
- ERA (pitchers)
- Extra base hits
- Fielding average
- Throwing speed (pitchers)
- RBIS
- Stolen bases
- Win/loss record (pitchers)

Swimming:

- Event—distance and best time
- Places—conference, invitational, regional, state

Tennis:

- Position—singles and doubles
- Handedness
- Record
- Places—conference, invitational, regional, state

Track and field:

- Event and best time
- Event and best distance
- Event and best height
- Places—conference, invitational, regional, state

Volleyball:

- Aces—number and average
- Assists
- Blocks
- Digs
- Kills

Wrestling:

- Record and weight
- Escapes
- Near falls—2 point and 3 point
- Reversals
- Pins and falls
- Takedowns
- Places—conference, invitational, regional, state

Speak to your high school coach about your goals and your exposure action plan. Unfortunately, some high school coaches do little or nothing to help their athletes with the recruiting process. While their support isn't essential for you to be successfully recruited, it can be very helpful.

If your coach is willing to make a comment for your profile, be sure it is short and hard-hitting. It should be about attitude, practice habits, coachability, etc. Keep the comments to one short paragraph. The paragraph should be the last item on your profile.

Also, you should affix a picture to the top right-hand corner of the profile. One in uniform is OK, but it should be close enough for your face to be easily seen. A high school graduation or similar picture is the best. A picture often creates a subtle, psychological familiarity between the coach and you. You are no longer just a name or a list of statistics.

Your profile must be clean and neat, grammatically correct, all words spelled correctly, and typed or computer-generated. Ask someone who is qualified (an English teacher is a good choice) to check and edit the components of your profile.

Sending profiles that don't follow these rules greatly reduces your chances to be successfully recruited.

THE COVER LETTER

5

A cover letter, the vehicle you use to sell yourself to coaches, must accompany your profile. As you prepare to create a cover letter, you should consider the following:

You have been building yourself for 17 or more years. Any person who has labored 17 years on a project would present it with great care and immense pride. A smart salesperson selling this project would be certain to present its strengths, value, and special features and benefits in order to obtain the full advantage that the project has earned and deserves.

Selling Yourself

A good sales presentation should show three important factors:

1. *Confidence.* Have confidence in the skills and abilities you have developed in your sport. Present those skills and abilities, demonstrating your confidence that they are equal to the task of positively contributing to the team's success.

2. *Respect.* Demonstrate your respect for coaches and recruiters and the institutions they represent. Few things more quickly destroy a prospect's chances to be offered an athletic tender or a financial aid award letter than a prospect who coaches consider

to be a verbally or mentally undisciplined prospect. These prospects are regarded as not coachable. The consequences are obvious.

3. *Humility.* Be proud of your accomplishments and achievements; you have worked hard and persistently to reach the level of skill you have achieved. While many people don't know the price you have paid, you and the coaches and recruiters know that the level of ability you possess is no accident. Remember! They know! So don't make coaches and recruiters experience you as a braggart, rather cause them to experience you as a coachable athlete who demonstrates humble pride.

Even though your home phone number is included in the profile, you should provide it in the cover letter as well. Tell coaches when the best time is to call either you or your parents. If your high school coach is willing to have coaches call him or her at home, mention the coach's number (include area code), as well as the best contact times.

The same editing, grammar, and spelling rules apply to your cover letter as those recommended for your profile. Keep your cover letter to one page.

If your cover letter appears to be mass-produced it is likely that it will receive less serious attention. The following devices will ensure that the coach knows the letter is written specifically to him or her:

- Use the college name.
- Use the college address.
- Use the team name—found in the College Athletic Directory in the back of the book.
- Use the coach's name.

A sample cover letter follows:

Sample Cover Letter

May 28, 2002

Mr. Clyde Wienersnots
Head Track Coach
Vogelheimer University
6676 West Benchbottom Street
Athletica, NH 04111

Dear Coach Wienersnots:

I would like to introduce myself to you. I am currently a junior sprinter and long jumper at Einars High School. I have spoken to a number of coaches and other qualified people concerning the Laser Track Program. They all say it's a good program.

Last year I qualified for the state meet in each event. While I didn't make it to finals, I have already improved on the performances this season. I am determined to win state meet medals in June. My personal best in the 100 meters is 10.64, achieved at the Spring Valley Invitational. My 200 meters personal best is 22.12, achieved during a home dual meet on May 4, 2000. I jumped 22 feet 9 inches at the Parker Relays. I expect my performances to continue to improve.

I scored a 23 on the ACT, have a 2.9 GPA in the NCAA core courses, a 3.1 cumulative GPA, and rank 61 in a class of 233. I plan to take the ACT again.

I believe my performance and my continued development demonstrate that I could contribute to your program. I would like to continue my track career at Vogelheimer, as well as pursue my educational and career goals.

I have enclosed my profile and a videotape of some of my recent competitions. I've also included next season's meet schedule so that you can evaluate me, if time permits. Please send me whatever materials are required for me to be further considered as a prospect for Laser Track and Field.

My home phone number is (502) 555-2573. I should be available on weekdays after 6:00 P.M. My coach, Bobo Otendoten, invites you to call him at school (502) 555-2200.

I look forward to hearing from you in the near future.

Sincerely,

Horace T. Bunkersnives
Enclosures

THE VIDEOTAPE 6

Team-sport coaches almost universally ask for a videotape. It is a quick, effective way to evaluate your skill, ability, intelligence, and intensity. Even some individual-event coaches (track, wrestling, swimming) request videotape. A well-produced videotape can generate great benefits for you. A poorly produced one does not help you accomplish your objective.

The best videotapes include five sections:

1. Video profile—an opening 30- to 40-second still shot of the top section of your profile. (Don't include the picture.)

2. Personal introduction—you, on camera, introducing yourself, giving a few personal statistics (name, age, high school, height, weight, graduation date, position and event, high school coach's name, ACT/SAT score, NCAA core course GPA, etc.) and a short statement similar to the following. Practice the statement—*out loud*!

   "Hi. I'm Morsly Horsefeather. I play defensive tackle and full-back for Homefield High School. I weigh 207 pounds and am 6 feet 1 inch tall. I graduate in June of 2000. My ACT score is 23, and my core course GPA is 2.6. My coach is Bobo Otendoten. I want to be considered as a prospect for Rumbler football. I hope you will agree that the tape shows that my level of play qualifies me to make a solid contribution to your program. Thanks for your time and consideration."

3. Competition—you competing in games, matches, or meets.

   • Team-Sport Competitors: two of your best games, start to finish. Include only the portions of the game in which you participate. Don't be tempted to cut or splice out poor performances. The coaches will detect it and wonder what it is that you're trying to hide. The consequences of creating suspicion should be obvious. Remember, coaches know that nobody plays a perfect game.
   • Event Competitors: 2 to 10 performances, depending on the event length (500 meter freestyle, 1,600 meter run) and technical requirements (hurdles, diving, parallel bars).

4. Highlights—10 to 15 of your season highlight plays or performances. These plays should demonstrate athletic ability, effort, versatility, and intensity—not just dramatic episodes. (Ten slam dunks or five goals scored against an inferior goalkeeper won't help you.) Highlights always follow game and performance sections.

5. Wrap-up—another 15- to 20-second segment of your profile. Get help in editing, splicing, dubbing, and special effects for your videotape. You may even want to use a professional or experienced videographer. Sometimes, all the help you need may be found in your high school media department. However, if you can't find help or can't afford it, still send the best video you can if a coach requests one.

SENDING CREDENTIALS

7

Where should I send my credentials? Before you can answer this question, you must ask and answer a few preliminary planning questions:

1. Am I willing to attend a college far from home, or am I willing only to attend local or regional institutions?
2. Do I want to attend a small or large, public or private school?
3. At what level of competition do I realistically believe I can successfully compete—Division I, II, III, or National Association of Intercollegiate Athletics (NAIA)?
4. Is my choice of a major course of study more important than where I compete?

The answers to these questions can provide a frame of reference for you as you decide to which coaches you will send your profile. That's right! You should send your profile to a specific coach as opposed to sending it to the head coach of your sport at the college receiving your profile.

Use the list in the last section of the book to locate the information you need. If you use the foregoing suggestions, you should receive an excellent response; that is, unless you send profiles to only Division I programs. Then you can anticipate only limited response.

The truth is that if you are a senior and are currently competing in your sport season and you haven't been recruited by Division I schools, it is highly unlikely that you will be offered an athletic scholarship by a Division I coach.

You may however, be offered an invited "walk-on" status, perhaps with an inducement that if you do well your freshman year, you might get a scholarship the following year.

In most cases, the reality is that walk-on status usually means you will get to *practice* your sport for four years. You will rarely, if ever, compete in an intercollegiate contest.

But if you're satisfied with being a practice opponent (often known as "scout," "gray," or "hamburger squad") for the team's regular players, then go for it. Unless that is, your parents need your help in reducing the financial burden for a college education.

Sometimes a degree from a certain prestigious institution (e.g., Stanford, Notre Dame, Colgate) is sufficient motivation to "walk on." A painfully small percentage of walk-ons do receive scholarships and create for themselves an opportunity to play regularly.

Remember, having a substantial part of your college education paid for is no small accomplishment for you and no minor detail for your parents. If significant financial aid is a priority, you should strongly consider NCAA Division II and III and NAIA colleges.

How Many Colleges Should Receive My Credentials?

The greater your exposure, the greater your chances to be successfully recruited. Depending on your sport and your realistic appraisal of your ability, you should be exposed to a minimum of 30 colleges. A good number is 50. Even if your realistic appraisal causes you to conclude that you are a Division I prospect, you should send many profiles to Division II and III institutions, at least 15 to each level.

"But I want to compete in a glamorous, high-level, or prestigious program," you say. Meaning, of course, Division I. You truly may be qualified to compete in Division I, but, *the truth is that if you are a solid Division I prospect, you probably would have been recruited by Division I programs by now and wouldn't be reading this guide.*

Thirty or more colleges? Absolutely! Here's why. Coaches recruit prospects that fit their coaching philosophy, system, and style of play. Your abilities and objectives may not fit the coach's requirements. Also, coaches just aren't recruiting for every position or event every year, so there may be no need for a prospect in your position or event.

Even if you interest coaches with your credentials and they make contact with you, you may be low on the recruiting depth chart. You may not move up high enough on the chart to be recruited. Conversely, the more depth charts you are on, the better your chances to move up and eventually be recruited.

The truth is that every college you send credentials to won't contact you. If you follow the suggestions in this guide, your credentials will be in the hands of 30 or more coaches in the various divisions. This will produce the results you want and deserve. Very often, this part of the recruiting process is a numbers game. So, you must generate sufficient numbers to overwhelm the odds.

Credential Evaluation

When college coaches and recruiters receive your profile, cover letter, and video, they will look at them in the same way prospective employers look at résumés. Once the profile has been evaluated, coaches then consider their individual needs to determine their interest in you. Factors such as the number of graduating seniors on their roster, the players playing your position and competing in your event, and available financial aid, in addition to the previously mentioned academic and athletic criteria, all contribute to the degree of interest coaches will have in you as a prospect.

Interested Coach

If they are interested, most colleges will send you an introductory letter and/or questionnaire. The questionnaire is an important first step. You must understand, however, that its function is more of an elimination process as compared to the selection process. Remember, the only time you are technically offered a scholarship is by an athletic tender or a financial aid award letter.

The questionnaire sent by colleges serves several purposes; but, very importantly, it is a tool with which coaches determine your interest in the college and their program. An important factor considered by coaches is how quickly you respond to any contact, be it a letter, questionnaire, or phone call. (If you have *any* interest in a college, send the information requested *immediately*!)

Do whatever is requested quickly and accurately. When coaches must choose between student-athletes who are similar academically and athletically, they often choose the ones who have demonstrated discipline and maturity in their communications with the coach.

ORGANIZE, ORGANIZE, ORGANIZE

As you can appreciate, if you are contacted by each college you send your profile to, you will be receiving a lot of information. If you choose not to organize this information, you will eventually confuse programs and coaches and/or lose important information from phone calls, letters, or documents. Demonstrate some discipline. Get organized.

You must have a filing system for each college to which you send information. Manila file folders are a good beginning. On the tab, place the name of the college. On the left inside cover, place the address, coach(es) name(s), and phone number(s). A detailed review of the initial contact between you and the coach or recruiter is helpful. All contacts should be recorded on a communications log.

Record each contact from the institution: letter, document, visit (college coach at your high school, your college visit[s], or college coach comes to your home), or phone call. The recording should include date, time, coach or recruiter's name, and the content of the conversation and any planned next step in the process. Be prepared to listen and take great notes. Keep your logs clipped in chronological order.

The following communications log can be photocopied.

Communications Log

1. Date and time _____

2. Type of contact—letter, personal note, questionnaire, phone call, face-to-face visit; home, high school, college

   _____

3. Initiated by whom? _____

   _____

4. Recruiter or coach and college _____

   _____

5. Content of discussion _____

   _____

   _____

   _____

   _____

   _____

   _____

   _____

   _____

6. Next step: by coach/by me

   _____

   _____

   _____

   _____

Organizing your recruiting communications intelligently and efficiently is crucial to your success. This opportunity could be valued up to $100,000 over four or five years. The earning power of a college graduate as compared to a person with a high school education has recently been pegged at $1,700,000 over a lifetime.

The truth is that most student-athletes do not appreciate the value of their college education.

CRITICAL DOCUMENTS

Many shattered dreams lie strewn on the road to successful recruitment because prospects decide to *wait* until tomorrow to act on requests to send documents. *The truth is that coaches are looking for prospects with inner motivation, mature responsibility, and who are self-starters.*

You can anticipate a request for a number of documents to be sent to the:

- coach or recruiter
- institution's admissions department
- institution's financial aid department
- NCAA

The documents requested are normally required for admittance to the college, required by the financial aid office to begin awarding financial aid, or required to certify your eligibility to practice and/or participate in NCAA competition.

Document List

Any additional documents requested by the coach, admissions office, financial aid office, or the NCAA must be responded to *immediately*. The following list may not include all the documents required by the institutions you are considering.

Application Form

No financial aid will be awarded to you unless this form is completed and received by the admissions office. Financial aid offices are forbidden to generate awards until the prospect has been accepted by the admissions department. It is likely that the admissions form will request that you send an application fee. Call coaches and tell them that you *can't handle* the admission fee right now. Ask if they can help you get the fee deferred until you enroll. In many cases, coaches can help. Often they will suggest you send the application directly to them. Then they will deliver the form to the admissions office. As you will appreciate, if you follow the suggestions of this guide and seek acceptance at a number of colleges, sending a check of $15 to $75 along with each application can become quite expensive. Your goal should be to pay an application fee *only* to the college in which you ultimately enroll. If you are fortunate enough to receive a scholarship, often the application fee is waived.

Free Application for Federal Student Aid (FAFSA)

The FAFSA form can be found in your high school guidance office. Ask your counselor for it. When you receive it, immediately complete it with the help of your parent(s) or guardian. Be certain to complete all sections of the form. If it is incomplete, you will be asked to complete it by the U.S. Department of Education and the enrolling college before any financial aid other than an athletic scholarship can be awarded to you. Mail it in the enclosed envelope.

Some parents don't complete the FAFSA. They may believe they will not qualify for any type of aid because they guess their income is too high. Others may determine that they won't divulge the personal and tax return information requested on the FAFSA, which is similar to that on your tax return.

It is a mistake not to complete and mail the FAFSA. Unlike the IRS, which wants to take your money, colleges use the information on the FAFSA to give you money! *The truth is that many families with incomes in the six-figure range are receiving need-based financial aid.*

Factors other than income influence eligibility for federal or state financial aid. State financial aid is almost always calculated based on the formula the department of education's computers use to evaluate the information provided on the FAFSA. State financial aid standards are often less harsh than federal financial aid standards. Your financial aid forms are sent to a central processing unit in Illinois. Computers crunch the data and determine how much you can afford to pay. Personal, family, financial, or employment issues are not part of the calculation executed by the computer program. Many families miss opportunities to reduce the financial burden of a college education because they choose not to complete and mail the FAFSA.

Many colleges award institutional grants (discounts from the announced tuition, room and board [*sticker price*]) and other financial aid based on the information generated by the FAFSA. When information from the FAFSA is used as a baseline for awarding financial aid, this formula is called *federal methodology*. Even though this aid is from the college's financial aid budget, it was calculated with federal methodology. And often a college's need-based financial aid awarding standards are less rigid than either state or federal standards. When an institution uses its own unique formula for determining student need and consequently which students will receive tuition discounts, this is called *institutional methodology*.

If there is no baseline data like that generated from the FAFSA, often the conclusion drawn is that you should be a "full freight" student.

College Scholarship Service (CSS) Profile

About 800 colleges require incoming freshmen to complete a form called the CSS Profile. The CSS Profile questions provide the institution information that the FAFSA doesn't ask. These colleges use the information on the CSS Profile to help the director of financial aid determine how much of a discount from the sticker price you should receive. Like all other requests for documents from a college, complete it and send it immediately.

Student Aid Report (SAR)

This report is generated by the department of education's computers. The SAR is based on the information you and your parents include on the FAFSA. Your parent(s) or guardian will receive a copy of this report. A number of the colleges you are interested in will receive a copy of the SAR. You will have directed, by naming them in section G of the FAFSA, which colleges will receive a copy of the SAR on the FAFSA form completed by you and your parent(s).

When you receive your SAR (sometimes called Blue Forms, even though the colors of forms sometimes aren't blue), examine it: there may be mistakes on it that could cost you plenty. Also, call immediately to request another *free* copy of the SAR, (319) 337-5665.

You will discover a number called the *expected family contribution* (EFC). The college's financial aid office will calculate (federal methodology) the federal and state financial aid available to you from the EFC number and other information of the SAR. Remember, the EFC number should be a line item on your profile.

After receiving the SAR:

- Keep your copy in a place where it will remain neat and clean. You may have to make a number of photocopies of the SAR.
- Take a SAR with you on each visit you make to a college, even if you think the college has received a copy.
- Give a copy of your SAR to any coach, recruiter, or admissions counselor who visits you at school or at your home.

High School Transcript

The process of sending your transcript to a college is the responsibility of your high school guidance counselor. Even if you haven't finished high school, you should request that transcripts be sent to the admissions department of colleges that interest you. Final transcripts will be sent upon your graduation. Your GPA in the core course requirements, as identified by the NCAA and presented later in this guide, plays an important role in your eligibility to practice and compete.

Many types of financial aid are awarded based on your high school GPA. Does it make sense to be a good high school student and focus on achieving as high a GPA as possible? Remember, your GPA should be a line item on your profile.

ACT/SAT Scores

To be NCAA eligible, you must sit for the ACT/SAT on one or more of the *national testing dates*. Your counselor can give you the dates and locations of these tests. You can take the ACT/SAT as often as you want (on a national testing date) to achieve a score that will help you be NCAA eligible. (Refer to the academic eligibility section of your *NCAA Guide for the College-Bound Student-Athlete*.) Remember, your ACT/SAT scores should be a line item on your profile.

Again, ACT/SAT scores are sent to the college admissions department by your high school counselor. Like your GPA, your ACT/SAT scores play an important role in your eligibility to practice and compete. (Refer to the academic eligibility section of your *NCAA Guide for the College-Bound Student-Athlete.*) Also, like your GPA, many financial aid awards are based on the scores of these tests. Some colleges will allow you to retake the ACT or SAT test on the college campus to give you an opportunity to improve your score in order to increase your academic financial aid award. Ask the college admissions office if they offer this opportunity.

Remember, sitting for an ACT/SAT test on the college campus can't change an ACT/SAT score for the purposes of NCAA eligibility because it isn't given at a national testing date location. The ACT/SAT scores that the NCAA recognizes for the purpose of determining your eligibility are those scores earned on the *national testing dates only!*

Financial Aid Estimator (FAE)

Many Division II and III colleges use an FAE to provide preliminary information from which they can estimate the amount of financial aid you might need to be able to attend that institution. A coach, recruiter, or admissions counselor may send you an FAE. This document helps the coach make preliminary recruiting decisions based on the results of yours and other prospects' FAEs.

As you can appreciate, if the coach receives a requested FAE from a prospect who has similar academic and athletic qualifications as you and doesn't receive your FAE, guess who's going to be offered a scholarship.

Institutional Financial Aid Application Form

An institution may ask you to complete a financial aid application form even though you also have completed a FAFSA and a CSS Profile. Private schools often have financial aid available for special circumstances. Examples are: alumni sponsored scholarships, major field of study scholarships (e.g., nursing, engineering, elementary education), or scholarships from a religious institution that awards members of its faith.

NCAA Clearing House Form

This form, *Making Sure You Are Eligible to Participate in College Sports*, must be completed and sent to the NCAA with an $18 registration fee. The Clearing House certifies your eligibility to participate in practices and competition. You're not eligible in Division I or II without Clearing House certification, even if you meet the eligibility standards.

Coaches rarely offer any kind of financial aid to students who haven't been certified eligible by the NCAA Clearing House. You can get the form free from your guidance counselor, athletic director, or coach. If it's not available, call the NCAA Clearing House at (319) 337-1492 or (800) 638-3731, or www.ncaa.org for a free form.

You and the college coach will receive notice of your eligibility certification from the NCAA. You will be given a personal identification number (PIN). The PIN should be listed as a line item on your profile. (Refer to the profile model page.) On the NCAA Clearing House form, you will be asked which colleges you wish to be notified. The NCAA will notify those colleges you identify of your eligibility status.

10

COMMUNICATIONS ACTIVITIES

If college coaches or recruiters that you are interested in call, you should immediately write a short letter thanking them for "your interest in me as a recruit for your program." Tell them of your interest in both the college and the athletic program. If you have additional information (i.e., awards won, recent performances) about yourself you want to share, do it at this time. This is also a good time to include your upcoming competition schedule.

As indicated previously, you may receive more than one phone call from the same person or other people related to a program. *This is no accident!* Additional calls are good signals, but you haven't been recruited yet! You must continue to do your part. After a few contacts by a coach or recruiter, you will detect a pattern of questions that indicates an increasing level of interest and/or concerns. For example, asking:

- for a videotape of your last game or performance
- for your coach's home phone number
- if you plan to retake the ACT/SAT
- if you have applied for admission
- if you have sent transcripts and ACT/SAT scores to admissions
- about recent injury
- if you'd be willing to change playing positions in college
- you to send an SAR
- you to visit the institution

Try to anticipate questions. Write down what you feel are the kind of answers you want to give and practice them—out loud. As the recruiting season progresses, you'll discover that the recruiter's questions will also change, asking:

- if you would be willing to walk on
- if you get a partial scholarship will you commit to the program
- how much financial aid it will take for you to enroll

Some coaches stop calling or returning your calls. Others may send you handwritten notes (a positive sign). By following the suggestions in Chapter 8 about organization, you will be prepared for the changes and be ready to answer critical questions.

Communications Initiated by You

Whenever you are cited in the newspaper or other media, send another note to the coach (Coach, I thought you might be interested in the enclosed article, etc.), and include a photocopy of the article that presents you favorably.

You may telephone a college coach at your expense as often as you wish. You may visit a college campus (unofficial visit) as often as you wish. However, you must avoid creating the impression that you can be recruited with little or no financial aid or that you will accept loan-type aid only or that the financial aid office can "gap" you (offer you less financial aid than your certified need as indicated by the EFC number on the SAR). *You should be paying a total no more than the* EFC *number amount.*

THE VISIT

11

I f coaches are really serious about recruiting you, they will ask you to visit the campus. Always ask if they will be "handling" (not paying) the expenses for the visit. Remember, there are certain restrictions concerning *official*, that is to say, paid visits. Refer to your NCAA *Guide for the College-Bound Student-Athlete*. Remember, you can make as many unofficial visits to a campus as you wish, which means you handle your expenses. You may take one official visit per school and five total official visits.

Be sure you visit only colleges in which you are interested. It's unfair to waste other people's time; even more importantly, don't waste your own time. An official visit *must always* be followed by a sincere thank-you note, no matter if you're recruited by that college or not. After all, the program has invested time and financial and personnel resources in you.

On your visit, you must try to speak with faculty and staff in many different departments of the college, in particular:

- Admissions
- Financial aid
- Housing
- Athletics
- Department head of your intended major field of study

Be certain to examine all the facilities that will directly impact your life on that campus:

- Dorms
- Athletic facilities
- Dining facilities
- Laboratories
- Classrooms
- Student union
- Library

Get a feel for the campus ambiance, as well.

Recruiting Can Be Unfair!

While being asked to visit is a positive step toward being successfully recruited, a cold dousing of reality is needed here. As you now know, coaches are almost surely recruiting more than one prospect for any one position. You should be aware that it is highly unlikely that coaches will successfully recruit their first-choice prospect for a position or event. To protect themselves, most coaches have backup recruit lists, usually referred to as depth charts.

The problem for the prospect is that you may be a backup recruit, low on the depth chart, and never know it. You may well experience the same kind of reception and may be told the same things as the recruit who is number one on the coach's depth chart. This is known as being *strung along*.

At a recent Ultimate Recruiting Seminar designed for college coaches and recruiters, the following suggestion was part of the seminar content: "For every scholarship you have, you should be recruiting four prospective student-athletes." In other words, effective recruiting requires that recruiters and coaches string along three prospects.

That's why it is so important for you to *never, never* place your college future with one coach or college! That's why you need some options available to you until you are asked to commit to a college. Coaches will be shopping for prospects and keeping their options open; you must shop for coaches and programs keeping your options open, too. Remember, the recruiting process is often a numbers game: you must play the game, as well! Overwhelm the odds with massive numbers. College coaches commonly have 500 or more potential recruits on their initial mailing lists.

Tips

The wise prospect seeks answers to many important questions. While the coach or recruiter of the college will be your primary source for answers, be aware that other sources are also available. These include: other athletes (usually met while visiting the campus), college-produced introductory reading material, catalogs, and observations made on the campus. Arm yourself with this book by keeping it conveniently located at your telephone. Keep it with you (but out of sight) at all times when visiting a campus.

A word of caution: be careful not to appear that you are investigating the coaches. However, be sure to get the answers as they can provide you with the information from which you can make an informed and good decision. While coaches may string you along, it is rare that coaches will not be truthful when asked a direct question.

Questions

Before you commit to a coach or college, it is important that you get satisfactory answers to each of the following questions.

Athletic

How much time is spent in practice?

When does the season begin? End?

Are there additional training periods?

What are practice hours?

What are my off-season responsibilities?

Can I compete in other sports?

What's the team's past record?

What conference and division does the team compete in?

How many games or meets are there per season?

How often does the team travel?

Can he or she describe the athletic facilities? (Observe during your visit.)

What is the coach's philosophy?

What are your chances of regularly competing and when?

What position/event/class are you being considered for?

How many freshmen at your position are being recruited?

What position am I on the recruiting depth chart?

Will I be redshirted?

What are the housing arrangements for athletes?

Have you seen me play or compete?

Why do you think my skills fit into your program?

Academic

Are my career goals compatible with the college's majors and programs?

Am I allowed time to make up classes and tests missed because of the competition schedule?

Am I qualified to meet admission standards?

Are tutors provided for athletes?

What percent of freshmen graduate? Graduate with their class?

What is the college's policy toward student-athletes during summer session?

Will I have an academic adviser?

Will the coaches provide any guidance if I have academic problems?

How many hours of studying per day are average for my major?

Do professors teach?

Legal

Do I receive a written contract or tender?

If I get injured or become sick, will I lose my financial aid?

What medical expenses are covered by the college?

How many credits are required for me to be eligible to compete? Keep my financial aid?

What is the status of the college's relationship with the NCAA?

Financial

Is there academic or need-based financial aid available?

What is the amount of financial aid being offered?

For how many years is it being offered?

What criteria is used to determine renewal of aid?

What portion of the total (yearly/semester) cost is covered by the financial aid I will receive?

What expenses does the financial aid cover (e.g., tuition, room, board, books, special assessments, supplies)?

What sources and types of financial aid will be included in the total financial aid package, e.g., state, Pell, FSEOG (Federal Supplemental Education Opportunity Grant), institutional, special, awards, grants, loans?

Am I eligible for additional financial aid now? In future years?

If I need five years to graduate, will I continue to receive the same amount of financial aid as the other four years?

Evaluate

After your visit, you should review the visit by asking yourself the following questions:

Did the coach or recruiter say negative things about other schools in an attempt to persuade me to attend his or her college?

Were the coaches interested in my academic success?

What was the attitude of the players toward their coaches?

Does the institution satisfy my requirements?

Would I attend this college if I weren't an athlete?

Can I play here, or will I be a member of the gray (practice) squad?

12

UNDERSTANDING THE RECRUITING PROCESS

The recruiting process is fundamentally unfair. It is unfair for many reasons, but the primary ones are money and the school's ability to compete and win. Its unfairness impacts college coaches, high school coaches, prospects, and their families.

College coaches have to win to keep their jobs. No matter how this fact is shaded, colored, coated, nuanced, or denied, it is fundamental. It is the wellspring of the unfairness in the recruiting process. With few exceptions, college coaches coach because they love it. Very few coaches make the big money of the highly visible basketball and football coaches you hear about. Many coaches are hired as part-timers.

No matter what sport they coach, when their team competes against another team, *the score of the contest is kept. Winners and losers are easily identified.* If the coach's team loses too often, the coach will be dismissed, which usually means he or she will no longer have the opportunity to enjoy the experience of coaching. He or she will no longer get paid for doing what he or she loves to do. It is unlikely that this individual will find another coaching position.

The pressure on coaches to win is as intense today as it has ever been in college athletics. That pressure may be disguised better than in the past as the NCAA trumpets its laudable attempts to raise the academic standards for college prospects. Recently, the NCAA *News* has been running small strips declaring that "Winning Isn't Everything!" Right! Money is!

The NCAA is demanding academic integrity from the nation's colleges along with raised academic entrance standards in an effort to coerce them to pay greater attention to their student-athletes' educations. To its credit, the NCAA has successfully reduced the influence of supporters of athletic programs from participating in the recruiting process. Most administrators would agree, however, that they are under some pressure from the supporters of athletic interests (usually alumni and local businesses that benefit from game attendance) to develop and maintain winning programs. While many administrators resist overt pressure from boosters, it's difficult to resist the influence of donations (money) to institutional programs by boosters. When programs don't meet the expectation of boosters, something gives: usually the coach's job. Or the amount of donations. Guess which one gives first.

When coaches are dismissed, it is painful; it hurts! To avoid losing their jobs, they try to find ways to ensure that they win. Coaches who win usually don't get dismissed. One of the best ways to ensure a winning program is to have athletes on their team who are better than the athletes on opposing teams.

How do coaches get these better athletes? They recruit them! They know that other coaches are recruiting for the best athletes, too. They know that competing coaches are recruiting for their financial and professional lives. They know that the competition is intense! If they are to be successful in the recruiting battle, they must be prepared to do everything possible to recruit the best athletes they can find.

The truth is that a significant minority of college coaches violate the NCAA recruiting rules and regulations in order to stay competitive: in order keep their jobs. We hear of violations primarily in the highly visible Division I revenue-producing sports, but coaches in other sports and other divisions stretch the limits of the NCAA rules, regulations and bylaws, as well. Some may say the foregoing is an exaggeration. The truth is it's not.

Because recruiting is so intense, many people get hurt along the way. It is unlikely that any coach intentionally hurts a prospect, yet because of the mechanics of the recruiting process and the high stakes involved, prospects and their families get hurt.

As an example, if a coach follows the recommendation of the Ultimate Recruiting Seminar, three of four prospects are being strung along. I confess! This past recruiting year (1998–99), I strung along four athletes while my number-one- *(must have)* choice considered which of the many offers she would accept. She accepted our program's offer late into the recruiting season. Then I called the others to tell them the bad news.

Recruiting Agony

Despite your best efforts, it is likely that you will experience some pain. It goes with the territory. This book can help you avoid getting hurt. It also provides you with the understanding and the tools to be successfully recruited by a college, a program, and a coach that is best for you.

First, by following *A Parent's and Student-Athlete's Guide to Athletic Scholarships*, you will be found!! Why? Because every college coach you send your credentials to will know *who* you are, *where* you are, *what* you can do, and *what they can expect* from you when you begin competing in college. Second, few colleges have the budgets or the scouts to be able to locate all the prospects who would be qualified to compete in their program. It's this simple! College coaches cannot possibly know where all potential prospects for their program are.

The number of qualified prospects coaches learn about depends on the size of the college, the program, interested alumni, number of assistants, and the recruiting budget. Coaches of small- and medium-sized colleges and programs want to locate qualified prospects just as desperately as the coaches in the larger institutions. Unfortunately, smaller schools have smaller budgets and less personnel.

They need help! You need help! By sending your credentials, you provide them with the help they need *and*, you help yourself!

Other than the largest Division I programs, few programs have a sufficient level of funding so that they can make full-ride athletic financial aid offers to the prospects they are recruiting. This is especially true for Division II colleges. (The assertions by Division III colleges concerning no athletic scholarships or financial aid based on athletic ability at Division III colleges requires a separate section, which will follow.)

Consequently, these restrictions cause the coach to be careful about who will be offered scholarships or financial aid awards. The cheaper coaches can recruit good prospects, the more funds available to recruit additional prospects. This means coaches increase their chances to have better athletes than their competition and ultimately, they can produce a winning program and keep their jobs!

13

WHY PROSPECTS AND FAMILIES GET HURT

Prospects don't understand their value in the recruiting market-place. They don't know how to interpret the meaning (both the obvious and hidden) of all the calls, letters, promises, and other communications from college recruiters. They don't know when they are being strung along or when they are being told the truth.

You can be intensely recruited with letters, personal notes, and phone calls for months and suddenly hear nothing because you were being strung along.

Protect Yourself

1. Until you have an offer in writing (award letter, contract, or tender) and until you make a commitment to a coach, you must *always* create the impression that you are considering other colleges' offers. In fact, you should always have at least one backup in case of an unpleasant surprise.

   Why? Sometimes, if a coach believes that you are being recruited by other coaches and you are at or near the top of his or her recruiting depth chart, the coach (or some other official at the college) may offer additional incentives (financial aid) for you to choose his or her program.

   If coaches believe you have no options, often they will try to recruit you for as little as possible. In that way, they can use the

unused resources that you didn't receive for some other recruit
who is bargaining more effectively than you.

2. Remember, ask coaches if they are recruiting other athletes for
   the same position. Why? This question signals the coaches that
   you have a grasp of a fact basic to recruiting: that most coaches
   are recruiting (and usually saying the same things to) more
   than one prospect. (Someone's being strung along here! Is it
   you?)

   If coaches really want you, they will know that you
   understand the foregoing facts and may be eager to make you
   an offer that is satisfactory to you.

3. Gain admittance to several colleges that you have visited and
   you feel have the right ingredients for you to be a successful
   student-athlete.

   Why? If you are admitted to a number of institutions that
   are recruiting you, you have two important benefits.

   - The coach can begin working early with other departments
     (i.e., admissions, financial aid, athletic, housing) in order to
     ensure you receive all the financial aid and other benefits to
     which you are entitled.
   - You can honestly tell the coach that you have been accepted
     at other colleges that are recruiting you.

Sleazy Recruiting Tactics

While most college coaches wish to be a positive influence on the student-athletes they coach and are fundamentally honest, a few of them
have little interest in you beyond you helping them have a winning
program and keeping their jobs. These are harsh comments about
some of my colleagues in the coaching ranks; but, it is sadly the truth.
Be alert for them.

The following points can help you recognize sleazy recruiting tac-
tics and, therefore, coaches to avoid:

1. The coach has a "booster" contact you or tells you that a
   "fan" will contact you about the program. The NCAA is making
   a concerted effort to eliminate from the recruiting process
   those persons who have "an interest" in the program. Even if
   you are offered nothing by them, which is highly unlikely, you

are in violation of the NCAA guidelines. The NCAA severely punishes those who violate the booster rules. Even if you just talk to a booster, you jeopardize your future with the NCAA. Refer to the NCAA *Guide for College-Bound Student-Athletes.*

2. Your best friend can walk on. These coaches have no interest in you or your friend. They are manipulating you by dangling a false hope in front of your friend.

3. Coaches may promise you a starting position your freshman year. Or guarantee that you will be an all-American, national champion, or have a professional career in sports primarily because you compete for them. (Remember, there is a difference between a guarantee and a statement about your potential.)

4. Coaches may "trash, slam, or bum rap" other colleges, programs, or coaches. If the coaches can't persuade you to join their program because of its qualities and their coaching ability, you'd be a fool to enroll.

5. Some coaches may tell you that the academic program in the field of study you plan to pursue is the "best in the nation." Use your high school counselor or a number of publications to check the accuracy of that statement.

6. Some coaches may promise you easy courses, easy professors, and no academic pressure. These coaches have little concern about your future beyond helping their program. By making your academic requirements easy, the coach has done you no favor. After all, you are going to do more important things in your life than compete in athletic contests.

An Important Word of Caution

If you or your parents accept money or any kind of gift from a school representative, you will be declared ineligible to compete in the NCAA.

14

AWARDING OF ATHLETIC FINANCIAL AID

Virtually all colleges that sponsor a sport that competes on the intercollegiate level want that sport program to be successful. To enjoy the benefits of a winning program, some level of recruiting is required. The level, intensity, directness, and operation of collegiate recruiting by any particular school are affected by a number of factors.

As you have learned, NCAA Division I and II offer designated athletic scholarships of some monetary value applied toward the cost of the tuition and/or fees of the institution awarding the financial aid. Division I often offers full rides, although they sometimes split some athletic scholarships and offer partial rides. Division II programs offer full rides much less often than does Division I. They split up their athletic scholarships more often than Division I. As you now know, NCAA rules restrict the number of athletic scholarships in each sport for both Division I and II. And Division II is allowed fewer athletic scholarships in nearly every sport than Division I.

When you are being recruited by a Division I or II college, the recruiters and coaches will discuss financial aid in terms of athletic scholarships. Usually Division II coaches will discuss additional financial aid in other terms, as well, such as need, academics, special talent, minority, merit, leadership, institutional grants, loans (e.g., Stafford, Perkins, PLUS).

Division II institutions more often than Division I schools combine one of the foregoing types of financial aid with an athletic scholarship in order to increase the total amount of financial aid to a prospect. The greater the nonathletic financial aid, the greater the chance of recruiting another prospect. However, unlike Division III institutions, Division I and II colleges usually don't negotiate an increase in the nonathletic categories of financial aid. The category left open for negotiations is usually the athletic award.

As you discuss and negotiate financial aid, paying close attention to your financial aid arithmetic, be sure you are combining all types of financial aid in order to calculate the total financial aid package. When you and the coach agree on the athletic scholarship, he or she and the athletic director will notify the college financial aid office of the amount offered. This is accomplished by sending an initial *athletic tender* to the financial aid office.

The financial aid office then combines the athletic scholarship with the financial aid you will be awarded in the other categories. You will receive two documents indicating the awarding of financial aid:

1. *Award Letter*. This document (see following sample) itemizes each financial aid award in every category (e.g., athletic, academic, work study, loan, institutional grant) you will receive if you choose to attend that college. You will be asked to confirm your decision to attend by accepting the award letter or signing a letter of intent or both.

Sample Financial Aid Award Letter

Bunkersnives University
Financial Aid Award

April 30, 2001

Bunkersnives University is pleased to offer you financial aid assistance for the academic year 2001–2002. This award becomes binding and official only when this form is completed and returned to the Financial Aid Office. Please carefully examine the accompanying information prepared for recipients of financial assistance prior to accepting any or all of this financial aid award.

Morsly Horsefeather
1 Prospect Street
Athletica, PA 12321

Accept/Decline (circle one)

Bunkersnives University Grant	$6,500	ACCEPT	DECLINE
Founders Grant	$1,000	ACCEPT	DECLINE
Leadership Award	$ 500	ACCEPT	DECLINE
Recognition Award	$ 800	ACCEPT	DECLINE
Alumni Grant	$ 500	ACCEPT	DECLINE
Diversity Grant	$1,000	ACCEPT	DECLINE
Pell Grant	$2,000	ACCEPT	DECLINE
Work Study (Potential Earnings)	$2,400	ACCEPT	DECLINE
Federal Stafford Student Loan	$2,625	MUST APPLY	

The white copy of this form must be signed and returned to the Financial Aid Office by May 15, 2001. After this date, Bunkersnives University cannot guarantee the receipt of any of the funds offered in this award. Deadline extensions may be granted upon written request until June 1. For additional information, contact your financial aid officer.

Statement of Purpose and Responsibility

I declare that I will use any funds I receive under the Pell Grant, FSEOG, College Work Study, Stafford Student Loan, Perkins Loan, PLUS Loan, or any other funds, awards, or loans administered by the University's Financial Aid Office only for expenses connected with attendance at Bunkersnives University. I understand that I am responsible for repayment of any portion of payments made to me that cannot be used to meet educational expenses connected to attendance at Bunkersnives University.

No Title IV financial aid will be awarded unless the following statement is completed.

I certify that I am not required to register with the Selective Service, because (check one)

____ I am a female.

____ I am in the armed services on active duty (National Guard members are not considered to be on active duty).

____ I have not reached my 18th birthday.

____ I was born before 1960.

____ I am a permanent resident of the Trust Territory of the Pacific Islands or Northern Mariana Islands.

____ I am registered with the Selective Service.

I accept the above captioned awards and authorize Bunkersnives University to directly credit my fee account with applicable state, federal, university, and/or outside agency funds in accordance with current regulations. I declare that I am not in default on any educational loan and owe no refund on any grant funds previously received for the purpose of attending Bunkersnives University. I certify that if I receive a Pell Grant, as a condition of acceptance of said Grant, I will not engage in unlawful manufacture, distribution, dispensation, possession, or use of a controlled substance during the period during which the Pell Grant is in effect.

I understand that I must maintain full-time enrollment (12 or more hours) each semester to receive any and all Bunkersnives University Grants. I will reference the Undergraduate Bulletin concerning refund policies of all financial aid received should I withdraw or reduce my hours to less than 12.

Signature _____ Date _____

List any other financial aid, scholarships, or loans you are receiving not listed on this award letter.

_____

_____

_____

2. *Athletic Tender.* This document (see following sample) has two purposes:
   - To describe the type and amount of athletic financial aid (*and only the amount of athletic financial aid*) you will receive if you choose to attend that college.
   - To secure your attendance at the institution and to bar you from competing at any other NCAA institution.

Sample Athletic Tender of Financial Aid

Flamingo State University
Athletic Tender for Financial Aid

Name_____   Date_____

Street_____   __ Initial __ Renewal

City, State, Zip   _____ Academic Year

_____

_____

Sport_____   _____ Enrollment Date

This tender represents all commitments to you by Flamingo State University and is subject to:

1. Fulfillment of admission requirements of the University
2. Fulfillment of NCAA academic eligibility requirements
3. Fulfillment of financial aid requirements as codified by the NCAA and Flamingo State University

This tender covers the following as checked:

_____ Full Grant: Includes tuition and all fees, standard double occupancy room, and board (meal plan 3)

_____ Partial Grant of $_____

You will be eligible for a year-to-year renewal of the Tender according to the University's renewal policies at the end of the academic year.

If you accept this Tender, please return (3) signed copies to the University Athletic Director no later than _____.

Signed_____
         Athletic Director

Signed_____
         Director of Financial Planning

Acceptance Notification

THIS TENDER IS CONTINGENT UPON THE SUBMISSION OF THE FREE APPLICATION FOR STUDENT AID (FAFSA).

I accept this Tender. I declare that I have not accepted any other Tender of Financial Aid from another NCAA institution.

I understand that:

1. The value of this Tender shall not exceed the value of the permissible FSU and NCAA expenses applicable to ISSC and Pell Grant awards.
2. The Aid provided in the Tender will be canceled if I sign a professional sports contract or accept money for playing in an athletic contest.

Signed _____   _____   _____
                       Student   Date   Social Security Number

Signed _____   _____
                Parent/Legal Guardian   Date

    You can sign the award letter, and even though it is unethical, you could decide to attend a different institution. If you sign the athletic tender and or the national letter of intent, you can compete only at that NCAA institution. Do not sign one without knowing the contents of the other. If you do sign one without knowing the contents of the other, you lose virtually all your negotiating leverage. The best insurance is to sign the two of them at the same time.

15

NEGOTIATING
GUIDELINES

Negotiations require some careful balancing and delicate control. Use the following guidelines to ensure that you are in control:

- Be sure coaches always know that the amount of the financial aid award will be a critical factor in choosing a college. (A parent might say, "Coach, I don't mean to be audacious, but it's important to me that you know I need/expect financial aid for my son/daughter.")

- Be sure coaches know that no commitment will be made until an award letter, tender, or contract is forthcoming. ("Coach, I mean no offense, and I'm confident you understand when I say we can't make a final commitment to you until we receive the award letter [Division III] or the athletic tender [Division I or II]. Is that fair?")

   The truth is that few people, including coaches, enjoy being perceived as unfair. It's important to ask, "Is that fair?" This seemingly innocuous sales technique has a powerful effect on the receiver of its message. *(If coaches say no, they are unfair.)*

- Always tell coaches that their institution is your number-one-choice. ("Coach, as you know, you are our number-one-choice, but it's important to us that all the issues, including financial aid, get satisfactorily resolved.")

- If you must have more aid, or feel you can negotiate more, do it with the coach or recruiter. The basis for further negotiation should be the athletic tender, with the objective to increase the amount of the tender.

   "Coach, after carefully calculating the total financial aid package offered in the tender/award letter, I need a little more help. I need another $500/$1,000/$2,000. Can you handle that additional amount?" Then be quiet! The first one who talks after the question is asked *loses*!

Negotiating Is Selling

The coach and the institution are generally in a position to put psychological pressure on you. They recognize that they are in a position of power and control and are usually quick to take advantage of the psychological stress you feel. You need a psychological counterforce to level the playing field.

Successful salespeople know what device to employ when they want to put the ball into the prospect or customer's court (i.e., make them buy the product or service they are selling). One of the most powerful psychological stressors known to man, this device is: *silence*!

A salesperson will ask a closing question such as, "Would you like to take the shoes home?" When the customer doesn't answer right away, say 15 seconds, the timid salesperson can't stand the pressure of no one talking and breaks the silence. The moment he or she starts talking, the sale is lost. The wise and courageous salesperson *remains silent* and forces the customer to talk first. When the customer talks, often he or she says yes.

Know When to Be Quiet

Sometimes the coach will ask a question. This is a good signal. It demonstrates the coach's interest in you, and it provides you with the opportunity to ask another closing question.

A coach might ask a question similar to, "I can't go $2,000. If I could increase the award letter by $1,000, would that be OK?" (Notice that the coach has asked a closing question. That is to say, he wants you to say, "Yes." That's in the coach's best interest.)

Only you know the answer to the question. If your answer is no, say, "No." Now the ball is back in the coach's court. If you sense the coach is bluffing with that type of question, *be quiet*.

Colleges give away close to $9 billion of their own funds for financial aid each year. If you want more money (a discount on tuition) than what you are initially offered, *you must ask for it*! Otherwise your financial aid package will not be increased!

If the coach suggests that you sign either of the documents (athletic tender or financial aid award letter), you must decline. "Well, go ahead and sign the award letter, and I'll see what I can do."

Your answer should be, "Coach, it's important to me to see if you can secure the increase with a new financial aid award. If you can, I'll sign both the award letter and the athletic tender at the same time. Is that fair?" Or, "Coach, I mean no disrespect, but I'd rather sign an award letter and the athletic tender that both show the additional amount as awarded. Is that fair?"

If the coach refuses to budge, you've lost nothing. Don't be afraid that the coach will become angry or withdraw the offer. (You have the documents in your hands. Signing them legally compels the institution.) Most coaches expect people to negotiate and usually respect those that negotiate aggressively, yet fairly.

Belligerence and threatening will accomplish nothing. Many parents don't realize that it's unimportant to financial aid counselors whether you attend the institution as it doesn't affect keeping their jobs. Admission counselors have to generate certain predetermined numbers. If they don't, jobs can be lost.

Sometimes you might have to appeal your financial aid package with a financial aid officer. Normally, the coach recruiting you will prepare you for the appeal interview.

Remember, the awarding of financial aid is a marketing tool used to increase or sustain enrollment. If you are being recruited by a small- to medium-sized private college, the following bold question often provokes outstanding results: "Isn't it better for the college to have a student enrolled who is receiving enhanced financial aid rather than having an empty seat or an empty bed?" *Be quiet!*

Pleading and groveling are counterproductive. You must always be reasonable and calm, and remain in control!

FINANCIAL AID LIMITS

16

The NCAA limits financial aid for each sport in both Division I and Division II. Athletic financial aid is counted by the NCAA in two categories:

1. *Head Count Sports*—used for some Division I sports. Any athlete who receives institutional financial aid, no matter the amount of aid, is counted as one. Head count limit sports exist *only* in Division I.

   - I-A Football: 85
   - I-AA Football: 63
   - Men's Basketball: 13
   - Ice Hockey: 30 counters/18 equivalencies
   - Women's Basketball: 15
   - Women's Gymnastics: 12
   - Women's Tennis: 8
   - Women's Volleyball: 12

2. *Equivalency Sports*—any sports not listed above. Generally, this means that one full grant-in-aid (full ride) can be divided among more than one student-athlete. Listings of equivalency limits for the remaining Division I sports and Division II sports follow.

Equivalency Limits for the Remaining Division I Sports

Men's Sports	Equivalency	Women's Sports	Equivalency
Baseball	11.7	Archery	5.0
Cross Country/ Track	12.6	Badminton	6.0
		Bowling	5.0
Fencing	4.5	Cross Country/ Track	18.0
Golf	4.5		
Gymnastics	6.3	Fencing	5.0
Ice Hockey	18.0	Field Hockey	12.0
Lacrosse	12.6	Golf	6.0
Rifle	3.6	Ice Hockey	18.0
Skiing	6.3	Lacrosse	12.0
Soccer	9.9	Rowing	20.0
Swimming	9.9	Skiing	7.0
Tennis	4.5	Soccer	12.0
Volleyball	4.5	Softball	12.0
Water Polo	4.5	Squash	5.0
Wrestling	9.9	Swimming	14.0
		Synchronized Swimming	5.0
		Team Handball	10.0
		Water Polo	8.0

Some Division I institutions offer cross country but not track and field. These institutions may offer 5.0 equivalencies for men and 6.0 equivalencies for women in cross country.

Equivalency Limits for the Remaining Division II Sports

Men's Sports	Equivalency	Women's Sports	Equivalency
Baseball	9.0	Archery	5.0
Basketball	10.0	Badminton	8.0
Cross Country/ Track	12.6	Basketball	10.0
		Bowling	5.0
Fencing	4.5	Cross Country/ Track	12.6
Football	36.0		
Golf	3.6	Fencing	4.5
Gymnastics	5.4	Field Hockey	6.3
Ice Hockey	13.5	Golf	5.4
Lacrosse	10.8	Gymnastics	6.0
Rifle	3.6	Ice Hockey	18.0
Skiing	6.3	Lacrosse	9.9
Soccer	9.0	Rowing	20.0
Swimming	8.1	Skiing	6.3
Team Handball	12.0	Soccer	9.9
Tennis	4.5	Softball	7.2
Volleyball	4.5	Squash	9.0
Water Polo	4.5	Swimming	8.1
Wrestling	9.0	Synchronized Swimming	5.0
		Tennis	6.0
		Volleyball	8.0
		Water Polo	8.0

All Division II sports are considered equivalency sports.

17

SPECIAL RECRUITING CONSIDERATIONS FOR THE THREE MAJOR SPORTS

Football, basketball, and baseball are the three sports that dominate the American media's attention. These sports all originated in America and each has a rich history of great players, great plays, great games, and zealous fans. Because of their traditions and history, each of the games is experiencing intense media coverage that in no small part motivates young people with athletic interest to aim for participation, if not glory, by competing in one of the sports.

Not long ago, basketball and football players aspiring to the professional leagues, learned and perfected their craft while in college. Aspiring baseball players, however, developed their major league skills at the minor league level. Few college baseball players went on to become major league stars.

While professional football leagues have wisely maintained their policy of drafting players from college, professional basketball leagues have begun drafting high school players who are college basketball prospects. Both sports allow college underclassmen to announce their availability for their sport's draft. More baseball players are emerging from the college ranks, although the best prospects are inundated with offers of money to forego their college educations and continue their development in the minor leagues.

Football, basketball, and baseball are securely woven into the sports culture of America and are the goal for most aspiring American athletes. Because of this, special attention must be paid to the necessary preparation required to become a prospect and to the recruiting circumstances unique to each.

Football

Many high school football players who are college prospects get strung along as they seek roster positions and financial aid. Remember, coaches aren't trying to harm any prospect; their priority is fielding a winning team.

Good college football coaches create a prospect depth chart for the positions for which they are recruiting. (Computer software is available that helps coaches organize both a depth chart and a prospect chart.) Their preference would be to recruit the prospect who is their first choice (number one on the position depth chart). They know, however, that often they will lose their first choice to another college, so they need to have a second and third choice, perhaps even more.

To be certain that coaches keep all the prospects on the depth chart strongly considering their program, they usually treat all prospects as if they were their first choice. If you happen to be the coach's third or fourth choice, you may think you're as good as successfully recruited because of the way the coach talks to you. But, more likely than not, the phone calls and promises will abruptly stop because the coach has successfully recruited a prospect higher on the position depth chart.

You must never allow yourself to be strung along. You must ask early in the recruiting process where you are listed on the recruiting depth chart for your position. Coaches rarely deceive a prospect when asked a direct question. If you are, for example, listed as number three, but you really want to join that program, tell the coach that you want him or her to continue considering you for the roster position. You also want to increase your leverage in the process.

"Coach, I appreciate that you think there might be another player that can play my position better than me. Your program is my first choice, and I look forward to demonstrating that I'm the type of player you're looking for. I'm talking to (two, three) other coaches about their programs, so if you choose not to include me in your plans, would you please let me know so I can sign with another college?" Then, be quiet.

While your profile is important, football coaches rarely recruit players without first seeing a videotape of them playing. That is why the creation of a video is so vital to your being successfully recruited. Refer back to the section concerning creating an effective videotape.

Many football coaches sponsor or attend football camps or combines. Combines are usually organized around a number of activities that allow attending coaches to evaluate speed, power, courage, and strength of prospects. Camps are designed with football skill development as the primary objective. Many coaches attend the best camps in search of prospects. The wise football prospect will be certain to attend at least one camp and one combine.

Basketball

Basketball is the toughest recruiting challenge for a prospect. Why? There are fewer roster positions and scholarships available than most other major sports.

If it is important to you to play intercollegiate basketball (as opposed to practicing as the "scout squad" against the real team), you will want to maintain a higher level of flexibility in your negotiations with the coach. Because of the number of scholarships available, wise prospects have three to four potential programs they are negotiating with in order to ensure a roster position and a solid financial aid package.

As with football, videotape is an essential ingredient to your successful recruitment. Create yours carefully, using the suggestions provided in the videotape section.

Include in your video episodes of ball-handling drills; demonstrate your shooting ability, using every shot you have developed. This is especially important to centers and power forwards as they need to demonstrate they can face the basket and score as well as possess shots that begin with their back to the basket. Players in these positions must also demonstrate that they can and will score in the face of an opponent.

As in football, participation at prestigious or elite camps is essential to creating massive exposure. Shoot-outs are also great venues for basketball exposure. If your coach doesn't enter your team in a summer shoot-out, ask him or her to enter one in your area.

Coaches like shoot-outs for scouting purposes as it gives them the opportunity to observe their prospect really playing basketball with all its intensity and skill, demanding the best of the players.

Baseball

No matter how accomplished you are in the field, no matter your speed from home to first or in the outfield, no matter how strong or accurate your throwing arm (unless you're a pitcher), if you can't hit the baseball, you won't be recruited! Learn to hit! If you *can* hit, learn to hit better!

Batting cages, baseball camps that emphasize hitting, hitting coaches, hitting instructional videos and books, and batting tees and wiffle balls should all be a part of your preparation to be a successfully recruited baseball prospect.

Baseball camps and summer leagues are a must for the aspiring intercollegiate baseball prospect. Your video must emphasize your hitting ability. If you are a pitcher, you must emphasize the speed of your fastball as well as its location.

18

SOLVING THE DIVISION III ATHLETIC FINANCIAL AID MYSTERY

Illicit Financial Aid Casts Shadow on Division III

from the NCAA *News* (date):

The Division III subcommittee of the NCAA Presidents Commission is presently considering restructuring in the areas of governance, membership, and championships, in addition to strengthening Division III transfer-eligibility legislation.

After reading the August 2, 1996, memorandum from the chair of the subcommittee, it is apparent that a sizeable part of its agenda deals with providing fair competition within the Division III membership. Though the committee's structural proposal for governance does include a "committee on eligibility and infractions," there was no mention of any emphasis on eliminating a major cause of our tilted playing field, that cause being illegal financial aid given to Division III student-athletes.

Whether it is because there are no television contracts or no large amounts of money involved, there seems to be either a naive assumption that financial aid violations do not occur at the Division III level or a lack of desire to resolve or even acknowledge the problem.

Well, there is a problem, it is of significant dimensions, and not much is being done about it.

The regulations concerning financial aid for student-athletes are defined clearly in the NCAA *Manual.* Bylaw 15.01.10 states that Division III institutions shall award financial aid to student-athletes only on the basis of financial need shown by the recipient. Bylaw 15.4 delineates the situations in which athletic ability is not allowed to be a criterion for awarding financial aid.

Yet, in the name of winning, some Division III coaches and administrators are sacrificing their personal and professional integrity, as well as putting the reputations of their schools at risk, by awarding excessive financial aid to student-athletes under the guise of leadership, merit, or presidential (or other inventive titles) scholarships.

No matter what the competitive level or reward for winning, these violations of the financial aid rules have no justification. The present Division III administrative restructuring process provides the NCAA with a great and timely opportunity to increase the emphasis on dealing with these violations and those who commit them.

It is also our responsibility as coaches and administrators to deal with the rule breakers. We are supposed to be builders of character, examples of commitment, and role models for the acceptance of responsibility.

We know violations are occurring. Many of us know some who are guilty.

Yet, for some reason closely akin to the misguided principle of "honor among thieves," we have allowed and abetted behavior we would not accept from our players or our children.

Chris Murphy, Head Basketball Coach
Maine Maritime Academy

NCAA regulations and bylaws disallow Division III institutions from awarding financial aid based on athletic ability. However, it is important to recognize that most students participating in sports at the Division III level are receiving substantial financial aid packages. Many of these financial aid awards are at or near full-ride levels.

And as Coach Murphy's editorial comment letter to the NCAA *News* clearly and frustratingly states, many Division III schools award excessive financial aid to student-athletes so the school can enjoy the benefits of a student-athlete's athletic ability, even though Division III colleges are forbidden by bylaw 15.4 to award financial aid based on athletic ability.

This aspect of recruiting is as integral to the process as a campus visit. It isn't going to change! Wise prospects and their parents will take advantage of it. You'll learn how in this chapter.

The NCAA regulations impacting the types and amounts of financial aid that Division III colleges can award student-athletes must also be available to all students. The regulations of NCAA Rule 15.4.9 state: "The composition of the financial aid package offered to a student-athlete shall be *consistent* (my italics) with the established policy of the institution's financial aid office for all students. . . ."[1]

Rule 15.4.9 (c) states: "The financial aid package for a particular student-athlete cannot be *clearly distinguishable* (my italics) from the *general pattern* (my italics) of all financial aid for all recipients (of financial aid) at the institution. . . ."[2]

Rule 15.4.9 (a) states: "A member institution *shall not consider* (my italics) athletic ability as a criterion in the formulation of the financial aid package. . . ."[3]

NCAA Division III coaches or recruiters are obliged to tell you that they can't/don't offer scholarships for athletic ability (i.e., athletic

1. NCAA *Manual*, NCAA, 1996, 219.
2. Ibid.
3. Ibid.

scholarship). Still, substantial financial aid will often be awarded to a prospective student-athlete. A potential financial aid award for a prospective student-athlete by an NCAA Division III school will never be discussed with you in terms of athletic scholarships or athletic ability. Many of these institutions have learned how to use the scholarship "name game." Play along!

Financial aid will likely be discussed in terms of merit awards, leadership awards, academic and honors awards, loans, employment, "awards of circumstance," and institutional awards. Institutional awards have many names; some of the more common names are: presidential award, founders grant, trustees award, leadership scholarship.

Many colleges offer an *institutional grant*. Some offer more than one, each grant being given different names. This institutional grant, no matter what name the college chooses to give it, is a discount on the sticker price of that college. The grant often has the college's name as part of the grant title; but some colleges use very creative names (recently, a Division III coach publicly called them "inventive names" for awards and grants).

The meaning is clear. Many NCAA Division III institutions award financial aid to prospects because of athletic ability, but invent an award name so that it appears that the award is for some other criteria. Very simply, this method is used by NCAA Division III institutions to circumvent Rule 15.4.2 to make scholarship money available to students with athletic ability.

If a college offers institutional grants, they are often described in the scholarship description section of the college catalog. The description of the grants may be similar to the following statements: "The (Beezer Benchbottom) Presidential Grants—given to students to meet their gift eligibility as determined by their financial need and the name of the college/university's assistance packaging formula." Or, "Institutionally funded financial aid offered to students to defer their cost of an education." (Both are institutional methodology.)

This formula, while usually having financial aid award elements consistent with other institutions, is uniquely designed to meet the needs of the particular institution and its students. The institution alone decides what its needs are. The institution alone decides how it will structure its assistance packaging formula, according to its needs.

In other words, institutions are free to structure their assistance packaging formulas so they have considerable flexibility. Institutions are also free to name the financial aid grants they award any student or student-athlete for the purpose of either enhancing or concealing the real purpose of the financial aid award.

Directors of financial aid are staff members responsible for accomplishing the institution's enrollment goal. They usually have great latitude to be flexible in deciding which prospective student gets what level of assistance and from what category according to the assistance packaging formula. This latitude, literally written into the enabling federal legislation, is called *professional judgment.* Financial aid directors, using professional judgment, can change the rules whenever it suits their purpose.

The truth is that a great minority of Division III institutions use institutional needs; professional judgment; assistance packaging formulas; and other awarding devices, gimmicks, and methods to circumvent or bend NCAA recruiting rules and regulations.

College administrators, usually directors of financial aid, decide which prospects "meet" (qualify) within the "established criteria" of the financial aid assistance packaging formula. Just as importantly, these administrators decide the meaning for measuring the terms, "consideration," "clearly distinguishable," "consistent," and "general pattern" in designing the institution's award packaging formula. They are also given the freedom to use professional judgment.

The coach of a powerful Division III athletic program stated in a recent alumni newsletter, "If private schools choose to be marginal in their ethics when it comes to awarding scholarships and grants, they can have a pretty good financial aid package."

19

INTERDEPARTMENTAL COMMUNICATIONS

CAA Rule 15.4.2 states: "All forms of financial assistance for
student-athletes shall be handled through the regular college
agency or committee that administers financial aid for all students."[1]

Division III recruiting regulations forbid a coach or athletic director (or for that matter, any person interested in a particular athletic
program or from the athletic department) from communicating with
the college's financial aid department concerning financial aid for any
prospective student-athlete. This restriction is created to prevent athletic department representatives (coaches) from influencing or manipulating acceptance, enrollment, or a financial aid package on behalf
of any prospect.

The truth is that most Division III institutions tolerate this type of
communication. The truth is that some, in fact, encourage it or give
permission to certain coaches within an athletic department to recruit
top high school prospects.

Coaches recruit top prospects knowing full well that they can desig-
nate to financial aid directors those prospects who should be granted
large financial aid packages or sometimes nearly full rides.

Many names are given to the recruiting practice whereby Division
III coaches can recruit top prospects, promise them excellent financial

---

1. NCAA *Manual*, NCAA, 217.

aid packages, and know that financial aid directors will use their professional judgment and award prospects what coaches have already promised. The most common term for this is called *chipping*, as in blue chip.

Some football coaches have been known to "move the goalpost" for a highly prized prospect. Some softball coaches have recognized the benefits of "shading the pole" for a pitcher who will take their team to the next level.

Be alert the next time you watch a professional athletic contest. Listen for the athlete's names and colleges being announced prior to the battle. From time to time, you'll hear the name of a college that may be unfamiliar to you. Check the directory in this book. Often you will learn the NCAA division of that college is Division III or an NAIA institution.

Division III, as well as NAIA schools, are often competitive with many Division II and even some Division I programs. It is no accident that some of the nation's finest athletes can be found at these schools. Large financial aid packages often play a crucial role in a student-athlete's enrollment in an NCAA Division III or NAIA institution. So if you are convinced you are a Division I prospect, but you feel you are being overlooked or are being strung along, your best choice for continuing your education and your athletic career may well be at the Division III or NAIA level.

Other Benefits

Student-athletes often receive preferential treatment regarding admissions. You may not be as competitive academically as other students applying for admission and still be admitted to many Division III or NAIA colleges. Your status as an athletic prospect may cause you to receive a waiver of the academic entrance standards (e.g., SAT/ACT scores, GPA, class rank) required of other entering students.

Some athletic departments conform a little more closely to the regulations yet still make their wishes known concerning financial aid awards and waivers for good prospects. Some will inform the admissions department or a counselor concerning what the financial aid requirements are for enrolling a hot or blue-chip prospect. Admissions passes the information on to financial aid so that it can work the magic of financial aid flexibility.

Sometimes a list of desirable prospects mysteriously appears on the desk of the appropriate financial aid officer. Then the assistance packaging formula can, with proper flexibility, be fortuitously applied to those prospects' total financial aid packages.

If an institution is found to be significantly violating recruiting rules and regulations, to its credit, the NCAA will deal with the violating institution in the severest manner. *The truth is that the NCAA doesn't have the resources to monitor Division III institutions intensely enough to discover and punish those that are intentionally bending the rules.* The NCAA requests that violations be "self-reported" to the NCAA. Most often these self-reported violations are minor in nature and are usually followed by perfunctory NCAA action or no action taken. *The truth is that most major violations are reported to the NCAA from outside the athletic program or by student-athletes within the program.*

Do any Division III institutions obey the recruiting regulations? Yes! Of course. You can find them—often at the bottom of their conference's standings.

Some coaches of these compliant institutions write guest editorials in the NCAA *News*, a weekly newspaper sent to all NCAA members, pleading that the violations stop, asking that the playing field be level for all Division III institutions. The violations continue!

Many Division III programs do violate the spirit, if not the actual bylaws of the NCAA. You are now aware of this tendency to violate regulations, and you also know how to use the system that has been created because of the systemic violation of NCAA rules and regulations.

So there's good news and bad news. The bad news is violations are common. The good news is that if you know the system, you can take advantage of it so that you can get what you want and deserve.

One Exception

There is one minor exception in Division III that provides for athletic financial aid awards based on athletic ability. "The one exception is for endowment funds that Division III institutions received before January 1, 1979, and established specifically for student-athletes. You can offer awards with these funds, so long as you comply with the other policies related to financial aid."[1]

It should be clear that the NCAA attempts to regulate financial aid awards to student-athletes enrolling in Division III institutions. It

---

1. *Guide to Financial Aid*, NCAA, 1996, 162.

should be equally as clear that student-athletes enrolling in these colleges can and do receive financial aid. The NCAA creates the parameters within which Division III colleges are supposed to operate. Within these parameters each institution makes its own individual, unique financial aid award decisions. Often, decisions to award financial aid dramatically stretch or break the recruiting rules and regulations.

Division III's Pleasant Surprise

As the foregoing has noted, Division III institutions state that they don't (with the one designated exception) offer financial aid based on athletic ability. You have learned that all divisions (including Division III) have great flexibility in packaging financial aid awards.

You have also learned that many students attending Division III colleges are playing sports and receiving substantial financial aid. Athletic scholarships awarded by Division I and II institutions are usually awarded on a year-to-year basis. The coach is often the person who decides if your athletic financial aid is renewed.

Usually, the only way you can lose your financial aid when enrolled in a Division III institution is because your academic performance doesn't meet the institution's publicly announced standards. That standard is usually related to a student's GPA.

Poor performance during an athletic season should not be used as a reason or excuse for reducing the amount of a financial aid package. In fact, you should be able to quit the team and maintain your financial aid package as though you were still on the team. After all, if you weren't awarded any financial aid because of your athletic ability, how can you lose financial aid because you choose to no longer participate in athletics? Your Division III financial aid had nothing to do with you being a recruited student-athlete!

20

NEGOTIATE, NEGOTIATE, NEGOTIATE

You, too, can and should use the same flexibility that Division III assistance packaging formulas provide colleges' financial aid directors to use professional judgment and flexibility to get students the institution wants. Deciding to negotiate and knowing on what basis and what strategies to negotiate with can produce substantial benefits.

Remember, Division III coaches are obliged to tell you, and will always tell you, that the college doesn't offer athletic scholarships. After coaches have made this obligatory comment concerning no athletic scholarships, listen carefully to the next comments.

If these comments indicate that the college "creates excellent financial aid packages," or "works hard to be sure that our athletes get every dollar they're entitled to," or "we have lots of financial aid available," or "nobody can give you more financial aid than we can," or "we'll match any financial aid package you're offered" (many financial aid departments will actually request that you send a copy of your financial aid award letter from another school for the purpose of matching), or similar comments, *let the negotiations begin!*

Start your part of the initial negotiations with something like this: "Coach, you're our first choice. So I'm happy to hear that about financial aid because the amount of financial aid my son/daughter gets will be crucial in the enrollment decision we make."

Remember, when discussing financial aid with Division III coaches, you must *avoid* using the term *athletic scholarship* or any similar terms. This creates real difficulties for coaches. They may feel that it's not in the program's best interest to recruit your son or daughter if you appear confused about athletic financial aid protocol.

As you negotiate a financial aid package with a coach, recruiter, or financial aid officer, be sure you are prepared for the discussion by reviewing the suggestions and scripts presented previously. Have your questions ready.

Many parents make the unfortunate mistake of immediately asking, "How much financial aid is my son or daughter going to get?" This is a huge error because it immediately puts coaches on the defensive. Coaches probably have a good idea of what you can contribute to their program, but know nothing about your EFC number or other pertinent factors used in determining your financial aid package.

Ask first about academics, housing, cost per credit hour, instructor-to-pupil ratio, major fields of study available, food plan, percentage of program athletes who graduate in four/five years, etc. Remember, coaches are interested in the quality of their program, not about the financial aid concerns of any one prospect. It's likely that they are recruiting between two and four prospects for the position you want! Start smart!

Most coaches and financial aid departments are in no position to tell you how much financial aid will be forthcoming on the occasion of your first contact with them. They need transcripts and ACT/SAT scores, provided to the admissions office, and the Student Aid Report (SAR) made available to the financial aid office.

Only after these documents are in the hands of both admissions and financial aid counselors can they begin to determine the financial aid implications for you and your parents. Only then do they have the data to create a financial aid package, using federal and state government grants and loans (federal methodology) and institutional grants and scholarships (institutional methodology).

Be persistent, but be patient!

21

THE ULTIMATE NEGOTIATING WEAPON

Your ultimate negotiating weapon is provided to you free of charge by the college financial aid office, sometimes named the office of financial planning or financial planning office. That weapon is the *financial aid award form/letter*. It is a letter/form from the college that states by line item what financial aid awards, grants, loans, work-study program, etc., you are being offered. Refer to the Sample Financial Aid Award Letter in the chapter "Awarding of Athletic Financial Aid."

As you can see, the form is structured in such a way that you can indicate whether you accept or decline each item in the financial aid award package. The form identifies a date by which the completed form must be returned. If the financial aid offered on the financial aid award letter is not acceptable, or not what you agreed to with either the coach, admissions counselor, or financial aid officer, you must return it.

But first send a photocopied form *to the coach* with a note indicating why you've returned the letter/form, and ask him or her to help you get what you want and deserve. If the coach wants you on the team, it is likely that someone from the institution's financial aid office will be contacting you shortly to *review* your financial aid award package. Probably they will revise the financial aid award to better meet your needs.

This is typically the type of situation for serious negotiation! You must be ready to use all the negotiation strategies and techniques presented to you previously. Generally, what you receive with the (first) financial aid award letter is your individual *sticker price*—the price that institution hopes you will settle for. The sticker price can often be changed through negotiations. *Be prepared to negotiate!*

Here are some suggestions for your negotiation opener:

- "I'd love for my son/daughter to come to your college, it's his/her first choice and ours, too. For him/her to come there, we need a little more help than what is in the award letter. Could you take a look at the package and see if my son/daughter can be awarded an additional $500/$1,000/$3,000 or more?"

- "We've nearly got a deal here! We need an additional ($750) for my son/daughter to be able to attend the university. Can you review the package and see if in your professional judgment the amount of the award could be increased?"

- "I'm sorry, but I was under the impression that my son/daughter would qualify for ($12,500) in financial aid. The award letter only provides for an ($11,000) package. My son/daughter won't be able to attend unless he/she receives that level of help. That will be a shame because your college is our first choice."

The truth is that few colleges refuse to reconsider award letters/ forms. Most American colleges are under extreme pressure to enroll students. They discount tuition and accommodate other needs whenever possible.

On the other hand, if coaches can't get additional financial aid or don't want to ask the financial aid office for more aid, they will contact you. By their explanation, you will know that you have been awarded all you will receive from that institution. Then it's time to decide to accept the package or move on to another program's offer. You are negotiating with more than one college, aren't you?

Once you have made your decision about which college you will attend, it's important that you notify the other institutions that you've been negotiating with that you will be attending another school. This may well provide someone who is being strung along an opportunity to be recruited and receive financial aid based on his or her athletic ability.

Enrollment Dates

While a number of colleges close freshman enrollment in late January to early February, most colleges continue searching for and enrolling students right up to the beginning of classes.

In the first chapter, a quote from *U.S. News & World Report* discussed the haggling that goes on between college admissions and financial aid departments with prospective students and their parents. Haggling equals negotiating, bargaining, compromising. There just aren't enough qualified high school students to create enough numbers for each college to enroll the number they'd like to enroll. There is ferocious competition among colleges to enroll qualified students (and sometimes not-so-qualified students). All colleges are motivated to get every prospective student they think they can enroll to enroll early.

One of the strategies used by admissions officers to encourage prospective students to enroll early is to tell students and their parents that they have an enrollment cutoff date and that no one is accepted after that date. *The truth is that most colleges will enroll students until they meet or exceed their required enrollment numbers. If they need to enroll students up to the day before classes to meet the enrollment quota, most will!*

Disinformation

Some high school guidance counselors have been persuaded to believe the self-serving statements in college brochures that are designed to cause you to hurry your decision. Too often they urge their students to make early decisions. This can often make students choose a college before they have sufficient information about other colleges so that they can make an informed enrollment decision.

Again, to be successfully recruited and receive the largest possible financial aid package, you must be negotiating with at least two (and it should be more) colleges for financial aid.

CONTRIBUTING TO MY
FUTURE SUCCESS

You can ensure the kind of future you want for yourself by understanding that those who are the most successful in life recognized that there is no substitute for the *will to prepare!*

How do you prepare? By committing to yourself, every day, that you will be the best student and the best athlete you can be. How can you accomplish that? You must *think, hustle, study, practice, concentrate, persist, focus, and win. You must always believe in yourself!*

Remember: *Winners never quit! Quitters never win!*

Often, a book of this type ends by wishing the reader good luck. The truth is that luck will have very little to do with your becoming a successfully recruited prospect. For that matter, luck will have little to do with your success and fulfillment as an adult.

Consider yourself lucky if you're not lazy. Consider yourself lucky if you don't quit. Consider yourself lucky if you believe in yourself.

Create your own luck. It has been said that luck is a place where preparation and opportunity come together. Follow the suggestions of this guide so you can be successfully recruited, continue your athletic career, and receive financial aid for your athletic ability.

Good courage, good skill, and good preparation!

FINANCIAL AID INFORMATION SOURCES

Finaid: Financial Aid Information Page at www.finaid.com
Worldwide College Scholarship Directory at www.800headstart.com,
e-mail: nsrs@aol.com
College Cost and Financial Aid at www.collegboard.org
Sallie Mae student loans at www.salliemae.com

GLOSSARY OF TERMS

Academic credentials. For the purposes of eligibility, they include ACT/SAT scores and core course GPA.

American College Testing (ACT) Assessment. A test designed to measure a prospect's ability in specific subject areas.

Athletic ability. A combination of above-average skill and excellent potential in a sport that is exhibited by a high school student-athlete.

Athletic credentials. Statistics, observable competition (video), measurable athletic skill (combines), and accomplishments created by a prospect.

Athletic tender. Document describing the amount of athletic financial aid being offered to a prospect.

Award letter. A letter or form describing by line item the different types of financial aid a prospect is being offered.

Blue-chip athlete. An athlete who demonstrates an ability to compete immediately on the college level and who exhibits potential to be a competitor of major impact on the team's chances for success.

Depth chart. A list of players in descending order used by coaches to place their first prospect choice down to their last prospect choice.

Discipline. Self-control exercised on a daily basis in order to focus on the achievement of a specific goal.

Discounted tuition. Any reduction in the announced tuition of the institution announcing the cost of tuition.

Educational services. All the services provided by an institution to its student body.

Equivalency sport. Sport where the grand total of available athletic financial aid is split among many athletes.

Expected family contribution (EFC). The amount of money a family is expected to contribute toward the student's total cost of a year's education. This amount is identified by the letters EFC on the Student Aid Report (SAR).

Exposure. The process of making coaches or recruiters aware of the athletic and academic accomplishments of a prospect.

Federal methodology. When information from the FAFSA is used as a baseline for awarding financial aid.

Financial aid. Any type of monetary assistance that reduces the announced cost (sticker price) of a year's tuition, fees, room and board, and other associated costs.

Financial aid award packaging formula. Each institution's system, comprising of and combining many factors, upon which is based the awarding of financial aid to students enrolling or matriculating in that institution.

Free Application for Federal Student Aid (FAFSA). The department of education's (DOE) initial application document used for the purpose of analyzing a student's educational funding need. It is a compilation of household and financial information used by the DOE computers to calculate the EFC and the SAR.

Full ride. A financial aid package that pays for all the costs associated with attending an institution. Also known as a full scholarship.

Gap. Being awarded less financial aid than what is certified as needed by the EFC number on the SAR.

Goal. An outcome one strives for through sacrifice and discipline to attain.

Gray squad. Team or group of athletes whose practice responsibility is to play against the first or second string in order to provide those teams with practice similar to an upcoming opponent.

Head count sports. When an athlete receives any amount of financial aid and is counted as one roster position. Only used in Division I.

Institutional methodology. When an institution uses its own unique formula for determining student need for the purpose of awarding financial aid.

Loan. Money borrowed to provide a discount in tuition. Except for agreed to circumstances, the borrowed money must be repaid after graduation.

Must have. First prospect choice of a coach. Number one on the coache's depth chart.

National Association of Intercollegiate Athletics (NAIA). An organization made up of a small number of institutions of higher education to standardize, monitor, and control the institutions within the organization. The institutions are separated into two divisions.

National Collegiate Athletic Association (NCAA). An organization made up of many institutions of higher education to standardize, monitor, and control the institutions within the organization. The institutions are separated into three divisions.

National testing date. The dates throughout the high school year on which all ACT or SAT tests are offered throughout the country.

National testing site. The places where the ACT or SAT tests are offered.

Official visit. One of five visits in which the college being visited handles the prospect's expenses.

Perkins loan. A loan taken from a lump sum of money given to a participating institution and offered to needy (financial aid director can define the term needy on a case-by-case basis) students by the enrolling college. The maximum loan per year is $3,000, has a 5 percent interest rate, and is deferred for nine months after a student leaves the institution.

Professional judgment. The authority of an institution's financial aid director to make tuition discount decisions on a case-by-case basis.

Prospect. Any high school athlete who has been contacted by any means by any institution for the purpose of exposing the athlete to the college or to encourage the athlete to consider the college for enrollment.

Recruit. Any student-athlete who has been contacted for the purpose of enrolling in an institution to participate in an athletic program.

Roster position. A designated place on a team as announced by the team's coach.

Scholastic Assessment Test (SAT). A test designed to measure a prospect's ability to handle college-level academic work.

Stafford loan. A loan with a maximum of $2,625 for the first year on which the federal government pays the loan interest. Repayment of principal and interest can be deferred up to six months after a student is no longer enrolled. A second Stafford loan does not subsidize the interest payment, so the interest accrues over the term of the loan.

Sticker price. The cost of a year's education announced by a college.

Strung along. Being treated by coaches or recruiters as though you are the first recruit choice when in fact you are farther down the depth chart.

Student Aid Report (SAR). The document created by the Federal government's computers from the household and financial information submitted on the FAFSA. Its primary function is to show the Expected Family Contribution (EFC).

Unofficial visit. A visit made by a prospect to a college when the expenses for the visit are handled by the prospect.

ALABAMA

ALABAMA, UNIVERSITY OF

	Men	**Women**
Box 870323	Baseball	Basketball
Tuscaloosa, AL 35487	Basketball	Cheerleading
Affiliation—NCAA I	Cross Country	Cross Country
(I-A Football)	Diving	Diving
Nickname—Crimson Tide	Football	Golf
Athletic Director—	Golf	Gymnastics
(205) 348-3697	Swimming	Soccer
	Tennis	Softball
	Track	Swimming
		Tennis
		Track
		Volleyball

ALABAMA, UNIVERSITY OF, BIRMINGHAM

	Men	**Women**
617 13th Street S	Baseball	Basketball
Birmingham, AL 35294-1160	Basketball	Cross Country
Affiliation—NCAA I	Football	Golf
(I-A Football)	Golf	Rifle
Nickname—Blazers	Soccer	Soccer
Athletic Director—	Tennis	Tennis
(205) 934-7252		Track
		Volleyball

ALABAMA, UNIVERSITY OF, HUNTSVILLE

	Men	**Women**
Spragins Hall	Baseball	Basketball
Huntsville, AL 35899	Basketball	Cross Country
Affiliation—NCAA II	Cross Country	Cheerleading
Nickname—Chargers	Ice Hockey	Soccer
Athletic Director—	Soccer	Softball
(256) 890-6144	Tennis	Tennis
		Volleyball

ALABAMA A&M UNIVERSITY

	Men	Women
PO Box 1597	Baseball	Basketball
4900 Meridan Street NW	Basketball	Cross Country
Normal, AL 35762-1597	Cross Country	Cheerleading
Affiliation—NCAA I	Football	Softball
Nickname—Bulldogs	Golf	Track
Athletic Director—	Soccer	Volleyball
(256) 851-5361	Tennis	
	Track	

ALABAMA STATE UNIVERSITY

	Men	Women
915 S. Jackson Street	Baseball	Basketball
Montgomery, AL 36104-5732	Basketball	Cross Country
Affiliation—NCAA I	Cross Country	Golf
(I-AA Football)	Football	Softball
Nickname—Hornets	Golf	Tennis
Athletic Director—	Tennis	Track
(334) 409-2322	Track	Volleyball

ATHENS STATE UNIVERSITY

	Men	Women
Pryor Street	Basketball	Softball
Athens, AL 35611		
Affiliation—NAIA I		
Nickname—Bears		
Athletic Director—		
(205) 233-8279		

AUBURN UNIVERSITY

	Men	Women
Corner of Samford and	Baseball	Basketball
Donahue	Basketball	Cross Country
PO Box 351	Cross Country	Diving
Auburn, AL 36831-0351	Diving	Golf
Affiliation—NCAA I	Football	Gymnastics
(I-A Football)	Golf	Soccer
Nickname—Tigers	Swimming	Softball
Athletic Director—	Tennis	Tennis
(334) 844-9891	Track	Track
		Volleyball

AUBURN UNIVERSITY, MONTGOMERY

7300 University Drive	**Men**	**Women**
Montgomery, AL 36117-3531	Baseball	Basketball
Affiliation—NAIA I	Basketball	Tennis
Nickname—Senators	Soccer	
Athletic Director—	Tennis	
(334) 244-3238		

BIRMINGHAM-SOUTHERN COLLEGE

900 Arkadelphia Road	**Men**	**Women**
Birmingham, AL 35254	Baseball	Cross Country
Affiliation—NAIA I	Basketball	Soccer
Nickname—Panthers	Cross Country	Tennis
Athletic Director—	Soccer	Volleyball
(205) 226-4936	Tennis	

CONCORDIA COLLEGE

1804 Green Street	**Men**	**Women**
Selma, AL 36703-3323	Baseball	Basketball
Nickname—Hornets	Basketball	Cheerleading
Athletic Director—		Softball
(334) 874-5741		

FAULKNER UNIVERSITY

5345 Atlanta Highway	**Men**	**Women**
Montgomery, AL 36109-3323	Baseball	Cheerleading
Affiliation—NAIA I	Basketball	Cross Country
Nickname—Eagles	Cross Country	Softball
Athletic Director—		Volleyball
(334) 260-6103		

HUNTINGDON COLLEGE

1500 W. Fairview Avenue	**Men**	**Women**
Montgomery, AL 36106-2114	Baseball	Basketball
Affiliation—NAIA I	Basketball	Golf
Nickname—Hawks	Cross Country	Soccer
Athletic Director—	Golf	Softball
(334) 833-4565	Soccer	Tennis
	Tennis	Volleyball

JACKSONVILLE STATE UNIVERSITY

700 Pelham Road N	Men	Women
Jacksonville, AL 36265-1602	Baseball	Basketball
Affiliation—NCAA I	Basketball	Cross Country
(I-AA Football)	Cross Country	Golf
Nickname—Gamecocks	Football	Rifle
Athletic Director—	Golf	Soccer
(256) 782-5365	Rifle	Tennis
	Tennis	Volleyball

JUDSON COLLEGE

Bibb Street	Women	
Marion, AL 36756	Basketball	Tennis
Affiliation—NCCAA	Golf	Volleyball
Nickname—Eagles	Softball	
Athletic Director—		
(334) 683-5159		

MILES COLLEGE

5500 Myron Massey Boulevard	Men	
Birmingham, AL 35208	Baseball	Football
Nickname—Golden Bears	Basketball	Tennis
Athletic Director—	Cross Country	Volleyball
(205) 929-1000 ext. 1513		

MOBILE, UNIVERSITY OF

PO Box 13220	Men	Women
Mobile, AL 36663-0220	Baseball	Basketball
Affiliation—NAIA I	Basketball	Cheerleading
Nickname—Rams	Cross Country	Cross Country
Athletic Director—	Golf	Golf
(334) 675-5990 ext. 279	Soccer	Soccer
	Track	Softball
		Tennis
		Track

MONTEVALLO, UNIVERSITY OF

Station 6600	Men	Women
Montevallo, AL 35115	Baseball	Basketball
Affiliation—NCAA II	Basketball	Golf
Nickname—Falcons	Golf	Soccer
Athletic Director—	Soccer	Tennis
(205) 665-6594		Volleyball

NORTH ALABAMA, UNIVERSITY OF

Athletic Drive	**Men**	**Women**
Florence, AL 35632	Baseball	Basketball
Affiliation—NCAA II	Basketball	Cross Country
Nickname—Lions	Cross Country	Soccer
Athletic Department—	Football	Softball
(256) 765-4397 ext. 4397	Golf	Tennis
	Tennis	Volleyball

SAMFORD UNIVERSITY

800 Lakeshore Drive	**Men**	**Women**
Birmingham, AL 35229	Baseball	Basketball
Affiliation—NCAA I	Basketball	Cheerleading
(I-AA Football)	Cross Country	Cross Country
Nickname—Bulldogs	Football	Golf
Athletic Director—	Golf	Soccer
(205) 870-2131	Tennis	Softball
	Track	Tennis
		Track
		Volleyball

SOUTH ALABAMA, UNIVERSITY OF

1107 HPELS Building	**Men**	**Women**
Mobile, AL 26688-1107	Baseball	Basketball
Affiliation—NCAA I	Basketball	Cheerleading
Nickname—Jaguars	Cross Country	Cross Country
Athletic Director—	Golf	Golf
(334) 460-7121	Soccer	Soccer
	Tennis	Tennis
	Track	Track
		Volleyball

SOUTHEASTERN BIBLE COLLEGE

3001 Highway 280 E	**Men**
Birmingham, AL 35243-4181	Basketball
Affiliation—NCCAA I	
Nickname—Sabers	
Athletic Director—	
(205) 970-9232	

SPRING HILL COLLEGE

4000 Dauphin Street	**Men**	**Women**
Mobile, AL 36608-1780	Baseball	Basketball
Affiliation—NAIA I	Basketball	Cross Country
Nickname—Badgers	Golf	Golf
Athletic Director—	Soccer	Soccer
(334) 380-3486	Tennis	Softball
		Tennis

STILLMAN COLLEGE

3600 Stillman Boulevard	**Men**	**Women**
Tuscaloosa, AL 35401-2602	Baseball	Basketball
Affiliation—NCAA III	Basketball	Tennis
Nickname—Tigers	Cross Country	Track
Athletic Director—	Tennis	Volleyball
(205) 366-8838 ext. 8838	Track	
	Volleyball	

TALLADEGA COLLEGE

627 Battle Street W	**Men**	**Women**
Talladega, AL 35160-2354	Baseball	Basketball
Affiliation—NAIA I	Basketball	Cheerleading
Nickname—Tornadoes	Cross Country	Cross Country
Athletic Director—	Golf	Golf
(256) 761-6239	Tennis	Tennis
	Volleyball	Track
		Volleyball

TROY STATE UNIVERSITY

University Avenue	**Men**	**Women**
Troy, AL 36082	Baseball	Basketball
Affiliation—NCAA I	Basketball	Cross Country
(I-AA Football)	Cross Country	Golf
Nickname—Trojans	Football	Soccer
Athletic Director—	Golf	Softball
(334) 670-3483	Tennis	Tennis
	Track	Track
		Volleyball

TUSKEGEE UNIVERSITY

321 James Center	**Men**	**Women**
Tuskegee Institute, AL 36068	Baseball	Basketball
Affiliation—NCAA II	Basketball	Cheerleading
Nickname—Golden Tigers	Cross Country	Cross Country
Athletic Director—	Football	Tennis
(334) 724-4800	Tennis	Track
	Track	Volleyball

WEST ALABAMA, UNIVERSITY OF

Station 5	**Men**	**Women**
Livingston, AL 35470	Baseball	Basketball
Affiliation—NCAA II	Basketball	Cross Country
Nickname—Tigers	Cross Country	Rodeo
Athletic Director—	Football	Softball
(205) 652-3784	Rodeo	Volleyball

ALASKA

ALASKA, UNIVERSITY OF, ANCHORAGE

3211 Providence Drive	**Men**	**Women**
Anchorage, AK 99508-4614	Basketball	Basketball
Affiliation—NCAA II	Cross Country	Cheerleading
(Div. I Hockey)	Ice Hockey	Gymnastics
Nickname—Seawolves	Skiing	Skiing
Athletic Director—	Swimming	Volleyball
(907) 786-1225		

ALASKA, UNIVERSITY OF, FAIRBANKS

PO Box 757440	**Men**	**Women**
Fairbanks, AK 99775-7440	Basketball	Basketball
Affiliation—NCAA II	Cross Country	Cross Country
(Div. I Hockey)	Ice Hockey	Rifle
Nickname—Nanooks	Rifle	Skiing
Athletic Director—	Skiing	Volleyball
(907) 474-6810		

ARIZONA

AMERICAN INDIAN COLLEGE

10020 N. 15th Avenue	**Men**	**Women**
Phoenix, AZ 85021-2107	Basketball	Basketball
Affiliation—NCAA, NCCAA, SWCC	Cross Country	Volleyball
Nickname—Warriors	Volleyball	
Athletic Director—		
(602) 944-3335		

ARIZONA, UNIVERSITY OF

PO Box 210096, McKale Center	**Men**	**Women**
Tucson, AZ 85721-0096	Baseball	Basketball
Affiliation—NCAA I	Basketball	Cross Country
(I-A Football)	Cross Country	Diving
Nickname—Wildcats	Diving	Golf
Athletic Director—	Football	Gymnastics
(520) 621-4622	Golf	Soccer
	Swimming	Softball
	Tennis	Swimming
	Track	Tennis
		Track
		Volleyball

ARIZONA BIBLE COLLEGE

1718 W. Maryland Avenue	**Men**	**Women**
Phoenix, AZ 85015-1701	Basketball	Basketball
Affiliation—NCCAA		Volleyball
Nickname—Falcons		
Athletic Director—		
(602) 242-6400		

ARIZONA STATE UNIVERSITY

PO Box 872505
Tempe, AZ 85287-2505
Affiliation—NCAA I
  (I-A Football)
Nickname—Sun Devils
Athletic Director—
  (602) 965-6360

Men	Women
Baseball	Basketball
Basketball	Cheerleading
Cross Country	Cross Country
Diving	Diving
Football	Golf
Golf	Gymnastics
Swimming	Soccer
Tennis	Softball
Track	Swimming
Wrestling	Tennis
	Track
	Volleyball

GRAND CANYON UNIVERSITY

3300 W. Camelback Road
Phoenix, AZ 85017-3030
Affiliation—NCAA II
  (Div. I Baseball)
Nickname—Antelopes
Athletic Director—
  (602) 589-2806

Men	Women
Baseball	Basketball
Basketball	Cross Country
Golf	Soccer
Soccer	Tennis
	Track
	Volleyball

NORTHERN ARIZONA UNIVERSITY

Box 15400
Flagstaff, AZ 86011
Affiliation—NCAA I
  (I-AA Football)
Nickname—Lumberjacks
Athletic Director—
  (520) 523-5353

Men	Women
Basketball	Basketball
Cross Country	Cheerleading
Diving	Cross Country
Football	Diving
Swimming	Golf
Tennis	Soccer
Track	Swimming
	Tennis
	Track
	Volleyball

SOUTHWESTERN COLLEGE

2625 E. Cactus Road
Phoenix, AZ 85032-7042
Affiliation—NCCAA II
Nickname—Eagles
Athletic Director—
  (602) 992-6101

Men	Women
Basketball	Volleyball

ARKANSAS

ARKANSAS, UNIVERSITY OF, FAYETTEVILLE

	Men	Women
Broyles Athletic Center	Baseball	Basketball
Fayetteville, AR 72701	Basketball	Cheerleading
Affiliation—NCAA I	Cheerleading	Cross Country
(I-A Football)	Cross Country	Diving
Nickname—Razorbacks	Football	Golf
Athletic Director—Men	Golf	Soccer
(501) 575-2755	Tennis	Softball
Athletic Director—Women	Track	Swimming
(501) 575-4959		Tennis
		Track
		Volleyball

ARKANSAS, UNIVERSITY OF, LITTLE ROCK

	Men	Women
2801 S. University Avenue	Baseball	Cheerleading
Little Rock, AR 72204-1000	Basketball	Cross Country
Affiliation—NCAA I	Cross Country	Diving
Nickname—Trojans	Golf	Golf
Athletic Director—	Tennis	Soccer
(501) 569-3167	Track	Swimming
		Tennis
		Track
		Volleyball

ARKANSAS, UNIVERSITY OF, MONTICELLO

	Men	Women
Box 3066 UAM	Baseball	Basketball
Monticello, AR 71656-0001	Basketball	Cross Country
Affiliation—NCAA II	Football	Softball
Nickname—Weevils	Golf	Tennis
Athletic Director—		
(870) 460-1058		

ARKANSAS, UNIVERSITY OF, PINE BLUFF

	Men	Women
N. University Drive	Baseball	Basketball
Pine Bluff, AR 71601	Basketball	Cross Country
Affiliation—NAIA I, NCAA I	Cross Country	Golf
Nickname—Golden Lions	Football	Softball
Athletic Director—	Golf	Tennis
(870) 543-8114	Tennis	Track
	Track	Volleyball

ARKANSAS BAPTIST COLLEGE

1600 High Street	**Men**	**Women**
Little Rock, AR 72202	Baseball	Badminton
Affiliation—NSCAA	Basketball	Basketball
Nickname—Buffaloes	Cross Country	Bowling
Athletic Director—	Track	Cross Country
(501) 374-4750	Volleyball	Gymnastics
		Softball
		Track
		Volleyball

ARKANSAS STATE UNIVERSITY

PO Box 1000	**Men**	**Women**
State University, AR 72467	Baseball	Basketball
Affiliation—NCAA I	Basketball	Cross Country
(I-A Football)	Cross Country	Golf
Nickname—Indians	Football	Tennis
Athletic Director—	Golf	Track
(870) 972-3030	Track	Volleyball

ARKANSAS TECH UNIVERSITY

Highway 7	**Men**	**Women**
Russellville, AR 72801	Baseball	Basketball
Affiliation—NCAA II	Basketball	Cross Country
Nickname—Wonder Boys	Football	Tennis
Athletic Director—	Golf	Volleyball
(501) 968-0345		

CENTRAL ARKANSAS, UNIVERSITY OF

314 Western Avenue	**Men**	**Women**
Conway, AR 72035	Baseball	Basketball
Affiliation—NCAA II	Basketball	Cheerleading
Nickname—Bears	Football	Cross Country
Athletic Director—	Soccer	Soccer
(501) 450-3150		Softball
		Tennis
		Volleyball

HARDING COLLEGE

900 E. *Center Avenue*	**Men**	**Women**
Searcy, AR 72149-0002	Baseball	Basketball
Affiliation—NCAA II	Basketball	Cross Country
Nickname—Bisons	Cross Country	Soccer
Athletic Director—	Football	Tennis
(501) 279-4305	Golf	Track
	Tennis	Volleyball
	Track	

HENDERSON STATE UNIVERSITY

PO Box 7630	**Men**	**Women**
Arkadelphia, AR 71999	Baseball	Basketball
Affiliation—NCAA II	Basketball	Cross Country
Nickname—Reddies	Football	Softball
Athletic Director—	Golf	Swimming
(870) 230-5161	Swimming	Tennis
	Tennis	Volleyball

HENDRIX COLLEGE

1600 Washington Avenue	**Men**	**Women**
Conway, AR 72032-4115	Baseball	Basketball
Affiliation—NCAA III	Basketball	Cheerleading
Nickname—Warriors	Cross Country	Cross Country
Athletic Director—	Golf	Golf
(501) 450-1315	Soccer	Soccer
	Swimming	Swimming
	Tennis	Tennis
		Track
		Volleyball

JOHN BROWN UNIVERSITY

2000 W. *University Street*	**Men**	**Women**
Siloam Springs, AR 72761-2112	Basketball	Basketball
Affiliation—NAIA I	Soccer	Cheerleading
Nickname—Golden Eagles	Swimming	Swimming
Athletic Director—	Tennis	Tennis
(501) 524-7305		Volleyball

LYON COLLEGE

Highland Avenue	**Men**	**Women**
Batesville, AR 72501	Basketball	Basketball
*Affiliation—*NAIA *I*	Cross Country	Cheerleading
Nickname—Scots	Golf	Cross Country
Athletic Director—	Soccer	Tennis
(870) 698-4201	Tennis	Volleyball
	Volleyball	

OUACHITA BAPTIST UNIVERSITY

Box 3788, 410 Ouachita Street	**Men**	**Women**
Arkadelphia, AR 71923-3200	Baseball	Basketball
*Affiliation—*NCAA *II*	Basketball	Cross Country
Nickname—Tigers	Cross Country	Diving
Athletic Director—	Diving	Swimming
(870) 245-5182	Football	Tennis
	Golf	Volleyball
	Swimming	
	Tennis	

OZARKS, UNIVERSITY OF THE

415 College Avenue	**Men**	**Women**
Clarksville, AR 72830	Baseball	Basketball
*Affiliation—*NCAA *III*	Basketball	Cross Country
Nickname—Eagles	Cross Country	Soccer
Athletic Director—	Golf	Softball
(501) 979-1325	Soccer	Tennis
	Tennis	

PHILANDER SMITH COLLEGE

812 W. 13th Street	**Men**	**Women**
Little Rock, AR 72202-3718	Basketball	Basketball
*Affiliation—*NAIA *I*	Golf	Cross Country
Nickname—Panthers	Track	Track
Athletic Director—	Volleyball	Volleyball
(501) 370-5348		

SOUTHERN ARKANSAS UNIVERSITY

100 E. University Street	**Men**	**Women**
Magnolia, AR 71753-2181	Baseball	Basketball
Affiliation—NCAA *II*	Basketball	Cheerleading
Nickname—Muleriders	Cross Country	Cross Country
Athletic Director—	Football	Softball
(870) 235-4132	Golf	Swimming
	Swimming	Tennis
	Track	Track
		Volleyball

CALIFORNIA

AZUSA PACIFIC UNIVERSITY

901 S. Alosta Avenue	**Men**	**Women**
Azusa, CA 91702-2701	Baseball	Basketball
Affiliation—NAIA *I*	Basketball	Cheerleading
Nickname—Cougars	Cross Country	Cross Country
Athletic Director—	Football	Soccer
(626) 812-3024	Soccer	Softball
	Tennis	Tennis
	Track	Track
		Volleyball

BETHANY COLLEGE

800 Bethany Drive	**Men**	**Women**
Scotts Valley, CA 95066-2820	Basketball	Basketball
Affiliation—NAIA *I*	Volleyball	Volleyball
Nickname—Bruins		
Athletic Director—		
(408) 438-3800		

BIOLA UNIVERSITY

13800 Biola Avenue	**Men**	**Women**
LaMirada, CA 90639	Baseball	Basketball
Affiliation—NAIA *I*	Basketball	Cross Country
Nickname—Eagles	Cross Country	Soccer
Athletic Director—	Soccer	Softball
(562) 906-4519	Swimming	Swimming
	Tennis	Tennis
	Track	Track
		Volleyball

CALIFORNIA, UNIVERSITY OF, BERKELEY

210 Memorial Stadium	**Men**	**Women**
Berkeley, CA 94720-4427	Baseball	Basketball
*Affiliation—*NCAA *I*	Basketball	Crew
(I-A Football)	Crew	Cross Country
Nickname—Golden Bears	Cross Country	Diving
Athletic Director—	Football	Field Hockey
(510) 642-0580	Golf	Golf
	Gymnastics	Gymnastics
	Rugby	Soccer
	Soccer	Softball
	Swimming	Swimming
	Tennis	Tennis
	Track	Track
	Water Polo	Volleyball
		Water Polo

CALIFORNIA, UNIVERSITY OF, DAVIS

Athletic Department	**Men**	**Women**
Davis, CA 95616	Baseball	Basketball
*Affiliation—*NCAA *II*	Basketball	Crew
Nickname—Aggies	Cross Country	Cross Country
Athletic Director—	Football	Gymnastics
(530) 752-1111	Golf	Lacrosse
	Soccer	Soccer
	Swimming	Softball
	Tennis	Swimming
	Track	Tennis
	Water Polo	Track
	Wrestling	Volleyball
		Water Polo

CALIFORNIA, UNIVERSITY OF, IRVINE

West Peltason and California	**Men**	**Women**
Irvine, CA 92697	Basketball	Basketball
*Affiliation—*NCAA *I*	Crew	Crew
Nickname—Anteaters	Cross Country	Cross Country
Athletic Director—	Golf	Sailing
(949) 824-6931	Sailing	Soccer
	Soccer	Swimming
	Swimming	Tennis
	Tennis	Track
	Track	Volleyball
	Volleyball	
	Water Polo	

CALIFORNIA, UNIVERSITY OF, LOS ANGELES

Morgan Center	**Men**	**Women**
325 Westwood Plaza	Baseball	Basketball
Los Angeles, CA 90095-1639	Basketball	Cross Country
Affiliation—NCAA I	Cross Country	Diving
(I-A Football)	Football	Golf
Nickname—Bruins	Golf	Soccer
Athletic Director—	Soccer	Softball
(310) 825-8699	Tennis	Swimming
	Track	Tennis
	Volleyball	Track
	Water Polo	Volleyball
		Water Polo

CALIFORNIA, UNIVERSITY OF, RIVERSIDE

900 University Avenue	**Men**	**Women**
Riverside, CA 92521	Baseball	Basketball
Affiliation—NCAA II	Basketball	Cross Country
Nickname—Highlanders	Cross Country	Softball
Athletic Director—	Tennis	Tennis
(909) 787-5496	Track	Track
		Volleyball

CALIFORNIA, UNIVERSITY OF, SAN DIEGO

9500 Gilman Drive	**Men**	**Women**
La Jolla, CA 92093-5003	Baseball	Basketball
Affiliation—NCAA III	Basketball	Crew
Nickname—Tritons	Crew	Cross Country
Athletic Director—	Cross Country	Diving
(619) 534-4211	Diving	Fencing
	Fencing	Soccer
	Golf	Softball
	Soccer	Swimming
	Swimming	Tennis
	Tennis	Track
	Track	Volleyball
	Volleyball	Water Polo
	Water Polo	

CALIFORNIA, UNIVERSITY OF, SANTA BARBARA

Department of Athletics	Men	Women
Santa Barbara, CA 93106	Baseball	Basketball
Affiliation—NCAA I	Basketball	Cross Country
Nickname—Gauchos	Cross Country	Diving
Athletic Director—	Diving	Gymnastics
(805) 893-3400	Golf	Lacrosse
	Gymnastics	Soccer
	Lacrosse	Softball
	Soccer	Swimming
	Swimming	Tennis
	Tennis	Track
	Track	Volleyball
	Volleyball	Water Polo
	Water Polo	

CALIFORNIA, UNIVERSITY OF, SANTA CRUZ

East Field House,	Men	Women
1156 High Street	Basketball	Basketball
Santa Cruz, CA 95064	Sailing	Cheerleading
Affiliation—NCAA III	Soccer	Soccer
Nickname—Banana Slugs	Swimming	Swimming
Athletic Director—	Tennis	Tennis
(408) 459-2531	Volleyball	Volleyball
	Water Polo	Water Polo

CALIFORNIA BAPTIST COLLEGE

8432 Magnolia Avenue	Men	Women
Riverside, CA 92504-3206	Baseball	Basketball
Affiliation—NAIA I	Basketball	Cheerleading
Nickname—Lancers	Cross Country	Cross Country
Athletic Director—	Golf	Soccer
(909) 343-4381	Soccer	Softball
	Tennis	Tennis
	Track	Track
	Volleyball	Volleyball

CALIFORNIA INSTITUTE OF TECHNOLOGY

1201 E. California Boulevard Pasadena, CA 91125 Affiliation—NCAA III Nickname—Beavers Athletic Director— (626) 395-6148	Men Baseball Basketball Cross Country Fencing Golf Soccer Swimming Tennis Track Volleyball Water Polo	Women Basketball Cross Country Fencing Swimming Tennis Track Volleyball

CALIFORNIA LUTHERAN UNIVERSITY

60 W. Olsen Road Thousand Oaks, CA 91360-2787 Affiliation—NCAA III Nickname—Kingsmen Athletic Director— (805) 493-3402	Men Baseball Basketball Cross Country Football Golf Soccer Tennis Track	Women Basketball Cross Country Soccer Softball Tennis Track Volleyball

CALIFORNIA MARITIME ACADEMY

200 Maritime Drive Vallejo, CA 94590 Affiliation—NAIA II Nickname—Keelhaulers Athletic Director— (707) 648-4261	Men Basketball Crew Golf Soccer Water Polo	Women Crew Volleyball

CALIFORNIA POLYTECHNIC STATE UNIVERSITY

1 Grand Avenue San Luis Obispo, CA 93407-9000 Affiliation—NCAA I (I-AA Football) Nickname—Mustangs Athletic Director— (805) 756-2923	Men Baseball Basketball Cross Country Football Soccer Swimming Tennis Track Wrestling	Women Basketball Cross Country Soccer Softball Swimming Tennis Track Volleyball

CALIFORNIA STATE POLYTECHNIC UNIVERSITY POMONA

3801 W. Temple Avenue	**Men**	**Women**
Pomona, CA 91768-2557	Baseball	Basketball
Affiliation—NCAA II	Basketball	Cross Country
Nickname—Broncos	Cross Country	Soccer
Athletic Director—	Soccer	Tennis
(909) 869-2811	Tennis	Track
	Track	Volleyball

CALIFORNIA STATE UNIVERSITY, BAKERSFIELD

9001 Stockdale Highway	**Men**	**Women**
Bakersfield, CA 93311-1022	Basketball	Cheerleading
Affiliation—NCAA II	Diving	Cross Country
(Div. I Wrestling)	Golf	Diving
Nickname—Roadrunners	Soccer	Soccer
Athletic Director—	Swimming	Softball
(805) 664-2188	Track	Swimming
	Wrestling	Tennis
		Track
		Volleyball
		Water Polo

CALIFORNIA STATE UNIVERSITY, CHICO

First and Orange	**Men**	**Women**
Chico, CA 95929	Baseball	Basketball
Affiliation—NCAA II	Basketball	Cross Country
Nickname—Wildcats	Cross Country	Soccer
Athletic Director—	Golf	Softball
(530) 898-5201	Soccer	Track
	Track	Volleyball

CALIFORNIA STATE UNIVERSITY, DOMINGUEZ HILLS

100 E. Victoria Street	**Men**	**Women**
Carson, CA 90747	Baseball	Basketball
Affiliation—NCAA II	Basketball	Cross Country
Nickname—Toros	Golf	Soccer
Athletic Director—	Soccer	Tennis
(310) 243-3893		Track
		Volleyball

CALIFORNIA STATE UNIVERSITY, FRESNO

	Men	**Women**
5305 N. Campus Drive	Baseball	Basketball
MG NG27	Basketball	Cheerleading
Fresno, CA 93740-8020	Cross Country	Cross Country
Affiliation—NCAA *I*	Football	Diving
(I-A Football)	Golf	Equestrian
Nickname—Bulldogs	Soccer	Soccer
Athletic Director—	Tennis	Softball
(209) 278-3178	Track	Swimming
	Wrestling	Tennis
		Track
		Volleyball

CALIFORNIA STATE UNIVERSITY, FULLERTON

	Men	**Women**
PO Box 6810	Baseball	Basketball
Fullerton, CA 92834-6810	Basketball	Cross Country
Affiliation—NCAA *I*	Cross Country	Fencing
Nickname—Titans	Fencing	Gymnastics
Athletic Director—	Soccer	Soccer
(714) 278-2777	Track	Softball
	Wrestling	Tennis
		Track
		Volleyball

CALIFORNIA STATE UNIVERSITY, HAYWARD

	Men	**Women**
25800 Carlos Bee Boulevard	Baseball	Basketball
Hayward, CA 94542-3001	Basketball	Cross Country
Affiliation—NCAA *III*	Cross Country	Soccer
Nickname—Pioneers	Soccer	Softball
Athletic Director—		Swimming
(510) 885-3038		Volleyball
		Water Polo

CALIFORNIA STATE UNIVERSITY, LONG BEACH

1250 N. Bellflower Boulevard	**Men**	**Women**
Long Beach, CA 90840-0006	Baseball	Basketball
Affiliation—NCAA I	Basketball	Cross Country
Nickname—49ers	Cross Country	Golf
Athletic Director—	Golf	Soccer
(562) 985-7976	Track	Softball
	Volleyball	Tennis
	Water Polo	Track
		Volleyball
		Water Polo

CALIFORNIA STATE UNIVERSITY, LOS ANGELES

5151 State University Drive	**Men**	**Women**
Los Angeles, CA 90032-4226	Baseball	Basketball
Affiliation—NCAA II	Basketball	Cross Country
Nickname—Golden Eagles	Cross Country	Soccer
Athletic Director—	Soccer	Tennis
(213) 343-3080	Tennis	Track
	Track	Volleyball

CALIFORNIA STATE UNIVERSITY, MONTEREY BAY

100 Campus Circle	**Men**	**Women**
Seaside, CA 93955-8000	Basketball	Basketball
Affiliation—NAIA II	Cross Country	Cross Country
Nickname—Otters	Golf	Golf
Athletic Director—	Rugby	Volleyball
(408) 582-3400	Soccer	

CALIFORNIA STATE UNIVERSITY, NORTHRIDGE

18111 Nordhoff Street	**Men**	**Women**
Northridge, CA 91330-8276	Baseball	Basketball
Affiliation—NCAA I	Basketball	Cross Country
(I-AA Football)	Cross Country	Diving
Nickname—Matadors	Diving	Golf
Athletic Director—	Football	Soccer
(818) 677-3208	Golf	Softball
	Soccer	Swimming
	Swimming	Tennis
	Track	Track
	Volleyball	Volleyball

CALIFORNIA STATE UNIVERSITY, SACRAMENTO

6000 J Street	**Men**	**Women**
Sacramento, CA 95819-6099	Baseball	Basketball
Affiliation—NCAA I	Basketball	Crew
(I-AA Football)	Cross Country	Cross Country
Nickname—Hornets	Football	Golf
Athletic Director—	Golf	Gymnastics
(916) 278-6348	Soccer	Soccer
	Tennis	Softball
	Track	Tennis
		Track
		Volleyball

CALIFORNIA STATE UNIVERSITY, SAN BERNARDINO

5500 University Parkway	**Men**	**Women**
San Bernardino, CA	Baseball	Basketball
92407-7500	Basketball	Cross Country
Affiliation—NCAA II	Golf	Soccer
Nickname—Coyotes	Soccer	Softball
Athletic Director—		Tennis
(909) 880-5011		Volleyball
		Water Polo

CALIFORNIA STATE UNIVERSITY, STANISLAUS

801 W. Monte Vista Avenue	**Men**	**Women**
Turlock, CA 95382-0256	Baseball	Basketball
Affiliation—NCAA II	Basketball	Cheerleading
Nickname—Warriors	Cross Country	Cross Country
Athletic Director—	Golf	Soccer
(209) 667-3566	Soccer	Softball
		Track
		Volleyball

CHAPMAN UNIVERSITY

	Men	Women
333 N. Glassell Street	Baseball	Basketball
Orange, CA 92866-1011	Basketball	Crew
Affiliation—NCAA III	Crew	Cross Country
Nickname—*Panthers*	Cross Country	Soccer
Athletic Director—	Football	Softball
(714) 997-6789	Golf	Swimming
	Lacrosse	Tennis
	Soccer	Track
	Swimming	Volleyball
	Tennis	
	Water Polo	

CHRISTIAN HERITAGE COLLEGE

	Men	Women
2100 Greenfield Drive	Basketball	Basketball
El Cajon, CA 92019-1161	Cross Country	Cross Country
Affiliation—NAIA, NCCAA I	Soccer	Volleyball
Nickname—*Hawks*		
Athletic Director—		
(619) 441-2200 ext. 1185		

CLAREMONT MCKENNA COLLEGE

	Men	Women
500 E. 9th Street	Baseball	Basketball
Claremont, CA 91711-5903	Basketball	Cross Country
Affiliation—NCAA III	Cross Country	Diving
Nickname—*Stags*	Football	Soccer
Athletic Director—	Golf	Softball
(909) 607-2220	Soccer	Swimming
	Swimming	Tennis
	Tennis	Track
	Track	Volleyball
	Water Polo	Water Polo

CONCORDIA UNIVERSITY

	Men	Women
1530 Concordia West	Baseball	Basketball
Irvine, CA 92612-3203	Basketball	Cross Country
Affiliation—NAIA I	Cross Country	Soccer
Nickname—*Eagles*	Soccer	Softball
Athletic Director—	Track	Track
(714) 854-8002 ext. 423		Volleyball

DOMINICAN COLLEGE OF SAN RAFAEL

50 Acacia Avenue	Men	Women
San Rafael, CA 94901-2230	Basketball	Basketball
Affiliation—NAIA	Cross Country	Cross Country
Nickname—Penguins	Soccer	Soccer
Athletic Director—	Tennis	Tennis
(415) 485-3230		Volleyball

FRESNO PACIFIC UNIVERSITY

1717 S. Chestnut Avenue	Men	Women
Fresno, CA 93702-4709	Basketball	Basketball
Affiliation—NAIA I	Cross Country	Cross Country
Nickname—Sunbirds	Soccer	Track
Athletic Director—	Track	Volleyball
(209) 453-2009		

HOLY NAMES COLLEGE

3500 Mountain Boulevard	Men	Women
Oakland, CA 94619-1627	Basketball	Basketball
Affiliation—NAIA II	Cross Country	Cross Country
Nickname—Hawks	Golf	Volleyball
Athletic Director—		
(510) 436-1491		

HUMBOLDT STATE UNIVERSITY

1 Harpst Street	Men	Women
Arcata, CA 95521	Basketball	Basketball
Affiliation—NCAA II	Cross Country	Crew
Nickname—Lumberjacks	Football	Cross Country
Athletic Director—	Soccer	Soccer
(707) 826-3666	Track	Softball
		Track
		Volleyball

LA SIERRA UNIVERSITY

4700 Pierce Street	Men	Women
Riverside, CA 92505-3331	Basketball	Basketball
Affiliation—NAIA	Gymnastics	Volleyball
Nickname—Golden Eagles	Soccer	
Athletic Director—	Tennis	
(732) 785-2295	Volleyball	

LA VERNE, UNIVERSITY OF

1950 3rd Street	**Men**	**Women**
La Verne, CA 91750-4401	Baseball	Basketball
Affiliation—NCAA III	Basketball	Cross Country
Nickname—Leopards	Cross Country	Soccer
Athletic Director—	Football	Softball
(909) 593-3511	Golf	Swimming
	Soccer	Tennis
	Swimming	Track
	Tennis	Volleyball
	Track	Water Polo
	Volleyball	
	Water Polo	

LOYOLA MARYMOUNT UNIVERSITY

7900 Loyola Boulevard	**Men**	**Women**
Los Angeles, CA 90045-2659	Baseball	Basketball
Affiliation—NCAA I	Basketball	Crew
Nickname—Lions	Crew	Cross Country
Athletic Director—	Cross Country	Soccer
(310) 338-2765	Golf	Softball
	Soccer	Swimming
	Swimming	Tennis
	Tennis	Volleyball
	Volleyball	
	Water Polo	

MASTER'S COLLEGE

21726 Placerita Canyon Road	**Men**	**Women**
Santa Clarita, CA 91321-1200	Baseball	Basketball
Affiliation—NAIA I	Basketball	Cross Country
Nickname—Mustangs	Cross Country	Soccer
Athletic Director—	Soccer	Volleyball
(805) 259-0942		

MENLO COLLEGE

1000 El Camino Real	**Men**	**Women**
Atherton, CA 94027-4300	Baseball	Basketball
Affiliation—NCAA III	Basketball	Cross Country
Nickname—Oaks	Cross County	Soccer
Athletic Director—	Football	Softball
(650) 688-3770	Golf	Tennis
	Soccer	Track
	Tennis	Volleyball
	Track	

MILLS COLLEGE

5000 MacArthur Boulevard	**Women**	
Oakland, CA 94613	Crew	Swimming
Affiliation—NCAA III	Cross Country	Tennis
Nickname—Cyclones	Soccer	Track
Athletic Director—		
(510) 430-2197		

NOTRE DAME, COLLEGE OF

1500 Ralston Avenue	**Men**	**Women**
Belmont, CA 94002-1908	Basketball	Basketball
Affiliation—NAIA	Cross Country	Cross Country
Nickname—Argonauts	Soccer	Softball
Athletic Director—	Tennis	Tennis
(650) 508-3685	Track	Track
		Volleyball

OCCIDENTAL COLLEGE

1600 Campus Road	**Men**	**Women**
Los Angeles, CA 90041-3314	Baseball	Basketball
Affiliation—NCAA III	Basketball	Cross Country
Nickname—Tigers	Cross Country	Soccer
Athletic Director—	Football	Softball
(213) 259-2699	Golf	Swimming
	Soccer	Tennis
	Swimming	Track
	Tennis	Volleyball
	Track	Water Polo
	Water Polo	

PACIFIC, UNIVERSITY OF THE

3601 Pacific Avenue	**Men**	**Women**
Stockton, CA 95211	Baseball	Basketball
Affiliation—NCAA I	Basketball	Cross Country
Nickname—Tigers	Golf	Field Hockey
Athletic Director—	Swimming	Soccer
(209) 946-2222	Tennis	Softball
	Volleyball	Swimming
	Water Polo	Tennis
		Volleyball
		Water Polo

PACIFIC CHRISTIAN COLLEGE
INTERNATIONAL UNIVERSITY

2500 Nutwood Avenue	**Men**	**Women**
Fullerton, CA 92831-3104	Basketball	Basketball
Affiliation—NCCAA I, NAIA II	Soccer	Soccer
Nickname—Royals	Tennis	Softball
Athletic Director—Men	Volleyball	Tennis
(714) 879-3901 ext. 288		Volleyball
Athletic Director—Women		
(714) 879-3901 ext. 270		

PATTEN COLLEGE

2433 Coolidge Avenue	**Men**	**Women**
Oakland, CA 94601-2699	Basketball	Basketball
Affiliation—NAIA II	Cross Country	Cross Country
Nickname—Lions	Golf	Golf
Athletic Director—	Soccer	Soccer
(510) 533-8300 ext. 286		Softball

PEPPERDINE UNIVERSITY

24255 Pacific Coast Highway	**Men**	**Women**
Malibu, CA 90263	Baseball	Basketball
Affiliation—NCAA I	Basketball	Cross Country
Nickname—Waves	Cross Country	Diving
Athletic Director—	Golf	Golf
(310) 456-4242	Soccer	Soccer
	Tennis	Swimming
	Volleyball	Tennis
	Water Polo	Volleyball

POINT LOMA NAZARENE UNIVERSITY

3900 Lomaland Drive	**Men**	**Women**
San Diego, CA 92106-2810	Baseball	Basketball
Affiliation—NAIA I	Basketball	Cross Country
Nickname—Crusaders	Cross Country	Softball
Athletic Director—	Golf	Tennis
(619) 849-2266	Soccer	Track
	Tennis	Volleyball
	Track	

POMONA-PITZER COLLEGES

Rains Center, 220 E. 6th Street	**Men**	**Women**
Claremont, CA 91711	Baseball	Basketball
Affiliation—NCAA *III*	Basketball	Cross Country
Nickname—*Sagehens*	Cross Country	Diving
Athletic Director—	Diving	Fencing
(909) 621-8016	Fencing	Golf
	Football	Lacrosse
	Golf	Soccer
	Lacrosse	Softball
	Soccer	Swimming
	Swimming	Tennis
	Tennis	Track
	Track	Volleyball
	Volleyball	Water Polo
	Water Polo	

REDLANDS, UNIVERSITY OF

PO Box 3080,	**Men**	**Women**
1200 E. Colton Avenue	Baseball	Basketball
Redlands, CA 92373-0999	Basketball	Cheerleading
Affiliation—NCAA *III*	Cross Country	Cross Country
Nickname—*Bulldogs*	Diving	Diving
Athletic Director—	Football	Lacrosse
(909) 335-4004	Golf	Soccer
	Soccer	Softball
	Swimming	Swimming
	Tennis	Tennis
	Track	Track
	Water Polo	Volleyball
		Water Polo

SAINT MARY'S COLLEGE OF CALIFORNIA

1928 Saint Mary's Road	**Men**	**Women**
Moraga, CA 94556-2715	Baseball	Basketball
Affiliation—NCAA *I*	Basketball	Crew
(I-AA Football)	Crew	Cross Country
Nickname—*Gaels*	Cross Country	Soccer
Athletic Director—	Football	Softball
(925) 631-4383	Golf	Tennis
	Rugby	Volleyball
	Soccer	
	Tennis	

SAN DIEGO, UNIVERSITY OF

5998 Alcala Park	Men	Women
San Diego, CA 92110-2429	Baseball	Basketball
Affiliation—NCAA I	Basketball	Crew
(I-AA Football)	Crew	Cross Country
Nickname—Toreros	Cross Country	Diving
Athletic Director—	Football	Soccer
(619) 260-2930	Golf	Softball
	Soccer	Swimming
	Tennis	Tennis
		Volleyball

SAN DIEGO STATE UNIVERSITY

5500 Campanile Drive	Men	Women
San Diego, CA 92182	Baseball	Basketball
Affiliation—NCAA I	Basketball	Cheerleading
(I-AA Football)	Football	Crew
Nickname—Aztecs	Golf	Cross Country
Athletic Director—	Soccer	Golf
(619) 594-3019	Tennis	Soccer
	Volleyball	Softball
		Swimming
		Tennis
		Track
		Volleyball
		Water Polo

SAN FRANCISCO, UNIVERSITY OF

2130 Fulton Street	Men	Women
San Francisco, CA 94117-1080	Baseball	Basketball
Affiliation—NCAA I	Basketball	Cross Country
Nickname—Dons	Cross Country	Golf
Athletic Director—	Golf	Rifle
(415) 422-6891	Rifle	Soccer
	Soccer	Tennis
	Tennis	Volleyball

SAN FRANCISCO STATE UNIVERSITY

1600 Holloway Avenue *San Francisco, CA 94132-4041* *Affiliation*—NCAA II *Nickname—Gators* *Athletic Director—* *(415) 338-2218*	**Men** Baseball Basketball Cross Country Soccer Swimming Track Wrestling	**Women** Basketball Cross Country Soccer Softball Swimming Tennis Track Volleyball

SAN JOSE CHRISTIAN COLLEGE

790 S. 12th Street *San Jose, CA 95112-2304* *Affiliation*—NCCAA, NBCAA *Athletic Director—* *(408) 293-9058*	**Men** Basketball Volleyball

SAN JOSE STATE UNIVERSITY

1 Washington Square *San Jose, CA 95112-3613* *Affiliation*—NCAA I *(I-A Football)* *Nickname—Spartans* *Athletic Director—* *(408) 924-1200*	**Men** Baseball Basketball Cross Country Football Golf Judo Soccer	**Women** Basketball Cheerleading Cross Country Diving Golf Gymnastics Soccer Softball Swimming Tennis Volleyball Water Polo

SANTA CLARA UNIVERSITY

500 El Camino *Santa Clara, CA 95053* *Affiliation*—NCAA I *Nickname—Broncos* *Athletic Director—* *(408) 554-5344*	**Men** Baseball Basketball Crew Cross Country Golf Soccer Tennis Water Polo	**Women** Basketball Crew Cross Country Golf Soccer Softball Tennis Volleyball

SIMPSON COLLEGE

2211 College View Drive	Men	Women
Redding, CA 96003-8601	Baseball	Basketball
Affiliation—NCCAA II, NAIA II	Basketball	Soccer
Nickname—Vanguards	Golf	Softball
Athletic Director—	Soccer	Volleyball
(530) 224-5600	Volleyball	

SONOMA STATE UNIVERSITY

1801 E. Cotati Avenue	Men	Women
Rohnert Park, CA 94928-3613	Baseball	Basketball
Affiliation—NCAA II	Basketball	Cross Country
Nickname—Cossacks	Soccer	Soccer
Athletic Director—	Tennis	Softball
(707) 664-2521		Tennis
		Track
		Volleyball

SOUTHERN CALIFORNIA, UNIVERSITY OF

103 Heritage Hall	Men	Women
Los Angeles, CA 90089	Basketball	Basketball
Affiliation—NCAA I	Baseball	Crew
(I-A Football)	Diving	Cross Country
Nickname—Trojans	Football	Diving
Athletic Director—	Golf	Golf
(213) 740-3843	Swimming	Soccer
	Tennis	Swimming
	Track	Tennis
	Volleyball	Track
	Water Polo	Volleyball
		Water Polo

STANFORD UNIVERSITY

Stanford, CA 94305	**Men**	**Women**
*Affiliation—*NCAA *I*	Baseball	Basketball
(I-A Football)	Basketball	Crew
Nickname—Cardinals	Crew	Cross Country
Athletic Director—	Cross Country	Diving
(650) 723-4596	Diving	Fencing
	Fencing	Field Hockey
	Football	Golf
	Golf	Gymnastics
	Gymnastics	Lacrosse
	Soccer	Soccer
	Swimming	Softball
	Tennis	Swimming
	Track	Tennis
	Volleyball	Track
	Water Polo	Volleyball

VANGUARD UNIVERSITY OF SOUTHERN CALIFORNIA

55 Fair Drive	**Men**	**Women**
Costa Mesa, CA 92626-6520	Baseball	Basketball
*Affiliation—*NAIA *I*	Basketball	Cross Country
Nickname—Lions	Cross Country	Soccer
Athletic Director—	Soccer	Softball
(714) 556-3610 ext. 279	Tennis	Tennis
	Track	Track
		Volleyball

WESTMONT COLLEGE

955 La Paz Road	**Men**	**Women**
Santa Barbara, CA 93108-1089	Basketball	Basketball
*Affiliation—*NAIA *I*	Cross Country	Cheerleading
Nickname—Warriors	Soccer	Cross Country
Athletic Director—	Tennis	Soccer
(805) 565-6010	Track	Tennis
		Track
		Volleyball

WHITTIER COLLEGE

13406 Philadelphia Street	**Men**	**Women**
Whittier, CA 90608-0634	Baseball	Basketball
*Affiliation—*NCAA III	Basketball	Cross Country
Nickname—Poets	Cross Country	Lacrosse
Athletic Director—	Football	Soccer
(562) 907-4271	Golf	Softball
	Lacrosse	Swimming
	Soccer	Tennis
	Swimming	Track
	Tennis	Volleyball
	Track	Water Polo
	Water Polo	

COLORADO

ADAMS STATE COLLEGE

Plachy Hall, Stadium Drive	**Men**	**Women**
Alamosa, CO 81102	Basketball	Basketball
*Affiliation—*NCAA II	Cross Country	Cheerleading
Nickname—Grizzlies	Football	Cross Country
Athletic Director—	Golf	Softball
(719) 587-7271	Track	Track
	Wrestling	Volleyball

COLORADO, UNIVERSITY OF

Campus Box 368	**Men**	**Women**
Boulder, CO 80309	Basketball	Basketball
*Affiliation—*NCAA I	Cross Country	Cross Country
(I-A Football)	Football	Golf
Nickname—Buffalos	Golf	Skiing
Athletic Director—	Skiing	Soccer
(303) 492-7930	Tennis	Tennis
	Track	Track
		Volleyball

COLORADO, UNIVERSITY OF, COLORADO SPRINGS

PO Box 7150, 1420 Austin Bluffs	**Men**	**Women**
Colorado Springs, CO 80933	Basketball	Basketball
*Affiliation—*NCAA II	Cross Country	Cross Country
Nickname—Mountain Lions	Golf	Softball
Athletic Director—	Soccer	Tennis
(719) 262-3575	Tennis	Volleyball

COLORADO CHRISTIAN UNIVERSITY

180 S. Garrison Street	**Men**	**Women**
Lakewood, CO 80226-1053	Basketball	Basketball
Affiliation—NCAA II	Cross Country	Cross Country
Nickname—Cougars	Golf	Soccer
Athletic Director—	Soccer	Tennis
(303) 238-5388 ext. 221		Volleyball

COLORADO COLLEGE

12 E. Cache La Poudre Street	**Men**	**Women**
Colorado Springs, CO 80909	Basketball	Basketball
Affiliation—NCAA III	Cross Country	Cross Country
(Div. I Hockey)	Football	Lacrosse
Nickname—Tigers	Ice Hockey	Soccer
Athletic Director—	Lacrosse	Softball
(719) 389-6476	Soccer	Swimming
	Swimming	Tennis
	Tennis	Track
	Track	Volleyball

COLORADO SCHOOL OF MINES

Volk Gymnasium, 1500 Illinois	**Men**	**Women**
Golden, CO 80401-1887	Baseball	Basketball
Affiliation—NCAA II	Basketball	Cross Country
Nickname—Orediggers	Cross Country	Softball
Athletic Director—	Football	Swimming
(303) 273-3363	Golf	Track
	Soccer	Volleyball
	Swimming	
	Tennis	
	Track	
	Wrestling	

COLORADO STATE UNIVERSITY

Fort Collins, CO 80523-0015	**Men**	**Women**
Affiliation—NCAA I	Basketball	Basketball
(I-A Football)	Cross Country	Cheerleading
Nickname—Rams	Football	Cross Country
Athletic Director—	Golf	Diving
(970) 491-5300	Track	Golf
		Softball
		Swimming
		Tennis
		Track
		Volleyball

DENVER, UNIVERSITY OF

2201 S. Asbury Avenue	**Men**	**Women**
Denver, CO 80210-4304	Basketball	Basketball
*Affiliation—*NCAA *II*	Golf	Golf
(Div. I Hockey)	Ice Hockey	Gymnastics
Nickname—Pioneers	Lacrosse	Lacrosse
Athletic Director—	Skiing	Skiing
(303) 871-3399	Soccer	Soccer
	Swimming	Swimming
	Tennis	Tennis
		Volleyball

FORT LEWIS COLLEGE

1000 Rim Drive	**Men**	**Women**
Durango, CO 81301-3999	Basketball	Basketball
*Affiliation—*NCAA *II*	Cross Country	Cross Country
Nickname—Skyhawks	Football	Soccer
Athletic Director—	Golf	Softball
(970) 247-7571	Soccer	Volleyball

MESA STATE COLLEGE

1175 Texas Avenue	**Men**	**Women**
Grand Junction, CO	Baseball	Basketball
81501-7605	Basketball	Cross Country
*Affiliation—*NCAA *II*	Football	Golf
Nickname—Mavericks	Tennis	Soccer
Athletic Director—		Softball
(970) 248-1278		Tennis
		Volleyball

METROPOLITAN STATE COLLEGE OF DENVER

PO Box 173362, Campus Box 9	**Men**	**Women**
Denver, CO 80217-3362	Baseball	Basketball
*Affiliation—*NCAA *II*	Basketball	Soccer
Nickname—Roadrunners	Soccer	Swimming
Athletic Director—	Swimming	Tennis
(303) 556-8300	Tennis	Volleyball

NORTHERN COLORADO, UNIVERSITY OF

Butler-Hancock Hall	**Men**	**Women**
Greeley, CO 80639	Baseball	Basketball
Affiliation—NCAA II	Basketball	Cheerleading
Nickname—Bears	Football	Cross Country
Athletic Director—	Golf	Golf
(970) 351-2534	Tennis	Soccer
	Track	Softball
	Wrestling	Swimming
		Tennis
		Track
		Volleyball

REGIS UNIVERSITY

Athletic Department,	**Men**	**Women**
3333 Regis Boulevard	Baseball	Basketball
Denver, CO 80221	Basketball	Cross Country
Affiliation—NCAA II	Cross Country	Soccer
Nickname—Rangers	Golf	Softball
Athletic Director—	Lacrosse	Volleyball
(303) 458-4070	Soccer	

SOUTHERN COLORADO, UNIVERSITY OF

2200 Bonforte Boulevard	**Men**	**Women**
Pueblo, CO 81001-4901	Baseball	Basketball
Affiliation—NCAA II	Basketball	Soccer
Nickname—Thunderwolves	Golf	Softball
Athletic Director—	Soccer	Tennis
(719) 549-2730	Tennis	Volleyball
	Wrestling	

UNITED STATES AIR FORCE ACADEMY

2169 Field House Drive,	**Men**	**Women**
Suite 100	Baseball	Basketball
Air Force Academy, CO 80840	Basketball	Cross Country
Affiliation—NCAA I	Cross Country	Diving
(I-A Football)	Diving	Fencing
Nickname—Falcons	Fencing	Gymnastics
Athletic Director—	Football	Rifle
(719) 333-4008	Golf	Soccer
	Gymnastics	Swimming
	Ice Hockey	Tennis
	Lacrosse	Track
	Rifle	Volleyball
	Soccer	
	Swimming	
	Tennis	
	Track	
	Water Polo	
	Wrestling	

WESTERN STATE COLLEGE OF COLORADO

1 College Heights	**Men**	**Women**
Gunnison, CO 81231	Basketball	Basketball
Affiliation—NCAA II	Cross Country	Cross Country
Nickname—Mountaineers	Football	Skiing
Athletic Director—	Skiing	Track
(970) 943-2079	Track	Volleyball
	Wrestling	

CONNECTICUT

ALBERTUS MAGNUS COLLEGE

700 Prospect Street	**Men**	**Women**
New Haven, CT 06511-1224	Baseball	Basketball
Affiliation—NCAA III	Basketball	Softball
Nickname—Falcons	Soccer	Swimming
Athletic Director—	Swimming	Tennis
(203) 874-0255	Tennis	Volleyball

BRIDGEPORT, UNIVERSITY OF

120 Waldemere Avenue	**Men**	**Women**
Bridgeport, CT 06601-2449	Baseball	Basketball
*Affiliation—*NCAA *II*	Basketball	Cross Country
Nickname—Purple Knights	Cross Country	Gymnastics
Athletic Director—	Soccer	Soccer
(203) 576-4059		Softball
		Volleyball

CENTRAL CONNECTICUT STATE UNIVERSITY

1615 Stanley Street	**Men**	**Women**
New Britain, CT 06053-2439	Baseball	Basketball
*Affiliation—*NCAA *I*	Basketball	Cheerleading
(I-AA Football)	Cross Country	Cross Country
Nickname—Blue Devils	Diving	Golf
Athletic Director—	Football	Soccer
(860) 832-3000	Golf	Softball
	Soccer	Swimming
	Swimming	Tennis
	Tennis	Track
	Track	Volleyball

CONNECTICUT, UNIVERSITY OF

2095 Hillside Road	**Men**	**Women**
Storrs, CT 06269-2095	Baseball	Basketball
*Affiliation—*NCAA *I*	Basketball	Cross Country
(I-AA Football)	Cross Country	Diving
Nickname—Huskies	Diving	Field Hockey
Athletic Director—	Football	Lacrosse
(860) 486-2725	Golf	Rowing
	Ice Hockey	Soccer
	Soccer	Softball
	Swimming	Swimming
	Tennis	Tennis
	Track	Track
		Volleyball

CONNECTICUT COLLEGE

270 Mihegan Avenue	**Men**	**Women**
New London, CT 06320-4125	Basketball	Basketball
Affiliation—NCAA *III*	Crew	Crew
Nickname—Camels	Cross Country	Cross Country
Athletic Director—	Diving	Diving
(860) 439-2666	Ice Hockey	Field Hockey
	Lacrosse	Ice Hockey
	Sailing	Lacrosse
	Soccer	Sailing
	Squash	Soccer
	Swimming	Squash
	Tennis	Swimming
	Track	Tennis
		Track
		Volleyball

EASTERN CONNECTICUT STATE UNIVERSITY

Windham Street	**Men**	**Women**
Willimantic, CT 06226	Baseball	Basketball
Affiliation—NCAA *III*	Basketball	Cheerleading
Nickname—Warriors	Cross Country	Cross Country
Athletic Director—	Lacrosse	Field Hockey
(860) 465-5222	Soccer	Lacrosse
	Track	Soccer
		Softball
		Swimming
		Tennis
		Track

FAIRFIELD UNIVERSITY

N. Benson Road	**Men**	**Women**
Fairfield, CT 06430	Baseball	Basketball
Affiliation—NCAA *I*	Basketball	Crew
(I-AA Football)	Cross Country	Cross Country
Nickname—Stags	Football	Diving
Athletic Director—	Golf	Field Hockey
(203) 254-4000 ext. 2101	Ice Hockey	Golf
	Lacrosse	Lacrosse
	Soccer	Soccer
	Swimming	Softball
	Tennis	Swimming
		Tennis
		Volleyball

HARTFORD, UNIVERSITY OF

200 Bloomfield Avenue	**Men**	**Women**
West Hartford, CT 06117-1545	Baseball	Basketball
Affiliation—NCAA *I*	Basketball	Cross Country
Nickname—Hawks	Cross Country	Golf
Athletic Director—	Golf	Soccer
(860) 768-4417	Lacrosse	Softball
	Soccer	Tennis
	Tennis	Track
	Track	Volleyball

NEW HAVEN, UNIVERSITY OF

300 Orange Avenue	**Men**	**Women**
West Haven, CT 06516-1916	Baseball	Basketball
Affiliation—NCAA *II*	Basketball	Cross Country
Nickname—Chargers	Cross Country	Soccer
Athletic Director—	Football	Softball
(203) 932-7020	Lacrosse	Tennis
	Soccer	Track
	Track	Volleyball

QUINNIPIAC COLLEGE

New Road	**Men**	**Women**
Hamden, CT 06518	Baseball	Basketball
Affiliation—NCAA *I*	Basketball	Cheerleading
Nickname—Braves	Cross Country	Cross Country
Athletic Director—	Golf	Field Hockey
(203) 281-8621	Ice Hockey	Lacrosse
	Lacrosse	Soccer
	Soccer	Softball
	Tennis	Tennis
		Volleyball

SACRED HEART UNIVERSITY

5151 Park Avenue	**Men**	**Women**
Fairfield, CT 96432-1023	Baseball	Basketball
Affiliation—NCAA *II*	Basketball	Bowling
Nickname—*Pioneers*	Crew	Cross Country
Athletic Director—	Cross Country	Field Hockey
(203) 365-7649	Football	Golf
	Golf	Lacrosse
	Ice Hockey	Soccer
	Lacrosse	Softball
	Soccer	Tennis
	Tennis	Track
	Track	Volleyball
	Volleyball	
	Wrestling	

SAINT JOSEPH'S COLLEGE

1678 Asylum Avenue	**Women**	
West Hartford, CT 06117	Basketball	Swimming
Affiliation—NCAA *III*	Cross Country	Tennis
Nickname—*Blue Jays*	Soccer	Volleyball
Athletic Director—	Softball	
(860) 232-3777		

SOUTHERN CONNECTICUT STATE UNIVERSITY

125 Wintergreen Avenue	**Men**	**Women**
New Haven, CT 05615-1059	Baseball	Basketball
Affiliation—NCAA *II*	Basketball	Cheerleading
Nickname—*Owls*	Cross Country	Cross Country
Athletic Director—	Football	Field Hockey
(203) 392-5250	Gymnastics	Gymnastics
	Soccer	Softball
	Swimming	Swimming
	Track	Track
	Wrestling	Volleyball

TEIKYO-POST UNIVERSITY

800 Country Club Road	**Men**	**Women**
Waterbury, CT 06708-3240	Baseball	Basketball
Affiliation—NAIA *II*	Basketball	Cross Country
Nickname—*Eagles*	Cross Country	Soccer
Athletic Director—	Soccer	Softball
(203) 596-4531		Volleyball

TRINITY COLLEGE

| *Summit Street,*
Ferris Athletic Center
Hartford, CT 06106
Affiliation—NCAA *III*
Nickname—Bantams
Athletic Director—
(860) 297-2055 | **Men**
Baseball
Basketball
Crew
Cross Country
Fencing
Football
Golf
Ice Hockey
Lacrosse
Soccer
Swimming
Tennis
Track
Water Polo
Wrestling | **Women**
Basketball
Crew
Cross Country
Fencing
Field Hockey
Ice Hockey
Lacrosse
Soccer
Softball
Squash
Swimming
Tennis
Track
Volleyball |

UNITED STATES COAST GUARD ACADEMY

| *15 Mohegan Avenue*
New London, CT 06320-4100
Affiliation—NCAA *III*
Nickname—Bears
Athletic Director—
(860) 444-8600 | **Men**
Baseball
Basketball
Crew
Cross Country
Football
Pistol
Rifle
Sailing
Soccer
Swimming
Tennis
Track
Wrestling | **Women**
Basketball
Crew
Cross Country
Pistol
Rifle
Sailing
Softball
Track
Volleyball |

WESLEYAN UNIVERSITY

Department of Physical	**Men**	**Women**
Education, 161 Cross Street	Baseball	Basketball
Middletown, CT 06459	Basketball	Crew
Affiliation—NCAA III	Crew	Cross Country
Nickname—Cardinals	Cross Country	Diving
Athletic Director—	Diving	Field Hockey
(860) 685-2896	Football	Golf
	Golf	Ice Hockey
	Ice Hockey	Lacrosse
	Lacrosse	Soccer
	Soccer	Softball
	Squash	Squash
	Swimming	Swimming
	Tennis	Tennis
	Track	Track
	Wrestling	Volleyball

WESTERN CONNECTICUT STATE UNIVERSITY

181 White Street	**Men**	**Women**
Danbury, CT 06810-6826	Baseball	Basketball
Affiliation—NCAA III	Basketball	Soccer
Nickname—Colonials	Football	Swimming
Athletic Director—	Soccer	Tennis
(203) 837-9013	Tennis	Volleyball

YALE UNIVERSITY

PO Box 208216,	**Men**	**Women**
Ray Tompkins House	Baseball	Basketball
New Haven, CT 06520-8216	Basketball	Crew
Affiliation—NCAA I	Crew	Cross Country
(I-AA Football)	Cross Country	Fencing
Nickname—Bulldogs	Diving	Field Hockey
Athletic Director—	Fencing	Golf
(203) 432-1414	Football	Gymnastics
	Golf	Ice Hockey
	Ice Hockey	Lacrosse
	Lacrosse	Soccer
	Soccer	Softball
	Squash	Squash
	Swimming	Swimming
	Tennis	Tennis
	Track	Track
		Volleyball

DELAWARE

DELAWARE, UNIVERSITY OF

Bob Carpenter Center,	**Men**	**Women**
610 S. College	Baseball	Basketball
Newark, DE 19716	Basketball	Cheerleading
*Affiliation—*NCAA *I*	Cross Country	Cross Country
(I-AA Football)	Diving	Diving
Nickname—Fightin' Blue Hens	Football	Field Hockey
Athletic Director—	Lacrosse	Lacrosse
(302) 831-4006	Soccer	Soccer
	Swimming	Softball
	Tennis	Swimming
	Track	Tennis
		Track
		Volleyball

DELAWARE STATE UNIVERSITY

Dupont Highway	**Men**	**Women**
Dover, DE 19901	Baseball	Basketball
*Affiliation—*NCAA *I*	Basketball	Cheerleading
(I-AA Football)	Cross Country	Cross Country
Nickname—Hornets	Football	Softball
Athletic Director—	Tennis	Tennis
(302) 739-4928	Track	Track
	Wrestling	Volleyball

GOLDEY-BEACOM COLLEGE

4701 Limestone Road	**Men**	**Women**
Wilmington, DE 19808-1927	Basketball	Softball
*Affiliation—*NAIA	Soccer	Volleyball
Nickname—Lightning		
Athletic Director—		
(302) 998-8814		

DISTRICT OF COLUMBIA

AMERICAN UNIVERSITY

4400 Massachusetts Avenue NW	**Men**	**Women**
Washington, DC 20016-8001	Basketball	Basketball
Affiliation—NCAA I	Cross Country	Cheerleading
Nickname—Eagles	Diving	Cross Country
Athletic Director—	Golf	Field Hockey
(202) 885-3033	Soccer	Lacrosse
	Swimming	Soccer
	Tennis	Swimming
	Wrestling	Tennis

CATHOLIC UNIVERSITY OF AMERICA

620 Michigan Avenue NE	**Men**	**Women**
Washington, DC 20064	Baseball	Basketball
Affiliation—NCAA III	Basketball	Cross Country
Nickname—Cardinals	Cross Country	Field Hockey
Athletic Director—	Football	Lacrosse
(202) 319-6047	Lacrosse	Soccer
	Soccer	Softball
	Swimming	Swimming
	Tennis	Tennis
	Track	Track
		Volleyball

DISTRICT OF COLUMBIA, UNIVERSITY OF

4200 Connecticut Avenue NW	**Men**	**Women**
Washington, DC 20008-1122	Basketball	Basketball
Affiliation—NCAA II	Cross Country	Cross Country
Nickname—Firebirds	Soccer	Tennis
Athletic Director—	Tennis	Volleyball
(202) 274-5024		

GALLAUDET UNIVERSITY

800 Florida Avenue NE	**Men**	**Women**
Washington, DC 20002-3660	Baseball	Basketball
Affiliation—NCAA III	Basketball	Cross Country
Nickname—Bison	Cross Country	Soccer
Athletic Director—	Football	Softball
(202) 651-5603	Soccer	Swimming
	Swimming	Tennis
	Tennis	Track
	Track	Volleyball
	Wrestling	

GEORGE WASHINGTON UNIVERSITY

600 22nd Street NW	**Men**	**Women**
Washington, DC 20037-2727	Baseball	Basketball
Affiliation—NCAA I	Basketball	Crew
Nickname—Colonials	Crew	Cross Country
Athletic Director—	Cross Country	Diving
(202) 994-6650	Diving	Gymnastics
	Golf	Soccer
	Soccer	Swimming
	Swimming	Tennis
	Tennis	Volleyball
	Water Polo	

GEORGETOWN UNIVERSITY

McDonough Arena	**Men**	**Women**
Washington, DC 20057	Baseball	Basketball
Affiliation—NCAA I	Basketball	Cheerleading
(I-AA Football)	Crew	Crew
Nickname—Hoyas	Cross Country	Cross Country
Athletic Director—	Diving	Diving
(202) 687-2435	Football	Field Hockey
	Golf	Sailing
	Lacrosse	Soccer
	Sailing	Swimming
	Soccer	Tennis
	Swimming	Track
	Tennis	Volleyball
	Track	

HOWARD UNIVERSITY

6th and Girard Streets NW	**Men**	**Women**
Washington, DC 20059	Baseball	Basketball
Affiliation—NCAA I	Basketball	Cross Country
(I-AA Football)	Cross Country	Lacrosse
Nickname—Bison	Football	Soccer
Athletic Director—	Soccer	Swimming
(202) 806-7140	Swimming	Tennis
	Tennis	Track
	Track	Volleyball
	Volleyball	

FLORIDA

BARRY UNIVERSITY

	Men	Women
11300 NE 2nd Avenue	Baseball	Basketball
Miami, FL 33161-6628	Basketball	Crew
Affiliation—NCAA II	Golf	Golf
Nickname—Buccaneers	Soccer	Soccer
Athletic Director—	Tennis	Softball
(305) 899-3554		Tennis
		Volleyball

BETHUNE-COOKMAN COLLEGE

	Men	Women
640 Dr. Mary McLeod Bethune	Baseball	Basketball
Boulevard	Basketball	Cross Country
Daytona Beach, FL 32114	Cross Country	Golf
Affiliation—NCAA I	Football	Softball
(I-A Football)	Golf	Tennis
Nickname—Wildcats	Tennis	Track
Athletic Director—	Track	Volleyball
(904) 255-1491 ext. 319	Volleyball	

CENTRAL FLORIDA, UNIVERSITY OF

	Men	Women
PO Box 16355	Baseball	Basketball
4000 Central Florida Boulevard	Basketball	Crew
Orlando, FL 32816-1635	Cross Country	Cross Country
Affiliation—NCAA I	Football	Golf
(I-A Football)	Golf	Soccer
Nickname—Golden Knights	Soccer	Tennis
Athletic Director—	Tennis	Track
(407) 823-5902		Volleyball

CLEARWATER CHRISTIAN

	Men	Women
3400 Gulf To Bay Boulevard	Baseball	Basketball
Clearwater, FL 33756-4514	Basketball	Softball
Affiliation—NCCAA II	Soccer	Volleyball
Nickname--Cougars		
Athletic Director—		
(727) 726-1153 ext. 211		

ECKERD COLLEGE

4200 54th Avenue S	Men	Women
Saint Petersburg, FL	Baseball	Basketball
44711-4744	Basketball	Cross Country
Affiliation—NCAA II	Golf	Soccer
Nickname—Tritons	Soccer	Softball
Athletic Director—	Tennis	Tennis
(813) 864-8252		Volleyball

EDWARD WATERS COLLEGE

1658 Kings Road	Men	Women
Jacksonville, FL 32209-6167	Baseball	Basketball
Affiliation—NAIA I	Basketball	Cross Country
Nickname—Tigers	Cross Country	Softball
Athletic Director—	Track	Track
(904) 366-2798		

EMBRY-RIDDLE AERONAUTICAL UNIVERSITY

University Fieldhouse	Men	Women
600 S. Clyde Morris Boulevard	Baseball	Soccer
Daytona Beach, FL 32114-3966	Basketball	Volleyball
Affiliation—NAIA	Golf	
(Div. II Basketball)		
Nickname—Eagles		
Athletic Director—		
(904) 226-6200		

FLAGLER COLLEGE

PO Box 1027, King Street	Men	Women
Saint Augustine, FL 32085-1027	Baseball	Basketball
Affiliation—NAIA II	Basketball	Cheerleading
Nickname—Saints	Cheerleading	Cross Country
Athletic Director—	Cross Country	Soccer
(904) 829-6481 ext. 252	Golf	Tennis
	Soccer	Volleyball
	Tennis	

FLORIDA, UNIVERSITY OF

	Men	Women
PO Box 14485	**Men**	**Women**
Gainesville, FL 32604-2485	Baseball	Basketball
Affiliation—NCAA I	Basketball	Cross Country
(I-A Football)	Cross Country	Diving
Nickname—Gators	Diving	Gymnastics
Athletic Director—	Football	Soccer
(352) 375-4683 ext. 6000	Golf	Softball
	Swimming	Swimming
	Tennis	Tennis
	Track	Track
		Volleyball

FLORIDA A&M UNIVERSITY

	Men	Women
Martin Luther King Jr.	**Men**	**Women**
Boulevard	Baseball	Basketball
Tallahassee, FL 32307	Basketball	Cheerleading
Affiliation—NCAA I	Cross Country	Cross Country
(I-AA Football)	Football	Softball
Nickname—Rattlers	Golf	Swimming
Athletic Director—	Swimming	Tennis
(850) 561-2165	Tennis	Track
	Track	Volleyball

FLORIDA ATLANTIC UNIVERSITY

	Men	Women
777 Glades Road	**Men**	**Women**
Boca Raton, FL 33431	Baseball	Basketball
Affiliation—NCAA I	Basketball	Cheerleading
Nickname—Owls	Cheerleading	Cross Country
Athletic Director—	Cross County	Diving
(561) 297-3710	Diving	Golf
	Football	Soccer
	Golf	Softball
	Soccer	Swimming
	Swimming	Tennis
	Tennis	Volleyball

FLORIDA INTERNATIONAL UNIVERSITY, UNIVERSITY PARK

	Men	Women
Tamiami Trail and	Baseball	Basketball
SW 107th Avenue	Basketball	Cross Country
Miami, FL 33199	Cross Country	Golf
*Affiliation—*NCAA *I*	Golf	Soccer
Nickname—Golden Panthers	Soccer	Softball
Athletic Director—	Tennis	Tennis
(305) 348-2761	Track	Track
		Volleyball

FLORIDA INSTITUTE OF TECHNOLOGY

	Men	Women
150 W. University Boulevard	Baseball	Basketball
Melbourne, FL 32901-6982	Basketball	Crew
*Affiliation—*NCAA *II*	Crew	Cross Country
Nickname—Panthers	Cross Country	Fencing
Athletic Director—	Fencing	Softball
(407) 674-8032	Soccer	Volleyball

FLORIDA MEMORIAL COLLEGE

	Men	Women
15800 NW 42nd Avenue	Baseball	Basketball
Opa Locka, FL 33054-6155	Basketball	Track
*Affiliation—*NAIA *II*	Track	Volleyball
Nickname—Lions		
Athletic Director—		
(305) 626-3690		

FLORIDA SOUTHERN COLLEGE

	Men	Women
111 Lake Hollingsworth Drive	Baseball	Basketball
Lakeland, FL 33801-5607	Basketball	Cross Country
*Affiliation—*NCAA *II*	Cross Country	Golf
Nickname—Moccasins	Golf	Soccer
Athletic Director—	Soccer	Softball
(941) 680-4254	Tennis	Tennis
		Volleyball

FLORIDA STATE UNIVERSITY

PO Box 2195, Moore Athletic Court	**Men**	**Women**
Tallahassee, FL 32316-2195	Baseball	Basketball
*Affiliation—*NCAA *I*	Basketball	Cheerleading
(I-A Football)	Crew	Cross Country
Nickname—Seminoles	Cross Country	Diving
Athletic Director—	Diving	Golf
(850) 644-1079	Football	Soccer
	Golf	Softball
	Swimming	Swimming
	Tennis	Tennis
	Track	Track
		Volleyball

JACKSONVILLE UNIVERSITY

University Boulevard N	**Men**	**Women**
Jacksonville, FL 32211	Baseball	Crew
*Affiliation—*NCAA *I*	Basketball	Cross Country
(I-AA Football)	Crew	Golf
Nickname—Dolphins	Cross Country	Soccer
Athletic Director—	Football	Tennis
(904) 745-7401	Golf	Track
	Soccer	Volleyball
	Tennis	
	Track	

LYNN UNIVERSITY

Trinity Hall,	**Men**	**Women**
3601 N. Military Trail	Baseball	Basketball
Boca Raton, FL 33431-5507	Basketball	Cross Country
*Affiliation—*NCAA *II*	Cross Country	Golf
Nickname—Fighting Knights	Golf	Soccer
Athletic Director—	Soccer	Softball
(561) 994-0770	Tennis	Tennis
		Volleyball

MIAMI, UNIVERSITY OF

5821 San Amaro Drive	**Men**	**Women**
Coral Gables, FL 33146-2436	Baseball	Basketball
Affiliation—NCAA I	Basketball	Crew
(I-A Football)	Crew	Cross Country
Nickname—Hurricanes	Cross Country	Diving
Athletic Director—	Diving	Golf
(305) 284-2673	Football	Soccer
	Swimming	Swimming
	Tennis	Tennis
	Track	Track

NORTH FLORIDA, UNIVERSITY OF

4567 Saint Johns Bluff Road S	**Men**	**Women**
Jacksonville, FL 32224-2645	Baseball	Basketball
Affiliation—NCAA II	Basketball	Cross Country
Nickname—Ospreys	Cross Country	Soccer
Athletic Director—	Golf	Softball
(904) 620-2833	Soccer	Tennis
	Tennis	Track
	Track	Volleyball

NOVA SOUTHEASTERN UNIVERSITY

3301 College Avenue	**Men**	**Women**
Fort Lauderdale, FL	Baseball	Basketball
33314-7721	Basketball	Cross Country
Affiliation—NAIA II	Cross Country	Soccer
Nickname—Knights	Golf	Softball
Athletic Director—	Soccer	Tennis
(954) 262-8250		Volleyball

PALM BEACH ATLANTIC COLLEGE

PO Box 24708	**Men**	**Women**
West Palm Beach, FL	Baseball	Basketball
33416-4708	Basketball	Cheerleading
Affiliation—NAIA II	Cross Country	Cross Country
Nickname—Sailfish	Golf	Soccer
Athletic Director—	Soccer	Softball
(561) 803-2525	Tennis	Tennis
		Volleyball

PENSACOLA CHRISTIAN COLLEGE

250 Brent Lane	**Men**	
Pensacola, FL 32503-2267	Basketball	Wrestling
*Affiliation—*NCCAA I	Volleyball	
Nickname—Eagles		
Athletic Director—		
(904) 478-8496		

ROLLINS COLLEGE

PO Box 2730	**Men**	**Women**
Winter Park, FL 32789-4499	Basketball	Basketball
*Affiliation—*NCAA II	Crew	Crew
Nickname—Tars	Cross Country	Cross Country
Athletic Director—	Golf	Golf
(407) 646-2198	Sailing	Soccer
	Skiing	Softball
	Soccer	Swimming
	Swimming	Tennis
	Tennis	Volleyball
		Water Polo

SAINT LEO COLLEGE

MC 2038, Box 6665	**Men**	**Women**
Saint Leo, FL 33574	Baseball	Basketball
*Affiliation—*NCAA II	Basketball	Softball
Nickname—Monarchs	Golf	Tennis
Athletic Director—	Soccer	Volleyball
(352) 588-8221	Tennis	

SAINT THOMAS UNIVERSITY

16400 NW 32nd Avenue	**Men**	**Women**
Opa Locka, FL 33054-6459	Baseball	Cheerleading
*Affiliation—*NAIA I, NAIA II	Basketball	Soccer
(Basketball)	Golf	Softball
Nickname—Bobcats	Soccer	Tennis
Athletic Director—	Tennis	Volleyball
(305) 628-6687		

SOUTH FLORIDA, UNIVERSITY OF

PED 214,	**Men**	**Women**
4202 S. Fowler Avenue	Baseball	Basketball
Tampa, FL 33620	Basketball	Cross Country
Affiliation—NCAA I	Cross Country	Golf
Nickname—Bulls	Football	Softball
Athletic Director—	Golf	Tennis
(813) 974-2791	Soccer	Track
	Tennis	Volleyball
	Track	

SOUTHEASTERN COLLEGE

1000 Longfellow Boulevard	**Men**	**Women**
Lakeland, FL 33801-6034	Baseball	Basketball
Affiliation—NCCAA I	Basketball	Volleyball
Nickname—Crusaders	Soccer	
Athletic Director—		
(941) 667-5138		

STETSON UNIVERSITY

421 N. Woodland Boulevard,	**Men**	**Women**
Unit 8359	Baseball	Basketball
DeLand, FL 32720-3757	Basketball	Crew
Affiliation—NCAA I	Crew	Cross Country
Nickname—Hatters	Cross Country	Golf
Athletic Director—	Golf	Soccer
(904) 822-8100	Soccer	Softball
	Tennis	Tennis
		Volleyball

TAMPA, UNIVERSITY OF

401 W. Kennedy Boulevard	**Men**	**Women**
Tampa, FL 33606-1450	Baseball	Basketball
Affiliation—NCAA II	Basketball	Crew
Nickname—Spartans	Crew	Cross Country
Athletic Director—	Cross Country	Soccer
(813) 253-6240	Golf	Softball
	Soccer	Swimming
	Swimming	Tennis
	Tennis	Volleyball

TRINITY BAPTIST COLLEGE

426 S. McDuff Avenue *Jacksonville, FL 32254-4234* *Affiliation—*NCCAA *II* *Nickname—Eagles* *Athletic Director—* *(904) 384-2206*	**Men** Basketball	**Women** Volleyball

WARNER SOUTHERN COLLEGE

5301 U.S. 27 South *Lake Wales, FL 33853* *Affiliation—*NAIA *II* *Nickname—Royals* *Athletic Director—* *(941) 638-1426*	**Men** Baseball Basketball Cross Country	**Women** Basketball Cross Country Volleyball

WEBBER COLLEGE

1201 Alternate Highway 27 S *Babson Park, FL 33827* *Affiliation—*NAIA *II* *Nickname—Warriors* *Athletic Director—* *(941) 638-2953*	**Men** Baseball Basketball Cross Country Golf Soccer Tennis	**Women** Basketball Golf Soccer Softball Tennis Volleyball

WEST FLORIDA, UNIVERSITY OF

11000 University Parkway *Pensacola, FL 32514-5732* *Affiliation—*NCAA *II* *Nickname—Argonauts* *Athletic Director—* *(904) 474-3003*	**Men** Baseball Basketball Cross Country Golf Soccer Tennis	**Women** Basketball Cross Country Soccer Softball Tennis

GEORGIA

AGNES SCOTT COLLEGE

141 S. College Avenue *Decatur, GA 30030* *Affiliation—*NCAA *III* *Nickname—Scotties* *Athletic Director—* *(404) 638-6359*	**Women** Basketball Cross Country Soccer	Tennis Volleyball

ALBANY STATE UNIVERSITY

504 College Drive	Men	Women
Albany, GA 31705-2717	Baseball	Basketball
Affiliation—NCAA II	Basketball	Cross Country
Nickname—Golden Rams	Cross Country	Track
Athletic Director—	Football	Volleyball
(912) 430-4762	Track	

ARMSTRONG ATLANTIC STATE UNIVERSITY

11935 Abercorn Street	Men	Women
Savannah, GA 31419-1909	Baseball	Basketball
Affiliation—NCAA II	Basketball	Cross Country
Nickname—Pirates	Cross Country	Softball
Athletic Director—	Tennis	Tennis
(912) 921-5258		Volleyball

ATLANTA CHRISTIAN COLLEGE

2605 Ben Hill Road	Men	Women
East Points, GA 30344-1900	Baseball	Basketball
Affiliation—NCCAA II	Basketball	Golf
Nickname—Chargers	Golf	Soccer
Athletic Director—	Soccer	Softball
(404) 669-2059	Tennis	Tennis
		Volleyball

AUGUSTA STATE UNIVERSITY

2500 Walton Way, #10	Men	Women
Augusta, GA 30904-4562	Baseball	Basketball
Affiliation—NCAA II	Basketball	Cross Country
(Div. I Golf)	Cross Country	Softball
Nickname—Jaguars	Golf	Tennis
Athletic Director—	Soccer	Volleyball
(706) 737-1626	Tennis	

BERRY COLLEGE

PO Box 5015	Men	Women
Mount Berry, GA 30149	Baseball	Basketball
Affiliation—NAIA I	Basketball	Cross Country
Nickname—Vikings	Cross Country	Soccer
Athletic Director—	Golf	Tennis
(706) 236-1721	Soccer	
	Tennis	
	Track	

BRENAU UNIVERSITY

1 Centennial Circle	**Women**	
Gainesville, GA 30501	Cross Country	Tennis
Affiliation—NAIA	Soccer	Volleyball
Nickname—Tigers		
Athletic Director—		
(770) 534-6230		

BREWTON PARKER COLLEGE

Highway 280	**Men**	**Women**
Mount Vernon, GA 30445	Baseball	Basketball
Affiliation—NAIA I	Basketball	Cross Country
Nickname—Wildcats	Soccer	Soccer
Athletic Director—	Tennis	Softball
(912) 583-3206		Tennis
		Volleyball

CLARK ATLANTA UNIVERSITY

J. P. Brawley Drive at Fair	**Men**	**Women**
Street SW	Baseball	Basketball
Atlanta, GA 30314	Basketball	Cross Country
Affiliation—NCAA II	Football	Tennis
Nickname—Panthers	Tennis	Track
Athletic Director—	Track	Volleyball
(404) 880-8126		

CLAYTON COLLEGE & STATE UNIVERSITY

PO Box 285	**Men**	**Women**
Morrow, GA 30260-1250	Basketball	Basketball
Affiliation—NCAA II	Cross Country	Cross Country
Nickname—Lakers	Golf	Soccer
Athletic Director—	Soccer	Tennis
(770) 961-3450		

COLUMBUS STATE UNIVERSITY

4225 University Avenue	**Men**	**Women**
Columbus, GA 31907-5645	Baseball	Basketball
Affiliation—NCAA II	Basketball	Cross Country
Nickname—Cougars	Cross Country	Softball
Athletic Director—	Golf	Tennis
(706) 565-2211	Tennis	

COVENANT COLLEGE

1500 Scenic Highway	**Men**	**Women**
Lookout Mountain, GA 30750	Basketball	Basketball
*Affiliation—*NAIA *II*	Cross Country	Cross Country
Nickname—Scots	Soccer	Soccer
Athletic Director—		Volleyball
(706) 820-1560 ext. 1513		

EMMANUEL COLLEGE

PO Box 129	**Men**	**Women**
Franklin Springs, GA 30639-0129	Baseball	Basketball
*Affiliation—*NAIA, NCCAA	Basketball	Softball
Nickname—Lions	Soccer	Tennis
Athletic Director—	Tennis	
(706) 245-3139		

EMORY UNIVERSITY

Woodruff Physical Education	**Men**	**Women**
Center	Baseball	Basketball
600 Asbury Circle	Basketball	Cross Country
Atlanta, GA 30322	Cross Country	Diving
*Affiliation—*NCAA *III*	Diving	Soccer
Nickname—Eagles	Golf	Softball
Athletic Director—	Soccer	Swimming
(404) 727-6532	Tennis	Tennis
	Track	Track
		Volleyball

FORT VALLEY STATE UNIVERSITY

State College Drive	**Men**	**Women**
Fort Valley, GA 31030	Basketball	Basketball
*Affiliation—*NCAA *II*	Cross Country	Tennis
Nickname—Wildcats	Football	Track
Athletic Director—	Tennis	Volleyball
(912) 825-6209	Track	
	Volleyball	

GEORGIA, UNIVERSITY OF

PO Box 1472	Men	Women
Athens, GA 30603-1472	Baseball	Basketball
Affiliation—NCAA I	Basketball	Cheerleading
(I-A Football)	Cross Country	Cross Country
Nickname—*Bulldogs*	Diving	Diving
Athletic Director—	Football	Golf
(706) 542-9037	Golf	Gymnastics
	Swimming	Soccer
	Tennis	Softball
	Track	Swimming
		Tennis
		Track
		Volleyball

GEORGIA COLLEGE

CBX 065	Men	Women
Milledgeville, GA 31061	Baseball	Basketball
Affiliation—NCAA II	Basketball	Cross Country
Nickname—*Bobcats*	Cross Country	Fencing
Athletic Director—	Fencing	Softball
(912) 445-6341	Golf	Tennis
	Tennis	

GEORGIA SOUTHERN UNIVERSITY

PO Box 8082	Men	Women
Stateboro, GA 30460	Baseball	Basketball
Affiliation—NCAA I	Basketball	Cross Country
(I-AA Football)	Cross Country	Diving
Nickname—*Eagles*	Diving	Soccer
Athletic Director—	Football	Softball
(912) 681-5047	Golf	Swimming
	Soccer	Tennis
	Swimming	Volleyball
	Tennis	

GEORGIA SOUTHWESTERN STATE UNIVERSITY

800 Wheatly Street	Men	Women
Americus, GA 31709-4635	Baseball	Basketball
Affiliation—NAIA I, NCAA II	Basketball	Cross Country
Nickname—*Hurricanes*	Cross Country	Softball
Athletic Director—	Tennis	Tennis
(912) 931-1360		Volleyball

GEORGIA STATE UNIVERSITY

1 Park South, Suite 840	**Men**	**Women**
Atlanta, GA 30303-2911	Baseball	Basketball
Affiliation—NCAA I	Basketball	Cheerleading
Nickname—Panthers	Cross Country	Cross Country
Athletic Director—	Golf	Golf
(404) 651-3173	Soccer	Soccer
	Tennis	Softball
	Wrestling	Tennis
		Volleyball

GEORGIA TECH

150 Bobby Dodd Way NW	**Men**	**Women**
Atlanta, GA 30332	Baseball	Basketball
Affiliation—NCAA I	Basketball	Cheerleading
(I-A Football)	Cross Country	Cross Country
Nickname—Yellow Jackets	Football	Softball
Athletic Director—	Golf	Swimming
(404) 894-5411	Swimming	Tennis
	Tennis	Track
	Track	Volleyball

KENNESAW STATE UNIVERSITY

1000 Chastain Road NW	**Men**	**Women**
Kennesaw, GA 30144-5588	Baseball	Basketball
Affiliation—NCAA II	Basketball	Cheerleading
Nickname—Owls	Cross Country	Cross Country
Athletic Director—	Golf	Softball
(770) 423-6210		Tennis

LA GRANGE COLLEGE

601 Broad Street	**Men**	**Women**
La Grange, GA 30240-2955	Baseball	Cheerleading
Affiliation—NAIA I	Basketball	Golf
Nickname—Panthers	Golf	Soccer
Athletic Director—	Soccer	Softball
(706) 812-7262	Swimming	Swimming
	Tennis	Tennis
		Volleyball

LIFE UNIVERSITY

1269 Barclay Circle SE	**Men**	**Women**
Marietta, GA 30060-2903	Basketball	Basketball
Affiliation—NAIA I	Cross Country	Cross Country
Nickname—Running Eagles	Golf	Track
Athletic Director—	Ice Hockey	
(770) 426-2765	Soccer	
	Rugby	
	Track	

MERCER UNIVERSITY

1400 Coleman Avenue	**Men**	**Women**
Macon, GA 31207	Baseball	Basketball
Affiliation—NCAA I	Basketball	Cross Country
Nickname—Bears	Cross Country	Golf
Athletic Director—	Golf	Soccer
(912) 752-2994	Rifle	Softball
	Soccer	Tennis
	Tennis	Volleyball

MOREHOUSE COLLEGE

830 Westview Drive SW	**Men**	
Atlanta, GA 30314-3773	Basketball	Football
Affiliation—NCAA II	Cheerleading	Tennis
Nickname—Tigers	Cross Country	Track
Athletic Director—		
(404) 215-2752		

MORRIS BROWN COLLEGE

643 Martin Luther King Jr.	**Men**	**Women**
Drive NW	Baseball	Basketball
Atlanta, GA 30314	Basketball	Cross Country
Affiliation—NCAA II	Cross Country	Tennis
Nickname—Wolverines	Football	Track
Athletic Director—	Tennis	Volleyball
(404) 220-3615	Track	

NORTH GEORGIA COLLEGE & STATE UNIVERSITY

Highway 60 S	**Men**	**Women**
Dahlonega, GA 30533	Basketball	Basketball
Affiliation—NAIA I	Cross Country	Cross Country
Nickname—Saints	Soccer	Soccer
Athletic Director—	Tennis	Softball
(706) 864-1627		Tennis

OGLETHORPE UNIVERSITY

4484 Peachtree Road NE	**Men**	**Women**
Atlanta, GA 30319-2737	Baseball	Basketball
Affiliation—NCAA III	Basketball	Cross Country
Nickname—Stormy Stanton	Cross Country	Golf
Athletic Director—	Golf	Soccer
(404) 364-8414	Soccer	Tennis
	Tennis	Track
	Track	Volleyball

PAINE COLLEGE

1235 15th Street	**Men**	**Women**
Augusta, GA 30901-3105	Baseball	Basketball
Affiliation—NCAA II	Basketball	Cross Country
Nickname—Lions	Cross Country	Softball
Athletic Director—	Track	Track
(706) 821-8353		Volleyball

PIEDMONT COLLEGE

PO Box 10	**Men**	**Women**
Demorest, GA 30535	Baseball	Basketball
Affiliation—NAIA I	Basketball	Soccer
Nickname—Lions	Soccer	Softball
Athletic Director—		Volleyball
(706) 778-3000 ext. 464		

SAVANNAH COLLEGE OF ART & DESIGN

PO Box 3146	**Men**	**Women**
Savannah, GA 31402-3146	Baseball	Basketball
Affiliation—NCAA III	Basketball	Crew
Nickname—Bees	Crew	Golf
Athletic Director—	Golf	Soccer
(912) 238-2432	Soccer	Softball
	Tennis	Tennis
		Volleyball

SAVANNAH STATE UNIVERSITY

State College Branch	**Men**	**Women**
Savannah, GA 31404	Baseball	Basketball
*Affiliation—*NCAA II	Basketball	Cheerleading
Nickname—Tigers	Cross Country	Cross Country
Athletic Director—	Football	Golf
(912) 353-5181	Golf	Tennis
	Tennis	Track
	Track	Volleyball

SHORTER COLLEGE

315 Shorter Avenue	**Men**	**Women**
Rome, GA 30165	Baseball	Basketball
*Affiliation—*NAIA I	Basketball	Cross Country
Nickname—Hawks	Cross Country	Tennis
Athletic Director—	Golf	
(706) 233-7347	Tennis	
	Track	

SOUTHERN POLYTECHNIC STATE UNIVERSITY

1100 S. Marietta Parkway SE	**Men**	
Marietta, GA 30060-2855	Baseball	Tennis
Nickname—Hornets		
Athletic Director—		
(770) 528-7350		

SPELMAN COLLEGE

Campus Box 1057,	**Women**	
350 Spelman Lane SW	Basketball	Tennis
Atlanta, GA 30314	Cheerleading	Track
*Affiliation—*NCAA II	Cross Country	Volleyball
Nickname—Jaguars	Golf	
Athletic Director—		
(404) 223-7674		

STATE UNIVERSITY OF WEST GEORGIA

Maple Street	**Men**	**Women**
Carrollton, GA 30118	Baseball	Basketball
*Affiliation—*NCAA II	Basketball	Cross Country
Nickname—Braves	Cross Country	Softball
Athletic Director—	Football	Tennis
(770) 836-6533	Tennis	Volleyball

THOMAS COLLEGE

	Men	Women
1501 Millpond Road	Baseball	Softball
Thomasville, GA 31792-7478	Basketball	Tennis
Affiliation—NAIA	Golf	
Nickname—Nighthawks	Soccer	
Athletic Director—		
(912) 226-1621 ext. 244		

TOCCOA FALLS COLLEGE

	Men	Women
PO Box 818	Baseball	Basketball
Toccoa Falls, GA 30598	Basketball	Soccer
Affiliation—NCCAA	Golf	Volleyball
Nickname—Eagles	Soccer	
Athletic Director—		
(706) 886-6831 ext. 5377		

VALDOSTA STATE UNIVERSITY

	Men	Women
Patterson Street	Baseball	Basketball
Valdosta, GA 31698	Basketball	Cross Country
Affiliation—NCAA II	Cross Country	Softball
Nickname—Blazers	Football	Tennis
Athletic Director—	Golf	Volleyball
(912) 333-5952	Tennis	

WESLEYAN COLLEGE

	Women	
4760 Forsyth Road	Basketball	Softball
Macon, GA 31210	Fencing	Tennis
Affiliation—NCAA III	Riding	Volleyball
Nickname—Pioneers	Soccer	
Athletic Director—		
(912) 757-5260		

HAWAII

BRIGHAM YOUNG UNIVERSITY (HAWAII)

	Men	Women
55-220 Kulanui Street	Basketball	Cross Country
Laie, HI 96762-1266	Cross Country	Softball
Affiliation—NCAA II, NAIA I	Soccer	Tennis
Nickname—Seasiders	Tennis	Volleyball
Athletic Director—		
(808) 293-3760		

CHAMINADE UNIVERSITY

3140 Walalae Avenue	**Men**	**Women**
Honolulu, HI 96816-1510	Basketball	Cross Country
Affiliation—NCAA II	Cross Country	Softball
Nickname—Silverswords	Tennis	Tennis
Athletic Director—	Water Polo	Volleyball
(808) 735-4790		

HAWAII, UNIVERSITY OF, HILO

200 W. Kawii Street	**Men**	**Women**
Hilo, HI 96720-4075	Baseball	Cheerleading
Affiliation—NCAA II	Basketball	Cross Country
(Div. I Baseball)	Cross Country	Softball
Nickname—Vulcans	Golf	Tennis
Athletic Director—	Tennis	Volleyball
(808) 974-7520		

HAWAII, UNIVERSITY OF, MANOA

1337 Lower Campus Road	**Men**	**Women**
Honolulu, HI 96822-2312	Baseball	Basketball
Affiliation—NCAA I	Basketball	Cheerleading
(I-A Football)	Diving	Cross Country
Nickname—Rainbows	Football	Diving
Athletic Director—Men	Golf	Golf
(808) 956-7301	Sailing	Sailing
Athletic Director—Women	Swimming	Soccer
(808) 956-4498	Tennis	Softball
	Volleyball	Swimming
		Tennis
		Volleyball
		Water Polo

HAWAII PACIFIC UNIVERSITY

1060 Bishop Street, #PH	**Men**	**Women**
Honolulu, HI 96813-3128	Baseball	Cheerleading
Affiliation—NCAA II	Basketball	Cross Country
Nickname—Sea Warriors	Cross Country	Soccer
Athletic Director—	Soccer	Softball
(808) 544-0221	Tennis	Tennis
		Volleyball

IDAHO

ALBERTSON COLLEGE

2112 Cleveland Boulevard	**Men**	**Women**
Caldwell, ID 83605-4432	Baseball	Basketball
Affiliation—NAIA II	Basketball	Golf
Nickname—Coyotes	Golf	Skiing
Athletic Director—	Soccer	Soccer
(208) 459-5850	Swimming	Swimming
	Tennis	Tennis
		Volleyball

BOISE STATE UNIVERSITY

1910 University Drive	**Men**	**Women**
Boise, ID 83725	Baseball	Basketball
Affiliation—NCAA I	Basketball	Cross Country
(I-A Football)	Cross Country	Golf
Nickname—Broncos	Football	Gymnastics
Athletic Director—	Golf	Soccer
(208) 385-1826	Tennis	Tennis
	Track	Track
	Wrestling	Volleyball

IDAHO, UNIVERSITY OF

Kibbie-ASUI Activity Center	**Men**	**Women**
Moscow, ID 83844	Basketball	Basketball
Affiliation—NCAA I	Cross Country	Cheerleading
(I-A Football)	Football	Cross Country
Nickname—Vandals	Golf	Golf
Athletic Director—	Tennis	Soccer
(208) 885-0200	Track	Tennis
		Track
		Volleyball

IDAHO STATE UNIVERSITY

Box 8173, Holt Arena	**Men**	**Women**
Pocatello, ID 83209	Basketball	Basketball
Affiliation—NCAA I	Cross Country	Cross Country
(I-AA Football)	Football	Golf
Nickname—Bengals	Golf	Soccer
Athletic Director—	Tennis	Tennis
(208) 236-4668	Track	Track
		Volleyball

LEWIS-CLARK STATE COLLEGE

500 8th Avenue Lewiston, ID 83501-2691 Affiliation—NAIA I, NCAA II Nickname—Warriors Athletic Director— (208) 799-2273	**Men** Baseball Basketball Cross Country Golf Rodeo Tennis	**Women** Basketball Cross Country Golf Rodeo Tennis Volleyball

NORTHWEST NAZARENE COLLEGE

623 Holly Street Nampa, ID 83686-5861 Affiliation—NAIA II Nickname—Crusaders Athletic Director— (208) 467-8348	**Men** Baseball Basketball Soccer	**Women** Basketball Cheerleading Soccer Tennis Volleyball

ILLINOIS

AUGUSTANA COLLEGE

3500 5th Avenue
Rock Island, IL 61201
Affiliation—NCAA III
Nickname—Vikings
Athletic Director—Men
  (309) 794-7527
Athletic Director—Women
  (309) 794-7529
	Men
	Baseball
	Basketball
	Cross Country
	Football
	Golf
	Soccer
	Swimming
	Tennis
	Wrestling
		Women
		Basketball
		Cross Country
		Golf
		Soccer
		Swimming
		Tennis
		Track
		Volleyball

AURORA UNIVERSITY

347 S. Gladstone Avenue Aurora, IL 60406-4877 Affiliation—NCAA III Nickname—Spartans Athletic Director— (630) 844-5111	**Men** Baseball Basketball Football Golf Soccer Tennis	**Women** Basketball Soccer Softball Tennis Volleyball

BARAT COLLEGE

	Men	Women
700 E. Westleigh Road	Basketball	Volleyball
Lake Forest, IL 60045-3263		
Affiliation—NAIA I		
Nickname—Bulldogs		
Athletic Director—		
(847) 604-6237		

BENEDICTINE UNIVERSITY

	Men	Women
5700 College Road	Baseball	Basketball
Lisle, IL 60532-2851	Basketball	Cross Country
Affiliation—NCAA III	Cross Country	Golf
Nickname—Eagles	Football	Soccer
Athletic Director—	Golf	Softball
(630) 829-6140	Ice Hockey	Swimming
	Soccer	Tennis
	Swimming	Track
	Tennis	Volleyball
	Track	

BLACKBURN COLLEGE

	Men	Women
700 College Avenue	Baseball	Basketball
Carlinville, IL 62626-1454	Basketball	Cheerleading
Affiliation—NCAA III	Cross Country	Cross Country
Nickname—Beavers	Football	Soccer
Athletic Director—	Golf	Softball
(217) 854-3231 ext. 4321	Soccer	Tennis
		Volleyball

BRADLEY UNIVERSITY

	Men	Women
Haussler Hall,	Baseball	Basketball
* 1501 Bradley Avenue*	Basketball	Cheerleading
Peoria, IL 61625	Cross Country	Cross Country
Affiliation—NCAA I	Diving	Diving
Nickname—Braves	Golf	Golf
Athletic Director—	Swimming	Softball
(309) 677-2670	Tennis	Swimming
	Track	Tennis
		Track
		Volleyball

CHICAGO, UNIVERSITY OF

	Men	Women
5640 S. University Avenue	Baseball	Basketball
Chicago, IL 60637-1524	Basketball	Cross Country
Affiliation—NCAA III	Cross Country	Soccer
Nickname—Maroons	Football	Softball
Athletic Director—	Soccer	Swimming
(773) 702-7684	Swimming	Tennis
	Tennis	Track
	Track	Volleyball
	Wrestling	

CHICAGO STATE UNIVERSITY

	Men	Women
9501 South King Drive	Baseball	Basketball
Chicago, IL 60628	Basketball	Cross Country
Affiliation—NCAA I	Cross Country	Golf
Nickname—Cougars	Golf	Tennis
Athletic Director—	Tennis	Track
(773) 995-2295	Track	Volleyball

CONCORDIA UNIVERSITY

	Men	Women
7400 Augusta Street	Baseball	Basketball
River Forest, IL 60305-1499	Basketball	Cross Country
Affiliation—NCAA III	Cross Country	Softball
Nickname—Cougars	Football	Tennis
Athletic Director—	Tennis	Track
(708) 209-3028	Track	Volleyball

DEPAUL UNIVERSITY

	Men	Women
1011 W. Belden Avenue	Basketball	Basketball
Chicago, IL 60614-3205	Cross Country	Cross Country
Affiliation—NCAA I	Golf	Soccer
Nickname—Blue Demons	Rifle	Softball
Athletic Director—	Soccer	Tennis
(773) 325-7502	Tennis	Track
	Track	Volleyball

DOMINICAN UNIVERSITY

7900 Division Street	**Men**	**Women**
River Forest, IL 60305-1066	Baseball	Basketball
Affiliation—NAIA I, NCAA III	Basketball	Soccer
Nickname—Stars	Soccer	Softball
Athletic Director—	Tennis	Tennis
(708) 524-6511	Volleyball	Volleyball

EASTERN ILLINOIS UNIVERSITY

600 Lincoln Avenue	**Men**	**Women**
Charleston, IL 61920-3011	Baseball	Basketball
Affiliation—NCAA I	Basketball	Cross Country
(I-AA Football)	Cross Country	Diving
Nickname—Panthers	Diving	Golf
Athletic Director—	Football	Soccer
(217) 581-2319	Golf	Softball
	Soccer	Swimming
	Swimming	Tennis
	Tennis	Track
	Track	Volleyball
	Wrestling	

ELMHURST COLLEGE

190 Prospect Avenue	**Men**	**Women**
Elmhurst, IL 60126-3271	Baseball	Basketball
Affiliation—NCAA III	Basketball	Cross Country
Nickname—Bluejays	Cross Country	Golf
Athletic Director—	Football	Soccer
(630) 617-3142	Golf	Softball
	Tennis	Tennis
	Track	Track
	Wrestling	Volleyball

EUREKA COLLEGE

300 E. College Avenue	**Men**	**Women**
Eureka, IL 61530-1562	Baseball	Basketball
Affiliation—NCAA III	Basketball	Diving
Nickname—Red Devils	Diving	Golf
Athletic Director—Men	Football	Soccer
(309) 467-6373	Golf	Softball
Athletic Director—Women	Soccer	Swimming
(309) 467-6374	Swimming	Tennis
	Tennis	Track
	Track	Volleyball

GREENVILLE COLLEGE

PO Box 159,	Men	Women
315 E. College Avenue	Baseball	Basketball
Greenville, IL 62246-0159	Basketball	Cross Country
Affiliation—NCCAA, NCAA III	Cross Country	Soccer
Nickname—Panthers	Football	Softball
Athletic Director—	Golf	Tennis
(618) 664-2800 ext. 4370	Soccer	Track
	Tennis	Volleyball
	Track	

ILLINOIS, UNIVERSITY OF, CHICAGO

901 W. Roosevelt Road	Men	Women
Chicago, IL 60608-1516	Baseball	Basketball
Affiliation—NCAA I	Basketball	Cross Country
Nickname—Flames	Cross Country	Gymnastics
Athletic Director—	Gymnastics	Softball
(312) 996-2695	Soccer	Swimming
	Swimming	Tennis
	Tennis	Volleyball

ILLINOIS, UNIVERSITY OF, SPRINGFIELD

PO Box 19243	Men	Women
Springfield, IL 62794-9243	Soccer	Basketball
Affiliation—NAIA I	Tennis	Tennis
Nickname—Prairie Stars		Volleyball
Athletic Director—		
(217) 206-6674		

ILLINOIS, UNIVERSITY OF, URBANA-CHAMPAIGN

1700 S. 4th Street	Men	Women
Champaign, IL 61820-6941	Baseball	Basketball
Affiliation—NCAA I	Basketball	Cross Country
(I-A Football)	Cross Country	Diving
Nickname—Fighting Illini	Football	Golf
Athletic Director—Men	Golf	Gymnastics
(217) 333-3631	Gymnastics	Soccer
Athletic Director—Women	Tennis	Swimming
(217) 333-0171	Track	Tennis
	Wrestling	Track
		Volleyball

ILLINOIS COLLEGE

1101 W. College Avenue
Jacksonville, IL 62650-2212
Affiliation—NCAA III
Nickname—Blueboys
Athletic Director—
  (217) 243-6651

Men	Women
Baseball	Basketball
Basketball	Cross Country
Cross Country	Golf
Football	Soccer
Golf	Softball
Soccer	Tennis
Tennis	Track
Track	Volleyball
Wrestling	

ILLINOIS INSTITUTE OF TECHNOLOGY

3300 S. Federal Street
Chicago, IL 60616-3732
Affiliation—NAIA I
Nickname—Scarlet Hawks
Athletic Director—
  (312) 567-3296

Men	Women
Baseball	Basketball
Basketball	Cross Country
Cross Country	Swimming
Swimming	Volleyball

ILLINOIS STATE UNIVERSITY

2660 Redbird Arena, #213
Normal, IL 61790-2660
Affiliation—NCAA I
  (I-AA Football)
Nickname—Redbirds
Athletic Director—
  (309) 438-3636

Men	Women
Baseball	Basketball
Basketball	Cross Country
Cross Country	Golf
Football	Gymnastics
Golf	Soccer
Tennis	Softball
Track	Swimming
	Tennis
	Track
	Volleyball

ILLINOIS WESLEYAN UNIVERSITY

PO Box 2900
Bloomington, IL 61702-2900
Affiliation—NCAA III
Nickname—Titans
Athletic Director—
  (309) 556-3345

Men	Women
Baseball	Basketball
Basketball	Cross Country
Cross Country	Golf
Football	Soccer
Golf	Softball
Soccer	Swimming
Swimming	Tennis
Tennis	Track
Track	Volleyball

JUDSON COLLEGE

1151 N. State Street	Men	Women
Elgin, IL 60123-1404	Basketball	Basketball
Affiliation—NAIA II, NCCAA	Cross Country	Cross Country
Nickname—Eagles	Soccer	Soccer
Athletic Director—		Softball
(847) 695-2500 ext. 3800		Tennis
		Volleyball

KENDALL COLLEGE

2408 Orrington Avenue	Men	Women
Evanston, IL 60201-2822	Basketball	Basketball
Affiliation—NAIA	Cross Country	Cross Country
Nickname—Vikings	Golf	Golf
Athletic Director—	Soccer	Soccer
(847) 866-1300 ext. 1375	Volleyball	Track
		Volleyball

KNOX COLLEGE

2 E. South Street	Men	Women
Galesburg, IL 61401-4928	Baseball	Basketball
Affiliation—NCAA III	Basketball	Cross Country
Nickname—Prairie Fire	Cross Country	Golf
Athletic Director—	Football	Soccer
(309) 341-7280	Golf	Softball
	Soccer	Swimming
	Swimming	Tennis
	Tennis	Track
	Track	Volleyball
	Wrestling	

LAKE FOREST COLLEGE

555 N. Sheridan Road	Men	Women
Lake Forest, IL 60045-2338	Basketball	Basketball
Affiliation—NCAA III	Cross Country	Cheerleading
Nickname—Foresters	Diving	Cross Country
Athletic Director—	Football	Diving
(847) 735-5290	Handball	Handball
	Ice Hockey	Soccer
	Soccer	Softball
	Swimming	Swimming
	Tennis	Tennis
		Volleyball

LEWIS UNIVERSITY

Route 53	**Men**	**Women**
Romeoville, IL 60441	Baseball	Basketball
Affiliation—NCAA II	Basketball	Cross Country
Nickname—Flyers	Cross Country	Golf
Athletic Director—	Golf	Soccer
(815) 836-5249	Soccer	Softball
	Swimming	Swimming
	Tennis	Tennis
	Track	Track
	Volleyball	Volleyball

LINCOLN CHRISTIAN COLLEGE

100 Campus View Drive	**Men**	**Women**
Lincoln, IL 62656-2111	Baseball	Basketball
Affiliation—NCCAA II	Basketball	Volleyball
Nickname—Preachers	Soccer	
Athletic Director—		
(217) 732-3168		

LOYOLA UNIVERSITY

6525 N. Sheridan Road	**Men**	**Women**
Chicago, IL 60626-5311	Basketball	Basketball
Affiliation—NCAA I	Bowling	Cross Country
Nickname—Ramblers	Cross Country	Golf
Athletic Director—	Golf	Soccer
(773) 508-2560	Soccer	Softball
	Track	Track
	Volleyball	Volleyball

MAC MURRAY COLLEGE

447 E. College Avenue	**Men**	**Women**
Jacksonville, IL 62650-2510	Baseball	Basketball
Affiliation—NCAA III	Basketball	Cross Country
Nickname—Highlanders	Cross Country	Soccer
Athletic Director—	Football	Softball
(217) 479-7143	Golf	Swimming
	Soccer	Tennis
	Swimming	Volleyball
	Tennis	
	Wrestling	

MCKENDREE COLLEGE

Price Convocation Center,	**Men**	**Women**
701 College Road	Baseball	Basketball
Lebanon, IL 62254-1212	Basketball	Cheerleading
*Affiliation—*NAIA *I*	Cross Country	Cross Country
Nickname—Bearcats	Football	Golf
Athletic Director—	Golf	Soccer
(618) 637-6871	Soccer	Softball
	Tennis	Tennis
	Track	Track
	Volleyball	Volleyball

MILLIKIN UNIVERSITY

1184 W. Main Street	**Men**	**Women**
Decatur, IL 62522-2039	Basketball	Basketball
*Affiliation—*NCAA *III*	Cross Country	Cross Country
Nickname—Big Blue	Football	Golf
Athletic Director—	Golf	Soccer
(217) 424-6344	Soccer	Softball
	Tennis	Swimming
	Track	Tennis
	Wrestling	Track
		Volleyball

MONMOUTH COLLEGE

700 E. Broadway	**Men**	**Women**
Monmouth, IL 61462-1963	Baseball	Basketball
*Affiliation—*NCAA *III*	Basketball	Cross Country
Nickname—Fighting Scots	Cross Country	Soccer
Athletic Director—	Football	Softball
(309) 457-2176	Soccer	Track
	Track	Volleyball
	Wrestling	

MOODY BIBLE INSTITUTE

820 N. La Salle Drive	**Men**	**Women**
Chicago, IL 60610-3214	Basketball	Basketball
*Affiliation—*NCCAA *II*	Soccer	Volleyball
Nickname—Archers	Volleyball	
Athletic Director—		
(312) 329-4451		

NORTH CENTRAL COLLEGE

30 N. Brainard College
Naperville, IL 60540-4607
Affiliation—NCAA III
Nickname—Cardinals
Athletic Director—
(630) 637-5500

Men
Baseball
Basketball
Cross Country
Football
Golf
Soccer
Swimming
Tennis
Track
Wrestling

Women
Basketball
Cross Country
Golf
Soccer
Softball
Swimming
Track
Volleyball

NORTH PARK UNIVERSITY

3225 W. Foster Avenue
Chicago, IL 60625-4810
Affiliation—NCAA III
Nickname—Vikings
Athletic Director—
(773) 244-5685

Men
Baseball
Basketball
Cross Country
Football
Golf
Soccer
Tennis
Track

Women
Basketball
Cheerleading
Cross Country
Golf
Soccer
Softball
Tennis
Track
Volleyball

NORTHEASTERN ILLINOIS UNIVERSITY

5500 N. Saint Louis Avenue
Chicago, IL 60625-4625
Affiliation—NCAA I
Nickname—Golden Eagles
Athletic Director—
(773) 794-3081

Men
Baseball
Basketball
Cross Country
Golf
Soccer
Swimming
Tennis

Women
Basketball
Cross Country
Golf
Softball
Swimming
Tennis
Volleyball

NORTHERN ILLINOIS UNIVERSITY

101 Evans Field House	**Men**	**Women**
DeKalb, IL 60115	Baseball	Basketball
Affiliation—NCAA I	Basketball	Cross Country
(I-A Football)	Diving	Diving
Nickname—Huskies	Football	Golf
Athletic Director—	Golf	Gymnastics
(815) 753-0888	Soccer	Soccer
	Swimming	Softball
	Tennis	Swimming
	Wrestling	Tennis
		Volleyball

NORTHWESTERN UNIVERSITY

1501 Central Street	**Men**	**Women**
Evanston, IL 60208-0840	Baseball	Basketball
Affiliation—NCAA I	Basketball	Cross Country
(I-A Football)	Diving	Fencing
Nickname—Wildcats	Football	Field Hockey
Athletic Director—	Golf	Golf
(847) 491-8880	Soccer	Soccer
	Swimming	Softball
	Tennis	Swimming
	Wrestling	Tennis
		Volleyball

OLIVET NAZARENE UNIVERSITY

240 E. Marsille	**Men**	**Women**
Kankakee, IL 60901	Baseball	Basketball
Affiliation—NAIA I	Basketball	Cheerleading
Nickname—Tigers	Cross Country	Cross Country
Athletic Director—	Football	Soccer
(815) 939-5372	Golf	Softball
	Soccer	Tennis
	Tennis	Track
	Track	Volleyball

PRINCIPIA COLLEGE

	Men	Women
1 Maybeck Place	Baseball	Basketball
Elsah, IL 62028-8714	Basketball	Cross Country
Affiliation—NCAA III	Cross Country	Golf
Nickname—Panthers	Football	Soccer
Athletic Director—	Golf	Softball
(618) 374-5025	Soccer	Swimming
	Swimming	Tennis
	Tennis	Track
	Track	Volleyball

QUINCY UNIVERSITY

	Men	Women
1800 College Avenue	Baseball	Basketball
Quincy, IL 62301-2670	Basketball	Cross Country
Affiliation—NCAA II	Cross Country	Soccer
Nickname—Hawks	Football	Softball
Athletic Director—	Soccer	Tennis
(217) 228-5290	Tennis	Volleyball
	Volleyball	

ROBERT MORRIS COLLEGE

	Men	Women
180 N. LaSalle Street	Baseball	Basketball
Chicago, IL 60601-2501	Basketball	Cross Country
Affiliation—NAIA II	Cross Country	Soccer
Nickname—Eagles		Softball
Athletic Director—		Volleyball
(312) 836-5015		

ROCKFORD COLLEGE

	Men	Women
5050 E. State Street	Baseball	Basketball
Rockford, IL 61108-2311	Basketball	Soccer
Affiliation—NCAA III	Golf	Softball
Nickname—Regents	Soccer	Swimming
Athletic Director—	Swimming	Tennis
(815) 226-4048	Tennis	Volleyball

SAINT FRANCIS, UNIVERSITY OF

500 Wilcox Street	**Men**	**Women**
Joliet, IL 60435-6169	Baseball	Basketball
Affiliation—NAIA I, NCAA II	Basketball	Cross Country
Nickname—Fighting Saints	Golf	Soccer
Athletic Director—	Soccer	Softball
(815) 744-2162	Tennis	Tennis
		Volleyball

SAINT XAVIER UNIVERSITY

3700 W. 103rd Street	**Men**	**Women**
Chicago, IL 60655-3105	Baseball	Cross Country
Affiliation—NAIA I	Basketball	Soccer
Nickname—Cougars	Football	Softball
Athletic Director—	Soccer	Volleyball
(773) 298-3000		

SOUTHERN ILLINOIS UNIVERSITY

Lingle Hall, Room 118	**Men**	**Women**
Carbondale, IL 62901	Baseball	Basketball
Affiliation—NCAA I	Basketball	Cross Country
(I-AA Football)	Cross Country	Diving
Nickname—Salukis	Diving	Golf
Athletic Director—	Football	Softball
(618) 453-7250	Golf	Swimming
	Swimming	Tennis
	Tennis	Track
	Track	Volleyball

SOUTHERN ILLINOIS UNIVERSITY

SIUE Box 1129	**Men**	**Women**
Edwardsville, IL 62026	Baseball	Basketball
Affiliation—NCAA II	Basketball	Cross Country
Nickname—Cougars	Cross Country	Golf
Athletic Director—	Soccer	Soccer
(618) 650-2869	Tennis	Softball
	Track	Tennis
	Wrestling	Track
		Volleyball

TRINITY CHRISTIAN COLLEGE

6601 W. College Drive	Men	Women
Palos Heights, IL 60463-1768	Baseball	Basketball
Affiliation—NAIA II, NCCAA I	Basketball	Soccer
Nickname—Trolls	Soccer	Softball
Athletic Director—		Volleyball
(708) 239-4779		

TRINITY INTERNATIONAL UNIVERSITY

2065 Half Day Road	Men	Women
Deerfield, IL 60015-1241	Baseball	Basketball
Affiliation—NAIA II	Basketball	Cross Country
Nickname—Trojans	Cross Country	Soccer
Athletic Director—	Soccer	Softball
(847) 317-7091	Tennis	Tennis
	Track	Track
	Volleyball	Volleyball

WESTERN ILLINOIS UNIVERSITY

103 Western Hall,	Men	Women
1 University Circle	Baseball	Basketball
Macomb, IL 61455	Basketball	Cheerleading
Affiliation—NCAA I	Cross Country	Cross Country
(I-AA Football)	Football	Diving
Nickname—Leathernecks	Golf	Soccer
Athletic Director—	Soccer	Softball
(309) 298-1106	Swimming	Swimming
	Tennis	Tennis
	Track	Track
		Volleyball

WHEATON COLLEGE

501 College Avenue	Men	Women
Wheaton, IL 60187-5501	Baseball	Basketball
Affiliation—NCAA III	Basketball	Cross Country
Nickname—Crusaders	Cross Country	Golf
Athletic Director—	Football	Soccer
(630) 752-5748	Golf	Softball
	Soccer	Swimming
	Swimming	Tennis
	Tennis	Track
	Track	Volleyball
	Wrestling	

INDIANA

ANDERSON UNIVERSITY

1100 E. 5th Street	**Men**	**Women**
Anderson, IN 46012-3462	Baseball	Basketball
*Affiliation—*NCAA *III*	Basketball	Cheerleading
Nickname—Ravens	Cross Country	Cross Country
Athletic Director—Men	Football	Golf
(765) 641-4483	Golf	Soccer
Athletic Director—Women	Soccer	Softball
(765) 641-4478	Tennis	Tennis
	Track	Track
		Volleyball

BALL STATE UNIVERSITY

2000 W. University Avenue	**Men**	**Women**
Muncie, IN 47306-1022	Baseball	Basketball
*Affiliation—*NCAA *I*	Basketball	Cross Country
(I-A Football)	Cross Country	Field Hockey
Athletic Director—	Football	Gymnastics
(765) 285-1671	Golf	Soccer
	Swimming	Softball
	Tennis	Swimming
	Track	Tennis
	Volleyball	Track
		Volleyball

BETHEL COLLEGE

1001 McKinley Avenue	**Men**	**Women**
Mishawaka, IN 46545	Baseball	Basketball
*Affiliation—*NAIA *II,* NCCAA *I*	Basketball	Cheerleading
Nickname—Pilots	Cross County	Cross Country
Athletic Director—	Golf	Soccer
(219) 257-3345	Soccer	Softball
	Tennis	Tennis
	Track	Track
		Volleyball

BUTLER UNIVERSITY

4600 Sunset Avenue	**Men**	**Women**
Indianapolis, IN 46208-3443	Baseball	Basketball
Affiliation—NCAA I	Basketball	Cross Country
(I-AA Football)	Cross Country	Golf
Nickname—Bulldogs	Football	Soccer
Athletic Director—	Golf	Softball
(317) 940-9940	Lacrosse	Swimming
	Soccer	Tennis
	Swimming	Track
	Tennis	Volleyball
	Track	

DEPAUW UNIVERSITY

Lilly Center,	**Men**	**Women**
702 S. College Street	Baseball	Basketball
Greencastle, IN 46135-1947	Basketball	Cross Country
Affiliation—NCAA III	Cross Country	Field Hockey
Nickname—Tigers	Football	Golf
Athletic Director—	Golf	Soccer
(765) 658-4961	Soccer	Softball
	Swimming	Swimming
	Tennis	Tennis
	Track	Track
		Volleyball

EARLHAM COLLEGE

801 National Road W	**Men**	**Women**
Richmond, IN 47374-4021	Baseball	Basketball
Affiliation—NCAA III	Basketball	Cross Country
Nickname—Quakers	Cross Country	Field Hockey
Athletic Director—	Football	Lacrosse
(765) 983-1489	Soccer	Soccer
	Tennis	Tennis
	Track	Track
		Volleyball

EVANSVILLE, UNIVERSITY OF

1800 Lincoln Avenue	**Men**	**Women**
Evansville, IN 47714-1506	Baseball	Basketball
*Affiliation—*NCAA I	Basketball	Cross Country
Nickname—Aces	Cross Country	Diving
Athletic Director—	Diving	Golf
(812) 479-2237	Golf	Soccer
	Soccer	Softball
	Swimming	Swimming
	Tennis	Tennis
		Volleyball

FRANKLIN COLLEGE

501 S. Monroe Street	**Men**	**Women**
Franklin, IN 46131-2512	Baseball	Basketball
*Affiliation—*NCAA III	Basketball	Cross Country
Nickname—Grizzlies	Cross Country	Golf
Athletic Director—Men	Football	Soccer
(317) 738-8121	Golf	Softball
Athletic Director—Women	Soccer	Tennis
(317) 738-8127	Tennis	Track
	Track	Volleyball

GOSHEN COLLEGE

1700 S. Main Street	**Men**	**Women**
Goshen, IN 46526-4724	Baseball	Basketball
*Affiliation—*NAIA II	Basketball	Cross Country
Nickname—Maple Leafs	Cross Country	Soccer
Athletic Director—Men	Golf	Softball
(219) 535-7493	Soccer	Tennis
Athletic Director—Women	Tennis	Track
(219) 535-7494	Track	Volleyball

GRACE COLLEGE

200 Seminary Drive	**Men**	**Women**
Winona Lake, IN 46590-1224	Baseball	Basketball
*Affiliation—*NAIA II, NCCAA I	Basketball	Cross Country
Nickname—Lancers	Cross Country	Soccer
Athletic Director—	Golf	Softball
(219) 372-5224	Soccer	Tennis
	Tennis	Track
	Track	Volleyball
	Volleyball	

HANOVER COLLEGE

PO Box 108, Main Street Hanover, IN 47243-0108 Affiliation—NCAA III Nickname—Panthers Athletic Director— (812) 866-7374	**Men** Baseball Basketball Cross Country Football Golf Soccer Tennis Track	**Women** Basketball Cross Country Field Hockey Golf Soccer Softball Tennis Track Volleyball

HUNTINGTON COLLEGE

2303 College Avenue Huntington, IN 46750-1237 Affiliation—NAIA II Nickname—Foresters Athletic Director— (219) 359-4282	**Men** Baseball Basketball Cross Country Golf Soccer Tennis Track	**Women** Basketball Cross Country Soccer Softball Tennis Track Volleyball

INDIANA INSTITUTE OF TECHNOLOGY

1600 E. Washington Boulevard Fort Wayne, IN 46803-1228 Affiliation—NAIA II Nickname—Warriors Athletic Director— (219) 422-5561	**Men** Baseball Basketball Soccer	**Women** Basketball Soccer Softball

INDIANA STATE UNIVERSITY

200 S. 6th Street Terre Haute, IN 47807-4215 Affiliation—NCAA I (I-AA Football) Nickname—Sycamores Athletic Director— (812) 237-4040	**Men** Baseball Basketball Cross Country Football Tennis Track	**Women** Basketball Cross Country Softball Tennis Track Volleyball

INDIANA UNIVERSITY

Athletic Department,	Men	Women
Assembly Hall	Baseball	Basketball
Bloomington, IN 47408	Basketball	Cross Country
Affiliation—NCAA I	Cross Country	Diving
(I-A Football)	Diving	Golf
Nickname—*Hoosiers*	Football	Soccer
Athletic Director—*Men*	Golf	Softball
(812) 855-1966	Soccer	Swimming
Athletic Director—*Women*	Swimming	Tennis
(812) 855-4439	Tennis	Track
	Track	Volleyball
	Wrestling	

INDIANA UNIVERSITY, KOKOMO

2300 Washington Street	Men
Kokomo, IN 36902-3557	Basketball
Nickname—*Knights*	
Athletic Director—	
(765) 455-9203	

INDIANA UNIVERSITY, SOUTH BEND

1700 Mishawaka Avenue	Men	Women
South Bend, IN 46615-1408	Basketball	Basketball
Affiliation—NAIA I		
Nickname—*Titans*		
Athletic Director—		
(219) 288-6058		

INDIANA UNIVERSITY, SOUTHEAST

4201 Grant Line Road	Men	Women
New Albany, IN 47150-2158	Baseball	Basketball
Affiliation—NAIA II	Basketball	Cross Country
Nickname—*Grenadiers*	Cross Country	Tennis
Athletic Director—	Tennis	Volleyball
(812) 941-2432		

INDIANA UNIVERSITY EAST

2325 Chester Boulevard	Men	Women
Richmond, IN 47374-1220	Basketball	Basketball
Nickname—*Pioneers*		Softball
Athletic Director—		Volleyball
(765) 973-8366		

INDIANA UNIVERSITY-PURDUE UNIVERSITY, FORT WAYNE

2101 E. Coliseum Boulevard
Fort Wayne, IN 46805-1445
Affiliation—NCAA *II*
Nickname—*Mastodons*
Athletic Director—
(219) 481-6643

Men	Women
Baseball	Basketball
Basketball	Cheerleading
Cross Country	Cross Country
Soccer	Softball
Tennis	Tennis
Volleyball	Volleyball

INDIANA UNIVERSITY-PURDUE UNIVERSITY, INDIANAPOLIS

901 W. New York Street,
Suite 105
Indianapolis, IN 46202-5224
Affiliation—NCAA *I*
Nickname—*Metros*
Athletic Director—
(317) 274-0622

Men	Women
Baseball	Basketball
Basketball	Cheerleading
Cross Country	Cross Country
Diving	Diving
Golf	Soccer
Soccer	Softball
Swimming	Swimming
Tennis	Tennis
	Volleyball

INDIANA WESLEYAN UNIVERSITY

4201 S. Washington Street
Marion, IN 46953
Affiliation—NAIA *II,* NCCAA
Nickname—*Wildcats*
Athletic Director—*Men*
(765) 677-2317
Athletic Director—*Women*
(765) 677-2319

Men	Women
Baseball	Basketball
Basketball	Cross Country
Cross Country	Soccer
Golf	Softball
Soccer	Tennis
Tennis	Track
Track	Volleyball

INDIANAPOLIS, UNIVERSITY OF

1400 E. Hanna Avenue
Indianapolis, IN 46227-3630
Affiliation—NCAA *II*
Nickname—*Greyhounds*
Athletic Director—
(317) 788-3306

Men	Women
Baseball	Basketball
Basketball	Cross Country
Cross Country	Golf
Football	Soccer
Golf	Softball
Soccer	Tennis
Swimming	Track
Tennis	Volleyball
Track	
Wrestling	

MANCHESTER COLLEGE

604 E. *College Avenue*
North Manchester, IN
  46962-1276
Affiliation—NCAA III
Nickname—Spartans
Athletic Director—
  (219) 982-5000 ext. 5390
	Men
	Baseball
	Basketball
	Cross Country
	Football
	Golf
	Soccer
	Tennis
	Track
	Wrestling
		Women
		Basketball
		Cheerleading
		Cross Country
		Golf
		Soccer
		Softball
		Tennis
		Track
		Volleyball

MARIAN COLLEGE

3200 *Cold Spring Road* *Indianapolis, IN 46222-1960* *Affiliation—NAIA II* *Nickname—Knights* *Athletic Director—* *(317) 955-6118*	**Men** Baseball Basketball Cross Country Cycling Golf Soccer Tennis Track	**Women** Basketball Cheerleading Cross Country Cycling Soccer Softball Tennis Track Volleyball

NOTRE DAME, UNIVERSITY OF

Joyce Center
Notre Dame, IN 46556
Affiliation—NCAA I
  (I-A Football)
Nickname—Fighting Irish
Athletic Director—
  (219) 631-7546
	Men
	Baseball
	Basketball
	Cross Country
	Diving
	Fencing
	Football
	Golf
	Ice Hockey
	Lacrosse
	Soccer
	Swimming
	Tennis
	Track
		Women
		Basketball
		Cheerleading
		Crew
		Cross Country
		Diving
		Fencing
		Golf
		Lacrosse
		Soccer
		Softball
		Swimming
		Tennis
		Track
		Volleyball

OAKLAND CITY UNIVERSITY

	Men	Women
143 Lycretia Street	Baseball	Basketball
Oakland City, IN 47660	Basketball	Cross Country
Affiliation—NCAA II	Cross Country	Golf
Nickname—Mighty Oaks	Golf	Softball
Athletic Director—		Volleyball
(812) 749-1290		

PURDUE UNIVERSITY

	Men	Women
1790 Mackey Arena	Baseball	Basketball
West Lafayette, IN 47907-1790	Basketball	Cheerleading
Affiliation—NCAA I	Cross Country	Cross Country
(I-A Football)	Diving	Diving
Nickname—Boilermakers	Football	Golf
Athletic Director—	Golf	Soccer
(765) 494-3189	Swimming	Softball
	Tennis	Swimming
	Track	Tennis
	Wrestling	Track
		Volleyball

PURDUE UNIVERSITY, CALUMET

	Men	Women
2200 169th Street	Basketball	Basketball
Hammond, IN 46323-2068	Soccer	Volleyball
Affiliation—NAIA I		
Nickname—Lakers		
Athletic Director—		
(219) 989-2540		

PURDUE UNIVERSITY, NORTH CENTRAL CAMPUS

	Men	Women
1401 S. U.S. Highway 421	Baseball	Cross Country
Westville, IN 46391	Basketball	
Nickname—Centaurs	Cross Country	

ROSE-HULMEN INSTITUTE OF TECHNOLOGY

| *5500 Wabash Avenue*
Terre Haute, IN 47803-3920
Affiliation—NCAA III
Nickname—Fightin' Engineers
Athletic Director—
(812) 877-8270 | **Men**
Baseball
Basketball
Cross Country
Football
Golf
Rifle
Soccer
Swimming
Tennis
Track
Wrestling | **Women**
Basketball
Cross Country
Rifle
Swimming
Track
Volleyball |

SAINT FRANCIS, UNIVERSITY OF

| *2701 Spring Street*
Fort Wayne, IN 46808
Affiliation—NAIA II
Nickname—Cougars
Athletic Director—
(219) 434-7475 | **Men**
Baseball
Basketball
Cheerleading
Cross Country
Football
Golf
Soccer
Track | **Women**
Basketball
Cheerleading
Cross Country
Soccer
Softball
Tennis
Track
Volleyball |

SAINT JOSEPH'S COLLEGE

| *PO Box 875*
Rensselaer, IN 47978-0875
Affiliation—NCAA II
Nickname—Pumas
Athletic Director—
(219) 866-6286 | **Men**
Baseball
Basketball
Cross Country
Football
Golf
Soccer
Tennis
Track | **Women**
Basketball
Cross Country
Golf
Soccer
Tennis
Track
Volleyball |

SAINT MARY-OF-THE-WOODS COLLEGE

| *LeFer Hall, 1000 Saint Mary's*
Road
Saint Mary-of-the-Woods, IN
47876
Affiliation—NSCAA
Nickname—Pomeroys
Athletic Director—
(812) 535-5288 | **Women**
Basketball | Softball |

SAINT MARY'S COLLEGE

Angela Athletic Facility	**Women**	
Notre Dame, IN 46556	Basketball	Softball
*Affiliation—*NCAA *III*	Cross Country	Swimming
Nickname—Belles	Diving	Tennis
Athletic Director—	Golf	Track
(219) 284-5547	Soccer	Volleyball

SOUTHERN INDIANA, UNIVERSITY OF

8600 University Boulevard	**Men**	**Women**
Evansville, IN 47712-3534	Baseball	Basketball
*Affiliation—*NCAA *II*	Basketball	Cross Country
Nickname—Screaming Eagles	Cross Country	Golf
Athletic Director—	Golf	Soccer
(812) 464-1846	Soccer	Softball
	Tennis	Tennis
		Track
		Volleyball

TAYLOR UNIVERSITY

236 W. Reade Avenue	**Men**	**Women**
Upland, IN 46989-1001	Baseball	Basketball
*Affiliation—*NAIA *II,* NCCAA	Basketball	Cross Country
Nickname—Trojans	Cross Country	Soccer
Athletic Director—	Football	Softball
(765) 998-5311	Golf	Tennis
	Soccer	Track
	Tennis	Volleyball
	Track	

TAYLOR UNIVERSITY, FORT WAYNE

1025 W. Rudsill Boulevard	**Men**	**Women**
Fort Wayne, IN 46807-2197	Basketball	Basketball
*Affiliation—*NCCAA *I*	Cheerleading	Cheerleading
Nickname—Falcons	Soccer	Volleyball
Athletic Director—		
(219) 456-2111 ext. 32230		

TRI-STATE UNIVERSITY

	Men	Women
1 University Avenue	Baseball	Basketball
Angola, IN 46703-1764	Basketball	Cross Country
Affiliation—NAIA II	Cross Country	Golf
Nickname—Thunder	Football	Soccer
Athletic Director—	Golf	Softball
(219) 665-4143	Soccer	Swimming
	Swimming	Tennis
	Tennis	Track
	Track	Volleyball
	Volleyball	

VALPARAISO UNIVERSITY

	Men	Women
Athletic-Recreation Center	Baseball	Basketball
Valparaiso, IN 46383	Basketball	Cheerleading
Affiliation—NCAA I	Cross Country	Cross Country
(I-AA Football)	Football	Diving
Nickname—Crusaders	Soccer	Soccer
Athletic Director—	Swimming	Softball
(219) 464-6894	Tennis	Swimming
	Track	Tennis
		Track
		Volleyball

WABASH COLLEGE

	Men	
301 W. Wabash Avenue	Baseball	Soccer
Crawfordsville, IN 47933-2428	Basketball	Swimming
Affiliation—NCAA III	Cross Country	Tennis
Nickname—Little Giants	Football	Track
Athletic Director—	Golf	Wrestling
(765) 361-6221		

IOWA

BRIAR CLIFF COLLEGE

*3303 Rebecca Street,
  PO Box 2100
Sioux City, IA 51104-2324
Affiliation—NAIA II
Nickname—Chargers
Athletic Director—
  (712) 279-1706*

Men	**Women**
Baseball	Basketball
Basketball	Cheerleading
Cross Country	Cross Country
Golf	Golf
Soccer	Soccer
Track	Softball
Wrestling	Track
	Volleyball

BUENA VISTA UNIVERSITY

*610 W. 4th Street
Storm Lake, IA 50588-1713
Affiliation—NCAA III
Nickname—Beavers
Athletic Director—
  (712) 749-2253*

Men	**Women**
Baseball	Basketball
Basketball	Cross Country
Cross Country	Golf
Football	Soccer
Golf	Softball
Soccer	Swimming
Swimming	Tennis
Tennis	Track
Track	Volleyball
Wrestling	

CENTRAL COLLEGE

*812 University Street
Pella, IA 50219-1902
Affiliation—NCAA III
Nickname—Dutch
Athletic Director—
  (515) 628-5310*

Men	**Women**
Baseball	Basketball
Basketball	Cross Country
Cross Country	Golf
Football	Soccer
Golf	Softball
Soccer	Tennis
Tennis	Track
Track	Volleyball
Wrestling	

CLARKE COLLEGE

1550 Clarke Drive Dubuque, IA 52001-3117 Affiliation—NCAA III Nickname—Crusaders Athletic Director— (319) 588-6462	**Men** Baseball Basketball Cross Country Golf Skiing Soccer Tennis Volleyball	**Women** Basketball Cheerleading Cross Country Golf Skiing Soccer Softball Tennis Volleyball

COE COLLEGE

1220 1st Avenue NE Cedar Rapids, IA 52402-5008 Affiliation—NCAA III Nickname—Kohawks Athletic Director— (319) 399-8599	**Men** Baseball Basketball Cross Country Football Golf Soccer Swimming Tennis Track Wrestling	**Women** Basketball Cross Country Golf Soccer Softball Swimming Tennis Track Volleyball

CORNELL COLLEGE

600 1st Street W Mount Vernon, IA 52314-1006 Affiliation—NCAA III Nickname—Rams Athletic Director— (319) 895-4230	**Men** Baseball Basketball Cross Country Football Golf Soccer Tennis Track Wrestling	**Women** Basketball Cross Country Golf Soccer Softball Tennis Track Volleyball

DORDT COLLEGE

498 4th Avenue NE	Men	Women
Sioux Center, IA 51250-1606	Baseball	Basketball
Affiliation—NAIA II	Basketball	Cross Country
Nickname—Defenders	Cross Country	Soccer
Athletic Director—	Golf	Softball
(712) 722-6305	Soccer	Tennis
	Tennis	Track
	Track	Volleyball

DRAKE UNIVERSITY

25th and University	Men	Women
Des Moines, IA 50311	Basketball	Basketball
Affiliation—NCAA I	Cross Country	Cross Country
(I-AA Football)	Football	Softball
Nickname—Bulldogs	Golf	Tennis
Athletic Director—	Soccer	Track
(515) 271-2889	Tennis	Volleyball
	Track	

DUBUQUE, UNIVERSITY OF

2000 University Avenue	Men	Women
Dubuque, IA 52001-5099	Baseball	Basketball
Affiliation—NCAA III	Basketball	Cross Country
Nickname—Spartans	Cross Country	Golf
Athletic Director—	Football	Softball
(319) 589-3599	Golf	Tennis
	Tennis	Track
	Track	Volleyball
	Wrestling	

FAITH BAPTIST COLLEGE

1900 NW 4th Street	Men	Women
Ankeny, IA 50021-2152	Basketball	Basketball
Affiliation—NCCAA II	Soccer	Volleyball
Nickname—Eagles		
Athletic Director—		
(515) 964-0601		

GRACELAND COLLEGE

| 700 College Avenue
Lamoni, IA 50140-1611
Affiliation—NAIA II
Nickname—Yellowjackets
Athletic Director—
(515) 784-5106 | Men
Baseball
Basketball
Cross Country
Football
Golf
Soccer
Tennis
Track
Volleyball | Women
Basketball
Cross Country
Golf
Soccer
Softball
Tennis
Track
Volleyball |

GRAND VIEW COLLEGE

| 1200 Grandview Avenue
Des Moines, IA 50316-1529
Affiliation—NAIA I
Nickname—Vikings
Athletic Director—
(515) 263-2897 | Men
Baseball
Basketball
Soccer | Women
Basketball
Cheerleading
Soccer
Softball
Volleyball |

GRINNELL COLLEGE

| PO Box 805
Grinnell, IA 50112-0805
Affiliation—NCAA III
Nickname—Pioneers
Athletic Director—
(515) 269-3800 | Men
Baseball
Basketball
Cross Country
Football
Golf
Soccer
Swimming
Tennis
Track | Women
Basketball
Cross Country
Golf
Soccer
Softball
Swimming
Tennis
Track
Volleyball |

IOWA, UNIVERSITY OF

1 Elliott Drive	**Men**	**Women**
Iowa City, IA 52242	Baseball	Basketball
Affiliation—NCAA I	Basketball	Crew
(I-A Football)	Cross Country	Cross Country
Nickname—Hawkeyes	Diving	Diving
Athletic Director—Men	Football	Field Hockey
(319) 335-9435	Golf	Golf
Athletic Director—Women	Gymnastics	Gymnastics
(319) 335-9247	Swimming	Soccer
	Tennis	Softball
	Track	Swimming
	Wrestling	Tennis
		Track
		Volleyball

IOWA STATE UNIVERSITY

1800 S. 4th Street	**Men**	**Women**
Ames, IA 50011	Baseball	Basketball
Affiliation—NCAA I	Basketball	Cross Country
(I-A Football)	Cross Country	Golf
Nickname—Cyclones	Football	Gymnastics
Athletic Director—	Golf	Soccer
(515) 294-0123	Swimming	Softball
	Track	Swimming
	Wrestling	Tennis
		Track
		Volleyball

IOWA WESLEYAN COLLEGE

601 N. Main Street	**Men**	**Women**
Mount Pleasant, IA 52641-1348	Baseball	Basketball
Affiliation—NAIA I	Basketball	Cross Country
Nickname—Tigers	Cross Country	Golf
Athletic Director—	Football	Soccer
(319) 385-6303	Golf	Softball
	Soccer	Track
	Track	Volleyball

LORAS COLLEGE

	Men	Women
1450 Alta Vista Street	Baseball	Basketball
Dubuque, IA 52004-0178	Basketball	Cross Country
*Affiliation—*NCAA *III*	Cross Country	Golf
Nickname—Duhawks	Football	Soccer
Athletic Director—	Golf	Softball
(319) 588-7112	Soccer	Swimming
	Swimming	Tennis
	Tennis	Track
	Track	Volleyball
	Wrestling	

LUTHER COLLEGE

	Men	Women
700 College Drive	Baseball	Basketball
Decorah, IA 52101-1039	Basketball	Cross Country
*Affiliation—*NCAA *III*	Cross Country	Diving
Nickname—Norse	Diving	Golf
Athletic Director—	Football	Soccer
(319) 387-1575	Golf	Softball
	Soccer	Swimming
	Swimming	Tennis
	Tennis	Track
	Track	Volleyball
	Wrestling	

MARYCREST INTERNATIONAL UNIVERSITY

	Men	Women
1607 W. 12th Street	Basketball	Basketball
Davenport, IA 52804-4034	Soccer	Soccer
*Affiliation—*NAIA *II*	Volleyball	Softball
Nickname—Marauding Eagles		
Athletic Director—		
(319) 326-9596		

MORNINGSIDE COLLEGE

	Men	Women
1501 Morningside Avenue	Baseball	Basketball
Sioux City, IA 51106-1717	Basketball	Cheerleading
*Affiliation—*NCAA *II*	Cross Country	Cross Country
Nickname—Chiefs	Football	Golf
Athletic Director—	Track	Softball
(712) 274-5192		Tennis
		Track
		Volleyball

MOUNT MERCY COLLEGE

1330 Elmhurst Drive NE	**Men**	**Women**
Cedar Rapids, IA 52402-4763	Baseball	Basketball
Affiliation—NAIA II	Basketball	Cross Country
Nickname—Mustangs	Cross Country	Golf
Athletic Director—	Golf	Soccer
(319) 363-8213	Soccer	Softball
	Track	Track
		Volleyball

MOUNT SAINT CLARE COLLEGE

400 N. Bluff Boulevard	**Men**	**Women**
Clinton, IA 52732-3910	Baseball	Basketball
Affiliation—NAIA	Basketball	Cross Country
Nickname—Mounties	Cross Country	Golf
Athletic Director—	Golf	Soccer
(319) 242-4023	Soccer	Softball
	Tennis	Tennis
	Track	Track
	Wrestling	Volleyball

NORTHERN IOWA, UNIVERSITY OF

23rd and College	**Men**	**Women**
Cedar Falls, IA 50614	Baseball	Basketball
Affiliation—NCAA I	Basketball	Cheerleading
(I-AA Football)	Cross Country	Cross Country
Nickname—Panthers	Diving	Diving
Athletic Director—	Football	Golf
(319) 273-2470	Golf	Softball
	Swimming	Swimming
	Tennis	Tennis
	Track	Track
	Wrestling	Volleyball

NORTHWESTERN COLLEGE

	Men	Women
101 7th Street SW	Baseball	Basketball
Orange City, IA 51041-1923	Basketball	Cheerleading
Affiliation—NAIA II	Cross Country	Cross Country
Nickname—Red Raiders	Football	Golf
Athletic Director—	Golf	Soccer
(712) 737-7280	Soccer	Softball
	Tennis	Tennis
	Track	Track
	Wrestling	Volleyball

SAINT AMBROSE UNIVERSITY

	Men	Women
518 W. Locust Street	Baseball	Basketball
Davenport, IA 52803-2829	Basketball	Cross Country
Affiliation—NAIA II	Cross Country	Golf
Nickname—Fighting Bees	Football	Soccer
Athletic Director—	Golf	Softball
(319) 333-6233	Soccer	Tennis
	Tennis	Track
	Track	Volleyball
	Volleyball	

SIMPSON COLLEGE

	Men	Women
701 North C Street	Baseball	Basketball
Indianola, IA 50125-1202	Basketball	Cheerleading
Affiliation—NCAA III	Cross Country	Cross Country
Nickname—Storm	Football	Golf
Athletic Director—	Golf	Soccer
(515) 961-1620	Soccer	Softball
	Tennis	Swimming
	Track	Tennis
	Wrestling	Track
		Volleyball

UPPER IOWA UNIVERSITY

PO Box 1857	**Men**	**Women**
Fayette, IA 52142-1857	Baseball	Basketball
*Affiliation—*NCAA *III*	Basketball	Cross Country
Nickname—Peacocks	Cross Country	Golf
Athletic Director—	Football	Soccer
(319) 425-5227	Golf	Softball
	Soccer	Tennis
	Tennis	Track
	Track	Volleyball
	Wrestling	

VENNARD COLLEGE

8th Avenue East	**Men**	**Women**
University Park, IA 52595	Basketball	Basketball
Nickname—Cougars	Golf	Golf
Athletic Director—		Volleyball
(515) 673-8391		

WARTBURG COLLEGE

222 9th Street NW	**Men**	**Women**
Waverly, IA 50677-2215	Baseball	Basketball
*Affiliation—*NCAA *III*	Basketball	Cheerleading
Nickname—Knights	Cross Country	Cross Country
Athletic Director—	Football	Golf
(319) 352-8470	Golf	Soccer
	Soccer	Softball
	Tennis	Tennis
	Track	Track
	Wrestling	Volleyball

WESTMAR UNIVERSITY

1002 3rd Avenue SE	**Men**	**Women**
Le Mars, IA 51031-2651	Baseball	Basketball
*Affiliation—*NAIA	Basketball	Soccer
Nickname—Eagles	Football	Softball
Athletic Director—	Golf	Track
(712) 546-2575	Soccer	Volleyball
	Tennis	
	Track	
	Wrestling	

WILLIAM PENN COLLEGE

201 *Trueblood Avenue*	Men	Women
Oskaloosa, IA 52577	Baseball	Basketball
Affiliation—NCAA *III*	Basketball	Cross Country
Nickname—*Statesmen*	Cross Country	Golf
Athletic Director—*Men*	Football	Soccer
(515) 673-1018	Golf	Softball
Athletic Director—*Women*	Soccer	Tennis
(515) 673-1024	Tennis	Track
	Track	Volleyball
	Wrestling	

KANSAS

BAKER UNIVERSITY

PO Box 65	Men	Women
Baldwin City, KS 66006-0065	Baseball	Basketball
Affiliation—NAIA *II*	Basketball	Cheerleading
Nickname—*Wildcats*	Cross Country	Cross Country
Athletic Director—	Football	Dance
(785) 594-6451	Golf	Softball
	Soccer	Tennis
	Tennis	Track
	Track	Volleyball

BARCLAY COLLEGE

PO Box 288	Men	Women
Haviland, KS 67059-0288	Basketball	Basketball
Nickname—*Bears*	Soccer	
Athletic Director—	Volleyball	
(316) 862-5876		

BENEDICTINE COLLEGE

1020 N. 2nd Street	Men	Women
Atchison, KS 66002-1402	Baseball	Basketball
Affiliation—NAIA	Basketball	Soccer
(Div. II Football)	Football	Softball
Nickname—*Ravens*	Golf	Tennis
Athletic Director—	Soccer	Track
(913) 367-5340 ext. 2502	Tennis	Volleyball
	Track	

BETHANY COLLEGE

421 N. 1st Street	**Men**	**Women**
Linsborg, KS 67456-1831	Baseball	Basketball
*Affiliation—*NAIA *II*	Basketball	Cross Country
Nickname—Swedes	Cross Country	Soccer
Athletic Director—	Football	Softball
(785) 227-3380 ext. 8174	Golf	Tennis
	Soccer	Track
	Tennis	Volleyball
	Track	

BETHEL COLLEGE

300 E. 27th Street	**Men**	**Women**
North Newton, KS 67117-8061	Basketball	Basketball
*Affiliation—*NAIA *II*	Football	Soccer
Nickname—Threshers	Soccer	Tennis
Athletic Director—	Tennis	Track
(316) 284-5279	Track	Volleyball

EMPORIA STATE UNIVERSITY

12th and Commercial	**Men**	**Women**
Emporia, KS 66801	Baseball	Basketball
*Affiliation—*NCAA *II*	Basketball	Cheerleading
Nickname—Hornets	Cross Country	Cross Country
Athletic Director—	Football	Softball
(316) 341-5350	Tennis	Tennis
	Track	Track
		Volleyball

FORT HAYS STATE UNIVERSITY

600 Park Street	**Men**	**Women**
Hays, KS 67601-4009	Baseball	Basketball
*Affiliation—*NCAA *II*	Basketball	Cheerleading
Nickname—Tigers	Cross Country	Cross Country
Athletic Director—	Football	Softball
(785) 628-4050	Golf	Tennis
	Track	Track
	Wrestling	Volleyball

FRIENDS UNIVERSITY

2100 W. University Street	**Men**	**Women**
Wichita, KS 67213-3379	Baseball	Basketball
Affiliation—NAIA II	Basketball	Soccer
Nickname—Falcons	Football	Softball
Athletic Director—	Golf	Tennis
(316) 295-5700	Soccer	Volleyball
	Tennis	

KANSAS, UNIVERSITY OF

205 Wagnon Student	**Men**	**Women**
Athletic Center	Baseball	Basketball
Lawrence, KS 66045	Basketball	Cheerleading
Affiliation—NCAA I	Cross Country	Crew
(I-A Football)	Diving	Cross Country
Nickname—Jayhawks	Football	Diving
Athletic Director—	Golf	Golf
(785) 864-3143	Swimming	Rowing
	Tennis	Soccer
	Track	Softball
		Swimming
		Tennis
		Track
		Volleyball

KANSAS STATE UNIVERSITY

1800 College Avenue	**Men**	**Women**
Manhattan, KS 66502-3308	Baseball	Basketball
Affiliation—NCAA I	Basketball	Golf
(I-A Football)	Football	Rowing
Nickname—Wildcats	Golf	Tennis
Athletic Director—	Track	Track
(785) 532-6912		Volleyball

KANSAS WESLEYAN UNIVERSITY

100 E. Claflin Avenue	**Men**	**Women**
Salina, KS 67401-6146	Baseball	Basketball
Affiliation—NAIA II, NSEAA	Basketball	Cheerleading
Nickname—Coyotes	Cross Country	Cross Country
Athletic Director—	Football	Golf
(785) 827-5541 ext. 3131	Golf	Soccer
	Soccer	Softball
	Track	Track
		Volleyball

MCPHERSON COLLEGE

1600 E. Euclid Street	**Men**	**Women**
McPherson, KS 67460-3847	Basketball	Basketball
Affiliation—NAIA II	Cross Country	Cross Country
(Div. II Football)	Football	Golf
Nickname—Bulldogs	Golf	Soccer
Athletic Director—	Soccer	Tennis
(316) 241-0731	Tennis	Track
	Track	Volleyball

MIDAMERICA NAZARENE

2030 E. College Way	**Men**	**Women**
Olathe, KS 66062-1851	Baseball	Basketball
Affiliation—NAIA II, NCCAA,	Basketball	Cross Country
HAAC	Cross Country	Softball
Nickname—Pioneers	Football	Track
Athletic Director—	Track	Volleyball
(913) 782-3750 ext. 266		

NEWMAN UNIVERSITY

3100 McCormick Street	**Men**	**Women**
Wichita, KS 67213-2097	Baseball	Basketball
Affiliation—NAIA I	Basketball	Soccer
Nickname—Jets	Golf	Softball
Athletic Director—	Soccer	Volleyball
(316) 942-4291 ext. 289		

OTTAWA UNIVERSITY

1001 S. Cedar Street	**Men**	**Women**
Ottawa, KS 66067-3341	Baseball	Basketball
Affiliation—NAIA II	Basketball	Cross Country
Nickname—Braves	Cross County	Golf
Athletic Director—	Football	Soccer
(913) 242-5200 ext. 5423	Golf	Softball
	Soccer	Track
	Track	Volleyball

PITTSBURGH STATE UNIVERSITY

1701 S. Broadway Street	**Men**	**Women**
Pittsburgh, KS 66762-5856	Baseball	Basketball
Affiliation—NCAA *II*	Basketball	Cross Country
Nickname—Gorillas	Cross Country	Softball
Athletic Director—	Football	Track
(316) 235-4653	Golf	Volleyball
	Track	

SAINT MARY COLLEGE

4100 S. 4th Street	**Men**	**Women**
Leavenworth, KS 66048-5082	Basketball	Basketball
Affiliation—NAIA *I*	Soccer	Soccer
Athletic Director—	Tennis	Volleyball
(913) 682-5151 ext. 6160		

SOUTHWESTERN COLLEGE

100 College Street	**Men**	**Women**
Winfield, KS 67156-2443	Basketball	Basketball
Affiliation—NAIA *II*	Cross Country	Cross Country
Nickname—Moundbuilders	Football	Soccer
Athletic Director—	Golf	Tennis
(316) 221-8218	Soccer	Track
	Tennis	Volleyball
	Track	

STERLING COLLEGE

Gleason Center	**Men**	**Women**
Sterling, KS 67579	Baseball	Basketball
Affiliation—NAIA *II*	Basketball	Cross Country
Nickname—Warriors	Cross Country	Soccer
Athletic Director—	Football	Softball
(316) 278-4285	Soccer	Tennis
	Tennis	Track
	Track	Volleyball

TABOR COLLEGE

400 S. Jefferson Street	Men	Women
Hillsboro, KS 67063-1753	Baseball	Basketball
Affiliation—NAIA II	Basketball	Cross Country
Nickname—Bluejays	Cross Country	Soccer
Athletic Director—	Football	Softball
(316) 947-3121 ext. 1308	Golf	Tennis
	Soccer	Track
	Tennis	Volleyball
	Track	

WASHBURN UNIVERSITY

1700 SW College Avenue	Men	Women
Topeka, KS 66621	Baseball	Basketball
Affiliation—NCAA II	Basketball	Softball
Nickname—Ichabods	Football	Tennis
Athletic Director—	Golf	Volleyball
(785) 231-1010 ext. 1790	Tennis	

WICHITA STATE UNIVERSITY

Campus Box 18,	Men	Women
1845 Fairmount	Baseball	Basketball
Wichita, KS 67260	Basketball	Cross Country
Affiliation—NCAA I	Cross Country	Golf
Nickname—Shockers	Golf	Softball
Athletic Director—	Tennis	Tennis
(316) 978-3250	Track	Track
		Volleyball

KENTUCKY

ALICE LLOYD COLLEGE

100 Purpose Road	Men	Women
Pippa Passes, KY 41844-9701	Baseball	Basketball
Affiliation—NAIA II	Basketball	Cross Country
Nickname—Eagles	Cross Country	Softball
Athletic Director—	Golf	Tennis
(606) 368-2101 ext. 7109		

ASBURY COLLEGE

1 Macklem Drive
Wilmore, KY 40390-1152
Affiliation—NAIA II
Nickname—*Eagles*
Athletic Director—
   (606) 858-3511 ext. 2163

Men	Women
Baseball	Basketball
Basketball	Cross Country
Soccer	Softball
Swimming	Swimming
Tennis	Tennis
	Volleyball

BELLARMINE COLLEGE

201 Newburg Road
Louisville, KY 40205-1863
Affiliation—NCAA II
Nickname—*Knights*
Athletic Director—
   (502) 452-8036

Men	Women
Baseball	Basketball
Basketball	Field Hockey
Cross Country	Golf
Golf	Soccer
Soccer	Softball
Tennis	Tennis
Track	Track
	Volleyball

BEREA COLLEGE

CPO 2287
Berea, KY 40404
Affiliation—NAIA II
Nickname—*Mountaineers*
Athletic Director—
   (606) 986-9341 ext. 5424

Men	Women
Baseball	Basketball
Basketball	Cross Country
Cross Country	Soccer
Golf	Softball
Soccer	Swimming
Swimming	Tennis
Tennis	Track
Track	Volleyball

BRESCIA UNIVERSITY

717 Frederica Street
Owensboro, KY 42301-3019
Affiliation—NAIA I
Nickname—*Bearcats*
Athletic Director—*Men*
   (502) 686-4292
Athletic Director—*Women*
   (502) 686-4330

Men	Women
Baseball	Basketball
Basketball	Soccer
Golf	Softball
Soccer	Tennis
Tennis	Volleyball

CAMPBELLSVILLE UNIVERSITY

1 University Drive
Campbellsville, KY 42718-2190
Affiliation—NAIA I, NCCAA
Nickname—Tigers
Athletic Director—
(502) 789-5009

Men	Women
Baseball	Basketball
Basketball	Cheerleading
Cross Country	Cross Country
Football	Golf
Golf	Soccer
Soccer	Softball
Swimming	Swimming
Tennis	Tennis
	Volleyball

CENTRE COLLEGE

600 W. Walnut Street
Danville, KY 40422-1309
Affiliation—NCAA III
Nickname—Colonels
Athletic Director—
(606) 236-6081

Men	Women
Baseball	Basketball
Basketball	Cheerleading
Cross Country	Cross Country
Football	Field Hockey
Golf	Golf
Soccer	Soccer
Swimming	Softball
Tennis	Swimming
Track	Tennis
	Track
	Volleyball

CUMBERLAND COLLEGE

7526 College Station Drive
Williamsburg, KY 40769-1386
Affiliation—NAIA I
Nickname—Indians
Athletic Director—
(606) 539-4467

Men	Women
Baseball	Basketball
Basketball	Cheerleading
Cross Country	Cross Country
Football	Golf
Golf	Soccer
Soccer	Softball
Swimming	Swimming
Tennis	Tennis
Track	Track
Wrestling	Volleyball

EASTERN KENTUCKY UNIVERSITY

Lancaster Avenue	**Men**	**Women**
Richmond, KY 40475	Baseball	Basketball
*Affiliation—*NCAA *I*	Basketball	Cross Country
(I-AA Football)	Cross Country	Golf
Nickname—Colonels	Football	Softball
Athletic Director—	Golf	Tennis
(606) 622-2120	Tennis	Track
	Track	Volleyball

GEORGETOWN COLLEGE

400 E. College Street	**Men**	**Women**
Georgetown, KY 40324-1628	Baseball	Basketball
*Affiliation—*NAIA *I*	Basketball	Cheerleading
Nickname—Tigers	Cross Country	Cross Country
Athletic Director—	Football	Golf
(502) 863-8115	Golf	Soccer
	Soccer	Softball
	Tennis	Tennis
		Volleyball

KENTUCKY, UNIVERSITY OF

Memorial Coliseum	**Men**	**Women**
Lexington, KY 40506	Baseball	Basketball
*Affiliation—*NCAA *I*	Basketball	Cheerleading
(I-A Football)	Cross Country	Cross Country
Nickname—Wildcats	Diving	Diving
Athletic Director—	Football	Golf
(606) 257-8015	Golf	Gymnastics
	Rifle	Rifle
	Soccer	Soccer
	Swimming	Softball
	Tennis	Swimming
	Track	Tennis
		Track
		Volleyball

KENTUCKY CHRISTIAN COLLEGE

100 Academic Parkway	**Men**	**Women**
Grayson, KY 41143-2205	Basketball	Basketball
*Affiliation—*NCCAA *II*	Cross Country	Cross Country
Nickname—Knights	Soccer	Tennis
Athletic Director—	Tennis	Volleyball
(606) 474-3215		

KENTUCKY STATE UNIVERSITY

E. Main Street	**Men**	**Women**
Frankfort, KY 40601	Baseball	Basketball
Affiliation—NCAA II	Basketball	Cross Country
Nickname—Thoroughbreds	Cross Country	Softball
Athletic Director—	Football	Tennis
(502) 227-6014	Golf	Track
	Tennis	Volleyball
	Track	

KENTUCKY WESLEYAN COLLEGE

PO Box 1029,	**Men**	**Women**
3000 Fredericia Street	Baseball	Basketball
Owensboro, KY 42302-1039	Basketball	Cheerleading
Affiliation—NCAA II	Football	Golf
Nickname—Panthers	Golf	Soccer
Athletic Director—	Soccer	Softball
(502) 926-3111 ext. 401	Tennis	Tennis
		Volleyball

LINDSEY WILSON COLLEGE

210 Lindsey Wilson Street	**Men**	**Women**
Columbia, KY 42628-1223	Baseball	Basketball
Affiliation—NAIA I	Basketball	Bowling
Nickname—Blue Raiders	Bowling	Cross Country
Athletic Director—	Cross Country	Golf
(502) 384-8070	Golf	Soccer
	Soccer	Softball
	Tennis	Tennis
	Track	Track
		Volleyball

LOUISVILLE, UNIVERSITY OF

Student Activities Center	**Men**	**Women**
Louisville, KY 49292-0001	Baseball	Basketball
Affiliation—NCAA I	Basketball	Cheerleading
(I-A Football)	Cross Country	Crew
Nickname—Cardinals	Diving	Cross Country
Athletic Director—	Football	Diving
(502) 852-5732	Golf	Field Hockey
	Soccer	Golf
	Swimming	Soccer
	Tennis	Softball
	Track	Swimming
		Tennis
		Track
		Volleyball

MIDWAY COLLEGE

512 S. Stephens Street	**Women**	
Midway, KY 40347	Basketball	Tennis
Affiliation—NAIA II	Cross Country	Track
Nickname—Eagles	Soccer	Volleyball
Athletic Director—	Softball	
(606) 846-5387		

MOREHEAD STATE UNIVERSITY

University Boulevard	**Men**	**Women**
Morehead, KY 40351	Baseball	Basketball
Affiliation—NCAA I	Basketball	Cheerleading
(I-AA Football)	Cross Country	Cross Country
Nickname—Eagles	Football	Rifle
Athletic Director—	Golf	Soccer
(606) 783-2088	Rifle	Softball
	Tennis	Tennis
	Track	Track
		Volleyball

MURRAY STATE UNIVERSITY

Athletic Department, PO Box 9	**Men**	**Women**
Murray, KY 42071-0009	Baseball	Basketball
Affiliation—NCAA *I*	Basketball	Crew
(I-AA Football)	Cross Country	Cross Country
Nickname—*Racers*	Football	Golf
Athletic Director—	Golf	Rifle
(502) 762-6800	Rifle	Tennis
	Tennis	Track
	Track	Volleyball

NORTHERN KENTUCKY UNIVERSITY

Nunn Drive	**Men**	**Women**
Highland Heights, KY 41099	Baseball	Basketball
Affiliation—NCAA *II*	Basketball	Cross Country
Nickname—*Norse*	Cross Country	Soccer
Athletic Director—	Golf	Softball
(606) 572-5631	Soccer	Tennis
	Tennis	Volleyball

PIKEVILLE COLLEGE

214 Sycamore Street	**Men**	**Women**
Pikeville, KY 41501-1113	Baseball	Basketball
Affiliation—NAIA *I*	Basketball	Cross Country
Nickname—*Bears*	Cross Country	Softball
Athletic Director—	Golf	Tennis
(606) 432-9313	Tennis	Volleyball

SPALDING UNIVERSITY

851 S. 4th Street	**Men**	**Women**
Louisville, KY 40203-2115	Basketball	Basketball
Affiliation—NAIA *I*	Golf	Soccer
Nickname—*Pelicans*	Soccer	Softball
Athletic Director—		Volleyball
(502) 585-9911 ext. 163		

THOMAS MORE COLLEGE

333 Thomas More Parkway	**Men**	**Women**
Crestview Hills, KY 41017-3428	Baseball	Basketball
Affiliation—NCAA *III*	Basketball	Cheerleading
Nickname—*Saints*	Cross Country	Cross Country
Athletic Director—	Football	Soccer
(606) 344-3390	Soccer	Softball
	Tennis	Tennis
		Volleyball

TRANSYLVANIA UNIVERSITY

300 N. Broadway	**Men**	**Women**
Lexington, KY 40508-1797	Baseball	Basketball
Affiliation—NAIA I	Basketball	Cheerleading
Nickname—Pioneers	Cross Country	Cross Country
Athletic Director—	Diving	Diving
(606) 233-8270	Golf	Field Hockey
	Soccer	Golf
	Swimming	Soccer
	Tennis	Softball
		Swimming
		Tennis
		Volleyball

UNION COLLEGE

310 College Street	**Men**	**Women**
Barbourville, KY 40906-1410	Baseball	Basketball
Affiliation—NAIA	Basketball	Cheerleading
(NAIA *Div. II Football)*	Football	Golf
Nickname—Bulldogs	Golf	Soccer
Athletic Director—	Soccer	Softball
(606) 546-1211	Swimming	Tennis
	Tennis	Volleyball

WESTERN KENTUCKY UNIVERSITY

1 Big Red Way	**Men**	**Women**
Bowling Green, KY 42101-5730	Baseball	Basketball
Affiliation—NCAA I	Basketball	Cross Country
(I-AA Football)	Cross Country	Golf
Nickname—Hilltoppers	Football	Swimming
Athletic Director—	Golf	Tennis
(502) 745-3542	Soccer	Track
	Swimming	Volleyball
	Tennis	
	Track	

LOUISIANA

BAPTIST CHRISTIAN COLLEGE

PO Box 80224
Shreveport, LA 71148
Affiliation—NCCAA
Nickname—Warriors
Athletic Director—
   (318) 631-3512

Men
Basketball
Football

Track

CENTENARY COLLEGE

PO Box 41188
Shreveport, LA 71134-1188
Affiliation—NCAA I
Nickname—Gentlemen/Ladies
Athletic Director—
   (318) 869-5087

Men
Baseball
Basketball
Cross Country
Golf
Rifle
Soccer
Tennis

Women
Basketball
Cross Country
Golf
Gymnastics
Rifle
Soccer
Softball
Tennis
Volleyball

DILLARD UNIVERSITY

2601 Gentilly Boulevard
New Orleans, LA 70122-3043
Affiliation—NAIA I
Nickname—Blue Devils
Athletic Director—Men
   (504) 286-4753
Athletic Director—Women
   (504) 286-4752

Men
Basketball
Cross Country

Women
Basketball
Cross Country

FAITH BAPTIST COLLEGE

PO Box A, 300 S. Broadway
Church Point, LA 70525
Affiliation—NBCAA, NCCAA
Nickname—The "Force"
Athletic Director—
   (318) 684-6383

Men
Baseball
Basketball
Track

Women
Basketball
Volleyball

GRAMBLING STATE UNIVERSITY

PO Box 868	Men	Women
Grambling, LA 71245-0868	Baseball	Basketball
Affiliation—NCAA I	Basketball	Bowling
(I-AA Football)	Bowling	Cross Country
Nickname—Tigers	Cross Country	Golf
Athletic Director—	Football	Softball
(318) 274-2374	Golf	Tennis
	Swimming	Track
	Tennis	Volleyball
	Track	
	Volleyball	

LOUISIANA CHRISTIAN UNIVERSITY

PO Box 150	Men
Sunset, LA 70584-0150	Basketball
Nickname—Runnin' Royals	Soccer
Athletic Director—	
(318) 662-3818	

LOUISIANA COLLEGE

1140 College Drive	Men	Women
Pineville, LA 71360-5122	Baseball	Basketball
Affiliation—NAIA I	Basketball	Cross Country
Nickname—Wildcats	Cross Country	Tennis
Athletic Director—		
(318) 487-7131		

LOUISIANA STATE UNIVERSITY

PO Box 25095	Men	Women
Baton Rouge, LA 70894-5095	Baseball	Basketball
Affiliation—NCAA I	Basketball	Cross Country
(I-A Football)	Cross Country	Golf
Nickname—Fighting Tigers	Diving	Gymnastics
Athletic Director—	Football	Soccer
(225) 388-3600	Golf	Softball
	Swimming	Swimming
	Tennis	Tennis
	Track	Track
		Volleyball

LOUISIANA STATE UNIVERSITY, SHREVEPORT

1 University Place
Shreveport, LA 71115-2301
*Affiliation—*NAIA *I*
Nickname—Pilots
Athletic Director—
  (318) 798-4106

Men
Baseball

LOUISIANA TECH UNIVERSITY

PO Box 3046
Ruston, LA 71272-0001
*Affiliation—*NCAA *I*
  (I-A Football)
Nickname—Bulldogs
Athletic Director—
  (318) 257-3247

Men	**Women**
Baseball	Basketball
Basketball	Cross Country
Cross Country	Softball
Football	Tennis
Golf	Track
Track	Volleyball

LOYOLA UNIVERSITY

6363 Saint Charles Avenue
New Orleans, LA 70118-6143
*Affiliation—*NAIA *I*
Nickname—Wolfpack
Athletic Director—
  (504) 865-3137

Men	**Women**
Baseball	Basketball
Basketball	Cross Country
Cross Country	Soccer
Tennis	Tennis
Track	Track
	Volleyball

LYCOMING COLLEGE

Academy Street
Williamsport, LA 17701
*Affiliation—*NCAA *III*
Nickname—Warriors
Athletic Director—
  (717) 321-4260

Men	**Women**
Basketball	Basketball
Cross Country	Cheerleading
Football	Cross Country
Golf	Lacrosse
Lacrosse	Soccer
Soccer	Softball
Tennis	Swimming
Track	Tennis
Wrestling	Track
	Volleyball

MCNEESE STATE UNIVERSITY

Ryan Street	**Men**	**Women**
Lake Charles, LA 70609	Baseball	Basketball
Affiliation—NCAA I	Basketball	Cross Country
(I-AA Football)	Cross Country	Soccer
Nickname—*Cowboys*	Football	Softball
Athletic Director—	Golf	Tennis
(318) 475-5908	Track	Track
		Volleyball

NEW ORLEANS, UNIVERSITY OF

Lakefront Arena	**Men**	**Women**
New Orleans, LA 70148	Baseball	Basketball
Affiliation—NCAA I	Basketball	Cross Country
Nickname—*Privateers*	Cross Country	Golf
Athletic Director—	Golf	Tennis
(504) 280-7020	Tennis	Track
	Track	Volleyball

NICHOLLS STATE UNIVERSITY

PO Box 2032	**Men**	**Women**
Thibodaux, LA 70310	Baseball	Basketball
Affiliation—NCAA I	Basketball	Cross Country
(I-AA Football)	Cross Country	Soccer
Nickname—*Colonels*	Football	Softball
Athletic Director—	Golf	Tennis
(504) 448-4795	Track	Track
		Volleyball

NORTHEAST LOUISIANA UNIVERSITY

308 Stadium Drive	**Men**	**Women**
Monroe, LA 71209-9000	Baseball	Basketball
Affiliation—NCAA I	Basketball	Cross Country
(I-A Football)	Cross Country	Softball
Nickname—*Indians*	Football	Swimming
Athletic Director—	Golf	Tennis
(318) 342-5360	Skiing	Track
	Swimming	Volleyball
	Tennis	
	Track	

NORTHWESTERN STATE UNIVERSITY

Athletic Fieldhouse	**Men**	**Women**
Natchitoches, LA 71497	Baseball	Basketball
*Affiliation—*NCAA *I*	Basketball	Cross Country
(I-AA Football)	Cross Country	Soccer
Nickname—Demons	Football	Softball
Athletic Director—	Track	Tennis
(318) 357-5251		Track
		Volleyball

SOUTHEASTERN LOUISIANA UNIVERSITY

PO Box 309, Center of Hazel	**Men**	**Women**
and W. Dakota	Baseball	Basketball
Hammond, LA 70402	Basketball	Cross Country
*Affiliation—*NCAA *I*	Cross Country	Soccer
Nickname—Lions	Golf	Softball
Athletic Director—	Tennis	Tennis
(504) 549-3818	Track	Track

SOUTHERN UNIVERSITY

6400 Pree Drive	**Men**	**Women**
New Orleans, LA 70126-1009	Basketball	Basketball
*Affiliation—*NAIA *I*	Track	
Nickname—Knights		
Athletic Director—		
(504) 286-5195		

SOUTHERN UNIVERSITY AND A&M COLLEGE

PO Box 9942	**Men**	**Women**
Baton Rouge, LA 70813	Baseball	Basketball
*Affiliation—*NCAA *I*	Basketball	Cross Country
(I-AA Football)	Cross Country	Golf
Nickname—Jaguars	Football	Softball
Athletic Director—	Golf	Tennis
(504) 771-2722	Tennis	Track
	Track	Volleyball

SOUTHWESTERN LOUISIANA, UNIVERSITY OF

201 Reinhardt Drive	**Men**	**Women**
Lafayette, LA 70506-4252	Baseball	Basketball
*Affiliation—*NCAA *I*	Basketball	Cross Country
(I-A Football)	Cross Country	Softball
Nickname—Ragin' Cajuns	Football	Tennis
Athletic Director—	Golf	Track
(318) 482-5393	Tennis	Volleyball
	Track	

TULANE UNIVERSITY

James Wilson Jr. Center	**Men**	**Women**
New Orleans, LA 70118	Baseball	Basketball
*Affiliation—*NCAA *I*	Basketball	Cross Country
(I-A Football)	Cross Country	Golf
Nickname—Green Wave	Football	Soccer
Athletic Director—	Golf	Tennis
(504) 865-5501	Tennis	Track
	Track	Volleyball

XAVIER UNIVERSITY

7325 Palmetto Street	**Men**	**Women**
New Orleans, LA 70125-1056	Basketball	Basketball
*Affiliation—*NAIA *I*	Cross Country	Cross Country
Nickname—Gold Rush	Tennis	Tennis
Athletic Director—		
(504) 483-7300 ext. 7329		

MAINE

BATES COLLEGE

130 Central Avenue
Lewiston, ME 04240-6042
Affiliation—NCAA *III*
Nickname—Bobcats
Athletic Director—
    (207) 786-6341

Men	Women
Baseball	Basketball
Basketball	Crew
Cross Country	Cross Country
Crew	Diving
Diving	Field Hockey
Football	Golf
Golf	Lacrosse
Lacrosse	Skiing—Alpine/
Skiing—Alpine/	Nordic
Nordic	Soccer
Soccer	Softball
Squash	Squash
Swimming	Swimming
Tennis	Tennis
Track	Track
	Volleyball

BOWDOIN COLLEGE

9000 College Station
Brunswick, ME 04011
Affiliation—NCAA *III*
Nickname—Polar Bears
Athletic Director—
    (207) 725-3666

Men	Women
Baseball	Basketball
Basketball	Cross Country
Cross Country	Diving
Diving	Field Hockey
Football	Golf
Golf	Ice Hockey
Ice Hockey	Lacrosse
Lacrosse	Skiing—Nordic/
Sailing	Alpine
Skiing—Nordic/	Soccer
Alpine	Softball
Soccer	Swimming
Swimming	Tennis
Tennis	Track
Track	Volleyball
Volleyball	

COLBY COLLEGE

4900 Mayflower Hill	**Men**	**Women**
Waterville, ME 04901-8849	Baseball	Basketball
Affiliation—NCAA *III*	Basketball	Crew
Nickname—White Mules	Crew	Cross Country
Athletic Director—	Cross Country	Field Hockey
(207) 872-3364	Football	Golf
	Golf	Ice Hockey
	Ice Hockey	Lacrosse
	Lacrosse	Skiing—Nordic/
	Skiing—Nordic/	Alpine
	Alpine	Soccer
	Soccer	Softball
	Squash	Squash
	Swimming	Swimming
	Tennis	Tennis
	Track	Track
		Volleyball

HUSSON COLLEGE

1 College Circle	**Men**	**Women**
Bangor, ME 04401-2929	Baseball	Basketball
Affiliation—NAIA	Basketball	Cross Country
(Div. II Basketball)	Cross Country	Field Hockey
Nickname—Braves	Golf	Soccer
Athletic Director—	Lacrosse	Softball
(207) 941-7029	Soccer	Volleyball
	Tennis	

MAINE, UNIVERSITY OF, AUGUSTA

46 University Drive	**Men**	**Women**
Augusta, ME 04330-9488	Basketball	Basketball
Affiliation—NSCAA		
Nickname—Moose		
Athletic Director—		
(207) 621-3442		

MAINE, UNIVERSITY OF, FARMINGTON

35 High Street	Men	Women
Farmington, ME 04938-1911	Baseball	Basketball
Affiliation—NAIA II, NCAA II	Basketball	Cross Country
Nickname—Beavers	Cross Country	Field Hockey
Athletic Director—	Golf	Golf
(207) 778-7142	Soccer	Soccer
		Softball
		Volleyball

MAINE, UNIVERSITY OF, FORT KENT

25 Pleasant Street	Men	Women
Fort Kent, ME 04743-1222	Basketball	Basketball
Affiliation—NAIA	Cross Country	Field Hockey
Nickname—Bengals	Golf	Golf
Athletic Director—	Skiing	Skiing
(207) 834-7571	Soccer	Soccer
	Volleyball	
	Wrestling	

MAINE, UNIVERSITY OF, MACHIAS

9 O'Brien Avenue	Men	Women
Machias, ME 04654-1321	Basketball	Basketball
Affiliation—NAIA II	Soccer	Soccer
Nickname—Clippers		Volleyball
Athletic Director—		
(207) 255-1290		

MAINE, UNIVERSITY OF, ORONO

5747 Memorial Gym	Men	Women
Orono, ME 04469-5747	Baseball	Basketball
Affiliation—NCAA I	Basketball	Cheerleading
(I-AA Football)	Cross Country	Cross Country
Nickname—Black Bears	Diving	Diving
Athletic Director—	Football	Field Hockey
(207) 581-1057	Golf	Golf
	Ice Hockey	Ice Hockey
	Soccer	Soccer
	Swimming	Softball
	Track	Swimming
		Tennis
		Track

MAINE, UNIVERSITY OF, PRESQUE ISLE

181 Main Street	**Men**	**Women**
Presque Isle, ME 04769-2844	Baseball	Basketball
*Affiliation—*NAIA *I*	Basketball	Cross Country
Nickname—Owls	Cross Country	Soccer
Athletic Director—	Golf	Softball
(207) 768-9477	Soccer	Volleyball

MAINE MARITIME ACADEMY

Pleasant Street	**Men**	**Women**
Castine, ME 04420	Basketball	Basketball
*Affiliation—*NCAA *III*	Cross Country	Cross Country
Nickname—Mariners	Football	Sailing
Athletic Director—	Lacrosse	
(207) 326-2451	Soccer	
	Sailing	

NEW ENGLAND, UNIVERSITY OF

11 Hills Beach Road	**Men**	**Women**
Biddeford, ME 04005-9526	Basketball	Basketball
*Affiliation—*NAIA *II,* NCAA *III*	Cross Country	Cross Country
Nickname—Nor'Easters	Golf	Lacrosse
Athletic Director—	Lacrosse	Soccer
(207) 283-0171 ext. 2376	Soccer	Softball
		Volleyball

SAINT JOSEPH'S COLLEGE

278 Whites Bridge Road	**Men**	**Women**
Standish, ME 04084-5270	Baseball	Basketball
*Affiliation—*NCAA *III,* NAIA *II*	Basketball	Cross Country
Nickname—Monks	Cross Country	Field Hockey
Athletic Director—	Golf	Soccer
(207) 893-6670	Soccer	Softball
		Volleyball

SOUTHERN MAINE, UNIVERSITY OF

37 College Avenue	**Men**	**Women**
Gorham, ME 04038-1091	Baseball	Basketball
Affiliation—NCAA *III*	Basketball	Cheerleading
Nickname—*Huskies*	Cross Country	Cross Country
Athletic Director—	Golf	Field Hockey
(207) 780-5588	Ice Hockey	Golf
	Sailing	Ice Hockey
	Soccer	Soccer
	Tennis	Softball
	Track	Tennis
	Wrestling	Track
		Volleyball

THOMAS COLLEGE

W. River Road	**Men**	**Women**
Waterville, ME 04901	Baseball	Basketball
Affiliation—NAIA	Basketball	Field Hockey
Nickname—*Terriers*	Golf	Soccer
Athletic Director—	Soccer	Softball
(207) 873-0771	Tennis	Volleyball

UNITY COLLEGE

H C Box 1, Quaker Hill Road	**Men**	**Women**
Unity, ME 04988	Basketball	Cross Country
Affiliation—NSCAA	Cross Country	Volleyball
Nickname—*Rams*	Soccer	
Athletic Director—		
(207) 948-3131 ext. 237		

WESTBROOK COLLEGE

716 Stevens Avenue	**Men**	**Women**
Portland, ME 04103-2670	Basketball	Basketball
Affiliation—NAIA *II*	Cross Country	Softball
Nickname—*Wildcats*	Golf	
Athletic Director—		
(207) 797-7261		

MARYLAND

BOWIE STATE UNIVERSITY

	Men	Women
14000 Jericho Park Road	Baseball	Basketball
Bowie, MD 20715-3319	Basketball	Cross Country
Affiliation—NCAA II	Cross Country	Soccer
Nickname—Bulldogs	Football	Softball
Athletic Director—	Soccer	Track
(301) 464-6068	Track	Volleyball

CAPITOL COLLEGE

	Men
11301 Springfield Road	Basketball
Laurel, MD 20708-9758	Soccer
Nickname—Chargers	
Athletic Director—	
(301) 369-2800	

COLUMBIA UNION COLLEGE

	Men	Women
7600 Flower Avenue	Baseball	Basketball
Takoma Park, MD 20912-7796	Basketball	Cross Country
Nickname—Pioneers	Cross Country	Track
Athletic Director—	Soccer	Volleyball
(301) 891-4128	Track	
	Volleyball	

COPPIN STATE COLLEGE

	Men	Women
2500 W. North Avenue	Baseball	Basketball
Baltimore, MD 21216-3698	Basketball	Cheerleading
Affiliation—NCAA I	Cross Country	Cross Country
Nickname—Eagles	Tennis	Softball
Athletic Director—	Track	Tennis
(410) 383-5607	Wrestling	Track
		Volleyball

FROSTBURG STATE UNIVERSITY

Physical Education Center	**Men**	**Women**
Frostburg, MD 21532	Baseball	Basketball
Affiliation—NCAA III	Basketball	Cross Country
Nickname—Bobcats	Cross Country	Field Hockey
Athletic Director—	Football	Lacrosse
(301) 687-4462	Soccer	Soccer
	Swimming	Softball
	Tennis	Swimming
		Tennis
		Track
		Volleyball

GOUCHER COLLEGE

1021 Dulany Valley Road	**Men**	**Women**
Towson, MD 21204	Basketball	Basketball
Affiliation—NCAA III	Cross Country	Cross Country
Nickname—Gophers	Lacrosse	Field Hockey
Athletic Director—	Soccer	Lacrosse
(410) 337-6383	Swimming	Riding
	Tennis	Soccer
		Swimming
		Tennis
		Track
		Volleyball

HOOD COLLEGE

401 Rosemont Avenue	**Women**	
Frederick, MD 21701	Basketball	Swimming
Affiliation—NCAA III	Field Hockey	Tennis
Nickname—Blazers	Lacrosse	Volleyball
Athletic Director—	Soccer	
(301) 696-3499		

JOHNS HOPKINS UNIVERSITY

	Men	Women
3400 N. Charles Street	Baseball	Basketball
Baltimore, MD 21218-2608	Basketball	Crew
Affiliation—NCAA III	Crew	Cross Country
(Div. I Lacrosse)	Cross Country	Fencing
Nickname—Blue Jays	Fencing	Field Hockey
Athletic Director—	Football	Lacrosse
(410) 516-7490	Lacrosse	Soccer
	Soccer	Squash
	Swimming	Swimming
	Tennis	Tennis
	Track	Track
	Water Polo	Volleyball
	Wrestling	

LOYOLA COLLEGE

	Men	Women
4501 N. Charles Street	Basketball	Basketball
Baltimore, MD 21210-2601	Cross Country	Cross Country
Affiliation—NCAA I	Golf	Lacrosse
Nickname—Greyhounds	Lacrosse	Soccer
Athletic Director—	Soccer	Swimming
(410) 617-2553	Swimming	Tennis
	Tennis	Volleyball

MARYLAND, UNIVERSITY OF, BALTIMORE COUNTY

	Men	Women
100 Hilltop Circle	Baseball	Basketball
Baltimore, MD 21250	Basketball	Cross Country
Affiliation—NCAA I	Cross Country	Golf
Nickname—Retrievers	Golf	Lacrosse
Athletic Director—	Lacrosse	Soccer
(410) 455-2207	Soccer	Softball
	Swimming	Swimming
	Tennis	Tennis
	Track	Volleyball

MARYLAND, UNIVERSITY OF, COLLEGE PARK

	Men	Women
PO Box 295	Baseball	Basketball
College Park, MD 20741-0295	Basketball	Cheerleading
Affiliation—NCAA I	Cross Country	Cross Country
(I-A Football)	Diving	Diving
Nickname—Terrapins	Football	Field Hockey
Athletic Director—	Golf	Gymnastics
(301) 314-7075	Lacrosse	Lacrosse
	Soccer	Soccer
	Swimming	Softball
	Tennis	Swimming
	Track	Tennis
	Wrestling	Track
		Volleyball

MARYLAND, UNIVERSITY OF, EASTERN SHORE

	Men	Women
Tawes Gymnastics, Room 1109	Baseball	Basketball
Princess Anne, MD 21853	Basketball	Bowling
Affiliation—NCAA I	Cross Country	Cheerleading
Nickname—Hawks	Tennis	Cross Country
Athletic Director—	Track	Softball
(410) 651-6496		Tennis
		Track
		Volleyball

MORGAN STATE UNIVERSITY

	Men	Women
1700 E. Cold Spring Lane	Basketball	Basketball
Baltimore, MD 21251	Cross Country	Bowling
Affiliation—NCAA I	Football	Cheerleading
(I-AA Football)	Tennis	Cross Country
Nickname—Bears	Track	Softball
Athletic Director—		Tennis
(410) 319-3575		Track
		Volleyball

MOUNT SAINT MARY'S COLLEGE

16300 Old Emmitsburg Road	Men	Women
Emmitsburg, MD 21727-7700	Baseball	Basketball
Affiliation—NCAA I	Basketball	Cross Country
Nickname—Mountaineers	Cross Country	Golf
Athletic Director—	Golf	Lacrosse
(301) 447-5000	Lacrosse	Soccer
	Soccer	Softball
	Tennis	Tennis
	Track	Track

NOTRE DAME OF MARYLAND, COLLEGE OF

4701 N. Charles Street	Women	
Baltimore, MD 21210	Basketball	Swimming
Affiliation—NCAA III	Field Hockey	Tennis
Nickname—Gators	Lacrosse	Volleyball
Athletic Director—	Soccer	
(410) 532-3588		

SAINT MARY'S COLLEGE OF MARYLAND

Somerset Hall	Men	Women
Saint Mary's City, MD 20686	Baseball	Basketball
Affiliation—NCAA III	Basketball	Cheerleading
Nickname—Seahawks	Lacrosse	Field Hockey
Athletic Director—	Sailing	Lacrosse
(301) 862-0319	Soccer	Sailing
	Swimming	Soccer
	Tennis	Swimming
		Tennis
		Volleyball

SALISBURY STATE UNIVERSITY

1101 Camden Avenue	Men	Women
Salisbury, MD 21801-6800	Baseball	Basketball
Affiliation—NCAA III	Basketball	Cross Country
Nickname—Sea Gulls	Cross Country	Field Hockey
Athletic Director—	Football	Lacrosse
(410) 548-3503	Lacrosse	Soccer
	Soccer	Softball
	Swimming	Swimming
	Tennis	Tennis
	Track	Track
		Volleyball

TOWSON UNIVERSITY

8000 York Road	**Men**	**Women**
Baltimore, MD 21251	Baseball	Basketball
*Affiliation—*NCAA *I*	Basketball	Cross Country
(I-AA Football)	Cross Country	Field Hockey
Nickname—Tigers	Football	Gymnastics
Athletic Director—	Golf	Lacrosse
(410) 830-2758	Lacrosse	Soccer
	Soccer	Softball
	Swimming	Swimming
	Tennis	Tennis
	Track	Track
		Volleyball

UNITED STATES NAVAL ACADEMY

566 Brownson Road	**Men**	**Women**
Annapolis, MD 21402-5039	Baseball	Basketball
*Affiliation—*NCAA *I*	Basketball	Crew
(I-A Football)	Crew	Cross Country
Nickname—Mids, Midshipmen	Cross Country	Diving
Athletic Director—	Diving	Rifle
(410) 268-6220	Football	Sailing
	Golf	Soccer
	Gymnastics	Squash
	Lacrosse	Swimming
	Rifle	Track
	Sailing	Volleyball
	Soccer	
	Swimming	
	Tennis	
	Track	
	Water Polo	
	Wrestling	

VILLA JULIE COLLEGE

1525 Greenspring Valley Road	**Men**	**Women**
Stevenson, MD 21153-0641	Basketball	Basketball
Affiliation—NCAA III	Cross Country	Cheerleading
Nickname—Mustangs	Golf	Cross Country
Athletic Director—	Lacrosse	Field Hockey
(410) 602-7250	Soccer	Golf
	Tennis	Lacrosse
	Track	Soccer
	Volleyball	Tennis
		Track
		Volleyball

WASHINGTON BIBLE COLLEGE

6511 Princess Garden Parkway	**Men**	**Women**
Lanham, MD 20706-3538	Baseball	Basketball
Affiliation—NCCAA II	Basketball	Softball
Nickname—Cougars	Soccer	Volleyball
Athletic Director—	Volleyball	
(301) 552-1400 ext. 283		

WASHINGTON COLLEGE

300 Washington Avenue	**Men**	**Women**
Chestertown, MD 21620-1438	Baseball	Basketball
Affiliation—NCAA III	Basketball	Crew
Nickname—Sho'men	Crew	Field Hockey
Athletic Director—	Lacrosse	Lacrosse
(410) 778-7232	Rowing	Soccer
	Soccer	Softball
	Swimming	Swimming
	Tennis	Tennis
		Volleyball

WESTERN MARYLAND COLLEGE

	Men	Women
2 College Hill	Baseball	Basketball
Westminster, MD 21157-4303	Basketball	Cross Country
Affiliation—NCAA III	Cross Country	Field Hockey
Nickname—Terror	Football	Lacrosse
Athletic Director—	Golf	Soccer
(410) 857-2571	Lacrosse	Softball
	Soccer	Swimming
	Swimming	Tennis
	Tennis	Track
	Track	Volleyball
	Wrestling	

MASSACHUSETTS

AMERICAN INTERNATIONAL COLLEGE

	Men	Women
1000 State Street	Baseball	Basketball
Springfield, MA 01109-3189	Basketball	Cheerleading
Affiliation—NCAA II	Football	Field Hockey
Nickname—Yellow Jackets	Golf	Lacrosse
Athletic Director—	Ice Hockey	Soccer
(413) 747-6534	Lacrosse	Softball
	Soccer	Tennis
	Tennis	Volleyball
	Wrestling	

AMHERST COLLEGE

	Men	Women
PO Box 5000, Box 2230	Baseball	Basketball
Amherst, MA 01002-5000	Basketball	Cross Country
Affiliation—NCAA III	Crew	Field Hockey
Nickname—Lord Jeffs	Golf	Golf
Athletic Director—	Ice Hockey	Ice Hockey
(413) 542-2274	Lacrosse	Lacrosse
	Soccer	Soccer
	Swimming	Softball
	Tennis	Squash
	Squash	Swimming
		Tennis
		Track
		Volleyball

ANNA MARIA COLLEGE

Sunset Lane	Men	Women
Paxton, MA 01612	Baseball	Basketball
Affiliation—NCAA III	Basketball	Cheerleading
Nickname—Amcats	Cross Country	Cross Country
Athletic Director—	Golf	Golf
(508) 849-3447	Soccer	Soccer
		Softball
		Volleyball

ASSUMPTION COLLEGE

500 Salisbury Street	Men	Women
Worcester, MA 01609-1265	Baseball	Basketball
Affiliation—NCAA II	Basketball	Crew
Nickname—Greyhounds	Cross Country	Cross Country
Athletic Director—	Crew	Field Hockey
(508) 767-7416	Football	Lacrosse
	Golf	Soccer
	Ice Hockey	Softball
	Lacrosse	Tennis
	Soccer	Volleyball
	Tennis	

ATLANTIC UNION COLLEGE

Main Street	Men	Women
South Lancaster, MA 01561	Basketball	Basketball
Affiliation—NAIA II	Soccer	Volleyball
Nickname—Flames	Tennis	
Athletic Director—	Volleyball	
(508) 268-2142		

BABSON COLLEGE

Webster Center	Men	Women
Babson Park, MA 02157	Baseball	Basketball
Affiliation—NCAA III	Basketball	Cross Country
Nickname—Beavers	Cross Country	Field Hockey
Athletic Director—	Golf	Lacrosse
(781) 239-4528	Ice Hockey	Skiing
	Lacrosse	Soccer
	Skiing	Softball
	Soccer	Tennis
	Swimming	Track
	Tennis	

BECKER COLLEGE

3 Paxton Street Leicester, MA 01524-1105 Affiliation—Independent Nickname—Hawks Athletic Director— (508) 791-9241 ext. 464	**Men** Baseball Basketball Cross Country Soccer Tennis	**Women** Basketball Cross Country Equestrian Field Hockey Soccer Softball Volleyball

BENTLEY COLLEGE

175 Forest Street Waltham, MA 02452 Affiliation—NCAA II Nickname—Falcons Athletic Director— (781) 891-2332	**Men** Baseball Basketball Cross Country Football Golf Ice Hockey Lacrosse Soccer Swimming Tennis Track	**Women** Aquatics Basketball Cross Country Field Hockey Lacrosse Soccer Softball Swimming Tennis Track Volleyball

BOSTON COLLEGE

140 Commonwealth Avenue Chestnut Hill, MA 02167-3800 Affiliation—NCAA I (I-A Football) Nickname—Eagles Athletic Director— (617) 552-4680	**Men** Baseball Basketball Cross Country Fencing Football Golf Ice Hockey Lacrosse Skiing Soccer Swimming Tennis Track Volleyball Water Polo Wrestling	**Women** Basketball Cross Country Diving Fencing Field Hockey Golf Lacrosse Skiing Soccer Softball Tennis Track Volleyball

BOSTON UNIVERSITY

285 Babcock Street	Men	Women
Boston, MA 02215-1003	Basketball	Basketball
Affiliation—NCAA I	Crew	Crew, Novice
Nickname—Terriers	Cross Country	Crew
Athletic Director—	Golf	Cross Country
(617) 353-4630	Ice Hockey	Field Hockey
	Soccer	Golf
	Swimming	Lacrosse
	Tennis	Soccer
	Track	Softball
	Wrestling	Swimming
		Tennis
		Track

BRANDEIS UNIVERSITY

415 South Street, MS 007	Men	Women
Waltham, MA 02254-9110	Baseball	Basketball
Affiliation—NCAA III	Basketball	Cross Country
Nickname—Judges	Cross Country	Fencing
Athletic Director—	Fencing	Soccer
(781) 736-3632	Golf	Softball
	Sailing	Swimming
	Soccer	Tennis
	Swimming	Track
	Tennis	Volleyball
	Track	

BRIDGEWATER STATE COLLEGE

10 Summer Street	Men	Women
Bridgewater, MA 02325	Baseball	Basketball
Affiliation—NCAA III	Basketball	Cross Country
Nickname—Bears	Cross Country	Field Hockey
Athletic Director—	Football	Lacrosse
(508) 697-1352	Soccer	Soccer
	Swimming	Softball
	Tennis	Tennis
	Track	Track
	Wrestling	Volleyball

CLARK UNIVERSITY

950 Main Street	**Men**	**Women**
Worcester, MA 01610-1400	Baseball	Basketball
Affiliation—NCAA III	Basketball	Crew
Nickname—Cougars	Crew	Cross Country
Athletic Director—	Cross Country	Diving
(508) 793-7160	Diving	Field Hockey
	Lacrosse	Soccer
	Soccer	Softball
	Swimming	Swimming
	Tennis	Tennis
		Volleyball

CURRY COLLEGE

Blue Hill Avenue	**Men**	**Women**
Milton, MA 02186	Baseball	Basketball
Affiliation—NCAA III	Basketball	Cross Country
Nickname—Colonels	Cross Country	Soccer
Athletic Director—	Football	Softball
(617) 333-2109	Ice Hockey	Tennis
	Lacrosse	
	Soccer	
	Tennis	

EASTERN NAZARENE COLLEGE

23 E. Elm Avenue	**Men**	**Women**
Quincy, MA 02170-2905	Baseball	Basketball
Affiliation—NCAA III	Basketball	Cross Country
Nickname—Crusaders	Cross Country	Softball
Athletic Director—	Soccer	Tennis
(617) 745-3638	Tennis	Volleyball

ELMS COLLEGE

291 Springfield Street	**Men**	
Chicopee, MA 01013	Basketball	Soccer
Affiliation—NCAA III	Golf	Swimming
Athletic Director—		
(413) 594-9474		

EMERSON COLLEGE

100 Beacon Street	Men	Women
Boston, MA 02116-1501	Baseball	Basketball
Affiliation—NCAA III	Basketball	Golf
Nickname—Lions	Golf	Soccer
Athletic Director—	Lacrosse	Softball
(617) 824-8691	Soccer	Tennis
	Tennis	Volleyball

EMMANUEL COLLEGE

400 The Fenway	Women	
Boston, MA 02115	Basketball	Tennis
Affiliation—NCAA III	Soccer	Volleyball
Nickname—Saints	Softball	
Athletic Director—		
(617) 735-9985		

ENDICOTT COLLEGE

376 Hale Street	Men	Women
Beverly, MA 01915-2096	Baseball	Basketball
Affiliation—NCAA III	Basketball	Cross Country
Nickname—Power Gulls	Cross Country	Field Hockey
Athletic Director—	Lacrosse	Lacrosse
(978) 927-0585 ext. 2304	Soccer	Soccer
	Tennis	Softball
		Tennis
		Volleyball

FITCHBURG STATE COLLEGE

160 Pearl Street	Men	Women
Fitchburg, MA 01420	Baseball	Basketball
Affiliation—NCAA III	Basketball	Cross Country
Nickname—Falcons	Cross Country	Field Hockey
Athletic Director—	Football	Soccer
(978) 665-3314	Ice Hockey	Softball
	Soccer	Track
	Track	Volleyball

FRAMINGHAM STATE COLLEGE

100 State Street	**Men**	**Women**
Framingham, MA 01702-2460	Baseball	Basketball
Affiliation—NCAA II	Basketball	Cross Country
Nickname—Rams	Cross Country	Field Hockey
Athletic Director—	Football	Soccer
(508) 626-4614	Ice Hockey	Volleyball
	Soccer	

GORDON COLLEGE

255 Grapevine Road	**Men**	**Women**
Wenham, MA 01984-1813	Baseball	Basketball
Affiliation—NCAA III	Basketball	Field Hockey
Nickname—Fighting Scots	Lacrosse	Lacrosse
Athletic Director—	Soccer	Soccer
(978) 927-2306 ext. 4335	Swimming	Softball
	Tennis	Tennis
		Volleyball

HARVARD UNIVERSITY

65 North Harvard Street/Murr Court	**Men**	**Women**
Boston, MA 02163	Baseball	Basketball
Affiliation—NCAA I	Basketball	Crew
(I-AA Football)	Crew	Cross Country
Nickname—Crimson	Cross Country	Fencing
Athletic Director—	Diving	Field Hockey
(617) 495-4848	Fencing	Golf
	Football	Ice Hockey
	Ice Hockey	Lacrosse
	Lacrosse	Sailing
	Sailing	Soccer
	Skiing	Softball
	Soccer	Squash
	Squash	Swimming
	Swimming	Tennis
	Tennis	Track
	Track	Volleyball
	Volleyball	Water Polo
	Water Polo	
	Wrestling	

HOLY CROSS, COLLEGE OF THE

College Street	**Men**	**Women**
Worcester, MA 01610	Baseball	Basketball
Affiliation—NCAA *I*	Basketball	Cheerleading
(I-AA Football)	Crew	Crew
Nickname—*Crusaders*	Cross Country	Cross Country
Athletic Director—	Diving	Field Hockey
(508) 793-2571	Football	Lacrosse
	Golf	Soccer
	Ice Hockey	Softball
	Lacrosse	Swimming
	Soccer	Tennis
	Swimming	Track
	Tennis	Volleyball
	Track	

LASELL COLLEGE

1844 Commonwealth Avenue	**Men**	**Women**
Newton, MA 02166	Basketball	Basketball
Affiliation—NCAA *III*	Cross Country	Cross Country
Nickname—*Lasers*	Lacrosse	Soccer
Athletic Director—	Soccer	Softball
(617) 243-2147		Volleyball

MASSACHUSETTS, UNIVERSITY OF, AMHERST

Boyden Building	**Men**	**Women**
Amherst, MA 01003	Baseball	Basketball
Affiliation—NCAA *I*	Basketball	Cheerleading
(I-AA Football)	Cheerleading	Crew
Nickname—*Minutemen*	Cross Country	Cross Country
Athletic Director—	Diving	Diving
(413) 545-4086	Football	Field Hockey
	Gymnastics	Gymnastics
	Ice Hockey	Lacrosse
	Lacrosse	Skiing
	Skiing	Soccer
	Soccer	Softball
	Swimming	Swimming
	Tennis	Tennis
	Track	Track
	Water Polo	Volleyball
		Water Polo

MASSACHUSETTS, UNIVERSITY OF, DARTMOUTH

285 Old Westport Road	Men	Women
North Dartmouth, MA 02747	Baseball	Basketball
Affiliation—NCAA III	Basketball	Cross Country
Nickname—Corsairs	Cross Country	Field Hockey
Athletic Director—	Football	Soccer
(508) 999-8720	Golf	Softball
	Ice Hockey	Swimming
	Soccer	Tennis
	Swimming	Track
	Tennis	Volleyball
	Track	

MASSACHUSETTS, UNIVERSITY OF, HARBOR CAMPUS

100 Morrissey Boulevard	Men	Women
Boston, MA 02125-3300	Baseball	Basketball
Affiliation—NCAA III	Basketball	Cheerleading
Nickname—Beacons	Cross Country	Cross Country
Athletic Director—	Football	Soccer
(617) 287-7810	Ice Hockey	Softball
	Lacrosse	Tennis
	Soccer	Track
	Tennis	Volleyball
	Track	

MASSACHUSETTS COLLEGE OF LIBERAL ARTS

Church Street	Men	Women
North Adams, MA 01247	Baseball	Basketball
Affiliation—NCAA III	Basketball	Cross Country
Nickname—Mohawks	Cross Country	Soccer
Athletic Director—	Ice Hockey	Softball
(413) 662-5411	Soccer	Tennis

MASSACHUSETTS INSTITUTE OF TECHNOLOGY

PO Box 397404	Men	Women
Cambridge, MA 02139-7404	Baseball	Basketball
Affiliation—NCAA *III*	Basketball	Crew
Nickname—*Engineers*	Crew	Cross Country
Athletic Director—	Cross Country	Diving
(617) 253-4497	Diving	Fencing
	Fencing	Field Hockey
	Football	Gymnastics
	Golf	Lacrosse
	Gymnastics	Rifle
	Ice Hockey	Sailing
	Lacrosse	Soccer
	Pistol	Softball
	Rifle	Swimming
	Sailing	Tennis
	Skiing	Track
	Squash	Volleyball
	Swimming	
	Tennis	
	Track	
	Volleyball	
	Water Polo	
	Wrestling	

MASSACHUSETTS, UNIVERSITY OF, LOWELL

1 University Avenue	Men	Women
Lowell, MA 01854-2827	Baseball	Basketball
Affiliation—NCAA *II*	Basketball	Crew
(Div. I Ice Hockey)	Crew	Cross Country
Athletic Director—	Cross Country	Field Hockey
(978) 934-2310	Football	Soccer
	Golf	Softball
	Ice Hockey	Tennis
	Soccer	Track
	Tennis	Volleyball
	Track	
	Wrestling	

MASSACHUSETTS MARITIME ACADEMY

101 Academy Drive	**Men**	**Women**
Buzzards Bay, MA 02532-3405	Baseball	Crew
Affiliation—NCAA *III*	Crew	Cross Country
Nickname—Buccaneers	Cross Country	Rifle
Athletic Director—	Football	Sailing
(508) 830-5055	Lacrosse	Softball
	Rifle	Volleyball
	Sailing	
	Soccer	

MERRIMACK COLLEGE

351 Turnpike Street	**Men**	**Women**
North Andover,	Baseball	Basketball
MA 01845-5816	Basketball	Cheerleading
Affiliation—NCAA *II*	Cross Country	Cross Country
Nickname—Warriors	Football	Field Hockey
Athletic Director—	Ice Hockey	Golf
(978) 837-2344	Lacrosse	Lacrosse
	Soccer	Soccer
	Tennis	Softball
		Swimming
		Tennis
		Volleyball

MOUNT HOLYOKE COLLEGE

Kendall Hall	**Women**	
South Hadley, MA 01075	Basketball	Soccer
Affiliation—NCAA *III*	Crew	Softball
Nickname—Lyons	Cross Country	Squash
Athletic Director—	Field Hockey	Swimming
(413) 538-2310	Golf	Tennis
	Lacrosse	Track
	Riding	Volleyball

NICHOLS COLLEGE

Dudley Hill	**Men**	**Women**
Dudley, MA 01571	Baseball	Basketball
Affiliation—NCAA III	Basketball	Field Hockey
Nickname—Bison	Football	Lacrosse
Athletic Director—	Golf	Soccer
(508) 213-2271	Ice Hockey	Softball
	Lacrosse	Tennis
	Soccer	Track
	Tennis	
	Track	

NORTHEASTERN UNIVERSITY

219 Cabot Circle,	**Men**	**Women**
360 Huntington Avenue	Baseball	Basketball
Boston, MA 02115	Basketball	Crew
Affiliation—NCAA I	Crew	Cross Country
(I-AA Football)	Cross Country	Field Hockey
Nickname—Huskies	Football	Ice Hockey
Athletic Director—	Ice Hockey	Soccer
(617) 373-7590	Soccer	Swimming
	Track	Track
		Volleyball

PINE MANOR COLLEGE

400 Heath Street	**Women**	
Chestnut Hill, MA 02467	Basketball	Softball
Affiliation—NCAA III	Cross Country	Tennis
Nickname—Gators	Soccer	Volleyball
Athletic Director—		
(617) 731-7056		

REGIS COLLEGE

235 Wellesley Street	**Women**	
Weston, MA 02193	Basketball	Softball
Affiliation—NCAA III	Crew	Swimming
Nickname—Beacons	Cross Country	Tennis
Athletic Director—	Diving	Track
(781) 768-7147	Field Hockey	Volleyball
	Soccer	

SALEM STATE COLLEGE

352 Lafayette Street	Men	Women
Salem, MA 01970-5348	Baseball	Basketball
Affiliation—NCAA III	Basketball	Cross Country
Nickname—Vikings	Cross Country	Field Hockey
Athletic Director—	Golf	Sailing
(978) 542-6569	Ice Hockey	Soccer
	Lacrosse	Softball
	Sailing	Swimming
	Soccer	Tennis
	Swimming	Track
	Tennis	Volleyball
	Track	

SIMMONS COLLEGE

51 Commonwealth Avenue	Men	Women
Boston, MA 02115	Sailing	Basketball
Affiliation—NCAA III		Crew
Nickname—Sharks		Cross Country
Athletic Director—		Diving
(617) 521-1038		Field Hockey
		Soccer
		Softball
		Swimming
		Tennis
		Track
		Volleyball

SMITH COLLEGE

Ainsworth Gymnasium	Women	
Northampton, MA 01063	Basketball	Soccer
Affiliation—NCAA III	Crew	Softball
Nickname—Pioneers	Cross Country	Squash
Athletic Director—	Diving	Swimming
(413) 585-2701	Field Hockey	Tennis
	Lacrosse	Track
	Riding	Volleyball
	Skiing	

SPRINGFIELD COLLEGE

263 *Alden Street*	**Men**	**Women**
Springfield, MA 01109-3707	Baseball	Basketball
Affiliation—NCAA *III*	Basketball	Cross Country
Nickname—Pride	Cross Country	Diving
Athletic Director—	Diving	Field Hockey
(413) 748-3333	Football	Gymnastics
	Golf	Lacrosse
	Gymnastics	Soccer
	Lacrosse	Softball
	Soccer	Swimming
	Swimming	Tennis
	Tennis	Track
	Track	Volleyball
	Volleyball	
	Wrestling	

STONEHILL COLLEGE

320 *Washington Street*	**Men**	**Women**
North Easton, MA 02357-7800	Baseball	Basketball
Affiliation—NCAA *II*	Basketball	Cross Country
Nickname—Chieftains	Cross Country	Field Hockey
Athletic Director—	Football	Soccer
(508) 565-1391	Ice Hockey	Softball
	Soccer	Tennis
	Tennis	Track
	Track	Volleyball

SUFFOLK UNIVERSITY

41 *Temple Street*	**Men**	**Women**
Boston, MA 02114-4241	Baseball	Basketball
Affiliation—NCAA *III*	Basketball	Cheerleading
Nickname—Rams	Cross Country	Cross Country
Athletic Director—	Golf	Softball
(617) 573-8379	Ice Hockey	Tennis
	Soccer	Volleyball
	Tennis	

TUFTS UNIVERSITY

College Avenue	Men	Women
Medford, MA 02155	Baseball	Basketball
Affiliation—NCAA III	Basketball	Crew
Nickname—Jumbos	Crew	Cross Country
Athletic Director—	Cross Country	Fencing
(617) 627-3232	Football	Field Hockey
	Golf	Lacrosse
	Ice Hockey	Sailing
	Lacrosse	Soccer
	Sailing	Softball
	Soccer	Squash
	Squash	Swimming
	Swimming	Tennis
	Tennis	Track
	Track	Volleyball

WELLESLEY COLLEGE

Keohane Sports Center	Women	
Wellesley, MA 02181	Basketball	Soccer
Affiliation—NCAA III	Crew	Squash
Athletic Director—	Cross Country	Swimming
(781) 283-2001	Diving	Tennis
	Fencing	Volleyball
	Field Hockey	
	Lacrosse	

WENTWORTH INSTITUTE OF TECHNOLOGY

550 Huntington Avenue	Men	Women
Boston, MA 02115-5901	Baseball	Basketball
Affiliation—NCAA III	Basketball	Golf
Nickname—Leopards	Golf	Rifle
Athletic Director—	Ice Hockey	Soccer
(617) 989-4146	Rifle	Softball
	Soccer	Tennis
	Tennis	Volleyball
	Volleyball	

WESTERN NEW ENGLAND COLLEGE

1215 Wilbraham Road	**Men**	**Women**
Springfield, MA 01119-2654	Baseball	Basketball
Affiliation—NCAA *III*	Basketball	Bowling
Nickname—Golden Bears	Bowling	Field Hockey
Athletic Director—	Football	Lacrosse
(413) 782-1377	Golf	Soccer
	Ice Hockey	Softball
	Lacrosse	Swimming
	Soccer	Volleyball
	Swimming	
	Tennis	
	Volleyball	
	Wrestling	

WESTFIELD STATE COLLEGE

577 Western Avenue	**Men**	**Women**
Westfield, MA 01086	Baseball	Basketball
Affiliation—NCAA *III*	Basketball	Cheerleading
Nickname—Owls	Cross Country	Cross Country
Athletic Director—	Football	Diving
(413) 572-5406	Soccer	Soccer
	Track	Softball
		Swimming
		Tennis
		Volleyball

WHEATON COLLEGE

Eveyln D. Haas Athletic Center	**Men**	**Women**
Norton, MA 02766	Baseball	Basketball
Affiliation—NCAA *III*	Basketball	Cross Country
Nickname—Lyons	Cross Country	Field Hockey
Athletic Director—	Lacrosse	Lacrosse
(508) 285-8216	Soccer	Soccer
	Swimming	Softball
	Tennis	Swimming
	Track	Tennis
		Track
		Volleyball

WHEELOCK COLLEGE

200 *The Riverway*
Boston, MA 02215
Affiliation—NCAA III
Nickname—Wildcats
Athletic Director—
   (617) 734-5200

Women
Basketball   Softball
Field Hockey   Swimming

WILLIAMS COLLEGE

Spring Street, Lasell Gymnastics
Williamstown, MA 01267
Affiliation—NCAA III
Nickname—Ephs
Athletic Director—
   (413) 597-2366

Men	**Women**
Baseball	Basketball
Basketball	Crew
Crew	Cross Country
Cross County	Field Hockey
Football	Lacrosse
Golf	Skiing
Ice Hockey	Soccer
Lacrosse	Softball
Skiing	Squash
Soccer	Swimming
Squash	Tennis
Swimming	Track
Tennis	Volleyball
Track	
Wrestling	

WORCESTER POLYTECHNIC INSTITUTE

100 *Institute Road*
Worcester, MA 01609-2247
Affiliation—NCAA III
Nickname—Engineers
Athletic Director—
   (508) 831-5243

Men	**Women**
Baseball	Basketball
Basketball	Cross Country
Cross Country	Field Hockey
Football	Soccer
Golf	Softball
Soccer	Swimming
Swimming	Tennis
Tennis	Track
Track	Volleyball
Wrestling	

WORCESTER STATE COLLEGE

486 Chandler Street	**Men**	**Women**
Worcester, MA 01602-2832	Baseball	Basketball
Affiliation—NCAA III	Basketball	Cross Country
Nickname—Lancers	Cross Country	Field Hockey
Athletic Director—	Football	Soccer
(508) 929-8034	Golf	Softball
	Ice Hockey	Tennis
	Soccer	Track
	Tennis	Volleyball
	Track	

MICHIGAN

ADRIAN COLLEGE

110 S. Madison Street	**Men**	**Women**
Adrian, MI 49221-2518	Baseball	Basketball
Affiliation—NCAA III	Basketball	Cross Country
Nickname—Bulldogs	Cross Country	Golf
Athletic Director—	Football	Soccer
(517) 265-5161 ext. 4245	Golf	Tennis
	Soccer	Track
	Tennis	Volleyball
	Track	

ALBION COLLEGE

4830 Kellogg Court	**Men**	**Women**
Albion, MI 49224-5014	Baseball	Basketball
Affiliation—NCAA III	Basketball	Cross Country
Nickname—Britons	Cross Country	Golf
Athletic Director—Men	Golf	Soccer
(517) 629-0281 ext. 0500	Soccer	Softball
Athletic Director—Women	Swimming	Swimming
(517) 629-0281 ext. 0516	Tennis	Tennis
	Track	Track
		Volleyball

ALMA COLLEGE

614 W. Superior Street Alma, MI 48801-1511 Affiliation—NCAA III Nickname—Scots Athletic Director—Men (517) 463-7988 Athletic Director—Women (517) 463-7017	Men Baseball Basketball Cross Country Diving Football Golf Soccer Swimming Tennis Track	Women Basketball Cross Country Diving Golf Soccer Softball Swimming Tennis Track Volleyball

AQUINAS COLLEGE

1607 Robinson Road SE Grand Rapids, MI 49506-1741 Affiliation—NAIA I Nickname—Saints Athletic Director— (616) 459-8281 ext. 3107	Men Baseball Basketball Cross Country Golf Soccer Tennis Track	Women Basketball Cross Country Golf Soccer Softball Tennis Track Volleyball

CALVIN COLLEGE

3201 Burton Street SE Grand Rapids, MI 49546-4301 Affiliation—NCAA III Nickname—Knights Athletic Director—Men (616) 957-6176 Athletic Director—Women (616) 957-6223	Men Baseball Basketball Cross Country Golf Ice Hockey Soccer Swimming Tennis Track	Women Basketball Cross Country Golf Soccer Softball Swimming Tennis Track Volleyball

CENTRAL BIBLE COLLEGE

3000 N. Grant Avenue Springfield, MI 65803-1033 Affiliation—NCCAA II Nickname—Spartans Athletic Director— (417) 833-2551	Men Basketball Cross Country Soccer	Women Volleyball

CENTRAL MICHIGAN UNIVERSITY

Rose Center	**Men**	**Women**
Mount Pleasant, MI 48859	Baseball	Basketball
Affiliation—NCAA I	Basketball	Cross Country
(I-A Football)	Cross Country	Field Hockey
Nickname—Chippewas	Football	Gymnastics
Athletic Director—	Track	Soccer
(517) 774-3131	Wrestling	Softball
		Track
		Volleyball

CONCORDIA COLLEGE

4090 Geddes Road	**Men**	**Women**
Ann Arbor, MI 48105-2750	Baseball	Basketball
Affiliation—NAIA II, NCCAA I	Basketball	Cross Country
Nickname—Wolverines	Cross Country	Soccer
Athletic Director—	Soccer	Softball
(313) 995-7343		Volleyball

CORNERSTONE COLLEGE

1001 E. Beltline Avenue NE	**Men**	**Women**
Grand Rapids, MI 49525-5803	Baseball	Basketball
Affiliation—NAIA II	Basketball	Cheerleading
Nickname—Golden Eagles	Cross Country	Cross Country
Athletic Director—	Golf	Soccer
(616) 222-1412	Soccer	Softball
	Tennis	Volleyball

DETROIT COLLEGE OF BUSINESS

4801 Oakman Boulevard	**Men**	
Dearborn, MI 48126-3755	Golf	Soccer
Affiliation—NAIA I		
Nickname—Falcons		
Athletic Director—		
(313) 581-4400 ext. 389		

DETROIT MERCY, UNIVERSITY OF

	Men	Women
PO Box 19900	Baseball	Basketball
Detroit, MI 48219-0900	Basketball	Cross Country
*Affiliation—*NCAA *I*	Cross Country	Fencing
Nickname—Titans	Fencing	Soccer
Athletic Director—	Golf	Softball
(313) 993-1720	Soccer	Tennis
	Track	Track

EASTERN MICHIGAN UNIVERSITY

	Men	Women
Convocation Center	Baseball	Basketball
Ypsilanti, MI 48197	Basketball	Cross Country
*Affiliation—*NCAA *I*	Cross Country	Diving
(I-A Football)	Diving	Golf
Nickname—Eagles	Football	Gymnastics
Athletic Director—	Golf	Soccer
(734) 487-1050	Soccer	Softball
	Swimming	Swimming
	Tennis	Tennis
	Track	Track
	Wrestling	Volleyball

FERRIS STATE UNIVERSITY

	Men	Women
210 Sports Drive	Basketball	Basketball
Big Rapids, MI 49307-2741	Football	Cheerleading
*Affiliation—*NCAA *II*	Golf	Cross Country
(Div. I Hockey)	Ice Hockey	Golf
Nickname—Bulldogs	Tennis	Softball
Athletic Director—		Tennis
(616) 592-2970		Track
		Volleyball

GRACE BIBLE COLLEGE

	Men	Women
PO Box 910	Basketball	Basketball
Wyoming, MI 49509-0910	Soccer	Volleyball
*Affiliation—*NCCAA *II*		
Nickname—Tigers		
Athletic Director—		
(616) 538-1770		

GRAND VALLEY STATE UNIVERSITY

192 Fieldhouse	**Men**	**Women**
Allendale, MI 49401-9401	Baseball	Basketball
*Affiliation—*NCAA *II*	Basketball	Cheerleading
Nickname—Lakers	Cross Country	Cross Country
Athletic Director—	Diving	Diving
(616) 895-3259	Football	Golf
	Golf	Soccer
	Swimming	Softball
	Tennis	Swimming
	Track	Tennis
		Track
		Volleyball

GREAT LAKES CHRISTIAN COLLEGE

6211 W. Willow Highway	**Men**	**Women**
Lansing, MI 48917-1231	Baseball	Volleyball
*Affiliation—*NCCAA	Basketball	
Nickname—Crusaders	Soccer	
Athletic Director—		
(517) 321-0242		

HILLSDALE COLLEGE

201 Oak Street	**Men**	**Women**
Hillsdale, MI 49242-1361	Baseball	Basketball
*Affiliation—*NCAA *II*	Basketball	Cross Country
Nickname—Chargers	Cross Country	Soccer
Athletic Director—	Football	Softball
(517) 437-7364	Soccer	Swimming
	Tennis	Tennis
	Track	Track
		Volleyball

HOPE COLLEGE

PO Box 9000	Men	Women
Holland, MI 49422-9000	Baseball	Basketball
Affiliation—NCAA III	Basketball	Cheerleading
Nickname—Flying Dutchmen	Cross Country	Cross Country
Athletic Director—Men	Diving	Diving
(616) 395-7698	Football	Golf
Athletic Director—Women	Soccer	Soccer
(606) 395-7694	Swimming	Softball
	Tennis	Swimming
	Track	Tennis
		Track
		Volleyball

KALAMAZOO COLLEGE

1200 Academy Street	Men	Women
Kalamazoo, MI 49006-3291	Baseball	Basketball
Affiliation—NCAA III	Basketball	Cross Country
Nickname—Hornets	Cross Country	Golf
Athletic Director—Men	Football	Soccer
(616) 337-7091	Golf	Softball
Athletic Director—Women	Soccer	Swimming
(616) 337-7090	Swimming	Tennis
	Tennis	Volleyball

LAKE SUPERIOR STATE UNIVERSITY

650 W. Easterday Avenue	Men	Women
Sault Sainte Marie, MI	Basketball	Basketball
49783-1626	Cross Country	Cross Country
Affiliation—NCAA II	Golf	Softball
(Div. I Ice Hockey)	Ice Hockey	Tennis
Nickname—Lakers	Tennis	Track
Athletic Director—	Track	Volleyball
(906) 635-2627		

LAWRENCE TECH UNIVERSITY

21000 W. 10 Mile Road	Men
Southfield, MI 48075-1051	Golf
Nickname—Blue Devils	Soccer
Athletic Director—	
(248) 204-3850	

MADONNA UNIVERSITY

26600 Schoolcraft Road	**Men**	**Women**
Livonia, MI 48150-1176	Baseball	Basketball
Affiliation—NAIA	Basketball	Cross Country
Nickname—Crusaders	Soccer	Softball
Athletic Director—		Volleyball
(734) 432-5610		

MICHIGAN, UNIVERSITY OF

1000 S. State Street	**Men**	**Women**
Ann Arbor, MI 48109-2202	Baseball	Basketball
Affiliation—NCAA I	Basketball	Cheerleading
(I-A Football)	Cross Country	Crew
Nickname—Wolverines	Diving	Cross Country
Athletic Director—	Football	Diving
(734) 764-6270	Golf	Field Hockey
	Gymnastics	Golf
	Ice Hockey	Gymnastics
	Swimming	Soccer
	Tennis	Softball
	Track	Swimming
	Wrestling	Tennis
		Track
		Volleyball

MICHIGAN, UNIVERSITY OF, DEARBORN

4901 Evergreen Road	**Men**	**Women**
Dearborn, MI 48128-2406	Basketball	Basketball
Affiliation—NAIA II	Soccer	Cross Country
Nickname—Wolves		Volleyball
Athletic Director—		
(313) 593-5070		

MICHIGAN STATE UNIVERSITY

248 Jenison Field House *East Lansing, MI 48824-1025* *Affiliation*—NCAA *I* *(I-A Football)* *Nickname*—*Spartans* *Athletic Director*— *(517) 355-1623*	**Men** Baseball Basketball Cross Country Diving Football Golf Gymnastics Ice Hockey Soccer Swimming Tennis Track Wrestling	**Women** Basketball Cheerleading Crew Cross Country Diving Field Hockey Golf Gymnastics Soccer Swimming Tennis Track Volleyball

MICHIGAN TECH UNIVERSITY

1400 Townsend Drive *Houghton, MI 49931-1200* *Affiliation*—NCAA *II* *(Div. I Hockey)* *Nickname*—*Huskies* *Athletic Director*— *(906) 487-3070*	**Men** Basketball Cross Country Football Ice Hockey Skiing Tennis Track	**Women** Basketball Cross Country Skiing Tennis Track Volleyball

NORTHERN MICHIGAN UNIVERSITY

1401 Presque Isle Avenue *Marquette, MI 49855-5305* *Affiliation*—NCAA *II* *(Div. I Hockey)* *Nickname*—*Wildcats* *Athletic Director*— *(906) 227-1211*	**Men** Basketball Cross Country Football Golf Ice Hockey Skiing	**Women** Basketball Cheerleading Cross Country Skiing Soccer Swimming Tennis Volleyball

NORTHWOOD UNIVERSITY

	Men	Women
3225 Cook Road	Baseball	Basketball
Midland, MI 48640-2311	Basketball	Cross Country
Affiliation—NCAA II	Cross Country	Soccer
Nickname—Timberwolves	Football	Softball
Athletic Director—	Golf	Tennis
(517) 837-4389	Ice Hockey	Track
	Lacrosse	Volleyball
	Soccer	
	Tennis	
	Track	

OAKLAND UNIVERSITY

	Men	Women
Athletic Department	Baseball	Basketball
Rochester, MI 48309-4401	Basketball	Cheerleading
Affiliation—NCAA I	Cross Country	Cross Country
Nickname—Golden Grizzlies	Diving	Diving
Athletic Director—	Golf	Golf
(248) 370-3190	Soccer	Soccer
	Swimming	Softball
		Swimming
		Tennis
		Volleyball

OLIVET COLLEGE

	Men	Women
320 S. Main Street	Baseball	Basketball
Olivet, MI 49076-9721	Basketball	Cheerleading
Affiliation—NCAA III	Cross Country	Cross Country
Nickname—Comets	Football	Diving
Athletic Director—	Golf	Golf
(616) 749-7672	Soccer	Soccer
	Swimming	Softball
	Track	Swimming
	Wrestling	Tennis
		Track
		Volleyball

SAGINAW VALLEY STATE

7400 Bay Road	**Men**	**Women**
University Center, MI 48710	Baseball	Basketball
Affiliation—NCAA II	Basketball	Cross Country
Nickname—Cardinals	Bowling	Golf
Athletic Director—	Cross Country	Softball
(517) 791-7306	Football	Tennis
	Golf	Track
	Soccer	Volleyball
	Tennis	
	Track	
	Volleyball	

SIENA HEIGHTS UNIVERSITY

1247 E. Siena Heights Drive	**Men**	**Women**
Adrian, MI 49221-1755	Baseball	Basketball
Affiliation—NAIA I	Basketball	Cross Country
Nickname—Saints	Cross Country	Soccer
Athletic Director—	Golf	Softball
(517) 264-7876	Soccer	Track
	Track	Volleyball

SPRING ARBOR COLLEGE

Main Street	**Men**	**Women**
Spring Arbor, MI 49283	Baseball	Basketball
Affiliation—NAIA I	Basketball	Cross Country
Nickname—Cougars	Cross Country	Soccer
Athletic Director—Men	Golf	Softball
(517) 750-6503	Soccer	Tennis
Athletic Director—Women	Tennis	Track
(517) 750-6506	Track	Volleyball

WAYNE STATE UNIVERSITY

5101 John C. Lodge,	**Men**	**Women**
101 Matthael Building	Baseball	Basketball
Detroit, MI 48202-3489	Basketball	Cross Country
Affiliation—NCAA II	Cross Country	Diving
Nickname—Tartars	Diving	Fencing
Athletic Director—	Fencing	Softball
(313) 577-4280	Football	Swimming
	Golf	Tennis
	Swimming	Volleyball
	Tennis	

WESTERN MICHIGAN UNIVERSITY

Read Fieldhouse	**Men**	**Women**
Kalamazoo, MI 49008	Baseball	Basketball
*Affiliation—*NCAA *I*	Basketball	Cheerleading
(I-A Football)	Cross Country	Cross Country
Nickname—Broncos	Football	Golf
Athletic Director—	Ice Hockey	Gymnastics
(616) 387-3082	Soccer	Soccer
	Tennis	Softball
	Track	Tennis
		Track
		Volleyball

WILLIAM TYNDALE COLLEGE

35700 W. 12 Mile Road	**Men**	
Farmington Hills, MI	Basketball	Soccer
48331-3149		
Nickname—Lancers		
Athletic Director—		
(248) 553-7200		

MINNESOTA

AUGSBURG COLLEGE

2211 Riverside Avenue	**Men**	**Women**
Minneapolis, MN 55454-1350	Baseball	Basketball
*Affiliation—*NCAA *III*	Basketball	Cheerleading
Nickname—Auggies	Cross Country	Cross Country
Athletic Director—Men	Football	Golf
(612) 330-1243	Golf	Ice Hockey
Athletic Director—Women	Ice Hockey	Soccer
(612) 330-1248	Soccer	Softball
	Track	Track
	Wrestling	Volleyball

BEMIDJI STATE UNIVERSITY

1500 Birchmont Drive NE	**Men**	**Women**
Bemidji, MN 56601-2600	Baseball	Basketball
Affiliation—NCAA *II*	Basketball	Cheerleading
Nickname—Beavers	Football	Cross Country
Athletic Director—	Golf	Golf
(218) 755-3783	Ice Hockey	Ice Hockey
	Track	Soccer
		Softball
		Tennis
		Track
		Volleyball

BETHEL COLLEGE

3900 Bethel Drive	**Men**	**Women**
Saint Paul, MN 55112-6902	Baseball	Basketball
Affiliation—NCAA *III*	Basketball	Cross Country
Nickname—Royals	Cross Country	Soccer
Athletic Director—Men	Football	Softball
(612) 638-6396	Golf	Tennis
Athletic Director—Women	Ice Hockey	Track
(612) 638-6032	Soccer	Volleyball
	Tennis	
	Track	

CARLETON COLLEGE

1 N. College Street	**Men**	
Northfield, MN 55057-4001	Baseball	Soccer
Affiliation—NCAA *III*	Basketball	Swimming
Nickname—Knights	Cross Country	Tennis
Athletic Director—	Football	Track
(507) 646-4056	Golf	Wrestling

CONCORDIA COLLEGE

901 8th Street S	Men	Women
Moorhead, MN 56562	Baseball	Basketball
Affiliation—NCAA III	Basketball	Cheerleading
Nickname—Cobbers	Cross Country	Cross Country
Athletic Director—	Football	Golf
(218) 299-4435	Golf	Soccer
	Ice Hockey	Softball
	Soccer	Swimming
	Tennis	Tennis
	Track	Track
	Wrestling	Volleyball

CONCORDIA UNIVERSITY

275 Syndicate Street N	Men	Women
Saint Paul, MN 55104-5436	Baseball	Basketball
Affiliation—NAIA I, II	Basketball	Cross Country
Nickname—Cornets	Cross Country	Soccer
Athletic Director—	Football	Softball
(612) 641-8700	Soccer	Track
	Track	Volleyball

CROWN COLLEGE

6425 County Road 30	Men	Women
Saint Bonifacius, MN	Baseball	Basketball
55375-9002	Basketball	Cheerleading
Affiliation—NCCAA II	Cross Country	Cross Country
Nickname—Crusaders	Football	Golf
Athletic Director—	Golf	Soccer
(612) 446-4170	Soccer	Volleyball

GUSTAVUS ADOLPHUS COLLEGE

800 W. College Avenue	Men	Women
Saint Peter, MN 56082-1485	Baseball	Basketball
Affiliation—NCAA III	Basketball	Cross Country
Nickname—Gusties	Cross Country	Golf
Athletic Director—	Football	Gymnastics
(507) 933-7622	Golf	Soccer
	Ice Hockey	Softball
	Soccer	Swimming
	Swimming	Tennis
	Tennis	Track
	Track	Volleyball

HAMLINE UNIVERSITY

1536 Hewitt Avenue	**Men**	**Women**
Saint Paul, MN 55104-1205	Baseball	Basketball
Affiliation—NCAA III	Basketball	Cross Country
Nickname—Fighting Pipers	Cross Country	Gymnastics
Athletic Director—Men	Football	Ice Hockey
(612) 523-2326	Ice Hockey	Soccer
Athletic Director—Women	Soccer	Softball
(612) 523-2034	Swimming	Swimming
	Tennis	Tennis
	Track	Track
		Volleyball

MACALESTER COLLEGE

1600 Grand Avenue	**Men**	**Women**
Saint Paul, MN 55105-1801	Baseball	Basketball
Affiliation—NCAA III	Basketball	Cross Country
Nickname—Scots	Cross Country	Golf
Athletic Director—	Football	Soccer
(651) 696-6260	Golf	Softball
	Soccer	Swimming
	Swimming	Tennis
	Tennis	Track
	Track	Volleyball

MINNESOTA STATE UNIVERSITY, MANKATO

PO Box 8400, MSU 28	**Men**	**Women**
Mankato, MN 56002-8414	Baseball	Basketball
Affiliation—NCAA II	Basketball	Cross Country
(Div. I Hockey)	Cross Country	Golf
Nickname—Mavericks	Football	Ice Hockey
Athletic Director—Men	Golf	Soccer
(507) 389-1795	Ice Hockey	Softball
Athletic Director—Women	Swimming	Swimming
(507) 389-2018	Tennis	Tennis
	Track	Track
	Wrestling	Volleyball

MARTIN LUTHER COLLEGE

1995 Luther Court	**Men**	**Women**
New Ulm, MN 56073-3965	Baseball	Basketball
Affiliation—NCAA III	Basketball	Cross Country
Nickname—Knights	Cross Country	Soccer
Athletic Director—	Football	Softball
(507) 354-8221 ext. 256	Golf	Tennis
	Soccer	Track
	Tennis	Volleyball
	Track	
	Wrestling	

MINNESOTA, UNIVERSITY OF, CROOKSTON

Sports Center	**Men**	**Women**
Crookston, MN 56716	Baseball	Basketball
Affiliation—NCAA II	Basketball	Soccer
Nickname—Golden Eagles	Football	Softball
Athletic Director—	Ice Hockey	Tennis
(218) 281-6897		Volleyball

MINNESOTA, UNIVERSITY OF, DULUTH

10 University Drive	**Men**	**Women**
Duluth, MN 55812-2496	Baseball	Basketball
Affiliation—NCAA II	Basketball	Cheerleading
(Div. I Hockey)	Cross Country	Cross Country
Nickname—Bulldogs	Ice Hockey	Ice Hockey
Athletic Director—	Tennis	Soccer
(218) 726-8168	Track	Softball
		Track
		Volleyball

MINNESOTA, UNIVERSITY OF, MORRIS

	Men	Women
E. 2nd Street	Baseball	Basketball
Morris, MN 56267	Basketball	Cross Country
Affiliation—NCAA II	Football	Golf
Nickname—Cougars	Golf	Soccer
Athletic Director—	Tennis	Softball
(320) 589-6421	Track	Tennis
	Wrestling	Track
		Volleyball

MINNESOTA, UNIVERSITY OF, TWIN CITIES

	Men	Women
516 15th Avenue SE, Room 245	Baseball	Basketball
Minneapolis, MN 55455-0120	Basketball	Cross Country
Affiliation—NCAA I	Cross Country	Diving
(I-A Football)	Football	Golf
Nickname—Golden Gophers	Golf	Gymnastics
Athletic Director—Men	Gymnastics	Ice Hockey
(612) 625-3536	Ice Hockey	Soccer
Athletic Director—Women	Swimming	Softball
(612) 624-4044	Tennis	Swimming
	Track	Tennis
	Wrestling	Track
		Volleyball

MINNESOTA BIBLE COLLEGE

	Men	Women
920 Mayowood Road SW	Baseball	Softball
Rochester, MN 55902-2382	Basketball	Tennis
Nickname—Royals	Golf	Volleyball
Athletic Director—	Tennis	
(507) 288-4563		

MOORHEAD STATE UNIVERSITY

	Men	Women
17th Street and 9th Avenue S	Basketball	Basketball
Moorhead, MN 56563	Cross Country	Cross Country
Affiliation—NCAA II	Football	Golf
Nickname—Dragons	Track	Soccer
Athletic Director—	Wrestling	Softball
(218) 236-2622		Swimming
		Tennis
		Track
		Volleyball

NORTH CENTRAL BIBLE COLLEGE

910 *Elliot Avenue S*	**Men**	**Women**
Minneapolis, MN 55404-1322	Baseball	Basketball
Affiliation—NCCAA II	Basketball	Cheerleading
Athletic Director—	Golf	Volleyball
(612) 343-4755	Soccer	

NORTHWESTERN COLLEGE

3003 *Snelling Avenue N*	**Men**	**Women**
Saint Paul, MN 55113-1598	Baseball	Basketball
Affiliation—NAIA II, NCCAA	Basketball	Cross Country
Nickname—Eagles	Cross Country	Soccer
Athletic Director—	Football	Softball
(651) 631-5219	Golf	Track
	Soccer	Volleyball
	Tennis	
	Track	

PILLSBURY BAPTIST BIBLE COLLEGE

315 *S. Grove Avenue*	**Men**	**Women**
Owatonna, MN 55060-3068	Baseball	Basketball
Affiliation—NCCAA	Basketball	Softball
Nickname—Comets	Golf	Volleyball
Athletic Director—	Soccer	
(507) 451-2710 ext. 211		

SAINT BENEDICT, COLLEGE OF

37 *S. College Avenue*	**Women**	
Saint Joseph, MN 56374	Basketball	Softball
Affiliation—NCAA III	Cross Country	Swimming
Nickname—Blazers	Golf	Tennis
Athletic Director—	Ice Hockey	Track
(320) 363-5301	Soccer	Volleyball

SAINT CATHERINE, COLLEGE OF

2004 *Randolph Avenue*	**Women**	
Saint Paul, MN 55105	Basketball	Swimming
Affiliation—NCAA III	Cross Country	Tennis
Nickname—Wildcats	Hockey	Track
Athletic Director—	Soccer	Volleyball
(612) 690-8771	Softball	

SAINT CLOUD STATE UNIVERSITY

720 4th Avenue S	**Men**	**Women**
Saint Cloud, MN 56301-4442	Baseball	Basketball
*Affiliation—*NCAA *II*	Basketball	Cross Country
(Div. I Hockey)	Cross Country	Diving
Nickname—Huskies	Diving	Golf
Athletic Director—	Football	Skiing
(320) 255-3102	Golf	Soccer
	Ice Hockey	Softball
	Swimming	Swimming
	Tennis	Tennis
	Track	Track
	Wrestling	Volleyball

SAINT JOHN'S UNIVERSITY

PO Box 7277,	**Men**	
#1 Champion Drive	Baseball	Ice Hockey
Collegeville, MN 56321-7277	Basketball	Soccer
*Affiliation—*NCAA *III*	Cross Country	Swimming
Nickname—Johnnies	Diving	Tennis
Athletic Director—	Football	Track
(320) 363-2500	Golf	Wrestling

SAINT MARY'S UNIVERSITY

700 Terrace Heights, 362	**Men**	**Women**
Winona, MN 55987-1321	Baseball	Basketball
*Affiliation—*NCAA *III*	Basketball	Cross Country
Nickname—Cardinals	Cross Country	Golf
Athletic Director—	Golf	Skiing
(507) 457-1578	Ice Hockey	Soccer
	Skiing	Softball
	Soccer	Swimming
	Swimming	Tennis
	Tennis	Track
	Track	Volleyball

SAINT OLAF COLLEGE

1520 Saint Olaf Avenue	**Men**	**Women**
Northfield, MN 55057-1574	Baseball	Basketball
Affiliation—NCAA III	Basketball	Cross Country
Nickname—Oles, Lions	Cross Country	Golf
Athletic Director—	Ice Hockey	Skiing
(507) 646-3250	Skiing	Soccer
	Soccer	Softball
	Swimming	Swimming
	Tennis	Tennis
	Track	Track
	Wrestling	Volleyball

SAINT SCHOLASTICS, COLLEGE OF

1200 Kenwood Avenue	**Men**	**Women**
Duluth, MN 55811-4199	Baseball	Basketball
Affiliation—NCAA III, NAIA II	Basketball	Cross Country
Nickname—Saints	Cross Country	Soccer
Athletic Director—	Ice Hockey	Softball
(218) 723-6551	Soccer	Tennis
	Tennis	Volleyball

SAINT THOMAS, UNIVERSITY OF

Mail #5003,	**Men**	**Women**
2115 Summit Avenue	Baseball	Basketball
Saint Paul, MN 55105	Basketball	Cross Country
Affiliation—NCAA III	Cross Country	Golf
Nickname—Tommies	Football	Ice Hockey
Athletic Director—	Golf	Soccer
(612) 962-5901	Ice Hockey	Softball
	Soccer	Swimming
	Swimming	Tennis
	Tennis	Track
	Track	Volleyball
	Wrestling	

SOUTHWEST STATE UNIVERSITY

1501 State Street	**Men**	**Women**
Marshall, MN 56258-3306	Baseball	Basketball
Affiliation—NCAA II	Basketball	Golf
Nickname—Golden Mustangs	Football	Soccer
Athletic Director—	Wrestling	Softball
(507) 537-7984		Tennis
		Volleyball

WINONA STATE UNIVERSITY

PO Box 5838	**Men**	**Women**
Winona, MN 55987-0838	Baseball	Basketball
Affiliation—NCAA II	Basketball	Cross Country
Nickname—Warriors	Football	Golf
Athletic Director—	Golf	Gymnastics
(507) 457-5212	Tennis	Soccer
		Softball
		Tennis
		Track
		Volleyball

MISSISSIPPI

ALCORN STATE UNIVERSITY

1000 ASU Drive, #510	**Men**	**Women**
Lorman, MS 39096	Baseball	Basketball
Affiliation—NCAA I	Basketball	Bowling
(I-AA Football)	Cross Country	Cross Country
Nickname—Braves	Football	Golf
Athletic Director—	Golf	Softball
(601) 877-6509	Tennis	Tennis
	Track	Track
	Volleyball	Volleyball

BELHAVEN COLLEGE

1500 Peachtree Street	**Men**	**Women**
Jackson, MS 39202-1754	Baseball	Basketball
Affiliation—NAIA I	Basketball	Cross Country
Nickname—Blazers	Cross Country	Soccer
Athletic Director—	Football	Softball
(601) 965-7025	Golf	Tennis
	Soccer	Volleyball
	Tennis	
	Volleyball	

BLUE MOUNTAIN COLLEGE

201 North Main Street	**Women**	
Blue Mountain, MS 38610	Basketball	Tennis
Affiliation—NAIA		
Nickname—Toppers		
Athletic Director—		
(601) 685-4771 ext. 46		

DELTA STATE UNIVERSITY

	Men	Women
PO Box A-3	Baseball	Basketball
Cleveland, MS 38733	Basketball	Cross Country
Affiliation—NCAA II	Football	Softball
Nickname—Statesmen	Golf	Swimming
Athletic Director—	Swimming	Tennis
(601) 846-4301	Tennis	

JACKSON STATE UNIVERSITY

	Men	Women
1325 John R. Lynch Street	Baseball	Basketball
Jackson, MS 39217-0510	Basketball	Cross Country
Affiliation—NCAA I	Cross Country	Golf
(I-AA Football)	Football	Softball
Nickname—Tigers	Golf	Tennis
Athletic Director—	Tennis	Track
(601) 968-7031	Track	Volleyball

MILLSAPS COLLEGE

	Men	Women
1701 N. State Street	Baseball	Basketball
Jackson, MS 39210	Basketball	Cheerleading
Affiliation—NCAA III	Cross Country	Cross Country
Nickname—Majors	Football	Golf
Athletic Director—	Golf	Soccer
(601) 974-1190	Soccer	Tennis
	Tennis	Volleyball

MISSISSIPPI, UNIVERSITY OF

	Men	Women
Athletic Department	Baseball	Basketball
University, MS 38677	Basketball	Cross Country
Affiliation—NCAA I	Cross Country	Golf
(I-A Football)	Football	Rifle
Nickname—Ole Miss Rebels	Golf	Soccer
Athletic Director—	Tennis	Softball
(601) 232-7546	Track	Tennis
		Track
		Volleyball

MISSISSIPPI COLLEGE

	Men	Women
PO Box 4049	Baseball	Basketball
Clinton, MS 39058	Basketball	Cross Country
Affiliation—NCAA III	Cross Country	Soccer
Nickname—Choctaws	Football	Softball
Athletic Director—	Soccer	Tennis
(601) 925-3342	Tennis	Volleyball

MISSISSIPPI STATE UNIVERSITY

	Men	Women
PO Box 5327	Baseball	Basketball
Mississippi State,	Basketball	Cross Country
MS 39762-5327	Cross Country	Golf
Affiliation—NCAA I	Football	Soccer
(I-A Football)	Golf	Softball
Nickname—Bulldogs	Tennis	Tennis
Athletic Director—	Track	Track
(601) 325-2532		Volleyball

MISSISSIPPI UNIVERSITY FOR WOMEN

	Women	
Box 1636	Basketball	Tennis
Columbus, MS 39701	Softball	Volleyball
Affiliation—NCAA II		
Nickname—Blues		
Athletic Director—		
(601) 329-8554		

MISSISSIPPI VALLEY STATE UNIVERSITY

	Men	Women
14000 Highway 82W	Baseball	Basketball
Itta Bena, MS 38941	Basketball	Cheerleading
Affiliation—NCAA I	Cross Country	Cross Country
(I-AA Football)	Football	Golf
Nickname—Delta Devils	Golf	Softball
Athletic Director—	Tennis	Tennis
(601) 254-9041 ext. 3551	Track	Track
		Volleyball

RUST COLLEGE

150 E. Rust Avenue	**Men**	**Women**
Holly Springs, MS 38635-2330	Baseball	Basketball
Affiliation—NCAA III	Basketball	Cross Country
Nickname—Bearcats	Cross Country	Tennis
Athletic Director—	Tennis	Volleyball
(601) 252-4661 ext. 4014	Track	

SOUTHERN MISSISSIPPI, UNIVERSITY OF

Fairchild Fieldhouse, University	**Men**	**Women**
Boulevard, Box 5017	Baseball	Basketball
Hattiesburg, MS 39406-5017	Basketball	Cheerleading
Affiliation—NCAA I	Cross Country	Cross Country
(I-A Football)	Football	Golf
Nickname—Golden Eagles	Golf	Soccer
Athletic Director—	Tennis	Softball
(601) 266-5017	Track	Tennis
		Track
		Volleyball

TOUGALOO COLLEGE

PO Box 23,	**Men**	**Women**
500 W. County Line Road	Basketball	Basketball
Tougaloo, MS 39174-0023	Cross Country	Cross Country
Affiliation—NAIA I		
Nickname—Bulldogs		
Athletic Director—		
(601) 977-7809		

WILLIAM CAREY COLLEGE

Tuscan Avenue	**Men**	**Women**
Hattiesburg, MS 39401	Baseball	Basketball
Affiliation—NAIA I	Basketball	Soccer
Nickname—Crusaders	Soccer	Softball
Athletic Director—		
(601) 582-6415		

MISSOURI

AVILA COLLEGE

11901 Wornall Road	**Men**	**Women**
Kansas City, MO 64145-1007	Baseball	Basketball
Affiliation—NAIA II	Basketball	Soccer
Nickname—Midlands	Soccer	Softball
Athletic Director—		Volleyball
(816) 942-8400 ext. 2356		

BAPTIST BIBLE COLLEGE

628 E. Kearney Street	**Men**	**Women**
Springfield, MO 65803-3426	Basketball	Basketball
Affiliation—NCCAA II	Soccer	Cheerleading
Nickname—Patriots		Volleyball
Athletic Director—		
(417) 268-6060 ext. 6038		

CALVARY BIBLE COLLEGE

15800 Calvary Road	**Men**	**Women**
Kansas City, MO 64147	Baseball	Basketball
Affiliation—NCCAA	Basketball	Volleyball
Nickname—Warriors	Golf	
Athletic Director—	Soccer	
(816) 322-5152 ext. 1209	Tennis	

CENTRAL CHRISTIAN COLLEGE

911 Urbandale Drive E	**Men**	**Women**
Moberly, MO 65270	Basketball	Basketball
Nickname—Heralds	Soccer	Volleyball
Athletic Director—		
(660) 263-3900		

CENTRAL METHODIST COLLEGE

411 CMC Square	**Men**	**Women**
Fayette, MO 65248	Baseball	Basketball
Affiliation—NAIA *II*	Basketball	Cheerleading
Nickname—Eagles	Cross Country	Cross Country
Athletic Director—	Football	Golf
(660) 248-6221	Golf	Soccer
	Soccer	Softball
	Tennis	Tennis
	Track	Track
		Volleyball

CENTRAL MISSOURI STATE

500 Washington Street	**Men**	**Women**
Warrensburg, MO 64093	Baseball	Basketball
Affiliation—NCAA *II*	Basketball	Cheerleading
Nickname—Mules	Cross Country	Cross Country
Athletic Director—	Football	Soccer
(660) 543-4112	Golf	Softball
	Track	Track
	Wrestling	Volleyball

COLUMBIA COLLEGE

1001 Rogers Street	**Men**	**Women**
Columbia, MO 65201-4580	Basketball	Softball
Affiliation—NAIA *I*	Soccer	Volleyball
Nickname—Cougars	Volleyball	
Athletic Director—		
(573) 875-7200		

CONCORDIA SEMINARY

801 De Mun Avenue	**Men**	
Saint Louis, MO 63105-3168	Basketball	Tennis
Nickname—Preachers		
Athletic Director—		
(314) 505-7215		

CULVER-STOCKTON COLLEGE

1 College Hill	**Men**	**Women**
Canton, MO 63435-1257	Baseball	Basketball
Affiliation—NAIA II	Basketball	Golf
Nickname—Wildcats	Football	Softball
Athletic Director—	Golf	Volleyball
(217) 231-6393	Soccer	

DRURY COLLEGE

900 N. Benton Avenue	**Men**	**Women**
Springfield, MO 65802-3712	Basketball	Soccer
Affiliation—NCAA II	Golf	Swimming
Nickname—Panthers	Soccer	Tennis
Athletic Director—	Swimming	Volleyball
(417) 873-7294	Tennis	

EVANGEL UNIVERSITY

1111 N. Glenstone Avenue	**Men**	**Women**
Springfield, MO 65802-2125	Baseball	Basketball
Affiliation—NAIA II	Basketball	Cheerleading
Nickname—Crusaders	Cross Country	Cross Country
Athletic Director—	Football	Golf
(417) 865-2811 ext. 7285	Track	Softball
		Track
		Volleyball

FONTBONNE COLLEGE

6800 Wydown Boulevard	**Men**	**Women**
Saint Louis, MO 63105-3098	Baseball	Basketball
Affiliation—NCAA III	Basketball	Cheerleading
Nickname—Griffins	Cross Country	Cross Country
Athletic Director—	Golf	Soccer
(314) 889-1444	Soccer	Softball
	Tennis	Tennis
		Volleyball

HANNIBAL-LA GRANGE COLLEGE

2800 Palmyra Road	**Men**	**Women**
Hannibal, MO 63401-1940	Baseball	Basketball
Affiliation—NAIA I, NCCAA I	Basketball	Soccer
Nickname—Trojans	Golf	Softball
Athletic Director—	Soccer	Volleyball
(573) 221-3575 ext. 308		

HARRIS-STOWE STATE

3026 Laclede Avenue	Men	Women
Saint Louis, MO 63103-2136	Baseball	Basketball
Affiliation—NAIA I	Basketball	Soccer
Nickname—Hornets	Soccer	Track
Athletic Director—		Volleyball
(314) 340-3530		

LINCOLN UNIVERSITY

820 Chestnut Street	Men	Women
Jefferson City, MO 65102-0029	Baseball	Basketball
Affiliation—NCAA II	Basketball	Cross Country
Nickname—Blue Tigers	Golf	Softball
Athletic Director—	Soccer	Tennis
(573) 681-5342	Track	Track

LINDENWOOD UNIVERSITY

209 Kingshighway Street	Men	Women
Saint Charles, MO 63301-1693	Baseball	Basketball
Affiliation—NAIA I	Basketball	Cross Country
Nickname—Lions	Cross Country	Golf
Athletic Director—	Football	Soccer
(314) 949-4980	Golf	Softball
	Soccer	Track
	Track	Volleyball
	Wrestling	

MARYVILLE UNIVERSITY OF SAINT LOUIS

13550 Conway Road	Men	Women
Saint Louis, MO 63141-7232	Baseball	Basketball
Affiliation—NCAA III	Basketball	Cross Country
Nickname—Saints	Cross Country	Golf
Athletic Director—	Golf	Soccer
(314) 529-9484	Tennis	Softball
		Tennis
		Volleyball

MESSENGER COLLEGE

PO Box 4050	Men	Women
Joplin, MO 64803-4050	Basketball	Basketball
Affiliation—NBCAA, MCCAA II	Volleyball	Volleyball
Nickname—Eagles		
Athletic Director—		
(417) 624-7070 ext. 108		

MISSOURI, UNIVERSITY OF

PO Box 677, Hearnes Center	Men	Women
Columbia, MO 65205-0677	Baseball	Basketball
Affiliation—NCAA I	Basketball	Cross Country
(I-A Football)	Football	Golf
Nickname—Tigers	Golf	Gymnastics
Athletic Director—	Swimming	Softball
(573) 882-6501	Tennis	Swimming
	Track	Tennis
	Wrestling	Track
		Volleyball

MISSOURI, UNIVERSITY OF, KANSAS CITY

5100 Rockhill Road	Men	Women
Kansas City, MO 64110-2446	Basketball	Basketball
Affiliation—NCAA I	Cross Country	Cross Country
Nickname—Kangaroos	Golf	Golf
Athletic Director—	Rifle	Rifle
(816) 235-1036	Soccer	Softball
	Tennis	Tennis
	Track	Track
		Volleyball

MISSOURI, UNIVERSITY OF, ROLLA

Athletic Department	Men	Women
Rolla, MO 65409	Baseball	Basketball
Affiliation—NCAA II	Basketball	Cross Country
Nickname—Miners	Cross Country	Soccer
Athletic Director—	Football	Softball
(573) 341-4175	Golf	Track
	Soccer	
	Swimming	
	Tennis	
	Track	

MISSOURI, UNIVERSITY OF, ST. LOUIS

8001 Natural Bridge Road	Men	Women
Saint Louis, MO 63121-4401	Baseball	Basketball
Affiliation—NCAA II	Basketball	Golf
Nickname—Rivermen	Golf	Soccer
Athletic Director—	Soccer	Softball
(314) 516-5657	Tennis	Tennis
		Volleyball

MISSOURI BAPTIST COLLEGE

	Men	Women
1 College Park Drive	Baseball	Basketball
Saint Louis, MO 63141-8698	Basketball	Cheerleading
Affiliation—NAIA I	Golf	Soccer
Nickname—Spartans	Soccer	Softball
Athletic Director—		Volleyball
(314) 434-8262 ext. 4211		

MISSOURI SOUTHERN STATE COLLEGE

	Men	Women
3950 Newman Road	Baseball	Basketball
Joplin, MO 64801-1512	Basketball	Cross Country
Affiliation—NCAA II	Cross Country	Soccer
Nickname—Lions	Football	Softball
Athletic Director—	Golf	Tennis
(417) 625-9570	Soccer	Track
	Track	Volleyball

MISSOURI VALLEY COLLEGE

	Men	Women
500 E. College Street	Baseball	Basketball
Marshall, MO 65340-3109	Basketball	Cross Country
Affiliation—NAIA II	Cross Country	Soccer
Nickname—Vikings	Football	Softball
Athletic Director—	Rodeo	Track
(660) 831-4219	Soccer	Volleyball
	Track	
	Wrestling	

MISSOURI WESTERN STATE

	Men	Women
4525 Downs Drive	Baseball	Basketball
Saint Joseph, MO 64507-2246	Basketball	Softball
Affiliation—NCAA II	Football	Tennis
Nickname—Griffons	Golf	Volleyball
Athletic Director—		
(816) 271-4482		

NORTHWEST MISSOURI STATE UNIVERSITY

	Men	Women
800 University Drive	Baseball	Basketball
Maryville, MO 64468-6015	Basketball	Cross Country
Affiliation—NCAA II	Cross Country	Softball
Nickname—Bearcats	Football	Tennis
Athletic Director—Men	Tennis	Track
(660) 562-1118	Track	Volleyball
Athletic Director—Women		
(660) 562-1298		

OZARK CHRISTIAN COLLEGE

	Men	Women
1111 N. Main Street	Basketball	Basketball
Joplin, MO 64801-1188	Soccer	Volleyball
Affiliation—NCCAA II		
Nickname—Ambassadors		
Athletic Director—		
(417) 624-2518 ext. 2301		

OZARKS, COLLEGE OF THE

	Men	Women
Opportunity Avenue	Baseball	Basketball
Point Lookout, MO 65726	Basketball	Cheerleading
Affiliation—NAIA II		Volleyball
Nickname—Bobcats		
Athletic Director—		
(417) 334-6411 ext. 4393		

PARK COLLEGE

	Men	Women
8700 NW River Park Drive,	Basketball	Basketball
Box 66	Cross Country	Cross Country
Parkville, MO 64152	Soccer	Soccer
Affiliation—NAIA I	Track	Softball
Nickname—Pirates	Volleyball	Track
Athletic Director—		Volleyball
(816) 741-2000 ext. 6492		

ROCKHURST COLLEGE

	Men	Women
1100 Rockhurst Road	Baseball	Basketball
Kansas City, MO 64110-2508	Basketball	Cross Country
Affiliation—NAIA, NCAA II	Cross Country	Golf
Nickname—Hawks	Golf	Soccer
Athletic Director—	Soccer	Tennis
(816) 501-4141	Tennis	Volleyball

SAINT LOUIS CHRISTIAN COLLEGE

1360 Grandview Drive	Men	Women
Florissant, MO 63033-6405	Baseball	Basketball
Affiliation—NCCAA II	Basketball	Volleyball
Nickname—Soldiers		
Athletic Director—		
(314) 837-6777		

SAINT LOUIS COLLEGE OF PHARMACY

4588 Parkview Place	Men	Women
Saint Louis, MO 63110-1029	Basketball	Volleyball
Affiliation—NAIA II		
Nickname—Eutectics		
Athletic Director—		
(314) 367-8700		

SAINT LOUIS UNIVERSITY

3672 W. Pine Boulevard	Men	Women
Saint Louis, MO 63108-3304	Baseball	Basketball
Affiliation—NCAA I	Basketball	Cross Country
Nickname—Billikens	Cross Country	Diving
Athletic Director—	Diving	Field Hockey
(314) 977-3167	Golf	Rifle
	Rifle	Soccer
	Soccer	Softball
	Swimming	Swimming
	Tennis	Tennis
		Volleyball

SOUTHEAST MISSOURI STATE UNIVERSITY

#1 University Plaza	Men	Women
Cape Girardeau, MO 63701	Baseball	Basketball
Nickname—Indians	Basketball	Cheerleading
Athletic Director—	Cross Country	Cross Country
(573) 651-2229	Football	Gymnastics
	Golf	Softball
	Track	Tennis
		Track
		Volleyball

SOUTHWEST BAPTIST UNIVERSITY

1600 University Avenue	**Men**	**Women**
Bolivar, MO 65613-2578	Baseball	Basketball
Affiliation—NCAA II	Basketball	Cheerleading
Nickname—Bearcats	Cross Country	Cross Country
Athletic Director—	Football	Soccer
(417) 326-1797	Golf	Softball
	Soccer	Tennis
	Tennis	Volleyball

SOUTHWEST MISSOURI STATE UNIVERSITY

901 S. National Avenue	**Men**	**Women**
Springfield, MO 65801-0027	Baseball	Basketball
Affiliation—NCAA I	Basketball	Cross Country
(I-AA Football)	Cross Country	Field Hockey
Nickname—Bears	Football	Golf
Athletic Director—	Golf	Soccer
(417) 836-5244	Soccer	Softball
	Swimming	Swimming
	Tennis	Tennis
	Track	Track
		Volleyball

TRUMAN STATE UNIVERSITY

100 E. Normal Street	**Men**	**Women**
Kirksville, MO 63501-4221	Baseball	Basketball
Affiliation—NCAA II	Basketball	Cheerleading
Nickname—Bulldogs	Cross Country	Cross Country
Athletic Director—	Football	Golf
(660) 785-4236	Golf	Soccer
	Soccer	Softball
	Swimming	Swimming
	Tennis	Tennis
	Track	Track
	Wrestling	Volleyball

WASHINGTON UNIVERSITY

Campus Box 1067,
* 1 Brookings Drive*
St. Louis, MO 63130
Affiliation—NCAA III
Nickname—Bears
Athletic Director—
* (314) 935-5185*

Men	Women
Baseball	Basketball
Basketball	Cross Country
Cross Country	Diving
Diving	Soccer
Football	Swimming
Soccer	Tennis
Swimming	Track
Tennis	Volleyball
Track	

WEBSTER UNIVERSITY

470 E. Lockwood Avenue
Webster Groves,
* MO 63119-3141*
Affiliation—NCAA III
Nickname—Gorloks
Athletic Director—
* (314) 968-6984*

Men	Women
Baseball	Basketball
Basketball	Cross Country
Cross Country	Golf
Golf	Softball
Soccer	Swimming
Tennis	Tennis
	Volleyball

WESTMINSTER COLLEGE

501 Westminster Avenue
Fulton, MO 65251-1299
Affiliation—NCAA III
Nickname—Blue Jays
Athletic Director—
* (573) 592-5301*

Men	Women
Baseball	Basketball
Basketball	Golf
Football	Rifle
Golf	Soccer
Rifle	Softball
Soccer	Tennis
Tennis	Volleyball

WILLIAM JEWELL COLLEGE

500 College Hill
Liberty, MO 64068-1843
Affiliation—NAIA II
Nickname—Cardinals
Athletic Director—
* (816) 781-7700 ext. 5284*

Men	Women
Baseball	Basketball
Basketball	Cheerleading
Cross Country	Cross Country
Football	Golf
Golf	Soccer
Soccer	Tennis
Tennis	Track
Track	Volleyball

WILLIAM WOODS UNIVERSITY

	Men	Women
200 W. 12th Street	Basketball	Basketball
Fulton, MO 65251-1004	Golf	Golf
*Affiliation—*NAIA *I*	Soccer	Soccer
Nickname—Owls	Volleyball	Softball
Athletic Director—		Tennis
(573) 592-4387		Volleyball

MONTANA

CARROLL COLLEGE

	Men	Women
1601 N. Benton Avenue	Basketball	Basketball
Helena, MT 59601-2821	Football	Soccer
*Affiliation—*NAIA *I*		Volleyball
Nickname—Fighting Saints		
Athletic Director—		
(406) 447-4401		

MONTANA, UNIVERSITY OF

	Men	Women
Harry Adams Field House	Basketball	Basketball
Missoula, MT 59812	Cross Country	Cross Country
*Affiliation—*NCAA *I*	Football	Golf
(I-AA Football)	Tennis	Soccer
Nickname—Grizzlies	Track	Tennis
Athletic Director—		Track
(406) 243-5331		Volleyball

MONTANA STATE UNIVERSITY, BILLINGS

	Men	Women
1500 N. 30th Street	Basketball	Basketball
Billings, MT 59012-0245	Cross Country	Cross Country
*Affiliation—*NCAA *II*	Soccer	Soccer
Nickname—Yellowjackets	Tennis	Tennis
Athletic Director—		Volleyball
(406) 657-2369		

MONTANA STATE UNIVERSITY, BOZEMAN

PO Box 173380	Men	Women
Bozeman, MT 59717-3380	Basketball	Basketball
Affiliation—NCAA I	Cross Country	Cross Country
(I-AA Football)	Football	Golf
Nickname—*Bobcats*	Rodeo	Rodeo
Athletic Director—	Tennis	Skiing
(406) 994-4221	Track	Tennis
		Track
		Volleyball

MONTANA STATE UNIVERSITY, NORTHERN

College Drive	Men	Women
Havre, MT 59501	Basketball	Basketball
Affiliation—NAIA I	Football	Cross Country
Nickname—*Northern Lights*	Rodeo	Golf
Athletic Director—	Wrestling	Rodeo
(406) 265-3720		Soccer
		Volleyball

MONTANA TECH OF THE UNIVERSITY OF MONTANA

Park Street	Men	Women
Butte, MT 59701	Basketball	Basketball
Affiliation—NAIA I	Football	Volleyball
Nickname—*Orediggers*		
Athletic Director—		
(406) 496-4266		

ROCKY MOUNTAIN COLLEGE

1511 Poly Drive	Men	Women
Billings, MT 59102-1739	Basketball	Basketball
Affiliation—NAIA I	Football	Skiing
Nickname—*Bears*	Golf	Volleyball
Athletic Director—	Skiing	
(406) 657-1124		

WESTERN MONTANA OF THE UNIVERSITY OF MONTANA

710 S. Atlantic Street	Men	Women
Dillon, MT 59725-3511	Basketball	Basketball
Affiliation—NAIA I	Football	Rodeo
Nickname—*Bulldogs*	Rodeo	Volleyball
Athletic Director—	Wrestling	
(406) 683-7412		

NEBRASKA

BELLEVUE UNIVERSITY

100 Galvin Road S	**Men**	**Women**
Bellevue, NE 68005-3058	Baseball	Soccer
Affiliation—NAIA	Basketball	Softball
Nickname—Bruins	Soccer	Volleyball
Athletic Director—		
(402) 293-3784		

CHADRON STATE COLLEGE

Armstrong Building, 1000 Main	**Men**	**Women**
Chadron, NE 69337-2667	Basketball	Basketball
Affiliation—NCAA II	Football	Golf
Nickname—Eagles	Track	Track
Athletic Director—	Wrestling	Volleyball
(308) 432-6345		

CONCORDIA COLLEGE

800 N. Columbia Avenue	**Men**	**Women**
Seward, NE 68434-1556	Baseball	Basketball
Affiliation—NAIA II	Basketball	Cross Country
Nickname—Bulldogs	Cross Country	Golf
Athletic Director—	Football	Soccer
(402) 643-7328	Golf	Softball
	Soccer	Tennis
	Tennis	Track
	Track	Volleyball

CREIGHTON UNIVERSITY

2500 California Plaza	**Men**	**Women**
Omaha, NE 68178	Baseball	Basketball
Affiliation—NCAA I	Basketball	Crew
Nickname—Bluejays	Cross Country	Cross Country
Athletic Director—	Golf	Golf
(402) 280-2720	Soccer	Soccer
	Tennis	Softball
		Tennis
		Volleyball

DANA COLLEGE

2848 College Drive Blair, NE 68008-1041 Affiliation—NAIA II Nickname—Vikings Athletic Director— (402) 426-7296	**Men** Baseball Basketball Cross Country Football Track Wrestling	**Women** Basketball Cross Country Soccer Track Volleyball

DOANE COLLEGE

1014 Boswell Avenue Crete, NE 68333 Affiliation—NAIA II Nickname—Tigers Athletic Director— (402) 826-8347	**Men** Baseball Basketball Cross Country Football Golf Tennis Track	**Women** Basketball Cross Country Golf Softball Tennis Track Volleyball

HASTINGS COLLEGE

7th and Turner Hastings, NE 68902 Affiliation—NAIA II Nickname—Broncos Athletic Director— (402) 461-7395	**Men** Baseball Basketball Cross Country Football Golf Soccer Tennis Track	**Women** Basketball Cheerleading Cross Country Golf Soccer Softball Tennis Track Volleyball

MIDLAND LUTHERAN COLLEGE

900 N. Clarkson Street Fremont, NE 68025-4254 Affiliation—NAIA II Nickname—Warriors Athletic Director— (402) 721-5480 ext. 6361	**Men** Baseball Basketball Cross Country Football Golf Tennis Track	**Women** Basketball Cross Country Golf Soccer Softball Tennis Track Volleyball

NEBRASKA, UNIVERSITY OF, KEARNEY

Health and Sports Center,	**Men**	**Women**
Highway 30 and 15th Avenue	Baseball	Basketball
Kearney, NE 68849	Basketball	Cross Country
Affiliation—NCAA II	Cross Country	Golf
Nickname—Antelopes	Football	Softball
Athletic Director—	Golf	Swimming
(308) 865-8332	Tennis	Tennis
	Track	Track
	Wrestling	Volleyball

NEBRASKA, UNIVERSITY OF, LINCOLN

103 S. Stadium	**Men**	**Women**
Lincoln, NE 68588	Baseball	Basketball
Affiliation—NCAA I	Basketball	Bowling
(I-A Football)	Cross Country	Cheerleading
Nickname—Cornhuskers	Football	Cross Country
Athletic Director—	Golf	Diving
(402) 472-3011	Gymnastics	Golf
	Swimming	Gymnastics
	Tennis	Soccer
	Track	Softball
	Wrestling	Swimming
		Tennis
		Track
		Volleyball

NEBRASKA, UNIVERSITY OF, OMAHA

60th and Dodge	**Men**	**Women**
Omaha, NE 68182	Baseball	Basketball
Affiliation—NCAA II	Basketball	Cheerleading
Nickname—Mavericks	Football	Cross Country
Athletic Director—	Ice Hockey	Diving
(402) 554-3389	Wrestling	Soccer
		Softball
		Swimming
		Track
		Volleyball

NEBRASKA WESLEYAN UNIVERSITY

5000 Saint Paul Avenue	**Men**	**Women**
Lincoln, NE 68504-2760	Baseball	Basketball
Affiliation—NCAA III, NAIA II	Basketball	Cross Country
Nickname—Plainsmen	Cross Country	Golf
Athletic Director—	Football	Soccer
(402) 465-2245	Golf	Softball
	Soccer	Tennis
	Tennis	Track
	Track	Volleyball

PERU STATE COLLEGE

PO Box 10	**Men**	**Women**
Peru, NE 68421-0010	Baseball	Basketball
Affiliation—NAIA II	Basketball	Softball
Nickname—Bobcats	Football	Volleyball
Athletic Director—		
(402) 872-2350		

UNION COLLEGE

3800 S. 48th Street	**Men**	**Women**
Lincoln, NE 68506-4300	Basketball	Volleyball
Athletic Director—	Golf	
(402) 486-2525		

WAYNE STATE COLLEGE

1111 Main Street	**Men**	**Women**
Wayne, NE 68787-1172	Baseball	Basketball
Affiliation—NCAA II	Basketball	Cross Country
Nickname—Wildcats	Cross Country	Golf
Athletic Director—	Football	Soccer
(402) 375-7520	Golf	Softball
	Track	Track
		Volleyball

WESLEY COLLEGE

120 N. State Street	**Men**	**Women**
Dover, NE 19901	Baseball	Basketball
Affiliation—NCAA *III*	Basketball	Cheerleading
Nickname—*Wolverines*	Football	Field Hockey
Athletic Director—	Golf	Golf
(302) 736-2557	Lacrosse	Lacrosse
	Soccer	Soccer
	Tennis	Softball
		Tennis

YORK COLLEGE

1125 E. 8th Street	**Men**	**Women**
York, NE 68467-2631	Baseball	Basketball
Affiliation—NAIA	Basketball	Cross Country
Nickname—*Panthers*	Cross Country	Soccer
Athletic Director—	Soccer	Softball
(402) 363-5720	Tennis	Tennis
	Track	Volleyball

NEVADA

NEVADA, UNIVERSITY OF, LAS VEGAS

PO Box 450001,	**Men**	**Women**
4504 Maryland Parkway	Baseball	Basketball
Las Vegas, NV 89154-0026	Basketball	Cheerleading
Affiliation—NCAA *I*	Diving	Cross Country
(I-A Football)	Football	Diving
Nickname—*Rebels*	Golf	Soccer
Athletic Director—	Soccer	Softball
(702) 895-4729	Swimming	Swimming
	Tennis	Tennis
		Track
		Volleyball

NEVADA, UNIVERSITY OF, RENO

Lawlor Annex Mailstop 232	**Men**	**Women**
Reno, NV 89557	Baseball	Basketball
Affiliation—NCAA I	Basketball	Cross Country
(I-A Football)	Football	Golf
Nickname—Wolf Pack	Golf	Rifle
Athletic Director—	Rifle	Skiing
(702) 784-6900	Skiing	Swimming
	Tennis	Tennis
		Track
		Volleyball

NEW HAMPSHIRE

COLBY-SAWYER COLLEGE

100 Main Street	**Men**	**Women**
New London, NH 03257-4612	Baseball	Basketball
Affiliation—NCAA III	Basketball	Equestrian
Nickname—Chargers	Riding	Lacrosse
Athletic Director—	Skiing	Skiing
(603) 526-3609	Soccer	Soccer
	Tennis	Tennis
	Track	Track
		Volleyball

DANIEL WEBSTER COLLEGE

20 University Drive	**Men**	**Women**
Nashua, NH 03063-1323	Baseball	Basketball
Affiliation—NCAA III	Basketball	Cross Country
Nickname—Eagles	Cross Country	Golf
Athletic Director—	Golf	Soccer
(603) 577-6571	Soccer	Softball
	Volleyball	Volleyball

DARTMOUTH COLLEGE

6083 Alumni Gym,	**Men**	**Women**
Wheelock Street	Baseball	Basketball
Hanover, NH 03755-3512	Basketball	Crew
Affiliation—NCAA *I*	Crew	Cross Country
(I-AA Football)	Cross Country	Diving
Nickname—*Bog Green*	Diving	Field Hockey
Athletic Director—	Football	Golf
(603) 646-2465	Golf	Ice Hockey
	Ice Hockey	Lacrosse
	Lacrosse	Rowing
	Sailing	Sailing
	Skiing—Alpine/	Skiing—Alpine/
	Nordic	Nordic
	Soccer	Soccer
	Squash	Softball
	Swimming	Squash
	Tennis	Swimming
	Track	Tennis
	Water Polo	Track
	Wrestling	Volleyball

FRANKLIN PIERCE COLLEGE

PO Box 60,	**Men**	**Women**
College Road, RFD 119	Baseball	Basketball
Rindge, NH 03461-0060	Basketball	Crew
Affiliation—NCAA *II*	Crew	Cross Country
Nickname—*Ravens*	Cross Country	Field Hockey
Athletic Director—	Golf	Golf
(603) 899-4080	Ice Hockey	Lacrosse
	Lacrosse	Soccer
	Soccer	Softball
	Tennis	Tennis
		Volleyball

KEENE STATE COLLEGE

229 Main Street	**Men**	**Women**
Keene, NH 03435	Baseball	Basketball
Affiliation—NCAA II	Basketball	Cross Country
Nickname—Owls	Cross Country	Field Hockey
Athletic Director—	Lacrosse	Lacrosse
(603) 358-2813	Soccer	Soccer
	Swimming	Softball
	Track	Swimming
		Track
		Volleyball

NEW ENGLAND COLLEGE

Clement Arena, 24 Bridge Street	**Men**	**Women**
Henniker, NH 03242-3202	Baseball	Basketball
Affiliation—NCAA III	Basketball	Field Hockey
Nickname—Pilgrims	Ice Hockey	Lacrosse
Athletic Director—	Lacrosse	Skiing
(603) 428-2292	Skiing	Soccer
	Soccer	Softball

NEW HAMPSHIRE, UNIVERSITY OF

Field House, 145 Main Street	**Men**	**Women**
Durham, NH 03824	Basketball	Basketball
Affiliation—NCAA I	Cross Country	Cheerleading
(I-AA Football)	Football	Crew
Nickname—Wildcats	Ice Hockey	Cross Country
Athletic Director—	Skiing	Field Hockey
(603) 862-2013	Soccer	Gymnastics
	Swimming	Ice Hockey
	Tennis	Lacrosse
	Track	Skiing
		Soccer
		Swimming
		Tennis
		Track
		Volleyball

NEW HAMPSHIRE COLLEGE

	Men	Women
2500 N. River Road	Baseball	Basketball
Hooksett, NH 03106-1067	Basketball	Cheerleading
Affiliation—NCAA II	Cross Country	Cross Country
Nickname—Penmen	Ice Hockey	Soccer
Athletic Director—	Lacrosse	Softball
(603) 624-1204	Soccer	Volleyball

NEW HAMPSHIRE TECHNICAL INSTITUTE

	Men	Women
Institute Drive	Baseball	Basketball
Concord, NH 03301	Basketball	Soccer
Affiliation—NSCAA	Soccer	Softball
Nickname—Capitols	Volleyball	Volleyball
Athletic Director—		
(603) 271-6428		

NOTRE DAME COLLEGE

	Men	Women
2321 Elm Street	Basketball	Basketball
Manchester, NH 03104-2213	Crew	Cross Country
Affiliation—NAIA	Soccer	Soccer
Nickname—Saints		Softball
Athletic Director—		
(603) 647-5500 ext. 240		

PLYMOUTH STATE COLLEGE

	Men	Women
Holderness Road	Baseball	Basketball
Plymouth, NH 03264	Basketball	Field Hockey
Affiliation—NCAA III	Football	Lacrosse
Nickname—Panthers	Ice Hockey	Skiing
Athletic Director—	Lacrosse	Soccer
(603) 535-2751	Skiing	Softball
	Soccer	Swimming
	Tennis	Tennis
	Wrestling	Volleyball

RIVIER COLLEGE

	Men	Women
420 Main Street	Baseball	Basketball
Nashua, NH 03060-5043	Basketball	Cross Country
Affiliation—NCAA III	Cross Country	Soccer
Nickname—Raiders	Soccer	Softball
Athletic Director—	Volleyball	Volleyball
(603) 888-1311 ext. 8257		

SAINT ANSELM COLLEGE

100 Saint Anselm Drive	Men	Women
Manchester, NH 03102-1308	Baseball	Basketball
Affiliation—NCAA II	Basketball	Cross Country
Nickname—Hawks	Cross Country	Golf
Athletic Director—	Football	Skiing
(603) 641-7800	Golf	Soccer
	Ice Hockey	Softball
	Lacrosse	Tennis
	Skiing	Volleyball
	Soccer	
	Tennis	
	Volleyball	

NEW JERSEY

BLOOMFIELD COLLEGE

467 Franklin Street	Men	Women
Bloomfield, NJ 07003-3425	Baseball	Basketball
Affiliation—NAIA II	Basketball	Cheerleading
Nickname—Deacons	Soccer	Soccer
Athletic Director—		Softball
(973) 748-9000 ext. 363		Volleyball

CALDWELL COLLEGE

9 Ryerson Avenue	Men	Women
Caldwell, NJ 07006-6185	Baseball	Basketball
Affiliation—NAIA II	Basketball	Golf
Nickname—Cougars	Golf	Soccer
Athletic Director—	Soccer	Softball
(973) 228-4424 ext. 264	Tennis	Tennis

CENTENARY COLLEGE

400 Jefferson Street	Men	Women
Hackettstown, NJ 07840-2184	Basketball	Basketball
Affiliation—NCAA III	Cross Country	Cross Country
Nickname—Cyclones	Equestrian	Equestrian
Athletic Director—	Golf	Golf
(908) 852-1400 ext. 2378	Lacrosse	Lacrosse
	Soccer	Soccer
	Wrestling	Softball
		Volleyball

DREW UNIVERSITY

36 Madison Avenue	**Men**	**Women**
Madison, NJ 07940-1434	Baseball	Basketball
Affiliation—NCAA III	Basketball	Cross Country
Nickname—Rangers	Cross Country	Fencing
Athletic Director—	Fencing	Field Hockey
(973) 408-3638	Lacrosse	Lacrosse
	Soccer	Soccer
	Swimming	Softball
	Tennis	Swimming
		Tennis

FAIRLEIGH DICKINSON UNIVERSITY, MADISON

285 Madison Avenue	**Men**	**Women**
Madison, NJ 07940-1006	Baseball	Basketball
Affiliation—NCAA III	Basketball	Cross Country
Nickname—Devils	Cross Country	Field Hockey
Athletic Director—	Football	Golf
(973) 443-8972	Golf	Lacrosse
	Lacrosse	Soccer
	Soccer	Softball
	Swimming	Swimming
	Tennis	Tennis
		Track

FAIRLEIGH DICKINSON UNIVERSITY, TEANECK

1000 River Road	**Men**	**Women**
Teaneck, NJ 07666-1914	Baseball	Basketball
Affiliation—NCAA I	Basketball	Cross Country
Nickname—Knights	Cross Country	Fencing
Athletic Director—	Golf	Tennis
(201) 692-2208	Soccer	Track
	Tennis	Volleyball
	Track	

FELICIAN COLLEGE

262 S. Main Street	**Men**	**Women**
Lodi, NJ 07644-2117	Basketball	Basketball
Affiliation—NAIA II, NCAA II	Soccer	Soccer
Nickname—Golden Falcons		Softball
Athletic Director—		
(973) 778-1190 ext. 6119		

GEORGIAN COURT COLLEGE

900 Lakewood Avenue	**Women**	
Lakewood, NJ 08710-2697	Basketball	Soccer
*Affiliation—*NAIA	Cross Country	Softball
Nickname—Lions		
Athletic Director—		
(732) 364-2200 ext. 683		

KEAN UNIVERSITY

1000 Morris Avenue	**Men**	**Women**
Union, NJ 07083	Baseball	Basketball
*Affiliation—*NCAA *III*	Basketball	Cheerleading
Nickname—Cougars	Football	Cross Country
Athletic Director—	Lacrosse	Field Hockey
(908) 527-2436	Soccer	Lacrosse
		Soccer
		Softball
		Swimming
		Tennis
		Track
		Volleyball

MONMOUTH UNIVERSITY

400 Cedar Avenue	**Men**	**Women**
West Long Branch,	Baseball	Basketball
NJ 07764-1804	Basketball	Cross Country
*Affiliation—*NCAA *I*	Cross Country	Field Hockey
(I-AA Football)	Football	Golf
Nickname—Hawks	Golf	Lacrosse
Athletic Director—	Soccer	Soccer
(732) 571-3415	Tennis	Softball
	Track	Tennis
		Track

MONTCLAIR STATE UNIVERSITY

Normal Avenue	**Men**	**Women**
Upper Montclair, NJ 07043	Baseball	Basketball
Affiliation—NCAA *III*	Basketball	Cheerleading
Nickname—*Red Hawks*	Cross Country	Cross Country
Athletic Director—	Football	Field Hockey
(973) 655-5234	Golf	Lacrosse
	Lacrosse	Skiing
	Soccer	Soccer
	Swimming	Softball
	Tennis	Swimming
	Track	Tennis
	Wrestling	Track
		Volleyball

NEW JERSEY, COLLEGE OF

PO Box 7718	**Men**	**Women**
Ewing, NJ 08628-0718	Baseball	Basketball
Affiliation—NCAA *III*	Basketball	Cross Country
Nickname—*Lions*	Cross Country	Field Hockey
Athletic Director—	Football	Lacrosse
(609) 771-2230	Golf	Soccer
	Soccer	Softball
	Swimming	Swimming
	Tennis	Tennis
	Track	Track
	Wrestling	

NEW JERSEY CITY UNIVERSITY

2039 John F. Kennedy	**Men**	**Women**
Boulevard	Baseball	Basketball
Jersey City, NJ 07305-1537	Basketball	Cross Country
Affiliation—NCAA *III*	Football	Soccer
Nickname—*Gothic Knights*	Soccer	Softball
Athletic Director—	Tennis	Track
(201) 200-3317	Volleyball	Volleyball

NEW JERSEY INSTITUTE OF TECHNOLOGY

80 Lock Street	Men	Women
Newark, NJ 07103-3507	Baseball	Basketball
Affiliation—NCAA II	Basketball	Cheerleading
Nickname—Highlanders	Fencing	Fencing
Athletic Director—	Soccer	Soccer
(973) 596-5727	Swimming	Swimming
	Tennis	Tennis
	Volleyball	

NORTHEASTERN BIBLE COLLEGE

12 Oak Lane	Men	Women
Essex Fells, NJ 07021-1004	Baseball	Basketball
Affiliation—NCCAA	Basketball	Softball
Nickname—Lancers	Golf	Volleyball
Athletic Director—	Soccer	
(973) 226-1074		

PRINCETON UNIVERSITY

PO Box 71, Jadwin Gym	Men	Women
Princeton, NJ 08544-0071	Baseball	Basketball
Affiliation—NCAA I	Basketball	Crew
(I-AA Football)	Crew	Cross Country
Nickname—Tigers	Cross Country	Diving
Athletic Director—	Diving	Fencing
(609) 258-3534	Fencing	Field Hockey
	Football	Golf
	Golf	Ice Hockey
	Ice Hockey	Lacrosse
	Lacrosse	Soccer
	Soccer	Softball
	Squash	Squash
	Swimming	Swimming
	Tennis	Tennis
	Track	Track
	Volleyball	Volleyball
	Water Polo	
	Wrestling	

RAMAPO COLLEGE OF NEW JERSEY

505 Ramapo Valley Road	**Men**	**Women**
Mahwah, NJ 07430-1623	Baseball	Basketball
Affiliation—NCAA III	Basketball	Cheerleading
Nickname—Roadrunners	Cross Country	Cross Country
Athletic Director—	Soccer	Soccer
(201) 529-7683	Tennis	Softball
	Track	Tennis
	Volleyball	Track
		Volleyball

RICHARD STOCKTON COLLEGE OF NEW JERSEY

PO Box 195, Jim Leeds Road	**Men**	**Women**
Pomona, NJ 08240	Baseball	Basketball
Affiliation—NCAA III	Basketball	Crew
Nickname—Ospreys	Cross Country	Cross Country
Athletic Director—	Lacrosse	Soccer
(609) 652-4217	Soccer	Softball
	Track	Track
		Volleyball

RIDER UNIVERSITY

2083 Lawrenceville Road	**Men**	**Women**
Lawrenceville, NJ 08648-3001	Baseball	Basketball
Affiliation—NCAA I	Basketball	Cross Country
Nickname—Broncs	Cross Country	Diving
Athletic Director—	Diving	Field Hockey
(609) 896-5338	Golf	Soccer
	Soccer	Softball
	Swimming	Swimming
	Tennis	Tennis
	Track	Track
	Wrestling	Volleyball

ROWMAN UNIVERSITY

201 Mullica Hill Road	**Men**	**Women**
Glassboro, NJ 08028-1701	Baseball	Basketball
Affiliation—NCAA *III*	Basketball	Cross Country
Nickname—Profs	Cross Country	Field Hockey
Athletic Director—	Football	Lacrosse
(609) 256-4676	Soccer	Soccer
	Swimming	Softball
	Track	Swimming
		Track
		Volleyball

RUTGERS, THE STATE UNIVERSITY OF NEW JERSEY

83 Rockefeller Road	**Men**	**Women**
Piscataway, NJ 08854-8053	Baseball	Basketball
Affiliation—NCAA *I*	Basketball	Cheerleading
(I-A Football)	Crew	Crew
Nickname—Scarlet Knights	Cross Country	Cross Country
Athletic Director—	Diving	Diving
(732) 445-8610	Fencing	Fencing
	Football	Field Hockey
	Golf	Golf
	Lacrosse	Gymnastics
	Soccer	Lacrosse
	Swimming	Soccer
	Tennis	Softball
	Track	Swimming
	Wrestling	Tennis
		Track
		Volleyball

RUTGERS UNIVERSITY, CAMDEN

3rd and Linden Street	**Men**	**Women**
Camden, NJ 08102	Baseball	Basketball
Affiliation—NCAA *III*	Basketball	Cross Country
Nickname—Scarlet Raptors	Cross Country	Soccer
Athletic Director—	Golf	Softball
(609) 225-6193	Soccer	Swimming
	Swimming	Track
	Track	Volleyball

RUTGERS UNIVERSITY, NEWARK

	Men	Women
Golden Dome Athletic Center,	Baseball	Basketball
42 Warren	Basketball	Softball
Newark, NJ 07102	Soccer	Tennis
Affiliation—NCAA III	Tennis	Volleyball
(Div. I Volleyball)	Volleyball	
Nickname—Scarlet Raiders		
Athletic Director—		
(973) 353-5474 ext. 203		

SAINT ELIZABETH, COLLEGE OF

	Women	
2 Convent Road	Basketball	Swimming
Morristown, NJ 07960-6989	Equestrian	Tennis
Affiliation—NCAA III	Soccer	Volleyball
Nickname—Eagles	Softball	
Athletic Director—		
(973) 290-4207		

SAINT PETE'S COLLEGE

	Men	Women
2641 John F. Kennedy	Baseball	Basketball
Boulevard	Basketball	Cheerleading
Jersey City, NJ 07306-5943	Bowling	Cross Country
Affiliation—NCAA I	Cross Country	Soccer
(I-AA Football)	Football	Softball
Nickname—Peacocks	Golf	Swimming
Athletic Director—	Soccer	Tennis
(201) 915-9098	Swimming	Track
	Tennis	Volleyball
	Track	

SETON HALL UNIVERSITY

	Men	Women
400 S. Orange Avenue	Baseball	Basketball
South Orange, NJ 07079-2646	Basketball	Cross Country
Affiliation—NCAA I	Cross Country	Diving
Nickname—Pirates	Diving	Soccer
Athletic Director—	Golf	Softball
(973) 761-9498	Soccer	Swimming
	Swimming	Tennis
	Tennis	Track
	Track	Volleyball
	Wrestling	

STEVENS INSTITUTE OF TECHNOLOGY

Castle on Houston	**Men**	**Women**
Hoboken, NJ 07030	Baseball	Basketball
Affiliation—NCAA III	Basketball	Cheerleading
Nickname—Ducks	Cross Country	Cross Country
Athletic Director—	Fencing	Fencing
(201) 216-5688	Lacrosse	Soccer
	Soccer	Swimming
	Swimming	Tennis
	Tennis	Track
	Track	Volleyball
	Volleyball	

WILLIAM PATERSON UNIVERSITY

300 Pompton Road	**Men**	**Women**
Wayne, NJ 07470-2103	Baseball	Basketball
Affiliation—NCAA III	Basketball	Cross Country
Nickname—Pioneers	Cross Country	Diving
Athletic Director—	Diving	Field Hockey
(973) 720-2356	Football	Soccer
	Soccer	Softball
	Swimming	Swimming
	Track	Track
	Volleyball	Volleyball

NEW MEXICO

EASTERN NEW MEXICO UNIVERSITY

Greyhound Arena, Station 17	**Men**	**Women**
Portales, NM 88130	Baseball	Basketball
Affiliation—NCAA II	Basketball	Cross Country
Nickname—Greyhounds	Cross Country	Softball
Athletic Director—	Football	Tennis
(505) 562-2121		Volleyball

NEW MEXICO, UNIVERSITY OF

South Campus
Albuquerque, NM 87131
Affiliation—NCAA I
  (I-A Football)
Nickname—Lobos
Athletic Director—
  (505) 925-5500

Men	Women
Baseball	Basketball
Basketball	Cross Country
Cross Country	Golf
Football	Skiing
Golf	Soccer
Gymnastics	Softball
Skiing	Swimming
Soccer	Tennis
Swimming	Track
Tennis	Volleyball
Track	
Wrestling	

NEW MEXICO HIGHLANDS UNIVERSITY

Athletic Department Field
  House
Las Vegas, NM 87701
Nickname—Cowboys
Athletic Director—
  (505) 454-3351

Men	Women
Baseball	Basketball
Basketball	Cross Country
Cross Country	Soccer
Football	Softball
	Volleyball

NEW MEXICO STATE UNIVERSITY

Box 30001, MSC 3145
Las Cruces, NM 88003-8001
Affiliation—NCAA I
  (I-A Football)
Nickname—Aggies
Athletic Director—
  (505) 646-1211

Men	Women
Baseball	Basketball
Basketball	Cross Country
Football	Diving
Golf	Golf
Tennis	Softball
	Swimming
	Tennis
	Track
	Volleyball

SOUTHWEST, COLLEGE OF THE

6610 N. Lovington Highway
Hobbs, NM 88240-9120
Affiliation—NAIA
Nickname—Mustangs
Athletic Director—
  (505) 392-6561

Men	Women
Baseball	Soccer
	Volleyball

WESTERN NEW MEXICO UNIVERSITY

	Men	Women
1000 W. College Avenue	Basketball	Basketball
Silver City, NM 88061-4158	Football	Golf
Affiliation—NCAA II	Golf	Softball
Nickname—Mustangs	Tennis	Tennis
Athletic Director—		Volleyball
(505) 538-6233		

NEW YORK

ADELPHI UNIVERSITY

	Men	Women
South Avenue	Baseball	Basketball
Garden City, NY 11530	Basketball	Cheerleading
Affiliation—NCAA II	Cross Country	Cross Country
(Div. I Soccer)	Golf	Soccer
Nickname—Panthers	Lacrosse	Softball
Athletic Director—	Soccer	Swimming
(516) 877-4231	Swimming	Tennis
	Tennis	Volleyball

ALBANY COLLEGE OF PHARMACY OF UNION UNIVERSITY

	Men	Women
106 New Scotland Avenue	Golf	Basketball
Albany, NY 12208	Soccer	Golf
Nickname—Panthers		Soccer
Athletic Director—		
(518) 445-3157		

ALFRED UNIVERSITY

	Men	Women
McLane Center	Basketball	Basketball
Alfred, NY 14802	Cross Country	Cross Country
Affiliation—NCAA III	Football	Field Hockey
Nickname—Saxons	Golf	Lacrosse
Athletic Director—	Lacrosse	Skiing
(607) 871-2193	Skiing	Soccer
	Soccer	Softball
	Swimming	Swimming
	Tennis	Tennis
	Track	Track
		Volleyball

BARD COLLEGE

Stevenson Gymnasium	Men	Women
Annandale On Hudson	Basketball	Basketball
Red Hook, NY 12571	Cross Country	Cross Country
Affiliation—NCAA III	Fencing	Fencing
Nickname—Raptors	Soccer	Soccer
Athletic Director—	Squash	Tennis
(914) 758-7528	Tennis	Volleyball

BARUCH COLLEGE

17 Lexington Avenue	Men	Women
New York, NY 10010-5518	Baseball	Basketball
Affiliation—NCAA III	Basketball	Cross Country
Nickname—Statesmen	Karate	Tennis
Athletic Director—	Tennis	Volleyball
(212) 387-1270	Volleyball	

CANSIUS COLLEGE

2001 Main Street	Men	Women
Buffalo, NY 14208-1035	Baseball	Basketball
Affiliation—NCAA I	Basketball	Cheerleading
(I-AA Football)	Cross Country	Crew
Nickname—Golden Griffins	Football	Cross Country
Athletic Director—	Golf	Lacrosse
(716) 888-2984	Ice Hockey	Rifle
	Lacrosse	Soccer
	Rifle	Softball
	Soccer	Swimming
	Tennis	Synchronized
	Track	Swimming
		Tennis
		Track
		Volleyball

CAZENOVIA COLLEGE

Lincklaen Street	Men	Women
Cazenovia, NY 13035	Baseball	Basketball
Affiliation—NCAA III	Basketball	Cheerleading
Nickname—Wildcats	Crew	Crew
Athletic Director—	Equestrian	Soccer
(315) 655-7142	Golf	Softball
	Soccer	Tennis
	Tennis	Volleyball

CLARKSON UNIVERSITY

Box 5830, Alumni Gym	**Men**	**Women**
Potsdam, NY 13699-5830	Baseball	Basketball
Affiliation—NCAA III	Basketball	Cross Country
(Div. I Hockey)	Cross Country	Lacrosse
Nickname—Golden Knights	Diving	Skiing
Athletic Director—	Golf	Soccer
(315) 268-6616	Ice Hockey	Swimming
	Lacrosse	Tennis
	Skiing	Volleyball
	Soccer	
	Swimming	
	Tennis	

COLGATE UNIVERSITY

13 Oak Drive	**Men**	**Women**
Hamilton, NY 13346-1338	Basketball	Basketball
Affiliation—NCAA I	Cross Country	Cheerleading
(I-AA Football)	Football	Cross Country
Nickname—Red Raiders	Golf	Diving
Athletic Director—	Ice Hockey	Field Hockey
(315) 228-7611	Lacrosse	Ice Hockey
	Soccer	Lacrosse
	Swimming	Soccer
	Tennis	Softball
	Track	Swimming
		Tennis
		Track
		Volleyball

COLUMBIA UNIVERSITY

Dodge Physical Fitness Center	**Men**	**Women**
3030 Broadway	Baseball	Archery
New York, NY 10027	Basketball	Basketball
Affiliation—NCAA I	Crew	Crew
(I-AA Football)	Cross Country	Cross Country
Nickname—Lions	Fencing	Diving
Athletic Director—	Football	Fencing
(212) 854-2537	Golf	Field Hockey
	Soccer	Lacrosse
	Swimming	Soccer
	Tennis	Swimming
	Track	Tennis
	Wrestling	Track
		Volleyball

CONCORDIA COLLEGE

171 White Plains Road	**Men**	**Women**
Bronxville, NY 10708-1923	Baseball	Basketball
Affiliation—NCAA II	Basketball	Soccer
Nickname—Clippers	Soccer	Softball
Athletic Director—	Tennis	Tennis
(914) 337-9300 ext. 2450	Volleyball	Volleyball

COOPER UNION, THE

30 Cooper Square, 6th Floor	**Men**
New York, NY 10003	Fencing
Nickname—Pioneers	
Athletic Director—	
(212) 353-4131	

CORNELL UNIVERSITY

Teagle Hall, Campus Road	**Men**	**Women**
Ithaca, NY 14853	Baseball	Basketball
Affiliation—NCAA I	Basketball	Crew
(I-AA Football)	Crew	Cross Country
Nickname—Big Red	Cross Country	Equestrian
Athletic Director—	Diving	Fencing
(607) 255-7265	Football	Field Hockey
	Golf	Golf
	Ice Hockey	Gymnastics
	Lacrosse	Ice Hockey
	Soccer	Lacrosse
	Swimming	Soccer
	Tennis	Softball
	Track	Swimming
	Wrestling	Tennis
		Track
		Volleyball
		Water Polo

DAEMEN COLLEGE

4380 Main Street	**Men**	**Women**
Amherst, NY 14226-3544	Basketball	Basketball
Affiliation—NAIA I		Volleyball
Nickname—Warriors		
Athletic Director—		
(716) 839-8346		

D'YOUVILLE COLLEGE

College Center, Porter Avenue	**Men**	**Women**
One D'Youville Square	Baseball	Basketball
Buffalo, NY 14201	Basketball	Cross Country
Affiliation—NSCAA, NCAA II	Cross Country	Golf
Nickname—Spartans	Golf	Softball
Athletic Director—	Volleyball	Volleyball
(716) 881-7789		

DOMINICAN COLLEGE

470 Western Highway	**Men**	**Women**
Orangeburg, NY 10962-1210	Baseball	Basketball
Affiliation—NAIA II	Basketball	Cheerleading
Nickname—Chargers	Cross Country	Soccer
Athletic Director—	Golf	Softball
(914) 398-3008	Soccer	Volleyball

DOWLING COLLEGE

150 Idle Hour Boulevard	**Men**	**Women**
Oakdale, NY 11769-1906	Baseball	Basketball
Affiliation—NCAA II	Basketball	Cheerleading
Nickname—Golden Lions	Crew	Crew
Athletic Director—	Golf	Softball
(516) 244-3317	Lacrosse	Tennis
	Soccer	Volleyball
	Tennis	

ELMIRA COLLEGE

One Park Place	**Men**	**Women**
Elmira, NY 14901-2085	Basketball	Basketball
Affiliation—NCAA III	Golf	Cheerleading
Nickname—Soaring Eagles	Ice Hockey	Field Hockey
Athletic Director—	Lacrosse	Lacrosse
(607) 735-1730	Soccer	Soccer
	Tennis	Softball
		Tennis
		Volleyball

FORDHAM UNIVERSITY

441 S. Fordham Road, Rose Hill
Bronx, NY 10458-5149
*Affiliation—*NCAA *I*
(I-AA Football)
Nickname—Rams
Athletic Director—
(718) 817-4300

Men	Women
Baseball	Basketball
Basketball	Cheerleading
Cross Country	Cross Country
Football	Rowing
Golf	Soccer
Soccer	Softball
Squash	Swimming
Swimming	Tennis
Tennis	Track
Track	Volleyball
Water Polo	

HAMILTON COLLEGE

198 College Hill Road
Clinton, NY 13323-1218
*Affiliation—*NCAA *III*
Nickname—Continentals
Athletic Director—
(315) 859-4114

Men	Women
Baseball	Basketball
Basketball	Crew
Crew	Cross Country
Cross Country	Diving
Diving	Field Hockey
Football	Golf
Golf	Ice Hockey
Ice Hockey	Lacrosse
Lacrosse	Soccer
Soccer	Softball
Squash	Squash
Swimming	Swimming
Tennis	Tennis
Track	Track
	Volleyball

HARTWICK COLLEGE

Binder Physical Education Center *Oneonta, NY 13820* *Affiliation—*NCAA *III* *(Div. I Soccer)* *Nickname—Hawks* *Athletic Director—* *(607) 431-4702*	**Men** Baseball Basketball Cross Country Diving Football Golf Lacrosse Soccer Swimming Tennis Track	**Women** Basketball Cheerleading Cross Country Field Hockey Golf Lacrosse Soccer Softball Swimming Tennis Track Volleyball

HILBERT COLLEGE

5200 S. Park Avenue *Hamburg, NY 14075-1519* *Affiliation—*NCAA *III* *Nickname—Hawks* *Athletic Director—* *(716) 649-7900 ext. 233*	**Men** Baseball Basketball Golf Soccer	**Women** Basketball Soccer Softball Volleyball

HOBART COLLEGE

300 Pulteney Street *Geneva, NY 14456-3304* *Affiliation—*NCAA *III* *Nickname—Statesmen* *Athletic Director—* *(315) 781-3565*	**Men** Basketball Crew Cross Country Football Golf	Ice Hockey Lacrosse Soccer Squash Tennis

HOFSTRA UNIVERSITY

Physical Fitness Center *Hempstead, NY 11549* *Affiliation—*NCAA *I* *(I-AA Football)* *Nickname—Flying Dutchmen* *Athletic Director—* *(516) 463-6753*	**Men** Baseball Basketball Cross Country Football Golf Lacrosse Soccer Tennis Wrestling	**Women** Basketball Cross Country Field Hockey Lacrosse Soccer Softball Tennis Volleyball

HOUGHTON COLLEGE

1 Willard Avenue	Men	Women
Houghton, NY 14744	Basketball	Basketball
Affiliation—NAIA I	Cross Country	Cross Country
Nickname—Highlanders	Soccer	Field Hockey
Athletic Director—	Track	Soccer
(716) 567-9645		Track

HUNTER COLLEGE OF THE CITY UNIVERSITY OF NEW YORK

695 Park Avenue	Men	Women
New York, NY 10021-5024	Basketball	Basketball
Affiliation—NCAA III	Cross Country	Cross Country
Nickname—Hawks	Fencing	Fencing
Athletic Director—	Soccer	Soccer
(212) 772-4783	Tennis	Softball
	Track	Swimming
	Volleyball	Tennis
	Wrestling	Track
		Volleyball

IONA COLLEGE

715 North Avenue	Men	Women
New Rochelle, NY 10801-1830	Baseball	Basketball
Affiliation—NCAA I	Basketball	Crew
(I-AA Football)	Crew	Cross Country
Nickname—Gaels	Cross Country	Soccer
Athletic Director—	Football	Softball
(914) 633-2311	Golf	Swimming
	Ice Hockey	Tennis
	Soccer	Track
	Swimming	Volleyball
	Tennis	
	Track	

ITHACA COLLEGE

Ceracche Athletics Center	**Men**	**Women**
Ithaca, NY 14650	Baseball	Basketball
*Affiliation—*NCAA *III*	Basketball	Crew
Nickname—Bombers	Crew	Cross Country
Athletic Director—	Cross Country	Diving
˙(607) 274-3209	Diving	Field Hockey
	Football	Gymnastics
	Lacrosse	Lacrosse
	Soccer	Soccer
	Swimming	Softball
	Tennis	Swimming
	Track	Tennis
		Track
		Volleyball

JOHN JAY COLLEGE OF CRIMINAL JUSTICE

899 10th Avenue	**Men**	**Women**
New York, NY 10019-1029	Baseball	Basketball
*Affiliation—*NCAA *III*	Basketball	Cross Country
Nickname—Bloodhounds	Cross Country	Rifle
Athletic Director—	Rifle	Softball
(212) 237-8000	Soccer	Swimming
	Swimming	Tennis
	Tennis	Volleyball
	Volleyball	

KEUKA COLLEGE

Weed Physical Arts Center	**Men**	**Women**
Keuka Park, NY 14478	Baseball	Basketball
*Affiliation—*NCAA *III*	Basketball	Soccer
Nickname—Warriors	Lacrosse	Synchronized
Athletic Director—	Soccer	Swimming
(315) 536-4111 ext. 5246		Volleyball

LE MOYNE COLLEGE

Springfield Road	**Men**	**Women**
Syracuse, NY 13214	Baseball	Basketball
Affiliation—NCAA *II*	Basketball	Cross Country
(Div. 1 Baseball)	Cross Country	Lacrosse
Nickname—*Dolphins*	Golf	Soccer
Athletic Director—	Lacrosse	Softball
(315) 445-4414	Soccer	Swimming
	Swimming	Tennis
	Tennis	Volleyball

LEHMAN COLLEGE

250 Bedford Park Boulevard W	**Men**	**Women**
Bronx, NY 10468-1527	Baseball	Basketball
Affiliation—NCAA *III*	Basketball	Cheerleading
Nickname—*Lighting*	Cross Country	Cross Country
Athletic Director—	Swimming	Softball
(718) 960-1117	Tennis	Swimming
	Track	Tennis
	Volleyball	Track
	Water Polo	Volleyball

LONG ISLAND UNIVERSITY, BROOKLYN CAMPUS

1 University Plaza	**Men**	**Women**
Brooklyn, NY 11201	Baseball	Basketball
Affiliation—NCAA *I*	Basketball	Cheerleading
Nickname—*Blackbirds*	Cross Country	Cross Country
Athletic Director—	Golf	Soccer
(718) 488-1030	Soccer	Softball
	Track	Tennis
		Track
		Volleyball

LONG ISLAND UNIVERSITY, C.W. POST CAMPUS

Post Campus,	**Men**	**Women**
720 Northern Boulevard	Baseball	Basketball
Brookville, NY 11548	Basketball	Cross Country
Affiliation—NCAA *II*	Cross Country	Field Hockey
Nickname—*Pioneers*	Football	Soccer
Athletic Director—	Lacrosse	Softball
(516) 299-2289	Soccer	Tennis
	Track	Track
		Volleyball

LONG ISLAND UNIVERSITY, SOUTHAMPTON CAMPUS

239 Montauk Highway	**Men**	**Women**
Southampton, NY 11968	Basketball	Basketball
Affiliation—NCAA II	Lacrosse	Soccer
Nickname—Colonials	Soccer	Softball
Athletic Director—	Tennis	Volleyball
(516) 287-8385	Volleyball	

MANHATTAN COLLEGE

Manhattan College Parkway	**Men**	**Women**
Riverdale, NY 10471	Baseball	Basketball
Affiliation—NCAA I	Basketball	Crew
Nickname—Jaspers	Crew	Cross Country
Athletic Director—	Cross Country	Lacrosse
(718) 862-8000	Golf	Soccer
	Lacrosse	Softball
	Soccer	Swimming
	Tennis	Tennis
		Track
		Volleyball

MANHATTANVILLE COLLEGE

2900 Purchase Street	**Men**	**Women**
Purchase, NY 10577-2103	Baseball	Basketball
Affiliation—NCAA III	Basketball	Equestrian
Nickname—Valiants	Golf	Field Hockey
Athletic Director—	Lacrosse	Lacrosse
(914) 323-5281	Soccer	Soccer
	Tennis	Softball
		Swimming
		Tennis
		Volleyball

MARIST COLLEGE

North Road	**Men**	**Women**
Poughkeepsie, NY 12601	Baseball	Basketball
Affiliation—NCAA *I*	Basketball	Crew
(I-AA Football)	Crew	Cross Country
Nickname—*Red Foxes*	Cross Country	Lacrosse
Athletic Director—	Football	Soccer
(914) 575-3304	Ice Hockey	Softball
	Lacrosse	Swimming
	Soccer	Tennis
	Swimming	Track
	Tennis	Volleyball
	Track	

MARYMOUNT COLLEGE

100 Marymount Avenue	**Women**	
Tarrytown, NY 10591	Basketball	Swimming
Nickname—*Saints*	Riding	Tennis
Athletic Director—	Softball	
(914) 332-8333		

MEDGAR EVERS COLLEGE

1150 Carroll Street	**Men**	**Women**
Brooklyn, NY 11225-2201	Basketball	Basketball
Affiliation—NCAA *III*	Cross Country	Cross Country
Nickname—*Cougars*	Soccer	Softball
Athletic Director—	Track	Track
(718) 270-6402		

MERCY COLLEGE

555 Broadway	**Men**	**Women**
Dobbs Ferry, NY 10522-1134	Baseball	Basketball
Affiliation—NCAA *II*	Basketball	Cross Country
Nickname—*Flyers*	Cross Country	Golf
Athletic Director—	Golf	Softball
(914) 674-7220	Soccer	Volleyball
	Tennis	

MOLLOY COLLEGE

1000 Hempstead Avenue	**Men**	**Women**
Rockville Centre,	Baseball	Basketball
NY 11570-1100	Basketball	Cheerleading
Affiliation—NCAA II	Cross Country	Cross Country
Nickname—Lions	Soccer	Equestrian
Athletic Director—		Soccer
(516) 256-2207		Softball
		Tennis
		Volleyball

MOUNT SAINT MARY COLLEGE

330 Powell Avenue	**Men**	**Women**
Newburgh, NY 12550-3412	Baseball	Basketball
Affiliation—NCAA III	Basketball	Soccer
Nickname—Knights	Soccer	Softball
Athletic Director—	Swimming	Swimming
(914) 569-3592	Tennis	Tennis
		Volleyball

MOUNT SAINT VINCENT, COLLEGE OF

Riverdale Avenue and 263rd	**Men**	**Women**
Street	Basketball	Basketball
Bronx, NY 10471	Cross Country	Cross Country
Affiliation—NCAA III	Tennis	Soccer
Nickname—Dolphins	Volleyball	Softball
Athletic Director—		Swimming
(718) 405-3410		Tennis
		Track
		Volleyball

NAZARETH COLLEGE

4245 East Avenue	**Men**	**Women**
Rochester, NY 14618	Basketball	Basketball
Affiliation—NCAA III	Diving	Cheerleading
Nickname—Golden Flyers	Golf	Field Hockey
Athletic Director—	Lacrosse	Golf
(716) 389-2195	Soccer	Lacrosse
	Swimming	Soccer
	Tennis	Swimming
		Tennis
		Volleyball

NEW ROCHELLE, COLLEGE OF

Castle Place	**Women**	
New Rochelle, NY 10805	Basketball	Tennis
Affiliation—NCAA III	Softball	Volleyball
Nickname—Blue Angels	Swimming	
Athletic Director—		
(914) 654-5315		

NEW YORK, CITY COLLEGE OF

138th Street and Convent	**Men**	**Women**
Avenue	Basketball	Basketball
New York, NY 10031	Cross Country	Cheerleading
Affiliation—NCAA III	Lacrosse	Cross Country
Nickname—Beavers	Soccer	Fencing
Athletic Director—	Tennis	Tennis
(212) 650-8230	Track	Track
	Volleyball	Volleyball

NEW YORK INSTITUTE OF TECHNOLOGY

PO Box 8000	**Men**	**Women**
Old Westbury, NY 11568-8000	Baseball	Basketball
Affiliation—NCAA II	Basketball	Cross Country
Nickname—Bears	Cross Country	Soccer
Athletic Director—	Lacrosse	Softball
(516) 686-7626	Soccer	Track
	Track	Volleyball

NEW YORK UNIVERSITY

Jerome S. Coles Sports Center	**Men**	**Women**
181 Mercer Street	Basketball	Basketball
New York, NY 10012-5499	Cross Country	Cheerleading
Affiliation—NCAA III	Diving	Cross Country
Nickname—Violets	Fencing	Diving
Athletic Director—	Golf	Fencing
(212) 998-2030	Soccer	Soccer
	Swimming	Swimming
	Tennis	Tennis
	Track	Track
	Volleyball	Volleyball
	Wrestling	

NIAGARA UNIVERSITY

PO Box 2009	Men	Women
Niagara University,	Baseball	Basketball
NY 14109-2009	Basketball	Cheerleading
Affiliation—NCAA I	Cross Country	Cross Country
Nickname—*Purple Eagles*	Golf	Ice Hockey
Athletic Director—	Ice Hockey	Lacrosse
(716) 286-8600	Soccer	Soccer
	Swimming	Softball
	Tennis	Swimming
		Tennis
		Volleyball

NYACK COLLEGE

1 S. Boulevard	Men	Women
Nyack, NY 10960-3604	Baseball	Basketball
Affiliation—NAIA II, NCCAA I	Basketball	Cross Country
Nickname—*The Purple Pride*	Cross Country	Soccer
Athletic Director—	Soccer	Softball
(914) 358-1710 ext. 181		Volleyball

PACE UNIVERSITY

861 Bedford Road	Men	Women
Pleasantville, NY 10570-2700	Baseball	Basketball
Affiliation—NCAA II	Basketball	Cheerleading
(Div. I Baseball)	Cross Country	Cross Country
Nickname—*Setters*	Football	Soccer
Athletic Director—	Lacrosse	Softball
(914) 773-3481	Tennis	Tennis
	Track	Track
		Volleyball

POLYTECHNIC UNIVERSITY

333 Jay Street	Men	Women
Brooklyn, NY 11201-2907	Baseball	Cross Country
Affiliation—NCAA III	Basketball	Judo
Nickname—*Blue Jays*	Cross Country	Tennis
Athletic Director—	Judo	Volleyball
(718) 637-5910	Soccer	
	Tennis	
	Volleyball	

PRACTICAL BIBLE COLLEGE

	Men	Women
PO Box 601 *Bible School Park,* *NY 13737-0601* *Affiliation—NCCAA II* *Nickname—Swordsmen* *Athletic Director—* *(607) 729-1581*	Basketball Soccer	Basketball

PRATT INSTITUTE

	Men	Women
200 Willoughby Avenue *Brooklyn, NY 11205-3817* *Affiliation—NCAA III* *Nickname—Cannoneers* *Athletic Director—* *(718) 636-3771*	Basketball Cross Country Soccer Tennis Track	Cross Country Soccer Tennis Track Volleyball

QUEENS COLLEGE

	Men	Women
65-30 Kissena Boulevard *Flushing, NY 11367-1575* *Affiliation—NCAA II* *Nickname—Knights* *Athletic Director—* *(718) 997-2770*	Baseball Basketball Cross Country Golf Swimming Tennis Track Volleyball Water Polo	Basketball Cross Country Soccer Softball Swimming Tennis Track Volleyball Water Polo

RENSSELAER POLYTECHNIC INSTITUTE

	Men	Women
AS&RC, 110 8th Street *Troy, NY 12180* *Affiliation—NCAA III* *Nickname—Engineers* *Athletic Director—Men* *(518) 276-6685* *Athletic Director—Women* *(518) 276-6257*	Baseball Basketball Cross Country Football Golf Ice Hockey Lacrosse Soccer Swimming Tennis Track	Basketball Cross Country Field Hockey Ice Hockey Lacrosse Soccer Softball Swimming Tennis Track

ROBERTS WESLEYAN COLLEGE

	Men	Women
2301 Westside Drive	Basketball	Basketball
Rochester, NY 14624-1933	Cross Country	Cross Country
Affiliation—NCCAA I, NAIA	Soccer	Soccer
Nickname—Raiders	Track	Track
Athletic Director—		Volleyball
(716) 594-6130		

ROCHESTER, UNIVERSITY OF

	Men	Women
Alumni Gymnasium	Baseball	Basketball
Rochester, NY 14627	Basketball	Cross Country
Affiliation—NCAA III	Cross Country	Field Hockey
Nickname—Yellowjackets	Football	Lacrosse
Athletic Director—	Golf	Soccer
(716) 275-4301	Soccer	Swimming
	Squash	Tennis
	Swimming	Track
	Tennis	Volleyball
	Track	

ROCHESTER INSTITUTE OF TECHNOLOGY

	Men	Women
51 Lomb Memorial Drive	Baseball	Basketball
Rochester, NY 14623-5603	Basketball	Cheerleading
Affiliation—NCAA III	Crew	Crew
Nickname—Tigers	Cross Country	Cross Country
Athletic Director—	Ice Hockey	Ice Hockey
(716) 475-2614	Lacrosse	Lacrosse
	Soccer	Soccer
	Swimming	Softball
	Tennis	Swimming
	Track	Tennis
	Wrestling	Track
		Volleyball

RUSSELL SAGE COLLEGE

	Women	
Robison Athletic & Recreation	Basketball	Tennis
Center, 45 Ferry Street	Soccer	Volleyball
Troy, NY 12180	Softball	
Affiliation—NCAA III		
Nickname—Gators		
Athletic Director—		
(518) 244-2274		

SAINT BONAVENTURE UNIVERSITY

PO Box G	**Men**	**Women**
Saint Bonaventure,	Baseball	Basketball
NY 14778-2287	Basketball	Cross Country
Affiliation—NCAA I	Cross Country	Soccer
Nickname—Bonnies	Golf	Softball
Athletic Director—	Soccer	Swimming
(716) 375-2282	Swimming	Tennis
	Tennis	Volleyball
	Volleyball	

SAINT FRANCIS COLLEGE

180 Remsen Street	**Men**	**Women**
Brooklyn, NY 11201-4305	Baseball	Basketball
Affiliation—NCAA I	Basketball	Cross Country
Nickname—Terriers	Cross Country	Softball
Athletic Director—	Soccer	Swimming
(718) 489-5365	Swimming	Tennis
	Tennis	Track
	Track	Volleyball
	Water Polo	Water Polo

SAINT JOHN'S UNIVERSITY

8000 Utopia Parkway	**Men**	**Women**
Jamaica, NY 11432-1335	Baseball	Basketball
Affiliation—NCAA I	Basketball	Cross Country
(I-AA Football)	Cross Country	Diving
Nickname—Red Storm	Fencing	Fencing
Athletic Director—	Football	Soccer
(718) 990-6224	Golf	Softball
	Soccer	Swimming
	Swimming	Tennis
	Tennis	Track
	Track	Volleyball

SAINT JOHN FISHER COLLEGE

3690 East Avenue	**Men**	**Women**
Rochester, NY 14618	Baseball	Basketball
Affiliation—NCAA III	Basketball	Cheerleading
Nickname—Cardinals	Cross Country	Cross Country
Athletic Director—	Football	Lacrosse
(716) 385-8309	Golf	Soccer
	Soccer	Softball
	Tennis	Tennis
		Volleyball

SAINT JOSEPH'S COLLEGE

245 Clinton Avenue	**Men**	**Women**
Brooklyn, NY 11205-3602	Basketball	Basketball
Nickname—Bears	Cross Country	Cross Country
Athletic Director—		Softball
(718) 636-6811		Volleyball

SAINT JOSEPHS COLLEGE

155 Roe Boulevard	**Men**	**Women**
Patchogue, NY 11772	Baseball	Basketball
Affiliation—NCAA III	Basketball	Cross Country
Nickname—Golden Eagles	Soccer	Equestrian
Athletic Director—	Tennis	Soccer
(516) 447-3290		Softball
		Tennis
		Volleyball

SAINT LAWRENCE UNIVERSITY

Park Street	**Men**	**Women**
Canton, NY 13517	Baseball	Basketball
Affiliation—NCAA III	Basketball	Cross Country
Nickname—Saints	Cross Country	Diving
Athletic Director—	Diving	Field Hockey
(315) 229-5877	Football	Ice Hockey
	Ice Hockey	Lacrosse
	Lacrosse	Riding
	Skiing	Skiing
	Soccer	Soccer
	Swimming	Swimming
	Tennis	Tennis
	Track	Volleyball

SAINT ROSE, THE COLLEGE OF

432 Western Avenue	**Men**	**Women**
Albany, NY 12203-1419	Baseball	Basketball
*Affiliation—*NCAA *II*	Basketball	Cheerleading
Nickname—Golden Knights	Cross Country	Cross Country
Athletic Director—	Soccer	Soccer
(518) 454-5282	Swimming	Softball
		Swimming
		Volleyball

SAINT THOMAS AQUINAS

125 Route 340	**Men**	**Women**
Sparkill, NY 10976-1041	Baseball	Basketball
*Affiliation—*NAIA *II*	Basketball	Soccer
Nickname—Spartans	Cross Country	Softball
Athletic Director—	Golf	Volleyball
(914) 398-4058	Soccer	

SARAH LAWRENCE

1 Mead Way	**Men**	**Women**
Bronxville, NY 10708-5931	Crew	Crew
Nickname—Gryphons	Cross Country	Cross Country
Athletic Director—	Equestrian	Equestrian
(914) 395-2560	Tennis	Tennis
		Volleyball

SIENA COLLEGE

515 Loudon Road	**Men**	**Women**
Loudonville, NY 12211-1459	Baseball	Basketball
*Affiliation—*NCAA *I*	Basketball	Cross Country
(I-AA Football)	Cross Country	Field Hockey
Nickname—Saints	Football	Golf
Athletic Director—	Golf	Lacrosse
(518) 783-2551	Lacrosse	Soccer
	Soccer	Softball
	Tennis	Tennis
		Volleyball

SKIDMORE COLLEGE

N. Broadway	**Men**	**Women**
Saratoga, NY 12866	Baseball	Basketball
Affiliation—NCAA *III*	Basketball	Crew
Nickname—Thoroughbreds	Crew	Field Hockey
Athletic Director—	Golf	Lacrosse
(518) 580-5370	Ice Hockey	Riding
	Lacrosse	Soccer
	Riding	Softball
	Soccer	Swimming
	Swimming	Tennis
	Tennis	Volleyball

STATE UNIVERSITY OF NEW YORK, ALBANY

1400 Washington Avenue	**Men**	**Women**
Albany, NY 12222-0100	Baseball	Basketball
Affiliation—NCAA *II*	Basketball	Cross Country
Nickname—Great Danes	Cross Country	Field Hockey
Athletic Director—	Football	Golf
(518) 442-2562	Lacrosse	Lacrosse
	Soccer	Soccer
	Track	Softball
		Tennis
		Track
		Volleyball

STATE UNIVERSITY OF NEW YORK, BINGHAMTON

PO Box 6000	**Men**	**Women**
Binghamton, NY 13902-6000	Baseball	Basketball
Affiliation—NCAA *II*	Basketball	Cross Country
Nickname—Colonials	Cross Country	Soccer
Athletic Director—	Golf	Softball
(607) 777-4255	Soccer	Swimming
	Tennis	Tennis
	Track	Track
	Wrestling	Volleyball

STATE UNIVERSITY OF NEW YORK, BUFFALO

	Men	Women
PO Box 605000, Alumni Arena	Basketball	Basketball
Buffalo, NY 14260-5000	Cross Country	Crew
Affiliation—NCAA I	Diving	Cross Country
(I-AA Football)	Football	Diving
Nickname—Bulls	Track	Soccer
Athletic Director—	Wrestling	Swimming
(716) 645-3445		Tennis
		Track
		Volleyball

STATE UNIVERSITY OF NEW YORK, NEW PALTZ

	Men	Women
Elting Gymnasium	Baseball	Basketball
New Paltz, NY 12561	Basketball	Cross Country
Affiliation—NCAA III	Cross Country	Lacrosse
Nickname—Hawks	Soccer	Soccer
Athletic Director—	Swimming	Softball
(914) 257-3910	Tennis	Swimming
	Volleyball	Tennis
		Volleyball

STATE UNIVERSITY OF NEW YORK, OSWEGO

	Men	Women
Route 104	Baseball	Basketball
Oswego, NY 13126	Basketball	Cross Country
Affiliation—NCAA III	Cross Country	Field Hockey
Nickname—Lakers	Diving	Lacrosse
Athletic Director—	Golf	Soccer
(315) 341-2378	Ice Hockey	Softball
	Lacrosse	Swimming
	Soccer	Tennis
	Swimming	Track
	Tennis	Volleyball
	Track	
	Wrestling	

STATE UNIVERSITY OF NEW YORK, STONY BROOK

USB Sports Center	Men	Women
Stony Brook, NY 11794	Baseball	Basketball
Affiliation—NCAA II	Basketball	Cross Country
(Div. I Lacrosse)	Cross Country	Diving
Nickname—Seawolves	Diving	Golf
Athletic Director—	Football	Soccer
(516) 632-7205	Lacrosse	Softball
	Soccer	Swimming
	Swimming	Tennis
	Tennis	Track
	Track	Volleyball

STATE UNIVERSITY OF NEW YORK COLLEGE AT BROCKPORT

350 New Campus Drive	Men	Women
Brockport, NY 14420-2989	Baseball	Basketball
Affiliation—NCAA III	Basketball	Cheerleading
Nickname—Golden Eagles	Cross Country	Cross Country
Athletic Director—	Football	Field Hockey
(716) 395-2579	Ice Hockey	Golf
	Soccer	Gymnastics
	Swimming	Lacrosse
	Track	Soccer
	Wrestling	Softball
		Swimming
		Tennis
		Track
		Volleyball

STATE UNIVERSITY OF NEW YORK COLLEGE AT BUFFALO

1300 Elmwood Avenue	Men	Women
Buffalo, NY 14222-1004	Basketball	Basketball
Affiliation—NCAA III	Cross Country	Cheerleading
Nickname—Bengals	Football	Cross Country
Athletic Director—	Ice Hockey	Lacrosse
(716) 878-6534	Soccer	Soccer
	Swimming	Softball
	Track	Swimming
		Tennis
		Track
		Volleyball

STATE UNIVERSITY OF NEW YORK
COLLEGE AT CORTLAND

Pashley Drive	**Men**	**Women**
Cortland, NY 13045	Baseball	Basketball
*Affiliation—*NCAA *III*	Basketball	Cross Country
Nickname—Red Dragons	Cross Country	Field Hockey
Athletic Director—	Football	Gymnastics
(607) 753-4953	Ice Hockey	Lacrosse
	Lacrosse	Soccer
	Soccer	Softball
	Swimming	Swimming
	Tennis	Tennis
	Wrestling	Track
		Volleyball

STATE UNIVERSITY OF NEW YORK
COLLEGE AT FREDONIA

Dods Hall	**Men**	**Women**
Fredonia, NY 14063	Baseball	Basketball
*Affiliation—*NCAA *III*	Basketball	Cheerleading
Nickname—Blue Devils	Cross Country	Cross Country
Athletic Director—	Ice Hockey	Lacrosse
(716) 673-3102	Soccer	Soccer
	Tennis	Softball
	Track	Tennis
		Track
		Volleyball

STATE UNIVERSITY OF NEW YORK
COLLEGE AT GENESEO

1 College Circle	**Men**	**Women**
Geneseo, NY 14454-1401	Basketball	Basketball
*Affiliation—*NCAA *III*	Cross Country	Cross Country
Nickname—Knights	Ice Hockey	Field Hockey
Athletic Director—	Lacrosse	Lacrosse
(716) 245-5345	Soccer	Soccer
	Swimming	Softball
	Track	Swimming
		Tennis
		Track
		Volleyball

STATE UNIVERSITY OF NEW YORK
COLLEGE AT OLD WESTBURY

PO Box 210	Men	Women
Old Westbury, NY 11568-0210	Baseball	Basketball
Affiliation—NCAA III	Basketball	Cross Country
Nickname—Panthers	Cross Country	Soccer
Athletic Director—	Soccer	Softball
(516) 876-3241	Tennis	Tennis
	Volleyball	Volleyball

STATE UNIVERSITY OF NEW YORK
COLLEGE AT ONEONTA

Ravine Parkway	Men	Women
Oneonta, NY 13820	Baseball	Basketball
Affiliation—NCAA III	Basketball	Cross Country
Nickname—Red Dragons	Cross Country	Field Hockey
Athletic Director—	Lacrosse	Lacrosse
(607) 436-3594	Soccer	Soccer
	Tennis	Softball
	Wrestling	Swimming
		Tennis
		Volleyball

STATE UNIVERSITY OF NEW YORK
COLLEGE AT PLATTSBURGH

101 Broad Street	Men	Women
Plattsburgh, NY 12901-2681	Basketball	Basketball
Affiliation—NCAA III	Cross Country	Cross Country
Nickname—Cardinals	Golf	Golf
Athletic Director—	Ice Hockey	Soccer
(518) 564-3140	Lacrosse	Softball
	Soccer	Swimming
	Swimming	Tennis
	Track	Track
		Volleyball

STATE UNIVERSITY OF NEW YORK
COLLEGE AT POTSDAM

Maxcy Hall	Men	Women
Potsdam, NY 13676	Basketball	Basketball
Affiliation—NCAA III	Diving	Cheerleading
Nickname—Bears	Ice Hockey	Diving
Athletic Director—	Lacrosse	Equestrian
(315) 267-2314	Soccer	Lacrosse
	Swimming	Soccer
		Swimming
		Tennis
		Volleyball

STATE UNIVERSITY COLLEGE
OF NEW YORK AT PURCHASE

Lincoln Avenue	Men	Women
Purchase, NY 10577	Basketball	Volleyball
Nickname—Panthers		
Athletic Director—		
(914) 251-6537		

STATE UNIVERSITY OF NEW YORK INSTITUTE OF
TECHNOLOGY, UTICA/ROME

PO Box 3050	Men	Women
Utica, NY 13504-3050	Baseball	Basketball
Affiliation—NCAA III	Basketball	Soccer
Nickname—Wildcats	Bowling	Softball
Athletic Director—	Golf	Tennis
(315) 792-7521	Soccer	Volleyball
	Tennis	

STATE UNIVERSITY OF NEW YORK MARITIME COLLEGE

6 Pennyfield Avenue	Men	Women
Bronx, NY 10465	Baseball	Basketball
Affiliation—NCAA III	Basketball	Crew
Nickname—Privateers	Crew	Cross Country
Athletic Director—	Cross Country	Rifle
(718) 409-7330	Lacrosse	Softball
	Rifle	Swimming
	Sailing	Volleyball
	Soccer	
	Swimming	
	Tennis	
	Wrestling	

STATEN ISLAND, COLLEGE OF

2800 Victory Boulevard
Staten Island, NY 10314-6609
Affiliation—NCAA III
Nickname—Dolphins
Athletic Director—
  (718) 982-3160

Men	Women
Baseball	Basketball
Basketball	Softball
Soccer	Swimming
Swimming	Tennis
Tennis	Volleyball

SYRACUSE UNIVERSITY

Manley Field House
Syracuse, NY 13244
Affiliation—NCAA I
  (I-A Football)
Nickname—Orangemen
Athletic Director—
  (315) 443-2385

Men	Women
Basketball	Basketball
Crew	Crew
Cross Country	Cross Country
Diving	Field Hockey
Football	Lacrosse
Lacrosse	Soccer
Soccer	Softball
Swimming	Swimming
Track	Tennis
Wrestling	Track
	Volleyball

UNION COLLEGE

Alumni Gym
Schenectady, NY 12308
Affiliation—NCAA III
  (Div. I Hockey)
Nickname—Dutchmen
Athletic Director—
  (518) 388-6284

Men	Women
Baseball	Basketball
Basketball	Crew
Crew	Cross Country
Cross Country	Diving
Diving	Field Hockey
Football	Lacrosse
Ice Hockey	Soccer
Lacrosse	Softball
Soccer	Swimming
Swimming	Tennis
Tennis	Track
Track	Volleyball

UNITED STATES MERCHANT MARINE ACADEMY

O'Hara Hall, Steamboat Road	**Men**	**Women**
Kings Point, NY 11024	Baseball	Basketball
Affiliation—NCAA III	Basketball	Crew
Nickname—Mariners	Crew	Pistol
Athletic Director—	Cross Country	Rifle
(516) 773-5454	Football	Sailing
	Golf	Softball
	Lacrosse	Swimming
	Pistol	Tennis
	Rifle	Track
	Sailing	Volleyball
	Soccer	
	Swimming	
	Tennis	
	Track	
	Volleyball	
	Water Polo	
	Wrestling	

UNITED STATES MILITARY ACADEMY

639 Howard Road	**Men**	**Women**
West Point, NY 10996	Baseball	Basketball
Affiliation—NCAA I	Basketball	Cross Country
(I-A Football)	Cross Country	Diving
Nickname—Black Knights,	Diving	Rifle
Army	Football	Soccer
Athletic Director—	Golf	Softball
(914) 938-3701	Gymnastics	Swimming
	Ice Hockey	Tennis
	Lacrosse	Track
	Rifle	Volleyball
	Soccer	
	Swimming	
	Tennis	
	Track	
	Wrestling	

UTICA COLLEGE OF SYRACUSE UNIVERSITY

1600 Burrstone Campus	**Men**	**Women**
Utica, NY 13502	Baseball	Cheerleading
Affiliation—NCAA *III*	Basketball	Cross Country
Nickname—*Pioneers*	Cross Country	Soccer
Athletic Director—	Golf	Softball
(315) 792-3051	Soccer	Swimming
	Swimming	Tennis
	Tennis	Volleyball

VASSAR COLLEGE

Box 259, 124 Raymond Avenue	**Men**	**Women**
Poughkeepsie, NY 12604-0259	Baseball	Basketball
Affiliation—NCAA *III*	Basketball	Crew
Nickname—*Brewers*	Crew	Cross Country
Athletic Director—	Cross Country	Diving
(914) 437-7452	Diving	Fencing
	Fencing	Field Hockey
	Lacrosse	Lacrosse
	Soccer	Soccer
	Squash	Swimming
	Swimming	Tennis
	Tennis	Track
	Track	Volleyball
	Volleyball	

WAGNER COLLEGE

One Campus Road	**Men**	**Women**
Staten Island, NY 10301-4428	Baseball	Basketball
Affiliation—NCAA *I*	Basketball	Cheerleading
(I-AA Football)	Cross Country	Cross Country
Nickname—*Seahawks*	Football	Golf
Athletic Director—	Golf	Lacrosse
(718) 390-3488	Ice Hockey	Soccer
	Lacrosse	Softball
	Tennis	Swimming
	Track	Tennis
	Wrestling	Track
		Volleyball

WELLS COLLEGE

PO Box 500	**Women**	
Aurora, NY 13026-0500	Field Hockey	Swimming
Affiliation—NCAA III	Lacrosse	Tennis
Nickname—The Express	Soccer	
Athletic Director—		
(315) 364-3410		

WILLIAM SMITH COLLEGE

Winn-Seeley Gymnastics,	**Women**	
300 Pulteney Street	Basketball	Sailing
Geneva, NY 14456	Crew	Soccer
Affiliation—NCAA III	Cross Country	Squash
Nickname—Herons	Field Hockey	Swimming
Athletic Director—	Lacrosse	Tennis
(315) 781-3500		

YESHIVA UNIVERSITY

500 W. 185th Street	**Men**	**Women**
New York, NY 10033-3201	Basketball	Basketball
Affiliation—NCAA III	Cross Country	Fencing
Nickname—Maccabees	Fencing	Tennis
Athletic Director—	Golf	
(212) 960-5211	Tennis	
	Track	
	Volleyball	
	Wrestling	

YORK COLLEGE OF THE CITY UNIVERSITY OF NEW YORK

94-20 Guy Brewer Boulevard	**Men**	**Women**
Jamaica, NY 11451	Basketball	Basketball
Affiliation—NCAA III	Cross Country	Cheerleading
Nickname—Cardinals	Soccer	Cross Country
Athletic Director—	Tennis	Tennis
(718) 262-5104	Track	Track
	Volleyball	Volleyball

NORTH CAROLINA

APPALACHIAN STATE UNIVERSITY

Owens Fieldhouse	**Men**	**Women**
Boone, NC 28608	Baseball	Basketball
Affiliation—NCAA I	Basketball	Cross Country
(I-AA Football)	Cross Country	Field Hockey
Nickname—Mountaineers	Football	Golf
Athletic Director—	Golf	Soccer
(828) 262-4010	Soccer	Tennis
	Tennis	Track
	Track	Volleyball
	Wrestling	

BARBER-SCOTIA COLLEGE

145 Cabarrus Avenue	**Men**	**Women**
Concord, NC 28025	Basketball	Basketball
Affiliation—NAIA I	Cross Country	Cross Country
Nickname—Sabers	Tennis	Softball
Athletic Director—	Track	Tennis
(704) 789-2900		Track
		Volleyball

BARTON COLLEGE

PO Box 5000	**Men**	**Women**
Wilson, NC 27893	Baseball	Basketball
Affiliation—NCAA II	Basketball	Cross Country
Nickname—Bulldogs	Cross Country	Soccer
Athletic Director—	Golf	Softball
(252) 399-6514	Soccer	Tennis
	Tennis	Volleyball

BELMONT ABBY COLLEGE

100 Belmont Mount Holly Road	**Men**	**Women**
Belmont, NC 28012-2702	Baseball	Basketball
Affiliation—NCAA II	Basketball	Cross Country
Nickname—Crusaders	Cross Country	Soccer
Athletic Director—	Golf	Softball
(704) 825-6809	Soccer	Tennis
	Tennis	Volleyball

BENNETT COLLEGE

900 E. Washington Street
Greensboro, NC 27402
Nickname—Bennett Belles
Athletic Director—
(910) 370-8710

Women	
Basketball	Volleyball

BREVARD COLLEGE

400 N. Broad Street
Brevard, NC 28712-3306
Affiliation—NJCAA/NAIA
Nickname—Tornadoes
Athletic Director—
(828) 884-8228

Men	Women
Baseball	Basketball
Basketball	Cross Country
Cross Country	Soccer
Golf	Softball
Soccer	Tennis
Tennis	Track
	Volleyball

CAMPBELL UNIVERSITY

PO Box 10, 217 Pope Street
Buies Creek, NC 27506-0010
Affiliation—NCAA I
Nickname—Fighting Camels
Athletic Director—
(910) 893-1326

Men	Women
Baseball	Basketball
Basketball	Cheerleading
Cross Country	Cross Country
Golf	Golf
Soccer	Soccer
Tennis	Softball
Track	Tennis
Wrestling	Track
	Volleyball

CATAWBA COLLEGE

W. Innes Street
Salisbury, NC 28144
Affiliation—NCAA II
Nickname—Indians
Athletic Director—
(704) 637-4474

Men	Women
Baseball	Basketball
Basketball	Cheerleading
Cross Country	Cross Country
Football	Field Hockey
Golf	Soccer
Lacrosse	Softball
Soccer	Swimming
Tennis	Tennis
	Volleyball

CHOWAN COLLEGE

PO Box 1848, Jones Drive	Men	Women
Murfreesboro, NC 27855	Baseball	Basketball
Affiliation—NCAA *III*	Basketball	Cross Country
Nickname—*Braves*	Football	Softball
Athletic Director—	Golf	Tennis
(919) 398-6273	Soccer	Volleyball
	Tennis	

DAVIDSON COLLEGE

PO Box 1750, 200 Baker Drive	Men	Women
Davidson, NC 28036-1750	Baseball	Basketball
Affiliation—NCAA *I*	Basketball	Cross Country
(I-AA Football)	Cross Country	Field Hockey
Nickname—*Wildcats*	Football	Lacrosse
Athletic Director—	Golf	Soccer
(704) 892-2373	Soccer	Swimming
	Swimming	Tennis
	Tennis	Track
	Track	Volleyball
	Wrestling	

DUKE UNIVERSITY

PO Box 90555	Men	Women
Cameron Indoor Stadium	Baseball	Basketball
Durham, NC 27708-0555	Basketball	Crew
Affiliation—NCAA *I*	Cross Country	Cross Country
(I-A Football)	Fencing	Fencing
Nickname—*Blue Devils*	Football	Field Hockey
Athletic Director—	Golf	Golf
(919) 684-2431	Lacrosse	Lacrosse
	Soccer	Soccer
	Swimming	Swimming
	Tennis	Tennis
	Track	Track
	Wrestling	Volleyball

EAST CAROLINA UNIVERSITY

Ficklen Drive	**Men**	**Women**
Greenville, NC 27858	Baseball	Basketball
Affiliation—NCAA *I*	Basketball	Cheerleading
(I-A Football)	Cross Country	Cross Country
Nickname—*Pirates*	Diving	Diving
Athletic Director—	Football	Soccer
(252) 328-4501	Golf	Softball
	Soccer	Swimming
	Swimming	Tennis
	Tennis	Track
	Track	Volleyball

EAST COAST BIBLE COLLEGE

6900 Wilkenson Boulevard	**Men**	**Women**
Charlotte, NC 28214-3100	Basketball	Basketball
Affiliation—NCCAA		
Athletic Director—		
(704) 394-2307		

ELIZABETH CITY STATE UNIVERSITY

1704 Weeksville Road	**Men**	**Women**
Elizabeth City, NC 27909-7806	Baseball	Basketball
Affiliation—NCAA *II*	Basketball	Cheerleading
Nickname—*Vikings*	Cross Country	Cross Country
Athletic Director—	Football	Golf
(252) 335-3229	Golf	Softball
	Track	Track
	Volleyball	Volleyball

ELON COLLEGE

2500 Campus Box	**Men**	**Women**
Elon College, NC 27244-2010	Baseball	Basketball
Affiliation—NCAA *II*	Basketball	Cross Country
Nickname—*Fightin' Christians*	Cross Country	Golf
Athletic Director—	Football	Soccer
(336) 584-2420	Golf	Softball
	Soccer	Tennis
	Tennis	Volleyball

FAYETTEVILLE STATE UNIVERSITY

	Men	Women
Newbold Station	**Men**	**Women**
1200 Murcheason Road	Basketball	Basketball
Fayetteville, NC 28301	Cross Country	Cross Country
Affiliation—NCAA II	Football	Softball
Nickname—Broncos	Golf	Volleyball
Athletic Director—		
(910) 486-1314		

GARDNER-WEBB UNIVERSITY

	Men	Women
Main Street	**Men**	**Women**
Boiling Springs, NC 28017	Baseball	Basketball
Affiliation—NCAA II	Basketball	Cheerleading
Nickname—Runnin' Bulldogs	Cross Country	Cross Country
Athletic Director—	Football	Golf
(704) 434-4342	Golf	Soccer
	Soccer	Softball
	Tennis	Tennis
	Wrestling	Volleyball

GREENSBORO COLLEGE

	Men	Women
815 W. Market Street	**Men**	**Women**
Greensboro, NC 27401-1823	Baseball	Basketball
Affiliation—NCAA III	Basketball	Cheerleading
Nickname—The Pride	Cross Country	Cross Country
Athletic Director—	Football	Lacrosse
(336) 272-7102 ext. 250	Golf	Soccer
	Lacrosse	Swimming
	Soccer	Tennis
	Tennis	Volleyball

GUILFORD COLLEGE

	Men	Women
5800 W. Friendly Avenue	**Men**	**Women**
Greensboro, NC 27410-4108	Baseball	Basketball
Affiliation—NCAA III	Basketball	Lacrosse
Nickname—Quakers	Football	Soccer
Athletic Director—	Golf	Tennis
(336) 316-2158	Lacrosse	Volleyball
	Soccer	
	Tennis	

HIGH POINT UNIVERSITY

University Station,	Men	Women
Montlieu Avenue	Baseball	Basketball
High Point, NC 27262	Basketball	Cross Country
Affiliation—NCAA I, NCAA II	Cross Country	Soccer
Nickname—Panthers	Golf	Tennis
Athletic Director—	Soccer	Track
(336) 841-9105	Tennis	Volleyball
	Track	

JOHNSON C. SMITH UNIVERSITY

100 Beatties Ford Road	Men	Women
Charlotte, NC 28216-5302	Baseball	Basketball
Affiliation—NCAA II	Basketball	Cheerleading
Nickname—Golden Bulls	Cross Country	Cross Country
Athletic Director—	Football	Golf
(704) 378-1209	Golf	Softball
	Tennis	Tennis
	Track	Track
	Volleyball	Volleyball

LEES-MCRAE COLLEGE

PO Box 128	Men	Women
Banner Elk, NC 28604-0128	Basketball	Basketball
Affiliation—NCAA II	Cross Country	Cross Country
Nickname—Bobcats	Golf	Skiing
Athletic Director—	Lacrosse	Soccer
(828) 898-8725	Skiing	Softball
	Soccer	Tennis
	Tennis	Volleyball

LENOIR-RHYNE COLLEGE

PO Box 7356	Men	Women
Hickory, NC 28603-7356	Baseball	Basketball
Affiliation—NCAA II	Basketball	Cross Country
Nickname—Bears	Cross Country	Golf
Athletic Director—	Football	Soccer
(828) 328-7128	Golf	Softball
	Soccer	Tennis
	Tennis	Volleyball

LIVINGSTONE COLLEGE

701 W. Monroe Street	**Men**	**Women**
Salisbury, NC 28144-5213	Basketball	Basketball
Affiliation—NCAA II	Cross Country	Cross Country
Nickname—Fighting Blue Bears	Football	Track
Athletic Director—	Track	Volleyball
(704) 638-5723	Volleyball	

MARS HILL COLLEGE

Bailey Street	**Men**	**Women**
Mars Hill, NC 28754	Baseball	Basketball
Affiliation—NCAA II	Basketball	Cross Country
Nickname—Lions	Cross Country	Soccer
Athletic Director—	Football	Softball
(828) 689-1215	Golf	Swimming
	Lacrosse	Tennis
	Soccer	Track
	Tennis	Volleyball
	Track	

MEREDITH COLLEGE

3800 Hillsborough Street	**Women**	
Raleigh, NC 27611	Basketball	Tennis
Affiliation—NCAA III	Soccer	Volleyball
Nickname—Angels	Softball	
Athletic Director—		
(919) 829-8311		

METHODIST COLLEGE

5400 Ramsey Street	**Men**	**Women**
Fayetteville, NC 28311-1420	Baseball	Basketball
Affiliation—NCAA III	Basketball	Cheerleading
Nickname—Monarchs	Cross Country	Cross Country
Athletic Director—	Football	Golf
(910) 630-7182	Golf	Soccer
	Soccer	Softball
	Tennis	Tennis
	Track	Track
		Volleyball

MONTREAT COLLEGE

405 Assembly Drive, Box 1267	**Men**	**Women**
Montreat, NC 28757	Baseball	Basketball
Affiliation—NAIA I, II	Basketball	Cross Country
Nickname—Cavaliers	Cross Country	Soccer
Athletic Director—	Golf	Softball
(828) 669-8011 ext. 3401	Soccer	Tennis
	Tennis	Volleyball

MOUNT OLIVE COLLEGE

634 Henderson Street	**Men**	**Women**
Mount Olive, NC 28365-1263	Baseball	Basketball
Affiliation—NCAA II	Basketball	Cross Country
Nickname—Trojans	Cross Country	Soccer
Athletic Director—	Golf	Softball
(919) 658-5056	Soccer	Tennis
	Tennis	Volleyball

NORTH CAROLINA, UNIVERSITY OF, ASHEVILLE

1 University Heights	**Men**	**Women**
Asheville, NC 28804-3251	Baseball	Basketball
Affiliation—NCAA I	Basketball	Cross Country
Nickname—Bulldogs	Cross Country	Soccer
Athletic Director—	Soccer	Tennis
(828) 251-6929	Tennis	Track
	Track	Volleyball

NORTH CAROLINA, UNIVERSITY OF, CHAPEL HILL

PO Box 2126	**Men**	**Women**
Chapel Hill, NC 27515-2126	Baseball	Basketball
Affiliation—NCAA I	Basketball	Crew
(I-A Football)	Cross Country	Cross Country
Nickname—Tar Heels	Fencing	Fencing
Athletic Director—	Football	Golf
(919) 962-6000	Golf	Gymnastics
	Lacrosse	Lacrosse
	Soccer	Soccer
	Swimming	Softball
	Tennis	Swimming
	Track	Tennis
	Volleyball	Track
	Wrestling	Volleyball

NORTH CAROLINA, UNIVERSITY OF, CHARLOTTE

9201 University City Boulevard	**Men**	**Women**
Charlotte, NC 28223	Baseball	Basketball
Affiliation—NCAA I	Basketball	Cross Country
Nickname—49ers	Cross Country	Soccer
Athletic Director—	Golf	Softball
(704) 547-4937	Soccer	Tennis
	Tennis	Track
	Track	Volleyball

NORTH CAROLINA, UNIVERSITY OF, GREENSBORO

PO Box 26168	**Men**	**Women**
337 HHP Building,	Baseball	Basketball
1500 Walker Road	Basketball	Cross Country
Greensboro, NC 27402-6168	Cross Country	Golf
Affiliation—NCAA I	Golf	Soccer
Nickname—Spartans	Soccer	Softball
Athletic Director—	Tennis	Tennis
(336) 334-5649	Track	Track
	Wrestling	Volleyball

NORTH CAROLINA, UNIVERSITY OF, PEMBROKE

1 University Drive	**Men**	**Women**
Pembroke, NC 28372	Baseball	Basketball
Affiliation—NCAA II	Basketball	Cross Country
Nickname—Braves	Cross Country	Softball
Athletic Director—	Football	Tennis
(910) 521-6334	Golf	Track
	Soccer	Volleyball
	Track	
	Wrestling	

NORTH CAROLINA, UNIVERSITY OF, WILMINGTON

	Men	Women
601 S. College Road	Baseball	Basketball
Wilmington, NC 28403-3201	Basketball	Cheerleading
Affiliation—NCAA I	Cross Country	Cross Country
Nickname—Seahawks	Diving	Diving
Athletic Director—	Golf	Golf
(910) 962-3230	Soccer	Soccer
	Swimming	Softball
	Tennis	Swimming
	Track	Tennis
		Track
		Volleyball

NORTH CAROLINA A&T STATE UNIVERSITY

	Men	Women
Corbett Sports Center	Baseball	Basketball
160 E. Market Street,	Basketball	Bowling
Moore Gym, Room 107	Cross Country	Cheerleading
Greensboro, NC 27411	Football	Cross Country
Affiliation—NCAA I	Tennis	Softball
(I-AA Football)	Track	Swimming
Nickname—Aggies		Tennis
Athletic Director—		Track
(336) 334-7686		Volleyball

NORTH CAROLINA CENTRAL UNIVERSITY

	Men	Women
18011 Fayetteville Street	Basketball	Basketball
Durham, NC 27707-3129	Cross Country	Cheerleading
Affiliation—NCAA II	Football	Cross Country
Nickname—Eagles	Golf	Softball
Athletic Director—	Tennis	Tennis
(919) 560-5427	Track	Track
		Volleyball

NORTH CAROLINA STATE UNIVERSITY

	Men	Women
Box 8501, Case Athletics Center	Baseball	Basketball
Raleigh, NC 27695-8501	Basketball	Cross Country
*Affiliation—*NCAA *I*	Cross Country	Diving
(I-A Football)	Football	Gymnastics
Nickname—Wolfpack	Golf	Soccer
Athletic Director—	Rifle	Swimming
(919) 515-2109	Soccer	Tennis
	Swimming	Track
	Tennis	Volleyball
	Track	
	Wrestling	

NORTH CAROLINA WESLEYAN

	Men	Women
3400 N. Wesleyan Boulevard	Baseball	Basketball
Rocky Mount, NC 27804-8677	Basketball	Soccer
*Affiliation—*NCAA *III*	Golf	Softball
Nickname—Battling Bishops	Soccer	Tennis
Athletic Director—	Tennis	Volleyball
(252) 985-5214		

PEACE COLLEGE

	Women	
15 E. Peace Street	Basketball	Volleyball
Raleigh, NC 27604	Tennis	
*Affiliation—*NCAA *III*		
Nickname—Pride		
Athletic Director—		
(919) 508-2223		

PFEIFFER UNIVERSITY

	Men	Women
Highway 52	Baseball	Basketball
Misenheimer, NC 28109	Basketball	Cross Country
*Affiliation—*NCAA *II*	Cross Country	Lacrosse
Nickname—Falcons	Golf	Soccer
Athletic Director—	Lacrosse	Softball
(704) 463-1360 ext. 2407	Soccer	Swimming
	Tennis	Tennis
		Volleyball

PIEDMONT BAPTIST COLLEGE

716 Franklin Street	**Men**	**Women**
Winston-Salem, NC 27101-5133	Basketball	Basketball
Affiliation—NCCAA II		Volleyball
Nickname—Conquerors		
Athletic Director—		
(336) 725-8344		

QUEENS COLLEGE

1900 Selwyn Avenue	**Men**	**Women**
Charlotte, NC 28274	Basketball	Basketball
Affiliation—NCAA II	Golf	Soccer
Nickname—Royals	Soccer	Softball
Athletic Director—	Tennis	Tennis
(704) 337-2510		Volleyball

ROANOKE BIBLE COLLEGE

714 1st Street	**Men**	**Women**
Elizabeth City, NC 27909-3926	Basketball	Basketball
Nickname—Flames	Golf	Volleyball
Athletic Director—	Volleyball	
(252) 334-2005		

SAINT ANDREWS PRESBYTERIAN COLLEGE

1700 Dogwood Mile Street	**Men**	**Women**
Laurinburg, NC 28352-5521	Baseball	Basketball
Affiliation—NCAA II	Basketball	Cross Country
Nickname—Knights	Cross Country	Equestrian
Athletic Director—	Equestrian	Soccer
(910) 277-5274	Golf	Softball
	Lacrosse	Tennis
	Soccer	Volleyball
	Tennis	
	Volleyball	

SAINT AUGUSTINE'S COLLEGE

1315 Oakwood Avenue	Men	Women
Raleigh, NC 27610-2247	Baseball	Basketball
Affiliation—NCAA II	Basketball	Cross Country
Nickname—Falcons	Cross Country	Golf
Athletic Director—	Golf	Softball
(919) 516-4171	Soccer	Tennis
	Tennis	Track
	Track	Volleyball
	Volleyball	

SALEM COLLEGE

601 S. Church Street	Women	
Winston-Salem, NC 27108	Cross Country	Swimming
Nickname—Spirits	Equestrian	Tennis
Athletic Director—	Field Hockey	Volleyball
(336) 721-2733	Soccer	

SHAW UNIVERSITY

118 E. South Street	Men	Women
Raleigh, NC 27601-2341	Baseball	Basketball
Affiliation—NCAA II	Basketball	Cross Country
Nickname—Bears	Cross Country	Softball
Athletic Director—	Tennis	Track
(919) 546-8281	Track	Volleyball

WAKE FOREST UNIVERSITY

PO Box 7265	Men	Women
Winston-Salem, NC 27109-7265	Baseball	Basketball
Affiliation—NCAA I	Basketball	Cheerleading
(I-A Football)	Cross Country	Cross Country
Nickname—Demon Deacons	Football	Field Hockey
Athletic Director—	Golf	Golf
(336) 758-5616	Soccer	Soccer
	Tennis	Tennis
	Track	Track
		Volleyball

WARREN WILSON COLLEGE

PO Box 9000,	Men	Women
701 Warren Wilson Road	Basketball	Basketball
Asheville, NC 28815-9000	Cross Country	Cheerleading
Nickname—Owls	Diving	Cross Country
Athletic Director—	Soccer	Diving
(704) 298-3325 ext. 270	Swimming	Soccer
		Swimming

WESTERN CAROLINA UNIVERSITY

Ramsey Center	Men	Women
Cullowhee, NC 28723	Baseball	Basketball
Affiliation—NCAA I	Basketball	Cross Country
(I-AA Football)	Cross Country	Golf
Nickname—Catamounts	Football	Tennis
Athletic Director—	Golf	Track
(828) 227-7338	Track	Volleyball

WINGATE UNIVERSITY

PO Box 3054, Camden Road	Men	Women
Wingate, NC 28174-0159	Baseball	Basketball
Affiliation—NCAA II	Basketball	Cross Country
Nickname—Bulldogs	Cross Country	Soccer
Athletic Director—	Football	Softball
(704) 233-8194	Golf	Swimming
	Lacrosse	Tennis
	Soccer	Volleyball
	Swimming	
	Tennis	

WINSTON-SALEM STATE UNIVERSITY

Station A, 601 Martin Luther	Men	Women
King Jr. Drive	Basketball	Basketball
Winston-Salem, NC 27102	Cross Country	Cheerleading
Affiliation—NCAA II	Football	Cross Country
Nickname—Rams	Tennis	Softball
Athletic Director—	Track	Tennis
(336) 750-2142		Track
		Volleyball

NORTH DAKOTA

DICKENSON STATE UNIVERSITY

291 Campus Drive
Dickinson, ND 58601-4853
Affiliation—NAIA II
Nickname—Blue Hawks
Athletic Director—
    (701) 227-2159

Men
Baseball
Basketball
Cross Country
Football
Golf
Tennis
Track
Wrestling

Women
Basketball
Cross Country
Golf
Softball
Tennis
Track
Volleyball

JAMESTOWN COLLEGE

PO Box 6088
Jamestown, ND 58402
Affiliation—NAIA II
Nickname—Jimmies
Athletic Director—
    (701) 252-3467 ext. 2445

Men
Baseball
Basketball
Cross Country
Football
Golf
Track
Wrestling

Women
Basketball
Cross Country
Softball
Track
Volleyball

MARY, UNIVERSITY OF

7500 University Drive
Bismarck, ND 58504-9658
Affiliation—NAIA II
Nickname—Marauders
Athletic Director—
    (701) 255-7500 ext. 376

Men
Baseball
Basketball
Cross Country
Football
Soccer
Tennis
Track
Wrestling

Women
Basketball
Cross Country
Soccer
Softball
Tennis
Track
Volleyball

MAYVILLE STATE UNIVERSITY

330 3rd Street NE
Mayville, ND 58257-1217
Affiliation—NAIA II
Nickname—Cornets
Athletic Director—
    (701) 786-4839

Men
Baseball
Basketball
Football

Women
Basketball
Softball
Volleyball

MINOT STATE UNIVERSITY

500 *University Avenue W* *Minot, ND 58707* *Affiliation*—NAIA *II* *Nickname*—*Beavers* *Athletic Director*— *(701) 858-3042*	**Men** Baseball Basketball Cross Country Football Tennis Track	**Women** Basketball Cross Country Golf Softball Tennis Track Volleyball

NORTH DAKOTA, UNIVERSITY OF

Box 9013, 2nd Avenue *Grand Forks, ND 58202* *Affiliation*—NCAA *II* *(Div. I Hockey)* *Nickname*—*Fighting Sioux* *Athletic Director*— *(701) 777-2234*	**Men** Baseball Basketball Cross Country Football Golf Ice Hockey Swimming Track Wrestling	**Women** Basketball Cross Country Golf Softball Swimming Tennis Track Volleyball

NORTH DAKOTA STATE UNIVERSITY

Bison Sports Arena, 16th *Avenue & University Drive N* *Fargo, ND 58105-5600* *Affiliation*—NCAA *II* *Nickname*—*Bison* *Athletic Director*—*Men* *(701) 231-8985* *Athletic Director*—*Women* *(701) 231-7807*	**Men** Baseball Basketball Cross Country Football Golf Track Wrestling	**Women** Basketball Cheerleading Cross Country Golf Soccer Softball Track Volleyball

TRINITY BIBLE COLLEGE

50 South 6th Avenue *Ellendale, ND 58436* *Affiliation*—NCCAA, NCAA *II* *Nickname*—*Lions* *Athletic Director*— *(701) 349-5777*	**Men** Basketball Cross Country Football Track Volleyball	**Women** Basketball Cross Country Track Volleyball

VALLEY CITY STATE UNIVERSITY

	Men	Women
101 College Street SW	Baseball	Basketball
Valley City, ND 58072-4024	Basketball	Cross Country
Affiliation—NAIA II	Cross Country	Softball
Nickname—Vikings	Football	Track
Athletic Director—	Track	Volleyball
(701) 845-7161	Wrestling	

OHIO

AKRON, UNIVERSITY OF

	Men	Women
JAR *Arena*	Baseball	Basketball
Akron, OH 44325-5201	Basketball	Cross Country
Affiliation—NCAA I	Cross Country	Rifle
(I-A Football)	Football	Softball
Nickname—Zips	Golf	Swimming
Athletic Director—	Rifle	Tennis
(330) 972-7080	Soccer	Volleyball
	Track	

ASHLAND UNIVERSITY

	Men	Women
401 College Boulevard	Baseball	Basketball
Ashland, OH 44805-3702	Basketball	Cheerleading
Affiliation—NCAA II	Cross Country	Cross Country
Nickname—Eagles	Football	Soccer
Athletic Director—	Golf	Softball
(419) 289-5959	Soccer	Swimming
	Swimming	Tennis
	Tennis	Track
	Track	Volleyball
	Wrestling	

BALDWIN-WALLACE COLLEGE

	Men	Women
275 Eastland Road	Baseball	Basketball
Berea, OH 44017-2005	Basketball	Cheerleading
Affiliation—NCAA III	Cross Country	Cross Country
Nickname—Yellow Jackets	Football	Golf
Athletic Director—Men	Golf	Soccer
(440) 826-2039	Soccer	Softball
Athletic Director—Women	Swimming	Swimming
(440) 826-3299	Tennis	Tennis
	Track	Track
	Wrestling	Volleyball

BLUFFTON COLLEGE

	Men	Women
280 W. College Avenue	Baseball	Basketball
Bluffton, OH 45817-1196	Basketball	Cross Country
Affiliation—NCAA III	Cross Country	Soccer
Nickname—Beavers	Football	Softball
Athletic Director—	Golf	Tennis
(419) 358-3226	Soccer	Track
	Tennis	Volleyball
	Track	
	Volleyball	

BOWLING GREEN STATE UNIVERSITY

	Men	Women
Perry Stadium	Baseball	Basketball
Bowling Green, OH 43404	Basketball	Cross Country
Affiliation—NCAA I	Cross Country	Diving
(I-A Football)	Diving	Golf
Nickname—Falcons	Football	Gymnastics
Athletic Director—	Golf	Soccer
(419) 372-2401	Ice Hockey	Softball
	Soccer	Swimming
	Swimming	Tennis
	Tennis	Track
	Track	Volleyball

CAPITAL UNIVERSITY

2199 S. Main Street
Columbus, OH 43209-3913
*Affiliation—*NCAA *III*
Nickname—Crusaders
Athletic Director—
  (614) 236-6538

Men	Women
Baseball	Basketball
Basketball	Cross Country
Cross Country	Soccer
Football	Softball
Golf	Tennis
Soccer	Volleyball
Tennis	
Wrestling	

CASE WESTERN RESERVE UNIVERSITY

10900 Euclid Avenue
Cleveland, OH 44106-7223
*Affiliation—*NCAA *III*
Nickname—Spartans
Athletic Director—
  (216) 368-2866

Men	Women
Baseball	Cross Country
Basketball	Fencing
Cross Country	Soccer
Fencing	Softball
Football	Swimming
Golf	Tennis
Soccer	Track
Swimming	Volleyball
Tennis	
Track	
Wrestling	

CEDARVILLE COLLEGE

PO Box 601
Cedarville, OH 45311-0601
*Affiliation—*NAIA *I,* NCCAA
Nickname—Yellow Jackets
Athletic Director—
  (937) 766-7759

Men	Women
Baseball	Basketball
Basketball	Cheerleading
Cross Country	Cross Country
Golf	Soccer
Soccer	Softball
Tennis	Tennis
Track	Track
	Volleyball

CENTRAL STATE UNIVERSITY

1400 Brush Row Road
Wilberforce, OH 45384
*Affiliation—*NAIA *I*
Nickname—Marauders
Athletic Director—
  (937) 376-5202

Men	Women
Baseball	Basketball
Basketball	Cheerleading
Football	Golf
Golf	Volleyball

CINCINNATI, UNIVERSITY OF

	Men	**Women**
PO Box 210021	Baseball	Basketball
Cincinnati, OH 45221-0021	Basketball	Cross Country
Affiliation—NCAA I	Cross Country	Diving
(I-AA Football)	Diving	Soccer
Nickname—Bearcats	Football	Swimming
Athletic Director—	Golf	Tennis
(513) 556-4603	Soccer	Track
	Swimming	Volleyball
	Track	

CINCINNATI BIBLE COLLEGE

	Men	**Women**
2700 Glenway Avenue	Basketball	Basketball
Cincinnati, OH 45204-1738	Golf	Volleyball
Affiliation—NCCAA II	Soccer	
Nickname—Golden Eagles		
Athletic Director—		
(513) 244-8101		

CIRCLEVILLE BIBLE COLLEGE

	Men	**Women**
PO Box 458,	Baseball	Basketball
1476 Lancaster Pike	Basketball	Volleyball
Circleville, OH 43113-0458	Soccer	
Affiliation—NCCAA II		
Nickname—Crusaders		
Athletic Director—		
(740) 477-7702		

CLEVELAND STATE UNIVERSITY

	Men	**Women**
2451 Euclid Avenue,	Baseball	Basketball
200 Prospect	Basketball	Cheerleading
Cleveland, OH 44115-2408	Diving	Cross Country
Affiliation—NCAA I	Fencing	Diving
Nickname—Vikings	Golf	Fencing
Athletic Director—	Soccer	Softball
(216) 687-5119	Swimming	Swimming
	Wrestling	Tennis
		Track
		Volleyball

DAYTON, UNIVERSITY OF

300 College Park	**Men**	**Women**
Dayton, OH 45469	Baseball	Basketball
Affiliation—NCAA I	Basketball	Cross Country
(I-AA Football)	Cross Country	Golf
Nickname—Flyers	Football	Soccer
Athletic Director—	Golf	Softball
(937) 229-2165	Soccer	Tennis
	Tennis	Track
		Volleyball

DEFIANCE COLLEGE

N. Clinton Street	**Men**	**Women**
Defiance, OH 43512	Baseball	Basketball
Affiliation—NCAA III	Basketball	Cross Country
Nickname—Yellow Jackets	Cross Country	Golf
Athletic Director—	Football	Soccer
(419) 783-2343	Golf	Softball
	Soccer	Tennis
	Tennis	Track
	Track	Volleyball

DENISON UNIVERSITY

PO Box M	**Men**	**Women**
Granville, OH 43023-0613	Baseball	Basketball
Affiliation—NCAA III	Basketball	Cross Country
Nickname—Big Red	Cross Country	Diving
Athletic Director—	Diving	Field Hockey
(740) 587-6428	Football	Lacrosse
	Golf	Soccer
	Lacrosse	Softball
	Soccer	Swimming
	Swimming	Tennis
	Tennis	Track
	Track	Volleyball

FINDLAY, UNIVERSITY OF

1000 N. Main Street	**Men**	**Women**
Findlay, OH 45840-3652	Baseball	Basketball
Affiliation—NCAA II, NAIA	Basketball	Cheerleading
Nickname—Oilers	Cross Country	Cross Country
Athletic Director—	Football	Golf
(419) 424-4651	Golf	Soccer
	Ice Hockey	Softball
	Soccer	Swimming
	Swimming	Tennis
	Tennis	Track
	Track	Volleyball
	Wrestling	

HEIDELBERG COLLEGE

310 E. Market Street	**Men**	**Women**
Tiffin, OH 44883-2434	Baseball	Basketball
Affiliation—NCAA III	Basketball	Cheerleading
Nickname—Student Princes	Cross Country	Cross Country
Athletic Director—	Football	Soccer
(419) 448-4607	Golf	Softball
	Soccer	Tennis
	Tennis	Track
	Track	Volleyball
	Wrestling	

HIRAM COLLEGE

PO Box 1777	**Men**	**Women**
Hiram, OH 44234-1777	Baseball	Basketball
Affiliation—NCAA III	Basketball	Cross Country
Nickname—Terriers	Cross Country	Diving
Athletic Director—	Diving	Golf
(330) 569-5345	Football	Soccer
	Golf	Softball
	Soccer	Swimming
	Swimming	Tennis
	Tennis	Track
	Track	Volleyball

JOHN CARROLL UNIVERSITY

20700 N. Park Boulevard	**Men**	**Women**
University Heights, OH	Baseball	Basketball
44118-4520	Basketball	Cheerleading
Affiliation—NCAA III	Cross Country	Cross Country
Nickname—Blue Streaks	Football	Soccer
Athletic Director—	Golf	Softball
(216) 397-4497	Soccer	Swimming
	Swimming	Tennis
	Tennis	Track
	Track	Volleyball
	Wrestling	

KENT STATE UNIVERSITY

PO Box 5190	**Men**	**Women**
Kent, OH 44242-0999	Baseball	Basketball
Affiliation—NCAA I	Basketball	Cheerleading
(I-A Football)	Cross Country	Cross Country
Nickname—Golden Flashes	Football	Field Hockey
Athletic Director—	Golf	Golf
(330) 672-3120	Track	Gymnastics
	Wrestling	Soccer
		Softball
		Track
		Volleyball

KENYON COLLEGE

Duff Street	**Men**	**Women**
Gambier, OH 43022	Baseball	Basketball
Affiliation—NCAA and NCAC	Basketball	Cross Country
Nickname—Lords	Cross Country	Field Hockey
Athletic Director—	Football	Lacrosse
(614) 427-5256	Golf	Soccer
	Lacrosse	Softball
	Soccer	Swimming
	Swimming	Tennis
	Tennis	Track
	Track	Volleyball

LAKE ERIE COLLEGE

391 W. Washington Street	**Men**	**Women**
Painesville, OH 44077-3309	Basketball	Basketball
Affiliation—NAIA *II*	Golf	Equestrian
Nickname—Storm	Soccer	Golf
Athletic Director—	Tennis	Soccer
(216) 639-7861		Softball
		Tennis
		Volleyball

MALONE COLLEGE

515 25th Street NW	**Men**	**Women**
Canton, OH 44709-3823	Baseball	Basketball
Affiliation—NAIA *II*	Basketball	Cross Country
Nickname—Pioneers	Cross Country	Soccer
Athletic Director—	Football	Softball
(330) 471-8296	Golf	Tennis
	Soccer	Track
	Tennis	Volleyball
	Track	

MARIETTA COLLEGE

215 5th Street	**Men**	**Women**
Marietta, OH 45750-4033	Baseball	Basketball
Affiliation—NCAA *III*	Basketball	Crew
Nickname—Pioneers	Crew	Soccer
Athletic Director—	Football	Softball
(740) 376-4701	Golf	Tennis
	Lacrosse	Volleyball
	Soccer	
	Tennis	

MIAMI UNIVERSITY

Millett Hall	**Men**	**Women**
Oxford, OH 45056	Baseball	Basketball
Affiliation—NCAA I	Basketball	Cross Country
(I-A Football)	Cross Country	Diving
Nickname—Red Hawks	Diving	Field Hockey
Athletic Director—	Football	Soccer
(513) 529-3113	Golf	Softball
	Ice Hockey	Swimming
	Soccer	Tennis
	Swimming	Track
	Tennis	Volleyball
	Track	
	Wrestling	

MOUNT ST. JOSEPH, COLLEGE OF

5701 Delhi Road	**Men**	**Women**
Cincinnati, OH 45233-1669	Baseball	Basketball
Affiliation—NCAA III	Basketball	Soccer
Nickname—Lions	Football	Softball
Athletic Director—	Tennis	Tennis
(513) 244-4311	Wrestling	Volleyball

MOUNT UNION COLLEGE

1972 Clark Avenue	**Men**	**Women**
Alliance, OH 44601-3929	Baseball	Basketball
Affiliation—NCAA III	Basketball	Cross Country
Nickname—Raiders	Cross Country	Soccer
Athletic Director—	Football	Softball
(330) 823-4880	Golf	Swimming
	Soccer	Tennis
	Swimming	Track
	Tennis	Volleyball
	Track	
	Wrestling	

MOUNT VERNON NAZARENE

800 Martinsburg Road	**Men**	**Women**
Mount Vernon, OH 43050-9509	Baseball	Basketball
Affiliation—NAIA II	Basketball	Softball
Nickname—Cougars	Golf	Volleyball
Athletic Director—	Soccer	
(740) 397-6862 ext. 3100		

MUSKINGUM COLLEGE

163 Stormont Street	**Men**	**Women**
New Concord, OH 43762-1118	Baseball	Basketball
Affiliation—NCAA III	Basketball	Cross Country
Nickname—Fighting Muskies	Cross Country	Soccer
Athletic Director—Men	Football	Softball
(740) 826-8325	Golf	Tennis
Athletic Director—Women	Soccer	Track
(740) 826-9324	Tennis	Volleyball
	Track	
	Wrestling	

NOTRE DAME COLLEGE OF OHIO

4545 College Road	**Women**	
South Euclid, OH 44121	Basketball	Tennis
Affiliation—NAIA	Soccer	Volleyball
Nickname—Blue Falcons	Softball	
Athletic Director—		
(216) 381-1680 ext. 306		

OBERLIN COLLEGE

200 Woodland Avenue	**Men**	**Women**
Oberlin, OH 44074	Baseball	Basketball
Affiliation—NCAA III	Basketball	Cross Country
Nickname—Yeomen	Cross Country	Field Hockey
Athletic Director—	Football	Lacrosse
(440) 775-8508	Lacrosse	Soccer
	Soccer	Swimming
	Swimming	Tennis
	Tennis	Track
	Track	Volleyball

OHIO DOMINICAN COLLEGE

1216 Sunbury Road	**Men**	**Women**
Columbus, OH 42319-2086	Baseball	Basketball
Affiliation—NAIA II	Basketball	Softball
Nickname—Panthers	Soccer	Volleyball
Athletic Director—		
(614) 251-4535		

OHIO NORTHERN UNIVERSITY

King Horn Center *Ada, OH 45810* *Affiliation—NCAA III* *Nickname—Polar Bears* *Athletic Director—* *(419) 772-2450*	**Men** Baseball Basketball Cross Country Football Golf Soccer Swimming Tennis Track Wrestling	**Women** Basketball Cross Country Golf Soccer Softball Swimming Tennis Track Volleyball

OHIO STATE UNIVERSITY

410 Woody Hayes Drive
Columbus, OH 43210-1104
Affiliation—NCAA I
    (I-A Football)
Nickname—Buckeyes
Athletic Director—
    (614) 292-2477
	Men
	Baseball
	Basketball
	Cross Country
	Diving
	Fencing
	Football
	Golf
	Gymnastics
	Ice Hockey
	Lacrosse
	Rifle
	Soccer
	Swimming
	Tennis
	Track
	Volleyball
	Wrestling
		Women
		Basketball
		Crew
		Cross Country
		Diving
		Fencing
		Field Hockey
		Golf
		Gymnastics
		Lacrosse
		Rifle
		Soccer
		Softball
		Swimming
		Tennis
		Track
		Volleyball

OHIO UNIVERSITY

Convocation Center
Athens, OH 45701
Affiliation—NCAA I
    (I-A Football)
Nickname—Bobcats
Athletic Director—
    (740) 593-0983
	Men
	Baseball
	Basketball
	Cross Country
	Diving
	Football
	Golf
	Swimming
	Track
	Wrestling
		Women
		Basketball
		Cross Country
		Diving
		Field Hockey
		Golf
		Soccer
		Softball
		Swimming
		Track
		Volleyball

OHIO WESLEYAN UNIVERSITY

61 S. Sandusky Street	Men	Women
Delaware, OH 43015-2333	Baseball	Basketball
Affiliation—NCAA III	Basketball	Cheerleading
Nickname—Battling Bishops	Cross Country	Cross Country
Athletic Director—	Football	Field Hockey
(740) 368-3000	Golf	Lacrosse
	Lacrosse	Soccer
	Soccer	Swimming
	Swimming	Tennis
	Tennis	Track
	Track	Volleyball

OTTERBEIN COLLEGE

160 Center Street	Men	Women
Westerville, OH 43081-1405	Baseball	Basketball
Affiliation—NCAA III	Basketball	Cross Country
Nickname—Cardinals	Cross Country	Soccer
Athletic Director—	Football	Softball
(614) 823-3518	Golf	Tennis
	Soccer	Track
	Tennis	Volleyball
	Track	

RIO GRANDE, UNIVERSITY OF

MSC-F34,	Men	Women
218 N. College Avenue	Baseball	Basketball
Rio Grande, OH 45674-3131	Basketball	Cheerleading
Affiliation—NAIA I	Cross Country	Cross Country
Nickname—Redmen	Soccer	Softball
Athletic Director—	Track	Track
(740) 245-5353 ext. 7220		Volleyball

SHAWNEE STATE UNIVERSITY

940 2nd Street	Men	Women
Portsmouth, OH 35662-4303	Baseball	Basketball
Affiliation—NAIA II	Basketball	Cross Country
Nickname—Bears	Cross Country	Softball
Athletic Director—	Golf	Tennis
(740) 355-2263	Soccer	Volleyball

TIFFIN UNIVERSITY

155 Miami Street	Men	Women
Tiffin, OH 44883-2109	Baseball	Basketball
Affiliation—NAIA II	Basketball	Cross Country
Nickname—Dragons	Cross Country	Soccer
Athletic Director—	Football	Softball
(419) 448-3452	Golf	Tennis
	Soccer	Track
	Tennis	Volleyball
	Track	

TOLEDO, UNIVERSITY OF

2801 W. Bancroft Street	Men	Women
Toledo, OH 43606-3328	Baseball	Basketball
Affiliation—NCAA I	Basketball	Golf
(I-A Football)	Cross Country	Soccer
Nickname—Rockets	Football	Softball
Athletic Director—	Golf	Tennis
(419) 530-4987	Swimming	Track
	Tennis	Volleyball
	Track	

URBANA UNIVERSITY

579 College Way	Men	Women
Urbana, OH 43078-2091	Baseball	Basketball
Affiliation—NAIA II	Basketball	Cheerleading
Nickname—Blue Knights	Football	Softball
Athletic Director—	Golf	Volleyball
(937) 484-1325	Soccer	

WALSH UNIVERSITY

202 Easton Street NW	Men	Women
North Canton, OH 44720-3396	Baseball	Basketball
Affiliation—NAIA II	Basketball	Cheerleading
Nickname—Cavaliers	Cross Country	Cross Country
Athletic Director—	Football	Soccer
(330) 490-7035	Golf	Softball
	Soccer	Swimming
	Tennis	Tennis
	Track	Track
		Volleyball

WILBERFORCE UNIVERSITY

1055 North Bickett Road	**Men**	**Women**
Wilberforce, OH 45384	Basketball	Basketball
Affiliation—NAIA I	Cross Country	Cheerleading
Nickname—Bulldogs	Golf	Cross Country
Athletic Director—	Track	Golf
(937) 376-2911 ext. 746		Track

WILMINGTON COLLEGE

251 Ludovic Street,	**Men**	**Women**
Pyle Center 1246	Baseball	Basketball
Wilmington, OH 45177	Basketball	Cross Country
Affiliation—NCAA III	Cross Country	Golf
Nickname—Quakers	Football	Soccer
Athletic Director—	Golf	Softball
(937) 382-6661 ext. 250	Soccer	Swimming
	Swimming	Tennis
	Tennis	Track
	Track	Volleyball
	Wrestling	

WITTENBERG UNIVERSITY

PO Box 720	**Men**	**Women**
Springfield, OH 45501-0720	Baseball	Basketball
Affiliation—NCAA III	Basketball	Cross Country
Nickname—Tigers	Cross Country	Field Hockey
Athletic Director—	Football	Lacrosse
(937) 327-6450	Golf	Soccer
	Lacrosse	Softball
	Soccer	Swimming
	Swimming	Tennis
	Tennis	Track
	Track	Volleyball

WOOSTER, THE COLLEGE OF

1267 Beall Avenue	**Men**	**Women**
Wooster, OH 44691-2393	Baseball	Basketball
Affiliation—NCAA *III*	Basketball	Cross Country
Nickname—*Fighting Scots*	Cross Country	Field Hockey
Athletic Director—	Football	Lacrosse
(330) 263-2500	Golf	Soccer
	Lacrosse	Swimming
	Soccer	Tennis
	Swimming	Track
	Tennis	Volleyball
	Track	

WRIGHT STATE UNIVERSITY

3640 Colonel Glenn Highway	**Men**	**Women**
Dayton, OH 45435	Baseball	Basketball
Affiliation—NCAA *I*	Basketball	Cheerleading
Nickname—*Raiders*	Cross Country	Cross Country
Athletic Director—	Diving	Soccer
(937) 775-2771	Golf	Softball
	Soccer	Swimming
	Swimming	Tennis
	Tennis	Volleyball

XAVIER UNIVERSITY

3800 Victory Parkway	**Men**	**Women**
Cincinnati, OH 45207-6114	Baseball	Basketball
Affiliation—NCAA *I*	Basketball	Cross Country
Nickname—*Musketeers*	Cross Country	Golf
Athletic Director—	Golf	Rifle
(513) 745-3414	Rifle	Soccer
	Soccer	Swimming
	Swimming	Tennis
	Tennis	Volleyball

YOUNGSTOWN STATE UNIVERSITY

One University Plaza	Men	Women
Youngstown, OH 44555	Baseball	Basketball
Affiliation—NCAA I	Basketball	Cross Country
(I-AA Football)	Cross Country	Diving
Nickname—Penguins	Football	Golf
Athletic Director—	Golf	Soccer
(330) 742-2385	Tennis	Softball
	Track	Swimming
		Tennis
		Track
		Volleyball

OKLAHOMA

BARTLESVILLE WESLEYAN

2201 Silverlake Road	Men	Women
Bartlesville, OK 74006-6233	Baseball	Basketball
Affiliation—NAIA II, NCCAA I	Basketball	Soccer
Nickname—Eagles	Golf	Volleyball
Athletic Director—	Soccer	
(918) 335-6259		

CAMERON UNIVERSITY

2800 W. Gore Boulevard	Men	Women
Lawton, OK 73505	Baseball	Basketball
Affiliation—NCAA II	Basketball	Softball
Nickname—Aggies	Golf	Tennis
Athletic Director—	Tennis	Volleyball
(580) 581-2460		

CENTRAL OKLAHOMA, UNIVERSITY OF

100 N. University Drive	Men	Women
Edmond, OK 73034-5207	Baseball	Basketball
Affiliation—NCAA II	Basketball	Cheerleading
Nickname—Broncos	Cross Country	Cross Country
Athletic Director—	Football	Soccer
(405) 341-2980 ext. 2501	Golf	Softball
	Tennis	Tennis
	Track	Track
	Wrestling	Volleyball

EAST CENTRAL UNIVERSITY

	Men	Women
E. 14th Street	Baseball	Basketball
Ada, OK 74820	Basketball	Cross Country
Affiliation—NAIA I, NCAA II	Cross Country	Soccer
Nickname—*Tigers*	Football	Softball
Athletic Director—	Golf	Tennis
(580) 332-8000 ext. 314	Tennis	

HILLSDALE FREE WILL BAPTIST COLLEGE

	Men	Women
PO Box 6343	Baseball	Basketball
Moore, OK 73153-0343	Basketball	Volleyball
Nickname—*Saints*		
Athletic Director—		
(405) 912-9000		

LANGSTON UNIVERSITY

	Men	Women
PO Box 175	Basketball	Basketball
Langston, OK 73050-0175	Football	Golf
Affiliation—NAIA I	Golf	Track
Nickname—*Lions*	Track	
Athletic Director—		
(405) 466-3263		

MID-AMERICA BIBLE COLLEGE

	Men	Women
3500 SW 119th Street	Baseball	Basketball
Oklahoma City, OK	Basketball	Volleyball
73170-4500		
Affiliation—NCCAA II		
Nickname—*Evangels*		
Athletic Director—		
(405) 691-3800		

NORTHEASTERN STATE UNIVERSITY

	Men	Women
600 N. Grand Avenue	Baseball	Basketball
Tahlequah, OK 74464-2301	Basketball	Golf
Affiliation—NCAA II	Football	Soccer
Nickname—*Redmen*	Golf	Softball
Athletic Director—	Soccer	Tennis
(918) 458-2071	Tennis	

NORTHWESTERN OKLAHOMA STATE

Oklahoma Boulevard	**Men**	**Women**
Akva, OK 73717	Baseball	Basketball
*Affiliation—*NAIA *I*	Basketball	Tennis
Nickname—Rangers	Football	
Athletic Director—	Tennis	
(405) 327-1700	Track	

OKLAHOMA, UNIVERSITY OF

180 W. Brooks, Room 201	**Men**	**Women**
Norman, OK 73019-6010	Baseball	Basketball
*Affiliation—*NCAA *I*	Basketball	Cheerleading
(I-A Football)	Cross Country	Cross Country
Nickname—Sooners	Football	Golf
Athletic Director—	Golf	Gymnastics
(405) 325-8383	Gymnastics	Soccer
	Tennis	Softball
	Track	Tennis
	Wrestling	Track
		Volleyball

OKLAHOMA, UNIVERSITY OF SCIENCE & ARTS OF

PO Box 82345	**Men**	**Women**
Chickasha, OK 73018	Basketball	Basketball
*Affiliation—*NAIA *I*	Tennis	
Nickname—Drovers		
Athletic Director—		
(405) 224-3140		

OKLAHOMA BAPTIST UNIVERSITY

500 W. University Street	**Men**	**Women**
Shawnee, OK 74804	Baseball	Basketball
*Affiliation—*NAIA *I*	Basketball	Cross Country
Nickname—Bison	Cross Country	Softball
Athletic Director—	Golf	Tennis
(405) 878-2132	Tennis	Track
	Track	

OKLAHOMA CHRISTIAN UNIVERSITY

PO Box 11000	**Men**	**Women**
Oklahoma City, OK	Baseball	Basketball
73136-1100	Basketball	Cheerleading
*Affiliation—*NAIA *I*	Cross Country	Cross Country
Nickname—Eagles	Golf	Soccer
Athletic Director—	Soccer	Softball
(405) 425-5361	Tennis	Tennis
	Track	Track

OKLAHOMA CITY UNIVERSITY

NW 23rd and Blackwelder	**Men**	**Women**
Oklahoma City, OK 73106	Baseball	Basketball
*Affiliation—*NAIA *I*	Basketball	Soccer
Athletic Director—	Golf	Softball
(405) 521-5302	Soccer	Tennis
	Tennis	

OKLAHOMA STATE UNIVERSITY

103 Gallagher-Iba Arena	**Men**	**Women**
Stillwater, OK 74078	Baseball	Basketball
*Affiliation—*NCAA *I*	Basketball	Cross Country
(I-A Football)	Cross Country	Golf
Nickname—Cowboys	Football	Soccer
Athletic Director—	Golf	Softball
(405) 744-7740	Tennis	Tennis
	Track	Track
	Wrestling	

ORAL ROBERTS UNIVERSITY

7777 S. Lewis Avenue	**Men**	**Women**
Tulsa, OK 74171-0003	Baseball	Basketball
*Affiliation—*NCAA *I*	Basketball	Cross Country
Nickname—Golden Eagles	Cross Country	Golf
Athletic Director—	Golf	Soccer
(918) 495-7007	Soccer	Tennis
	Tennis	Track
	Track	Volleyball

PANHANDLE STATE UNIVERSITY

PO Box 430	Men	Women
Goodwell, OK 73939-0430	Baseball	Basketball
Affiliation—NCAA II	Basketball	Cross Country
Nickname—Aggies	Football	Golf
Athletic Director—	Golf	Softball
(580) 349-2611 ext. 390		

PHILLIPS UNIVERSITY

University Station	Men	Women
Enid, OK 73701	Baseball	Basketball
Affiliation—NAIA I	Basketball	Cross Country
Nickname—Haymakers	Cross Country	Soccer
Athletic Director—	Golf	Softball
(405) 237-4433	Soccer	Tennis
	Tennis	Track
	Track	

SAINT GREGORY'S UNIVERSITY

1900 W. Macarthur Street	Men	Women
Shawnee, OK 74804	Baseball	Basketball
Affiliation—NAIA	Basketball	Soccer
Nickname—Cavaliers	Golf	Softball
Athletic Director—	Soccer	Tennis
(405) 878-5101		

SOUTHEASTERN OKLAHOMA STATE UNIVERSITY

University Boulevard	Men	Women
Durant, OK 74701	Baseball	Basketball
Affiliation—NCAA II	Basketball	Cheerleading
Nickname—Savages	Football	Cross Country
Athletic Director—	Tennis	Softball
(580) 924-0121 ext. 2311		Tennis
		Volleyball

SOUTHERN NAZARENE UNIVERSITY

6729 NW 39th Expressway	**Men**	**Women**
Bethany, OK 73008-2605	Baseball	Basketball
Affiliation—NAIA I	Basketball	Cross Country
Nickname—Redskins	Cross Country	Golf
Athletic Director—	Golf	Soccer
(405) 491-6339	Soccer	Softball
	Tennis	Tennis
	Track	Track
		Volleyball

SOUTHWESTERN OKLAHOMA STATE UNIVERSITY

100 Campus Drive	**Men**	**Women**
Weatherford, OK 73096-3001	Baseball	Basketball
Affiliation—NCAA II	Basketball	Cross Country
Nickname—Bulldogs	Football	Golf
Athletic Director—	Golf	Soccer
(580) 774-3068		Softball

TULSA, THE UNIVERSITY OF

600 S. College Avenue	**Men**	**Women**
Tulsa, OK 74101-3126	Basketball	Basketball
Affiliation—NCAA I	Cross Country	Cheerleading
(I-A Football)	Football	Cross Country
Nickname—Golden Hurricane	Golf	Golf
Athletic Director—	Soccer	Soccer
(918) 631-2381	Tennis	Softball
	Track	Tennis
		Track
		Volleyball

OREGON

CASCADE COLLEGE

9101 E. Burnside Street	**Men**	**Women**
Portland, OR 97216-1515	Basketball	Cross Country
Affiliation—NCCAA, NAIA	Cross Country	Soccer
Nickname—Thunderbirds	Soccer	Track
Athletic Director—	Track	Volleyball
(503) 255-1260		

CONCORDIA UNIVERSITY

2811 NE Holman Street Portland, OR 97211-6067 Affiliation—NAIA Nickname—Cavaliers Athletic Director— (503) 280-8516	**Men** Baseball Basketball Soccer	**Women** Basketball Soccer Softball Volleyball

EASTERN OREGON UNIVERSITY

1410 L Avenue La Grande, OR 97850-2899 Affiliation—NAIA II, NCAA III Nickname—Mountaineers Athletic Director— (541) 962-3363	**Men** Baseball Basketball Cross Country Football Track	**Women** Basketball Cross Country Softball Track Volleyball

EUGENE BIBLE COLLEGE

2155 Bailey Hill Road Eugene, OR 97405-1150 Nickname—Deacons Athletic Director— (503) 485-1780	**Men** Basketball Soccer	**Women** Volleyball

GEORGE FOX UNIVERSITY

414 N. Meridian Street Newberg, OR 97132-2625 Affiliation—NAIA II, NCAA III Nickname—Bruins Athletic Director— (503) 554-2911	**Men** Baseball Basketball Cross Country Soccer Tennis Track	**Women** Basketball Cross Country Soccer Softball Tennis Track Volleyball

LEWIS & CLARK COLLEGE

0615 SW Palatine Hill Road Portland, OR 97219-7879 Affiliation—NAIA II, NCAA III Nickname—Pioneers Athletic Director— (503) 768-7548	**Men** Baseball Basketball Cross Country Football Golf Swimming Tennis Track	**Women** Basketball Cross Country Golf Softball Swimming Tennis Track Volleyball

LINFIELD COLLEGE

	Men	Women
900 SE Baker Street	Baseball	Basketball
McMinnville, OR 97128-6808	Basketball	Cross Country
*Affiliation—*NAIA *II,* NCAA *III*	Cross Country	Golf
Nickname—Wildcats	Football	Lacrosse
Athletic Director—	Golf	Soccer
(503) 434-2421	Soccer	Softball
	Swimming	Swimming
	Tennis	Tennis
	Track	Track
		Volleyball

MULTNOMAH BIBLE COLLEGE

	Men	Women
8435 NE Glisan Street	Basketball	Basketball
Portland, OR 97220-5814	Soccer	Cheerleading
*Affiliation—*NCCAA *II*		Volleyball
Nickname—Ambassadors		
Athletic Director—		
(503) 251-5395		

NORTHWEST CHRISTIAN COLLEGE

	Men	Women
828 E. 11th Avenue	Basketball	Basketball
Eugene, OR 97401-3745		Softball
*Affiliation—*NCCAA *I,* NCSAA		Volleyball
Nickname—Crusaders		
Athletic Director—		
(541) 343-1641		

OREGON, UNIVERSITY OF

	Men	Women
Casanova Center,	Baseball	Basketball
2727 Leo Harris Parkway	Basketball	Cross Country
Eugene, OR 97401-8835	Cross Country	Golf
*Affiliation—*NCAA *I*	Football	Soccer
(I-A Football)	Golf	Softball
Nickname—Ducks	Tennis	Tennis
Athletic Director—	Track	Track
(541) 346-4481	Wrestling	Volleyball

OREGON INSTITUTE OF TECHNOLOGY

PO Box 2029	**Men**	**Women**
Klamath Falls, OR 97601-0502	Basketball	Cheerleading
Affiliation—NAIA II	Cross Country	Cross Country
Nickname—Hustlin' Owls	Track	Softball
Athletic Director—		Track
(541) 885-1625		Volleyball

OREGON STATE UNIVERSITY

Gill Coliseum	**Men**	**Women**
Corvallis, OR 97331-4105	Baseball	Basketball
Affiliation—NCAA I	Basketball	Crew
(I-A Football)	Crew	Golf
Nickname—Beavers	Football	Gymnastics
Athletic Director—	Golf	Soccer
(541) 737-7374	Soccer	Softball
	Wrestling	Swimming
		Volleyball

PACIFIC UNIVERSITY

2043 College Way	**Men**	**Women**
Forest Grove, OR 97116-1756	Baseball	Basketball
Affiliation—NCAA III	Basketball	Cross Country
Nickname—Boxers	Cross Country	Golf
Athletic Director—	Golf	Soccer
(503) 359-2767	Soccer	Softball
	Tennis	Tennis
	Track	Track
	Wrestling	Volleyball

PORTLAND, UNIVERSITY OF

5000 N. Willamette Boulevard	**Men**	**Women**
Portland, OR 97203-5723	Baseball	Basketball
Affiliation—NCAA I	Basketball	Cross Country
Nickname—Pilots	Cross Country	Golf
Athletic Director—	Golf	Soccer
(503) 283-7704	Soccer	Tennis
	Tennis	Track
	Track	Volleyball

PORTLAND STATE UNIVERSITY

PO Box 751	**Men**	**Women**
Portland, OR 97207-0751	Basketball	Basketball
Affiliation—NCAA I	Cross Country	Cross Country
(I-AA Football)	Football	Golf
Nickname—Vikings	Golf	Soccer
Athletic Director—	Track	Softball
(503) 725-2500	Wrestling	Tennis
		Track
		Volleyball

SOUTHERN OREGON UNIVERSITY

1250 Siskiyou Boulevard	**Men**	**Women**
Ashland, OR 97520-5010	Basketball	Basketball
Affiliation—NAIA	Cross Country	Cross Country
Nickname—Raiders	Football	Tennis
Athletic Director—	Track	Track
(541) 552-6236	Wrestling	Volleyball

WARNER PACIFIC COLLEGE

2219 SE 68th Avenue	**Men**	**Women**
Portland, OR 97215-4026	Baseball	Basketball
Affiliation—NAIA	Basketball	Softball
Nickname—Knights	Soccer	Volleyball
Athletic Director—	Volleyball	
(503) 775-4366		

WESTERN BAPTIST COLLEGE

5000 Deer Park Drive SE	**Men**	**Women**
Salem, OR 97301-9330	Baseball	Basketball
Affiliation—NAIA II, NCCAA	Basketball	Soccer
Nickname—Warriors	Soccer	Volleyball
Athletic Director—		
(503) 375-7021		

WESTERN OREGON UNIVERSITY

345 Monmouth Avenue S	**Men**	**Women**
Monmouth, OR 97361-2111	Baseball	Basketball
Affiliation—NAIA, NCAA II	Basketball	Cross Country
Nickname—Wolves	Cross Country	Soccer
Athletic Director—	Football	Softball
(503) 838-8252	Track	Track
		Volleyball

WILLAMETTE UNIVERSITY

900 State Street	**Men**	**Women**
Salem, OR 97301-3930	Baseball	Basketball
Affiliation—NCAA III	Basketball	Crew
Nickname—Bearcats	Crew	Cross Country
Athletic Director—	Cross Country	Golf
(503) 370-6217	Football	Soccer
	Golf	Softball
	Soccer	Swimming
	Swimming	Tennis
	Tennis	Track
	Track	Volleyball

PENNSYLVANIA

ALBRIGHT COLLEGE

PO Box 15234, N. 13th Street	**Men**	**Women**
Reading, PA 19612-5234	Baseball	Badminton
Affiliation—NCAA III	Basketball	Basketball
Nickname—Lions	Cross Country	Cheerleading
Athletic Director—	Football	Cross Country
(610) 921-7535	Golf	Field Hockey
	Soccer	Soccer
	Swimming	Softball
	Tennis	Swimming
	Track	Tennis
	Wrestling	Track
		Volleyball

ALLEGHENY COLLEGE

PO Box AC, 520 N. Main Street	**Men**	**Women**
Meadville, PA 16335-0034	Baseball	Basketball
Affiliation—NCAA III	Basketball	Cross Country
Nickname—Gators	Cross Country	Diving
Athletic Director—	Diving	Lacrosse
(814) 332-3350	Football	Soccer
	Golf	Softball
	Soccer	Swimming
	Swimming	Tennis
	Tennis	Track
	Track	Volleyball

ALLENTOWN COLLEGE

2755 Station Avenue	Men	Women
Center Valley, PA 18034-9566	Baseball	Basketball
Affiliation—NCAA III	Basketball	Cross Country
Nickname—Centaurs	Cross Country	Soccer
Athletic Director—	Golf	Softball
(610) 282-1335	Lacrosse	Tennis
	Soccer	Track
	Tennis	Volleyball
	Track	

ALVERNIA COLLEGE

400 Saint Bernadine Street	Men	Women
Reading, PA 19607-1737	Baseball	Basketball
Affiliation—NCAA III	Basketball	Cross Country
Nickname—Crusaders	Cross Country	Field Hockey
Athletic Director—	Golf	Soccer
(610) 796-8276	Soccer	Softball
	Tennis	Tennis
		Volleyball

BAPTIST BIBLE COLLEGE

538 Venard Road	Men	Women
Clarks Summit, PA 18411-1250	Basketball	Basketball
Affiliation—NCCAA II, NCAA III	Cross Country	Cheerleading
Nickname—Defenders	Soccer	Cross Country
Athletic Director—	Track	Soccer
(717) 586-2400	Wrestling	Track
		Volleyball

BEAVER COLLEGE

450 S. Easton Road	Men	Women
Glenside, PA 19038-3215	Baseball	Basketball
Affiliation—NCAA III	Basketball	Cross Country
Nickname—Scarlet Knights	Cross Country	Field Hockey
Athletic Director—	Golf	Lacrosse
(215) 572-2194	Soccer	Riding
	Swimming	Soccer
	Tennis	Softball
		Swimming
		Tennis
		Volleyball

BLOOMSBURG UNIVERSITY

400 E. 2nd Street	Men	Women
Bloomsburg, PA 17815-1301	Baseball	Basketball
*Affiliation—*NCAA *II*	Basketball	Cheerleading
Nickname—Huskies	Cross Country	Cross Country
Athletic Director—	Football	Field Hockey
(717) 389-4050	Soccer	Lacrosse
	Swimming	Soccer
	Tennis	Softball
	Track	Swimming
	Wrestling	Tennis
		Track

BRYN MAWR COLLEGE

Schwartz Gymnasium	Women	
Bryn Mawr, PA 19010	Badminton	Soccer
*Affiliation—*NCAA *III*	Basketball	Swimming
Nickname—Mawrters	Cross Country	Tennis
Athletic Director—	Field Hockey	Volleyball
(610) 526-5364	Lacrosse	

BUCKNELL UNIVERSITY

Moore Avenue	Men	Women
Lewisburg, PA 17837	Baseball	Basketball
*Affiliation—*NCAA *I*	Basketball	Cheerleading
(I-AA Football)	Crew	Crew
Nickname—Bison	Cross Country	Cross Country
Athletic Director—	Diving	Diving
(717) 524-1232	Football	Field Hockey
	Golf	Golf
	Lacrosse	Lacrosse
	Soccer	Soccer
	Swimming	Softball
	Tennis	Swimming
	Track	Tennis
	Water Polo	Track
	Wrestling	Volleyball
		Water Polo

CABRINI COLLEGE

610 King of Prussia Road	**Men**	**Women**
Radnor, PA 19087-3632	Basketball	Basketball
Affiliation—NCAA III	Cross Country	Cross Country
Nickname—Cavaliers	Golf	Field Hockey
Athletic Director—	Lacrosse	Lacrosse
(610) 971-8386	Soccer	Soccer
	Tennis	Softball
	Track	Tennis
		Track
		Volleyball

CALIFORNIA UNIVERSITY OF PENNSYLVANIA

250 University Avenue	**Men**	**Women**
California, PA 15419-1341	Baseball	Basketball
Affiliation—NCAA II	Basketball	Cross Country
Nickname—Vulcans	Cross Country	Soccer
Athletic Director—	Football	Softball
(724) 938-4351 ext. 4352	Soccer	Tennis
	Track	Track
		Volleyball

CARLOW COLLEGE

3333 5th Avenue	**Women**	
Pittsburgh, PA 15213	Basketball	Softball
Affiliation—NAIA	Crew	Tennis
Nickname—Celtics	Cross Country	Volleyball
Athletic Director—		
(412) 578-8826		

CARNEGIE MELLON UNIVERSITY

Tech and Frew	**Men**	**Women**
Pittsburgh, PA 15213	Basketball	Basketball
Affiliation—NCAA III	Cross Country	Cheerleading
Nickname—Tartans	Football	Cross Country
Athletic Director—	Golf	Soccer
(412) 268-8555	Soccer	Swimming
	Swimming	Tennis
	Tennis	Track
	Track	Volleyball

CHATHAM COLLEGE

Woodland Road	**Women**	
Pittsburgh, PA 15232	Basketball	Softball
*Affiliation—*NCAA *III*	Ice Hockey	Tennis
Nickname—Cougars	Soccer	Volleyball
Athletic Director—		
(412) 365-1635		

CHESTNUT HILL COLLEGE

Germantown Avenue	**Women**	
Philadelphia, PA 19118	Basketball	Softball
Athletic Director—	Field Hockey	Tennis
(215) 248-7060	Lacrosse	Volleyball

CHEYNEY UNIVERSITY

PO Box 350, Cheyney Road	**Men**	**Women**
Cheyney, PA 19319	Basketball	Basketball
*Affiliation—*NCAA *II*	Cross Country	Cross Country
Nickname—Wolves	Football	Tennis
Athletic Director—	Tennis	Track
(610) 399-2287	Track	Volleyball
	Wrestling	

CLARION UNIVERSITY

Wood Street, Tippin Gym,	**Men**	**Women**
Room 112	Baseball	Basketball
Clarion, PA 16214	Basketball	Cross Country
*Affiliation—*NCAA *II*	Cross Country	Diving
Nickname—Golden Eagles	Diving	Softball
Athletic Director—	Football	Swimming
(814) 226-1997	Golf	Tennis
	Swimming	Track
	Track	Volleyball
	Wrestling	

DELAWARE VALLEY COLLEGE

700 E. Butler Avenue	**Men**	**Women**
Doylestown, PA 18901-2607	Baseball	Basketball
Affiliation—NCAA *III*	Basketball	Cross Country
Nickname—*Aggies*	Cross Country	Field Hockey
Athletic Director—	Football	Soccer
(215) 486-2268	Golf	Softball
	Soccer	Track
	Track	Volleyball
	Wrestling	

DICKINSON COLLEGE

Kline Center, High Street	**Men**	**Women**
Carlisle, PA 17013	Baseball	Basketball
Affiliation—NCAA *III*	Basketball	Cross Country
Nickname—*Red Devils*	Cross Country	Field Hockey
Athletic Director—	Football	Lacrosse
(717) 245-1320	Golf	Soccer
	Lacrosse	Softball
	Soccer	Swimming
	Swimming	Tennis
	Tennis	Track
	Track	Volleyball

DREXEL UNIVERSITY

3141 Chestnut Street	**Men**	**Women**
Philadelphia, PA 19104-2816	Baseball	Basketball
Affiliation—NCAA *I*	Basketball	Crew
Nickname—*Dragons*	Crew	Cross Country
Athletic Director—	Cross Country	Diving
(215) 895-1999	Diving	Field Hockey
	Golf	Lacrosse
	Lacrosse	Soccer
	Soccer	Softball
	Swimming	Swimming
	Tennis	Tennis
	Track	Track
	Wrestling	Volleyball

DUQUESNE UNIVERSITY

600 Forbes Avenue	**Men**	**Women**
Pittsburgh, PA 15285	Baseball	Basketball
*Affiliation—*NCAA I	Basketball	Cheerleading
(I-AA Football)	Crew	Crew
Nickname—Dukes	Cross Country	Cross Country
Athletic Director—	Football	Lacrosse
(412) 396-5589	Golf	Rifle
	Ice Hockey	Soccer
	Rifle	Swimming
	Soccer	Tennis
	Swimming	Track
	Tennis	Volleyball
	Track	
	Wrestling	

EAST STROUDSBURG UNIVERSITY

Smith and Normal Street	**Men**	**Women**
East Stroudsburg, PA 18301	Baseball	Basketball
*Affiliation—*NCAA II	Basketball	Cheerleading
Nickname—Warriors	Cross Country	Cross Country
Athletic Director—	Football	Field Hockey
(717) 422-3642	Soccer	Lacrosse
	Tennis	Soccer
	Track	Softball
	Volleyball	Swimming
		Tennis
		Track
		Volleyball

EASTERN COLLEGE

1300 Eagle Road	**Men**	**Women**
Saint Davids, PA 19087-3617	Baseball	Basketball
*Affiliation—*NCAA III	Basketball	Cheerleading
Nickname—Eagles	Cross Country	Cross Country
Athletic Director—	Golf	Field Hockey
(610) 341-1785	Lacrosse	Golf
	Soccer	Lacrosse
	Tennis	Soccer
	Volleyball	Softball
		Tennis
		Volleyball

EDINBORO UNIVERSITY

Edinboro, PA 16444	**Men**	**Women**
Affiliation—NCAA II	Baseball	Basketball
Nickname—Fighting Scots	Basketball	Cheerleading
Athletic Director—	Cross Country	Cross Country
(814) 732-2776 ext. 223	Football	Soccer
	Golf	Softball
	Swimming	Swimming
	Tennis	Tennis
	Track	Track
	Wrestling	Volleyball

ELIZABETHTOWN COLLEGE

1 Alpha Drive	**Men**	**Women**
Elizabethtown, PA 17022-2298	Baseball	Basketball
Affiliation—NCAA III	Basketball	Cross Country
Nickname—Blue Jays	Cross Country	Field Hockey
Athletic Director—	Golf	Golf
(717) 361-1137	Soccer	Soccer
	Swimming	Softball
	Tennis	Swimming
	Track	Tennis
	Wrestling	Track
		Volleyball

FRANKLIN AND MARSHALL COLLEGE

Box 303, College Avenue	**Men**	**Women**
Lancaster, PA 17604	Baseball	Basketball
Affiliation—NCAA III	Basketball	Cross Country
Nickname—Diplomats	Cross Country	Field Hockey
Athletic Director—	Football	Golf
(717) 291-4102	Golf	Lacrosse
	Lacrosse	Soccer
	Soccer	Softball
	Squash	Swimming
	Swimming	Squash
	Tennis	Tennis
	Track	Track
	Wrestling	Volleyball

GANNON UNIVERSITY

University Square	**Men**	**Women**
Erie, PA 16541	Baseball	Basketball
Affiliation—NCAA II	Basketball	Cross Country
Nickname—Golden Knights	Cross Country	Golf
Athletic Director—	Football	Lacrosse
(814) 871-7453	Golf	Soccer
	Lacrosse	Softball
	Soccer	Swimming
	Swimming	Tennis
	Tennis	Volleyball
	Wrestling	

GENEVA COLLEGE

3200 College Avenue	**Men**	**Women**
Beaver Falls, PA 15010-3557	Baseball	Basketball
Affiliation—NAIA, NCCAA I	Basketball	Cross Country
Nickname—Golden Tornadoes	Cross Country	Soccer
Athletic Director—Men	Football	Softball
(724) 847-6648	Soccer	Tennis
Athletic Director—Women	Tennis	Track
(724) 847-6651	Track	Volleyball

GETTYSBURG COLLEGE

Campus Box 400	**Men**	**Women**
300 N. Washington Street	Baseball	Basketball
Gettysburg, PA 17325	Basketball	Cheerleading
Affiliation—NCAA III	Cross Country	Cross Country
Nickname—Bullets	Football	Field Hockey
Athletic Director—	Golf	Lacrosse
(717) 337-6530	Lacrosse	Soccer
	Soccer	Softball
	Swimming	Swimming
	Tennis	Tennis
	Track	Track
	Wrestling	Volleyball

GROVE CITY COLLEGE

100 Campus Drive
Grove City, PA 16127-2104
Affiliation—NCAA III
Nickname—Wolverines
Athletic Director—Men
  (724) 458-2126
Athletic Director—Women
  (724) 458-2129

Men
Baseball
Basketball
Cross Country
Football
Golf
Soccer
Swimming
Tennis
Track

Women
Basketball
Cross Country
Golf
Soccer
Softball
Swimming
Tennis
Track
Volleyball

GWYNEDD MERCY COLLEGE

Gwynedd Valley, PA 19437
Affiliation—NCAA III
Nickname—Griffins
Athletic Director—
  (215) 641-5574

Men
Baseball
Basketball
Cross Country
Golf
Soccer
Tennis

Women
Basketball
Cross Country
Field Hockey
Golf
Lacrosse
Softball
Tennis
Volleyball

HAVERFORD COLLEGE

370 Lancaster Avenue
Haverford, PA 19041-1336
Affiliation—NCAA III
Nickname—Fords
Athletic Director—
  (610) 869-1120

Men
Baseball
Basketball
Cricket
Cross Country
Fencing
Lacrosse
Soccer
Squash
Tennis
Track

Women
Basketball
Cross Country
Fencing
Field Hockey
Lacrosse
Soccer
Softball
Squash
Tennis
Track
Volleyball

HOLY FAMILY COLLEGE

Grant and Frankford Streets
Philadelphia, PA 19114
Affiliation—NAIA II
Nickname—Tigers
Athletic Director—
  (215) 632-8284

Men
Basketball
Golf
Soccer

Women
Basketball
Cheerleading
Cross Country
Soccer
Softball

IMMACULATA COLLEGE

	Women	
1135 King Road	Basketball	Softball
Immaculata, PA 19345	Cross Country	Tennis
Affiliation—NCAA III	Field Hockey	Volleyball
Nickname—Mighty Macs		
Athletic Director—		
(610) 647-4400 ext. 3736		

INDIANA UNIVERSITY OF PENNSYLVANIA

	Men	Women
Memorial Field House	Baseball	Basketball
Indiana, PA 15705	Basketball	Cheerleading
Affiliation—NCAA II	Cross Country	Cross Country
Nickname—Indians	Football	Field Hockey
Athletic Director—	Golf	Lacrosse
(724) 357-2751	Swimming	Soccer
	Track	Softball
		Swimming
		Tennis
		Track
		Volleyball

JUNIATA COLLEGE

	Men	Women
1700 Moore Street	Baseball	Basketball
Huntington, PA 16652-2119	Basketball	Cross Country
Affiliation—NCAA III	Football	Field Hockey
Nickname—Eagles	Soccer	Soccer
Athletic Director—	Track	Softball
(814) 641-3512	Volleyball	Swimming
		Tennis
		Track
		Volleyball

KING'S COLLEGE

N. *Main Street*	Men	Women
Wilkes-Barre, PA 18711	Baseball	Basketball
*Affiliation—*NCAA *III*	Basketball	Cross Country
Nickname—Monarchs	Cross Country	Field Hockey
Athletic Director—	Football	Lacrosse
(717) 287-5323	Golf	Rifle
	Lacrosse	Soccer
	Rifle	Softball
	Soccer	Swimming
	Swimming	Tennis
	Tennis	Volleyball
	Volleyball	
	Wrestling	

KUTZTOWN UNIVERSITY

Keystone Hall	Men	Women
Kutztown, PA 19530	Baseball	Basketball
*Affiliation—*NCAA *II*	Basketball	Cheerleading
Nickname—Golden Bears	Cross Country	Cross Country
Athletic Director—	Football	Field Hockey
(610) 683-4095	Soccer	Soccer
	Swimming	Softball
	Tennis	Swimming
	Track	Tennis
	Wrestling	Track
		Volleyball

LA ROCHE COLLEGE

9000 Babcock Boulevard	Men	Women
Pittsburgh, PA 15237-5808	Baseball	Basketball
*Affiliation—*NCAA *III*	Basketball	Cross Country
Nickname—Redhawks	Cross Country	Soccer
Athletic Director—	Golf	Softball
(412) 536-1011	Soccer	Tennis
		Volleyball

LA SALLE UNIVERSITY

PO Box 805, 1900 W. Olney	Men	Women
Philadelphia, PA 19105-0805	Baseball	Basketball
Affiliation—NCAA I	Basketball	Crew
Nickname—Explorers	Crew	Cross Country
Athletic Director—	Cross Country	Diving
(215) 951-1516	Diving	Field Hockey
	Football	Lacrosse
	Golf	Soccer
	Soccer	Softball
	Swimming	Swimming
	Tennis	Tennis
	Track	Track
		Volleyball

LAFAYETTE COLLEGE

Pierce and Hamilton	Men	Women
Easton, PA 18042	Baseball	Basketball
Affiliation—NCAA I	Basketball	Cheerleading
(I-AA Football)	Cross Country	Cross Country
Nickname—Leopards	Diving	Diving
Athletic Director—	Fencing	Fencing
(610) 330-5470	Football	Field Hockey
	Golf	Lacrosse
	Lacrosse	Soccer
	Soccer	Softball
	Swimming	Swimming
	Tennis	Tennis
	Track	Track
		Volleyball

LANCASTER BIBLE COLLEGE

901 Eden Road	Men	Women
Lancaster, PA 17601-5036	Baseball	Basketball
Affiliation—NCCAA II	Basketball	Cheerleading
Nickname—Chargers	Soccer	Softball
Athletic Director—		Volleyball
(717) 560-8267		

LEBANON VALLEY COLLEGE

101 N. College Avenue	Men	Women
Annville, PA 17003	Baseball	Basketball
Affiliation—NCAA III	Basketball	Cross Country
Nickname—Flying Dutchmen	Cross Country	Field Hockey
Athletic Director—	Football	Soccer
(717) 867-6261	Golf	Softball
	Ice Hockey	Swimming
	Soccer	Tennis
	Swimming	Track
	Tennis	Volleyball
	Track	
	Wrestling	

LEHIGH UNIVERSITY

641 Taylor Street	Men	Women
Bethlehem, PA 18015-3107	Baseball	Basketball
Affiliation—NCAA I	Basketball	Cheerleading
(I-AA Football)	Cross Country	Cross Country
Nickname—Engineers	Diving	Diving
Athletic Director—	Football	Field Hockey
(610) 758-4320	Golf	Lacrosse
	Lacrosse	Soccer
	Soccer	Softball
	Swimming	Swimming
	Tennis	Tennis
	Track	Track
	Wrestling	Volleyball

LINCOLN UNIVERSITY

PO Box 179	Men	Women
Lincoln University, PA	Baseball	Basketball
19352-0999	Basketball	Cheerleading
Affiliation—NCAA III	Bowling	Cross Country
Nickname—Lions	Cross Country	Tennis
Athletic Director—	Soccer	Track
(610) 932-8300 ext. 3382	Tennis	Volleyball
	Track	

LOCK HAVEN UNIVERSITY

Thomas Field House	**Men**	**Women**
Lock Haven, PA 17745	Baseball	Basketball
Affiliation—NCAA II	Basketball	Cross Country
(Div. I Wrestling)	Cross Country	Field Hockey
Nickname—Bald Eagles	Football	Lacrosse
Athletic Director—	Soccer	Soccer
(717) 893-2093	Track	Softball
	Wrestling	Swimming
		Track
		Volleyball

MANSFIELD UNIVERSITY

Academy Street	**Men**	**Women**
Mansfield, PA 16933	Baseball	Basketball
Affiliation—NCAA II	Basketball	Cross Country
Nickname—Mountaineers	Cross Country	Field Hockey
Athletic Director—	Football	Softball
(717) 662-4046	Track	Swimming
	Wrestling	Track

MARYWOOD UNIVERSITY

2300 Adams Avenue	**Men**	**Women**
Scranton, PA 18509-1598	Baseball	Basketball
Affiliation—NCAA III	Basketball	Cross Country
Nickname—Pacers	Cross Country	Field Hockey
Athletic Director—	Soccer	Soccer
(717) 961-4724	Tennis	Softball
		Tennis
		Volleyball

MERCYHURST COLLEGE

501 E. 38th Street	**Men**	**Women**
Erie, PA 16546	Baseball	Basketball
Affiliation—NCAA II	Basketball	Crew
Nickname—Lakers	Crew	Cross Country
Athletic Director—	Cross Country	Field Hockey
(814) 824-2226	Football	Lacrosse
	Golf	Soccer
	Ice Hockey	Softball
	Lacrosse	Tennis
	Soccer	Volleyball
	Tennis	
	Volleyball	

MESSIAH COLLEGE

College Avenue	Men	Women
Grantham, PA 17027	Baseball	Basketball
Affiliation—NCAA III	Basketball	Cross Country
Nickname—Falcons	Cross Country	Field Hockey
Athletic Director—	Golf	Lacrosse
(717) 691-6018	Lacrosse	Soccer
	Soccer	Softball
	Tennis	Tennis
	Track	Track
	Wrestling	Volleyball

MILLERSVILLE UNIVERSITY OF PENNSYLVANIA

PO Box 1002, N. George Street	Men	Women
Millersville, PA 17551-0302	Baseball	Basketball
Affiliation—NCAA II	Basketball	Cross Country
(Div. I Wrestling)	Cross Country	Field Hockey
Nickname—Marauders	Football	Lacrosse
Athletic Director—Men	Golf	Soccer
(717) 871-2359	Soccer	Softball
Athletic Director—Women	Tennis	Swimming
(717) 872-3402	Track	Tennis
	Wrestling	Track
		Volleyball

MISERICORDIA COLLEGE

Lake Street	Men	Women
Dallas, PA 18612	Baseball	Basketball
Affiliation—NCAA III	Basketball	Cheerleading
Nickname—Cougars	Cross Country	Cross Country
Athletic Director—	Golf	Field Hockey
(717) 674-6294	Soccer	Soccer
	Swimming	Softball
		Swimming
		Volleyball

MORAVIAN COLLEGE

1200 Main Street	**Men**	**Women**
Bethlehem, PA 18018-6614	Baseball	Basketball
Affiliation—NCAA III	Basketball	Cross Country
Nickname—Greyhounds	Cross Country	Field Hockey
Athletic Director—	Football	Soccer
(610) 861-1472	Golf	Softball
	Soccer	Tennis
	Tennis	Track
	Track	Volleyball

MOUNT ALOYSIUS COLLEGE

14 College Drive	**Men**	**Women**
Cresson, PA 16630-1900	Basketball	Basketball
Affiliation—NAIA I		Volleyball
Nickname—Mounties		
Athletic Director—		
(814) 886-6472		

MUHLENBERG COLLEGE

2400 W. Chew Street	**Men**	**Women**
Allentown, PA 18104-5564	Baseball	Basketball
Affiliation—NCAA III	Basketball	Cross Country
Nickname—Mules	Cross Country	Field Hockey
Athletic Director—	Football	Lacrosse
(610) 821-3379	Golf	Soccer
	Soccer	Softball
	Tennis	Tennis
	Track	Track
	Wrestling	Volleyball

NEUMANN COLLEGE

One Neumann Drive	**Men**	**Women**
Aston, PA 19014-1298	Baseball	Basketball
Affiliation—NCAA III	Basketball	Cross Country
Nickname—Knights	Cross Country	Field Hockey
Athletic Director—	Golf	Golf
(610) 558-5627	Ice Hockey	Lacrosse
	Lacrosse	Soccer
	Soccer	Softball
	Tennis	Tennis
		Volleyball

PENNSYLVANIA STATE UNIVERSITY, UNIVERSITY PARK

	Men	Women
Bryce Jordan Center	Baseball	Basketball
University Park, PA 16802	Basketball	Cross Country
Affiliation—NCAA I	Cross Country	Diving
(I-A Football)	Diving	Fencing
Nickname—Nittany Lions	Fencing	Field Hockey
Athletic Director—	Football	Golf
(814) 865-1086	Golf	Gymnastics
	Gymnastics	Lacrosse
	Lacrosse	Soccer
	Soccer	Softball
	Swimming	Swimming
	Tennis	Tennis
	Track	Track
	Volleyball	Volleyball
	Wrestling	

PENNSYLVANIA STATE UNIVERSITY, ERIE, BEHREND COLLEGE

	Men	Women
Station Road	Baseball	Basketball
Erie, PA 16563-5400	Basketball	Cross Country
Affiliation—NCAA III	Cross Country	Soccer
Nickname—Behrend Lions	Golf	Softball
Athletic Director—	Soccer	Tennis
(814) 898-6397	Tennis	Track
	Track	Volleyball

PENNSYLVANIA, UNIVERSITY OF

Weightman Hall N,	**Men**	**Women**
235 S. 33rd Street	Baseball	Basketball
Philadelphia, PA 19104	Basketball	Crew
Affiliation—NCAA I	Crew	Cross Country
(I-AA Football)	Cross Country	Diving
Nickname—Quakers	Diving	Fencing
Athletic Director—	Fencing	Field Hockey
(215) 898-6121	Football	Gymnastics
	Golf	Lacrosse
	Lacrosse	Soccer
	Soccer	Softball
	Squash	Squash
	Swimming	Swimming
	Tennis	Tennis
	Track	Track
	Wrestling	Volleyball

PHILADELPHIA, UNIVERSITY OF THE SCIENCES IN

600 S. 43rd Street	**Men**	**Women**
Philadelphia, PA 19104-4418	Baseball	Basketball
Affiliation—NAIA II	Basketball	Cheerleading
Athletic Director—	Cross Country	Cross Country
(215) 596-8916	Golf	Golf
	Rifle	Rifle
	Tennis	Softball
		Tennis
		Volleyball

PHILADELPHIA COLLEGE OF BIBLE

200 Manor Avenue	**Men**	**Women**
Langhorne, PA 19047-2943	Baseball	Basketball
Affiliation—NCCAA II	Basketball	Field Hockey
Nickname—Crimson Eagles	Soccer	Softball
Athletic Director—	Volleyball	Volleyball
(215) 702-4268		

PHILADELPHIA COLLEGE OF TEXTILES AND SCIENCE

School House Lane and Henry Avenue	**Men**	**Women**
Philadelphia, PA 19144-5444	Baseball	Basketball
Affiliation—NCAA *II*	Basketball	Field Hockey
(Div. I Soccer)	Golf	Lacrosse
Nickname—*Rams*	Soccer	Soccer
Athletic Director—	Tennis	Softball
(215) 951-2731		Tennis
		Volleyball

PITTSBURGH, UNIVERSITY OF

PO Box 7436	**Men**	**Women**
Pittsburgh, PA 15213-0436	Baseball	Basketball
Affiliation—NCAA *I*	Basketball	Cross Country
(I-A Football)	Cross Country	Diving
Nickname—*Panthers*	Diving	Gymnastics
Athletic Director—	Football	Soccer
(412) 648-8230	Soccer	Swimming
	Swimming	Tennis
	Track	Track
	Wrestling	Volleyball

PITTSBURGH, UNIVERTSITY OF, BRADFORD

300 Campus Drive	**Men**	**Women**
Bradford, PA 16701-2812	Baseball	Basketball
Affiliation—NCAA *III*	Basketball	Cross Country
Nickname—*Panthers*	Cross Country	Golf
Athletic Director—	Golf	Soccer
(814) 362-7523	Soccer	Softball
		Volleyball

PITTSBURGH, UNIVERSITY OF, GREENSBURG

1150 Mt. Pleasant Road	**Men**	**Women**
Greensburg, PA 15601-5860	Baseball	Basketball
Nickname—*Bobcats*	Basketball	Cheerleading
Athletic Director—	Golf	Softball
(724) 836-9949	Soccer	Tennis
		Volleyball

PITTSBURGH, UNIVERSITY OF, JOHNSTOWN

Sports Center	**Men**	**Women**
Johnstown, PA 15904	Baseball	Basketball
Affiliation—NCAA II	Basketball	Cheerleading
Nickname—Mountain Cats	Soccer	Cross Country
Athletic Director—	Wrestling	Track
(814) 269-2000		Volleyball

POINT PARK COLLEGE

201 Wood Street	**Men**	**Women**
Pittsburgh, PA 15222-1912	Baseball	Basketball
Affiliation—NAIA I	Basketball	Softball
Nickname—Pioneers	Soccer	
Athletic Director—		
(412) 392-3844		

ROBERT MORRIS COLLEGE

881 Narrows Run Road	**Men**	**Women**
Moon Township, PA	Basketball	Basketball
15108-1189	Cross Country	Cheerleading
Affiliation—NCAA I	Football	Crew
(I-AA Football)	Golf	Cross Country
Nickname—Colonials	Soccer	Soccer
Athletic Director—	Tennis	Softball
(412) 262-8302	Track	Tennis
		Track
		Volleyball

ROSEMONT COLLEGE

1400 Montgomery Avenue	**Women**	
Rosemont, PA 19010	Basketball	Tennis
Affiliation—NCAA III	Field Hockey	Volleyball
Nickname—Ramblers	Softball	
Athletic Director—		
(610) 527-0200 ext. 2360		

SAINT FRANCIS COLLEGE OF PENNSYLVANIA

PO Box 600,	Men	Women
Maurice Stokes Athletic	Basketball	Basketball
Center	Cross Country	Cross Country
Loretto, PA 15940-0600	Football	Diving
Affiliation—NCAA I	Golf	Golf
(I-AA Football)	Soccer	Soccer
Nickname—Red Flash	Tennis	Softball
Athletic Director—	Track	Swimming
(814) 472-3018	Volleyball	Tennis
		Track
		Volleyball

SAINT JOSEPH'S UNIVERSITY

5600 City Avenue	Men	Women
Philadelphia, PA 19131-1308	Baseball	Basketball
Affiliation—NCAA I	Basketball	Cheerleading
Nickname—Hawks	Crew	Crew
Athletic Director—	Cross Country	Cross Country
(610) 660-1707	Golf	Field Hockey
	Lacrosse	Lacrosse
	Soccer	Rowing
	Swimming	Soccer
	Tennis	Softball
	Track	Tennis
		Track

SAINT VINCENT COLLEGE

300 Fraser Purchase Road	Men	Women
Latrobe, PA 15650-2667	Baseball	Basketball
Affiliation—NAIA II	Basketball	Cross Country
Nickname—Bearcats	Cross Country	Lacrosse
Athletic Director—	Lacrosse	Soccer
(724) 539-9761 ext. 4580	Soccer	Softball
	Tennis	Volleyball

SCRANTON, UNIVERSITY OF

John Ling Center	**Men**	**Women**
Scranton, PA 18510	Baseball	Basketball
Affiliation—NCAA III	Basketball	Cross Country
Nickname—Royals	Cross Country	Field Hockey
Athletic Director—	Golf	Soccer
(717) 941-7440	Ice Hockey	Softball
	Lacrosse	Swimming
	Soccer	Tennis
	Swimming	Volleyball
	Tennis	
	Wrestling	

SETON HILL COLLEGE

Seton Hill Drive	**Women**	
Greensburg, PA 15601	Basketball	Softball
Affiliation—NAIA I	Cross Country	Tennis
Nickname—Spirit	Soccer	Volleyball
Athletic Director—		
(724) 838-4259		

SHIPPENSBURG UNIVERSITY

1871 Old Main Drive	**Men**	**Women**
Shippensburg, PA 17257-2200	Baseball	Basketball
Affiliation—NCAA II	Basketball	Cheerleading
Nickname—Raiders	Cross Country	Cross Country
Athletic Director—	Football	Field Hockey
(717) 532-1711	Soccer	Lacrosse
	Swimming	Soccer
	Track	Softball
	Wrestling	Swimming
		Tennis
		Track
		Volleyball

SLIPPERY ROCK UNIVERSITY

102 Morrow Field House	**Men**	**Women**
Slippery Rock, PA 16057	Baseball	Basketball
Affiliation—NCAA II	Basketball	Cross Country
Nickname—Rock	Cross Country	Field Hockey
Athletic Director—	Football	Soccer
(724) 738-2000	Golf	Softball
	Judo	Swimming
	Soccer	Tennis
	Swimming	Track
	Tennis	Volleyball
	Track	Water Polo
	Water Polo	
	Wrestling	

SUSQUEHANNA UNIVERSITY

514 University Avenue	**Men**	**Women**
Selinsgrove, PA 17870-1163	Baseball	Basketball
Affiliation—NCAA III	Basketball	Cheerleading
Nickname—Crusaders	Cross Country	Crew
Athletic Director—	Crew	Cross Country
(717) 372-4272	Football	Field Hockey
	Golf	Lacrosse
	Soccer	Soccer
	Swimming	Softball
	Tennis	Swimming
	Track	Tennis
		Track
		Volleyball

SWARTHMORE COLLEGE

500 College Avenue	**Men**	**Women**
Swarthmore, PA 19081-1306	Baseball	Badminton
Affiliation—NCAA III	Basketball	Basketball
Nickname—Garnet Tide	Cross Country	Cross Country
Athletic Director—	Football	Field Hockey
(610) 328-8222	Golf	Lacrosse
	Lacrosse	Soccer
	Soccer	Softball
	Swimming	Swimming
	Tennis	Tennis
	Track	Track
	Wrestling	Volleyball

TEMPLE UNIVERSITY

Vivaqua Hall, PO Box 2842	**Men**	**Women**
Philadelphia, PA 19122-0842	Baseball	Basketball
Affiliation—NCAA I	Basketball	Cheerleading
(I-A Football)	Crew	Crew
Nickname—Owls	Football	Fencing
Athletic Director—	Golf	Field Hockey
(215) 204-7759	Gymnastics	Gymnastics
	Soccer	Lacrosse
	Tennis	Soccer
	Track	Softball
		Tennis
		Track
		Volleyball

THIEL COLLEGE

75 College Avenue	**Men**	**Women**
Greenville, PA 16125	Baseball	Basketball
Affiliation—NCAA III	Basketball	Cross Country
Nickname—Tomcats	Cross Country	Golf
Athletic Director—	Football	Soccer
(724) 589-2139	Golf	Softball
	Tennis	Tennis
	Track	Track
	Wrestling	Volleyball

URSINUS COLLEGE

Main Street	**Men**	**Women**
Collegeville, PA 19426	Baseball	Basketball
Affiliation—NCAA III	Basketball	Cheerleading
Nickname—Bears	Cross Country	Cross Country
Athletic Director—	Football	Field Hockey
(610) 409-3606	Golf	Gymnastics
	Soccer	Lacrosse
	Swimming	Soccer
	Tennis	Softball
	Track	Swimming
	Wrestling	Tennis
		Track
		Volleyball

VALLEY FORGE CHRISTIAN

Charlestown Road	Men	Women
Phoenixville, PA 19460	Baseball	Basketball
*Affiliation—*NCCAA	Basketball	Cross Country
Nickname—Patriots	Cross Country	Softball
Athletic Director—	Soccer	Volleyball
(610) 917-1467		

VILLANOVA UNIVERSITY

800 Lancaster Avenue	Men	Women
Villanova, PA 19085-1603	Baseball	Basketball
*Affiliation—*NCAA *I*	Basketball	Crew
(I-AA Football)	Cross Country	Cross Country
Nickname—Wildcats	Football	Field Hockey
Athletic Director—	Golf	Lacrosse
(610) 519-4110	Ice Hockey	Soccer
	Lacrosse	Softball
	Soccer	Swimming
	Swimming	Tennis
	Tennis	Track
	Track	Volleyball
		Water Polo

WASHINGTON AND JEFFERSON COLLEGE

60 S. Lincoln Street,	Men	Women
Henry Memorial Court	Baseball	Basketball
Room 103	Basketball	Cross Country
Washington, PA 15301-4812	Cross Country	Golf
*Affiliation—*NCAA *III*	Football	Soccer
Nickname—Presidents	Golf	Softball
Athletic Director—	Lacrosse	Swimming
(724) 223-6054	Soccer	Tennis
	Swimming	Track
	Tennis	Volleyball
	Track	
	Volleyball	
	Wrestling	

WAYNESBURG COLLEGE

51 W. College Street	**Men**	**Women**
Waynesburg, PA 15370	Baseball	Basketball
Affiliation—NCAA III	Basketball	Cross Country
Nickname—Yellowjackets	Football	Golf
Athletic Director—Men	Golf	Soccer
(724) 852-3246	Soccer	Softball
Athletic Director—Women	Tennis	Tennis
(724) 852-3315	Wrestling	Volleyball

WEST CHESTER UNIVERSITY

Sturzebecker Health Science	**Men**	**Women**
Center	Baseball	Basketball
West Chester, PA 19383	Basketball	Cheerleading
Affiliation—NCAA II	Cross Country	Cross Country
Nickname—Golden Rams	Diving	Field Hockey
Athletic Director—	Football	Gymnastics
(610) 436-3555	Golf	Lacrosse
	Lacrosse	Soccer
	Soccer	Softball
	Swimming	Swimming
	Tennis	Tennis
	Track	Track
		Volleyball

WESTMINSTER COLLEGE

Market Street	**Men**	**Women**
New Wilmington, PA 16172	Baseball	Basketball
Affiliation—NCAA II	Basketball	Cross Country
Nickname—Titans	Cross Country	Softball
Athletic Director—	Football	Swimming
(724) 946-7308	Golf	Tennis
	Soccer	Volleyball
	Swimming	
	Tennis	
	Track	

WIDENER UNIVERSITY

One University Place	Men	Women
Chester, PA 19013	Baseball	Basketball
Affiliation—NCAA III	Basketball	Cross Country
Nickname—Pioneers	Cross Country	Field Hockey
Athletic Director—	Football	Lacrosse
(610) 449-4443	Golf	Soccer
	Lacrosse	Softball
	Soccer	Tennis
	Swimming	Track
	Tennis	Volleyball
	Track	

WILKES UNIVERSITY

PO Box 111	Men	Women
Wilkes Barre, PA 18766	Baseball	Basketball
Affiliation—NCAA III	Basketball	Field Hockey
Nickname—Colonels	Football	Golf
Athletic Director—	Golf	Soccer
(717) 408-4024	Soccer	Softball
	Tennis	Tennis
	Wrestling	Volleyball

WILSON COLLEGE

1015 Philadelphia Avenue	Women	
Chambersburg, PA 17201	Basketball	Softball
Affiliation—NCAA III	Equestrian	Tennis
Nickname—Phoenix	Field Hockey	Volleyball
Athletic Director—	Gymnastics	
(717) 262-2012		

YORK COLLEGE

Wolf Gym	Men	Women
York, PA 17405	Baseball	Basketball
Affiliation—NCAA III	Basketball	Cross Country
Nickname—Spartans	Cross Country	Field Hockey
Athletic Director—	Golf	Soccer
(717) 849-1614	Soccer	Softball
	Swimming	Swimming
	Tennis	Tennis
	Track	Track
	Wrestling	Volleyball

RHODE ISLAND

BROWN UNIVERSITY

Hope Street	**Men**	**Women**
Providence, RI 02912	Baseball	Basketball
Affiliation—NCAA I	Basketball	Crew
(I-AA Football)	Crew	Cross Country
Nickname—Bears	Cross Country	Diving
Athletic Director—	Diving	Fencing
(401) 863-2972	Fencing	Field Hockey
	Football	Golf
	Golf	Gymnastics
	Ice Hockey	Ice Hockey
	Lacrosse	Lacrosse
	Soccer	Skiing
	Squash	Soccer
	Swimming	Softball
	Tennis	Squash
	Track	Swimming
	Water Polo	Tennis
	Wrestling	Track
		Volleyball

BRYANT COLLEGE

1150 Douglas Pike	**Men**	**Women**
Smithfield, RI 02917-1291	Baseball	Basketball
Affiliation—NCAA II	Basketball	Cross Country
Nickname—Bulldogs	Cross Country	Soccer
Athletic Director—	Football	Softball
(401) 232-6070	Golf	Tennis
	Soccer	Track
	Tennis	Volleyball
	Track	

JOHNSON & WALES UNIVERSITY

8 Abbott Park Place	**Men**	**Women**
Providence, RI 02903-3703	Baseball	Basketball
Affiliation—NCAA III	Basketball	Cheerleading
Nickname—Wildcats	Cross Country	Cross Country
Athletic Director—Men	Golf	Soccer
(401) 598-1725	Ice Hockey	Softball
Athletic Director—Women	Soccer	Tennis
(401) 598-1715	Tennis	Volleyball
	Volleyball	
	Wrestling	

PROVIDENCE COLLEGE

River Avenue	**Men**	**Women**
Providence, RI 02918	Baseball	Basketball
Affiliation—NCAA *I*	Basketball	Cross Country
Nickname—*Friars*	Cross Country	Field Hockey
Athletic Director—	Golf	Ice Hockey
(401) 865-2500	Ice Hockey	Soccer
	Lacrosse	Softball
	Soccer	Swimming
	Swimming	Tennis
	Tennis	Track
	Track	Volleyball

RHODE ISLAND, UNIVERSITY OF

3 Keaney Road, Suite 1	**Men**	**Women**
Kingston, RI 02881-1111	Baseball	Basketball
Affiliation—NCAA *I*	Basketball	Cross Country
(I-AA Football)	Cross Country	Diving
Nickname—*Rams*	Diving	Field Hockey
Athletic Director—	Football	Gymnastics
(401) 874-5245	Golf	Soccer
	Soccer	Softball
	Swimming	Swimming
	Tennis	Tennis
	Track	Track
		Volleyball

RHODE ISLAND COLLEGE

600 Mount Pleasant Avenue	**Men**	**Women**
Providence, RI 02908-1924	Baseball	Basketball
Affiliation—NCAA *III*	Basketball	Cross Country
Nickname—*Anchormen*	Cross Country	Gymnastics
Athletic Director—	Soccer	Soccer
(401) 456-8007	Tennis	Softball
	Track	Tennis
	Wrestling	Track
		Volleyball

ROGER WILLIAMS UNIVERSITY

Old Ferry Road	**Men**	**Women**
Bristol, RI 02809	Baseball	Basketball
*Affiliation—*NCAA *III*	Basketball	Crew
Nickname—Hawks	Cross Country	Cross Country
Athletic Director—	Equestrian	Equestrian
(401) 254-3129	Golf	Golf
	Lacrosse	Sailing
	Sailing	Soccer
	Soccer	Softball
	Tennis	Tennis
	Volleyball	Volleyball
	Wrestling	

SALVE REGINA UNIVERSITY

100 Ochre Point Avenue	**Men**	**Women**
Newport, RI 02840-4149	Baseball	Basketball
*Affiliation—*NCAA *III*	Basketball	Cross Country
Nickname—Seahawks	Football	Equestrian
Athletic Director—	Golf	Field Hockey
(401) 847-6650 ext. 2268	Ice Hockey	Lacrosse
	Lacrosse	Sailing
	Soccer	Soccer
	Tennis	Softball
		Tennis
		Track

SOUTH CAROLINA

ALLEN UNIVERSITY

1530 Harden Street	**Men**	**Women**
Columbia, SC 29204-1057	Baseball	Cross Country
*Affiliation—*NAIA	Basketball	Track
Nickname—Yellow Jackets	Cross Country	
Athletic Director—	Track	
(803) 376-5745		

ANDERSON COLLEGE

Boulevard Street	**Men**	**Women**
Anderson, SC 29621	Baseball	Basketball
*Affiliation—*NAIA *I,* NCAA *II*	Basketball	Cross Country
Nickname—Trojans	Cross Country	Soccer
Athletic Director—	Golf	Softball
(864) 231-2023	Tennis	Tennis
	Wrestling	Volleyball

BENEDICT COLLEGE

Harden Street	**Men**	**Women**
Columbia, SC 29204	Baseball	Basketball
*Affiliation—*NAIA *I*	Basketball	Cross Country
Nickname—Tigers	Cross Country	Softball
Athletic Director—	Football	Track
(803) 253-5411	Golf	Volleyball
	Tennis	
	Track	

CHARLESTON SOUTHERN UNIVERSITY

PO Box 118087	**Men**	**Women**
Charleston, SC 29423-8087	Baseball	Basketball
*Affiliation—*NCAA *I*	Basketball	Cross Country
(I-AA Football)	Cross Country	Golf
Nickname—Buccaneers	Football	Soccer
Athletic Director—	Golf	Softball
(843) 863-7675	Soccer	Tennis
	Tennis	Track
	Track	Volleyball

CITADEL, THE

171 Moultrie Street	**Men**	**Women**
Charleston, SC 29409	Baseball	Volleyball
*Affiliation—*NCAA *I*	Basketball	
(I-AA Football)	Cross Country	
Nickname—Bulldogs	Football	
Athletic Director—	Golf	
(843) 953-5030	Soccer	
	Tennis	
	Track	
	Wrestling	

CLAFLIN COLLEGE

700 College Street NE	**Men**	**Women**
Orangeburg, SC 29115-4477	Basketball	Basketball
*Affiliation—*NAIA *I*	Track	Cross Country
Nickname—Panthers		Tennis
Athletic Director—		Track
(803) 534-2710		Volleyball

CLEMSON UNIVERSITY

	Men	Women
PO Box 31, 1 Perimeter Road	Baseball	Basketball
Clemson, SC 29633-0031	Basketball	Cross Country
Affiliation—NCAA I	Cross Country	Diving
(I-A Football)	Diving	Rowing
Nickname—Tigers	Football	Soccer
Athletic Director—	Golf	Swimming
(864) 656-2218	Soccer	Tennis
	Swimming	Track
	Tennis	Volleyball
	Track	

COASTAL CAROLINA UNIVERSITY

	Men	Women
PO Box 26154,	Baseball	Basketball
755 Highway 544	Basketball	Cross Country
Conway, SC 29528-6054	Cross Country	Golf
Affiliation—NCAA I	Golf	Softball
Nickname—Chanticleers	Soccer	Tennis
Athletic Director—	Tennis	Track
(843) 349-2813	Track	Volleyball

COKER COLLEGE

	Men	Women
College Avenue	Baseball	Basketball
Hartsville, SC 29550	Basketball	Cross Country
Affiliation—NCAA II	Cross Country	Soccer
Nickname—Cobras	Golf	Softball
Athletic Director—	Soccer	Tennis
(843) 383-8071	Tennis	Volleyball

COLLEGE OF CHARLESTON

	Men	Women
30 George Street	Baseball	Basketball
Charleston, SC 29401-1434	Basketball	Cross Country
Affiliation—NCAA I	Cross Country	Equestrian
Nickname—Cougars	Golf	Golf
Athletic Director—	Sailing	Sailing
(843) 953-8251	Soccer	Soccer
	Swimming	Softball
	Tennis	Swimming
		Tennis
		Volleyball

COLUMBIA COLLEGE

1301 Columbia College Drive	**Men**	
Columbia, SC 29230	Cross Country	Volleyball
Affiliation—NAIA	Tennis	
Nickname—Koalas		
Athletic Director—		
(803) 768-3861		

ERSKINE COLLEGE

PO Box 357	**Men**	**Women**
Due West, SC 29639-0357	Baseball	Basketball
Affiliation—NCAA II	Basketball	Cross Country
Nickname—Flying Fleet	Cross Country	Soccer
Athletic Director—	Soccer	Softball
(864) 379-8859	Tennis	Tennis

FRANCIS MARION UNIVERSITY

PO Box 100547	**Men**	**Women**
Florence, SC 29501-0547	Baseball	Basketball
Affiliation—NCAA II	Basketball	Cross Country
Nickname—Patriots	Cross Country	Soccer
Athletic Director—	Golf	Softball
(843) 661-1241	Soccer	Tennis
	Tennis	Track
	Track	Volleyball

FURMAN UNIVERSITY

3300 Poinsett Highway	**Men**	**Women**
Greenville, SC 29613-0002	Baseball	Basketball
Affiliation—NCAA I	Basketball	Cross Country
(I-AA Football)	Cross Country	Golf
Nickname—Paladins	Football	Soccer
Athletic Director—	Golf	Softball
(864) 294-2150	Soccer	Tennis
	Tennis	Track
	Track	Volleyball

LANDER UNIVERSITY

Stanley Avenue	**Men**	**Women**
Greenwood, SC 29649	Baseball	Basketball
Affiliation—NCAA II	Basketball	Cross Country
Nickname—Senators	Cross Country	Soccer
Athletic Director—	Soccer	Softball
(864) 388-8314	Tennis	Tennis
		Volleyball

LIMESTONE COLLEGE

1115 College Drive	**Men**	**Women**
Gaffney, SC 29340-3778	Baseball	Basketball
Affiliation—NAIA I, NCAA II	Basketball	Cheerleading
Nickname—Saints	Golf	Lacrosse
Athletic Director—	Lacrosse	Soccer
(864) 488-4561	Soccer	Softball
	Tennis	Tennis
		Volleyball

MORRIS COLLEGE

N. Main Street Extension	**Men**	**Women**
Sumter, SC 29150	Baseball	Basketball
Affiliation—NAIA I	Basketball	Softball
Nickname—Hornets	Track	Track
Athletic Director—		
(803) 775-9371		

NEWBERRY COLLEGE

2100 College Street	**Men**	**Women**
Newberry, SC 29108-2126	Baseball	Basketball
Affiliation—NCAA II	Basketball	Cheerleading
Nickname—Indians	Cross Country	Cross Country
Athletic Director—	Football	Golf
(803) 321-5155	Golf	Soccer
	Soccer	Softball
	Tennis	Tennis
	Volleyball	Volleyball

NORTH GREENVILLE COLLEGE

PO Box 1892	Men	Women
Tigerville, SC 29688-1892	Baseball	Basketball
Affiliation—NAIA	Basketball	Cheerleading
Nickname—Mounties	Football	Soccer
Athletic Director—	Golf	Softball
(864) 977-7018	Soccer	Tennis
	Tennis	Volleyball

PRESBYTERIAN COLLEGE

105 Ashland Avenue	Men	Women
Clinton, SC 29325-2994	Baseball	Basketball
Affiliation—NCAA II	Basketball	Cheerleading
Nickname—Blue Hose	Cross Country	Cross Country
Athletic Director—	Football	Soccer
(864) 833-8242	Golf	Softball
	Soccer	Tennis
	Tennis	Volleyball

SOUTH CAROLINA, UNIVERSITY OF

Rex Enright Athletic Center,	Men	Women
1300 Rosewood Drive	Baseball	Basketball
Columbia, SC 29208	Basketball	Cross Country
Affiliation—NCAA I	Diving	Diving
(I-A Football)	Football	Equestrian
Nickname—Fighting Gamecocks	Golf	Golf
Athletic Director—	Soccer	Soccer
(803) 777-8881	Swimming	Softball
	Tennis	Swimming
	Track	Tennis
		Track
		Volleyball

SOUTH CAROLINA, UNIVERSITY OF, AIKEN

171 University Parkway	Men	Women
Aiken, SC 29801-6309	Baseball	Basketball
Affiliation—NCAA II	Basketball	Cross Country
Nickname—Pacers	Cross Country	Soccer
Athletic Director—	Golf	Softball
(803) 648-6851 ext. 3406	Soccer	Tennis
	Tennis	Track

SOUTH CAROLINA, UNIVERSITY OF, SPARTANBURG

800 University Way	**Men**	**Women**
Spartanburg, SC 29303-4932	Baseball	Basketball
Affiliation—NCAA II	Basketball	Cross Country
Nickname—Rifles	Cross Country	Softball
Athletic Director—	Soccer	Tennis
(864) 503-5140	Tennis	Volleyball

SOUTH CAROLINA STATE UNIVERSITY

300 College Street NE	**Men**	**Women**
Orangeburg, SC 29117	Basketball	Basketball
Affiliation—NCAA I	Cross Country	Bowling
(I-AA Football)	Football	Cheerleading
Nickname—Bulldogs	Golf	Cross Country
Athletic Director—	Tennis	Softball
(803) 536-8578	Track	Tennis
		Track
		Volleyball

SOUTHERN WESLEYAN UNIVERSITY

1 Wesleyan Drive	**Men**	**Women**
Central, SC 29630	Baseball	Basketball
Affiliation—NAIA, NCCAA	Basketball	Cross Country
Nickname—Warriors	Cross Country	Softball
Athletic Director—	Golf	Volleyball
(803) 639-2453	Soccer	

VOORHEES COLLEGE

Voorhees Road	**Men**	**Women**
Demark, SC 29042	Baseball	Basketball
Affiliation—NAIA I	Basketball	Cheerleading
Nickname—Tigers	Cross Country	Cross Country
Athletic Director—	Track	Softball
(803) 793-3351 ext. 7348		Track
		Volleyball

WINTHROP UNIVERSITY

Winthrop Coliseum, Eden	**Men**	**Women**
Terrace	Baseball	Basketball
Rock Hill, SC 29733	Basketball	Cross Country
*Affiliation—*NCAA *I*	Cross Country	Golf
Nickname—Eagles	Golf	Softball
Athletic Director—	Soccer	Tennis
(803) 323-2129 ext. 226	Tennis	Track
	Track	Volleyball

WOFFORD COLLEGE

429 N. Church	**Men**	**Women**
Spartanburg, SC 29303-3663	Baseball	Basketball
*Affiliation—*NCAA *I*	Basketball	Cross Country
(I-AA Football)	Cross Country	Golf
Nickname—Terriers	Football	Soccer
Athletic Director—	Golf	Softball
(864) 597-4090	Soccer	Tennis
	Tennis	Track
	Track	Volleyball

SOUTH DAKOTA

AUGUSTANA COLLEGE

2001 S. Summit Avenue	**Men**	**Women**
Sioux Falls, SD 57191	Baseball	Basketball
*Affiliation—*NCAA *II*	Basketball	Cross Country
Nickname—Vikings	Cross Country	Softball
Athletic Director—	Football	Tennis
(605) 336-4315	Tennis	Track
	Track	Volleyball
	Wrestling	

BLACK HILLS STATE UNIVERSITY

PO Box 9924, 1200 University	**Men**	**Women**
Spearfish, SD 57799	Basketball	Basketball
*Affiliation—*NAIA *I*	Cross Country	Cheerleading
Nickname—Yellow Jackets	Football	Cross Country
Athletic Director—	Track	Track
(605) 642-6881		Volleyball

DAKOTA STATE UNIVERSITY

820 N. Washington Avenue *Madison, SD 57042-1735* *Affiliation—NAIA II* *Nickname—Trojans* *Athletic Director—* *(605) 256-5229*	**Men** Baseball Basketball Cross Country Football Golf Track	**Women** Basketball Cross Country Golf Softball Track Volleyball

DAKOTA WESLEYAN UNIVERSITY

1200 University Boulevard *Mitchell, SD 57301* *Affiliation—NAIA II* *Nickname—Tigers* *Athletic Director—* *(605) 995-2875*	**Men** Baseball Basketball Cross Country Football Golf Track Wrestling	**Women** Basketball Cheerleading Cross Country Golf Soccer Softball Track Volleyball

HURON UNIVERSITY

333 9th Street SW *Huron, SD 57350-2765* *Affiliation—NAIA II* *Nickname—Screaming Eagles* *Athletic Director—* *(605) 352-8721*	**Men** Baseball Basketball Football Soccer Track Wrestling	**Women** Basketball Cheerleading Soccer Softball Track Volleyball

MOUNT MARTY COLLEGE

1105 W. 8th Street *Yankton, SD 57078-3725* *Affiliation—NAIA II* *Nickname—Lancers* *Athletic Director—* *(605) 668-1529*	**Men** Baseball Basketball Cross Country Golf Track	**Women** Basketball Cross Country Golf Track Volleyball

NATIONAL AMERICAN UNIVERSITY

321 Kansas City Street *Rapid City, SD 57701-2820* *Affiliation—NAIA* *Nickname—Mavericks* *Athletic Director—* *(605) 394-4834*	**Men** Rodeo Soccer	**Women** Rodeo Soccer Volleyball

NORTHERN STATE UNIVERSITY

1200 S. Jay Street	**Men**	**Women**
Aberdeen, SD 57401-7155	Baseball	Basketball
Affiliation—NCAA II	Basketball	Cross Country
Nickname—Wolves	Cross Country	Golf
Athletic Director—	Football	Soccer
(605) 626-2488	Golf	Softball
	Tennis	Tennis
	Track	Track
	Wrestling	Volleyball

PRESENTATION COLLEGE

1500 N. Main Street	**Men**	**Women**
Aberdeen, SD 57401-1280	Basketball	Basketball
Affiliation—NAIA II		Volleyball
Nickname—Saints		
Athletic Director—		
(605) 229-8515		

SIOUX FALLS, UNIVERSITY OF

1101 W. 22nd Street	**Men**	**Women**
Sioux Falls, SD 57105-1600	Baseball	Basketball
Affiliation—NAIA II	Basketball	Cross Country
Nickname—Cougars	Cross Country	Soccer
Athletic Director—	Football	Softball
(605) 331-6656	Soccer	Tennis
	Tennis	Track
	Track	Volleyball

SOUTH DAKOTA, UNIVERSITY OF

414 E. Clark Street	**Men**	**Women**
Vermillion, SD 57069-2307	Baseball	Basketball
Affiliation—NCAA II	Basketball	Cross Country
Nickname—Coyotes	Cross Country	Softball
Athletic Director—	Football	Swimming
(605) 677-5951	Swimming	Tennis
	Tennis	Track
	Track	Volleyball

SOUTH DAKOTA SCHOOL OF MINES AND TECHNOLOGY

	Men	Women
501 E. Saint Joe Street	Basketball	Basketball
Rapid City, SD 57701-3901	Cross Country	Cross Country
*Affiliation—*NAIA *II*	Football	Track
Nickname—Hardrockers	Track	Volleyball
Athletic Director—		
(605) 394-2352		

SOUTH DAKOTA STATE UNIVERSITY

	Men	Women
16th Avenue and 11th Street	Baseball	Basketball
Brookings, SD 57007	Basketball	Cross Country
*Affiliation—*NCAA *II*	Cross Country	Golf
Nickname—Jackrabbits	Football	Softball
Athletic Director—	Golf	Swimming
(605) 688-5625	Swimming	Tennis
	Tennis	Track
	Track	Volleyball
	Wrestling	

TENNESSEE

AUSTIN PEAY STATE UNIVERSITY

	Men	Women
PO Box 4515	Baseball	Basketball
Clarksville, TN 37044	Basketball	Cross Country
*Affiliation—*NCAA *I*	Cross Country	Golf
(I-A Football)	Football	Rifle
Nickname—Governors	Golf	Softball
Athletic Director—	Tennis	Tennis
(931) 648-7904		Track
		Volleyball

BELMONT UNIVERSITY

	Men	Women
1900 Belmont Boulevard	Baseball	Basketball
Nashville, TN 37212-3758	Basketball	Cross Country
*Affiliation—*NCAA *I*	Cross Country	Golf
Nickname—Bruins	Golf	Soccer
Athletic Director—	Soccer	Softball
(615) 460-5547	Tennis	Tennis
		Track
		Volleyball

BETHEL COLLEGE

College Drive	**Men**	**Women**
McKenzie, TN 38201	Baseball	Basketball
*Affiliation—*NAIA *II,* NAIA *I*	Basketball	Soccer
Nickname—Wildcats	Football	Softball
Athletic Director—	Golf	
(901) 352-4203	Soccer	

BRYAN COLLEGE

Bryan Hill	**Men**	**Women**
Dayton, TN 37321	Basketball	Basketball
*Affiliation—*NAIA *I,* NCCAA	Soccer	Soccer
Nickname—Lions	Tennis	Tennis
Athletic Director—		Volleyball
(423) 775-7255		

CARSON-NEWMAN COLLEGE

2130 Branner Avenue	**Men**	**Women**
Jefferson City, TN 37760-2224	Baseball	Basketball
*Affiliation—*NCAA *II*	Basketball	Cross Country
Nickname—Eagles	Cross Country	Soccer
Athletic Director—	Football	Softball
(423) 471-3372	Golf	Tennis
	Soccer	Track
	Tennis	Volleyball
	Track	
	Wrestling	

CHRISTIAN BROTHERS UNIVERSITY

650 E. Parkway S	**Men**	**Women**
Memphis, TN 38104-5519	Baseball	Basketball
*Affiliation—*NCAA *II*	Basketball	Cross Country
Nickname—Buccaneers	Cross Country	Soccer
Athletic Director—	Golf	Softball
(901) 321-3374	Soccer	Tennis
	Tennis	Volleyball

CUMBERLAND UNIVERSITY

1 Cumberland Square	**Men**	**Women**
Lebanon, TN 37087-3408	Baseball	Basketball
*Affiliation—*NAIA *I*	Basketball	Cheerleading
Nickname—Bulldogs	Cross Country	Cross Country
Athletic Director—	Football	Golf
(800) 467-0562 ext. 1132	Golf	Soccer
	Soccer	Softball
	Tennis	Tennis
	Wrestling	Volleyball

EAST TENNESSEE STATE UNIVERSITY

University Drive and State of	**Men**	**Women**
Franklin	Baseball	Basketball
Johnson City, TN 37614	Basketball	Cheerleading
*Affiliation—*NCAA *I*	Cross Country	Cross Country
(I-AA Football)	Football	Golf
Nickname—Buccaneers	Golf	Soccer
Athletic Director—	Tennis	Tennis
(423) 439-4343	Track	Track
		Volleyball

FISK UNIVERSITY

17 Avenue N	**Men**	**Women**
Nashville, TN 37208	Baseball	Basketball
*Affiliation—*NCAA *III*	Basketball	Cheerleading
Nickname—Bulldogs	Cross Country	Cross Country
Athletic Director—	Golf	Tennis
(615) 329-8782	Tennis	Track
		Volleyball

FREED HARDEMAN UNIVERSITY

158 E. Main Street	**Men**	**Women**
Henderson, TN 38340-2306	Baseball	Basketball
*Affiliation—*NAIA *I*	Basketball	Softball
Nickname—Lions	Golf	Tennis
Athletic Director—	Tennis	Volleyball
(901) 989-6001		

JOHNSON BIBLE COLLEGE

	Men	Women
7900 Johnson Drive	Baseball	Basketball
Knoxville, TN 37998	Basketball	Volleyball
Affiliation—NCCAA II	Soccer	
Nickname—Evangels		
Athletic Director—		
(423) 573-4517		

KING COLLEGE

	Men	Women
1350 King College Road	Baseball	Basketball
Bristol, TN 37620-2632	Basketball	Soccer
Affiliation—NAIA II	Golf	Tennis
Nickname—Tornados	Soccer	Volleyball
Athletic Director—	Tennis	
(423) 652-4781		

KNOXVILLE COLLEGE

	Men	Women
901 College Street	Baseball	Basketball
Knoxville, TN 37921-4724	Basketball	Tennis
Affiliation—NCAA III	Football	Track
Nickname—Bulldogs	Track	
Athletic Director—	Volleyball	
(423) 524-6689		

LAMBUTH UNIVERSITY

	Men	Women
705 Lambuth Boulevard	Baseball	Basketball
Jackson, TN 38301-5280	Basketball	Cross Country
Affiliation—NAIA I	Cross Country	Soccer
(NAIA II Football)	Football	Softball
Nickname—Eagles	Golf	Tennis
Athletic Director—	Soccer	Volleyball
(901) 425-3433	Tennis	

LANE COLLEGE

	Men	Women
545 Lane Avenue	Baseball	Basketball
Jackson, TN 38301-4501	Basketball	Cheerleading
Affiliation—NCAA II	Cross Country	Cross Country
Nickname—Dragons	Football	Softball
Athletic Director—	Tennis	Tennis
(901) 426-7568	Track	Track
	Volleyball	Volleyball

LEE UNIVERSITY

1120 Ocoee Street	Men	Women
Cleveland, TN 37311	Baseball	Basketball
Affiliation—NAIA I, NCCAA	Basketball	Cheerleading
Nickname—Flames	Cross Country	Cross Country
Athletic Director—	Golf	Soccer
(423) 614-8440	Soccer	Softball
	Tennis	Tennis
		Volleyball

LEMOYNE-OWEN COLLEGE

807 Walker Avenue	Men	Women
Memphis, TN 38126-6510	Baseball	Basketball
Affiliation—NCAA II	Basketball	Cross Country
Nickname—Magicians	Cross Country	Track
Athletic Director—	Track	Volleyball
(901) 942-7327		

LINCOLN MEMORIAL UNIVERSITY

PO Box 2028,	Men	Women
Cumberland Gap Parkway	Baseball	Basketball
Harrogate, TN 37752	Basketball	Cheerleading
Affiliation—NCAA II	Cross Country	Cross Country
Nickname—Railsplitters	Golf	Golf
Athletic Director—	Soccer	Soccer
(423) 869-6299	Tennis	Softball
		Tennis
		Volleyball

LIPSCOME UNIVERSITY

3901 Granny White Pike	Men	Women
Nashville, TN 37204-3951	Baseball	Basketball
Affiliation—NAIA I	Basketball	Cheerleading
Nickname—Bison	Cross Country	Cross Country
Athletic Director—	Golf	Golf
(615) 269-1795	Tennis	Softball
		Tennis
		Volleyball

MARTIN METHODIST COLLEGE

	Men	Women
433 W. Madison Street	Baseball	Basketball
Pulaski, TN 38478-2716	Basketball	Cross Country
*Affiliation—*NAIA *I*	Cross Country	Soccer
Nickname—Indians	Golf	Softball
Athletic Director—	Soccer	Tennis
(931) 363-9872	Tennis	Volleyball

MARYVILLE COLLEGE

	Men	Women
502 E. Lamar Alexander	Baseball	Basketball
Parkway	Basketball	Soccer
Maryville, TN 37804-5907	Soccer	Softball
*Affiliation—*NCAA *III*	Tennis	Tennis
Nickname—Fighting Scots		Volleyball
Athletic Director—		
(423) 981-8280		

McCOY COLLEGE

	Men	Women
1106 16th Avenue S	Baseball	Basketball
Nashville, TN 37212-2305	Basketball	Softball
Nickname—Gentlemen/Ladies	Golf	Tennis
	Lacrosse	
	Soccer	
	Swimming	

MEMPHIS, UNIVERSITY OF

	Men	Women
570 Normal	Baseball	Basketball
Memphis, TN 38152	Basketball	Cross Country
*Affiliation—*NCAA *I*	Cross Country	Golf
(I-A Football)	Football	Rifle
Nickname—Tigers	Golf	Soccer
Athletic Director—	Rifle	Tennis
(901) 678-2234	Soccer	Track
	Tennis	Volleyball
	Track	

MIDDLE TENNESSEE STATE UNIVERSITY

MTSU Box 77,	**Men**	**Women**
1500 Greenland Drive	Baseball	Basketball
Murfreesboro, TN 37130-3180	Basketball	Cross Country
Affiliation—NCAA I	Cross Country	Soccer
(I-A Football)	Football	Softball
Nickname—Blue Raiders	Golf	Tennis
Athletic Director—	Tennis	Track
(615) 898-2450	Track	Volleyball

MILLIGAN COLLEGE

Toll Branch Road	**Men**	**Women**
Milligan College, TN 37682	Baseball	Basketball
Affiliation—NAIA II	Basketball	Soccer
Nickname—Buffaloes	Golf	Softball
Athletic Director—	Soccer	Tennis
(423) 461-8783	Tennis	Volleyball

RHODES COLLEGE

2000 N. Parkway	**Men**	**Women**
Memphis, TN 38112-1624	Baseball	Basketball
Affiliation—NCAA III	Basketball	Cross Country
Nickname—Lynx	Cross Country	Golf
Athletic Director—	Football	Soccer
(901) 843-3940	Golf	Softball
	Soccer	Tennis
	Tennis	Track
	Track	Volleyball

SOUTH, UNIVERSITY OF THE

735 University Avenue	**Men**	**Women**
Sewanee, TN 37383	Baseball	Basketball
Affiliation—NCAA III	Basketball	Cross Country
Nickname—Tigers	Cross Country	Field Hockey
Athletic Director—	Football	Golf
(615) 598-1388	Golf	Soccer
	Soccer	Swimming
	Swimming	Tennis
	Tennis	Track
	Track	Volleyball

TENNESSEE, UNIVERSITY OF

1720 Volunteer Boulevard	**Men**	**Women**
Knoxville, TN 37916-3716	Baseball	Basketball
Affiliation—NCAA I	Basketball	Crew
(I-A Football)	Cross Country	Cross Country
Nickname—Volunteers	Football	Diving
Athletic Director—Men	Golf	Golf
(423) 974-1224	Swimming	Soccer
Athletic Director—Women	Tennis	Softball
(423) 974-0001	Track	Swimming
		Tennis
		Track
		Volleyball

TENNESSEE, UNIVERSITY OF, CHATTANOOGA

615 McCallie Avenue	**Men**	**Women**
Chattanooga, TN 37403-2504	Basketball	Basketball
Affiliation—NCAA I	Cross Country	Cross Country
(I-AA Football)	Football	Soccer
Nickname—Mocs	Golf	Softball
Athletic Director—	Tennis	Tennis
(423) 755-4494	Track	Track
	Wrestling	Volleyball

TENNESSEE, UNIVERSITY OF, MARTIN

UT Martin Elm Center	**Men**	**Women**
Martin, TN 38238	Baseball	Basketball
Affiliation—NCAA I	Basketball	Cross Country
(I-AA Football)	Football	Rifle
Nickname—Skyhawks	Golf	Soccer
Athletic Director—	Rifle	Softball
(901) 587-7661	Tennis	Tennis
	Track	Track
		Volleyball

TENNESSEE STATE UNIVERSITY

3500 John A. Merritt Boulevard	**Men**	**Women**
Nashville, TN 37209-1500	Basketball	Basketball
Affiliation—NCAA I	Cross Country	Cross Country
(I-AA Football)	Football	Soccer
Nickname—Tigers	Golf	Softball
Athletic Director—	Tennis	Tennis
(615) 963-7750	Track	Track
	Volleyball	Volleyball

TENNESSEE TECHNOLOGICAL UNIVERSITY

	Men	Women
PO Box 5057	Baseball	Basketball
Cookeville, TN 38505	Basketball	Cross Country
Affiliation—NCAA I	Cross Country	Golf
(I-AA Football)	Football	Rifle
Nickname—Golden Eagles	Golf	Soccer
Athletic Director—	Rifle	Softball
(931) 372-3949	Rugby	Tennis
	Tennis	Track
	Track	Volleyball

TENNESSEE TEMPLE UNIVERSITY

	Men	Women
1815 Union Avenue	Baseball	Basketball
Chattanooga, TN 37404-3530	Basketball	Volleyball
Affiliation—NCCAA I	Soccer	
Nickname—Crusaders		
Athletic Director—		
(423) 493-4220		

TENNESSEE WESLEYAN COLLEGE

	Men	Women
Green Street	Baseball	Basketball
Athens, TN 37303	Basketball	Soccer
Affiliation—NAIA	Golf	Softball
Nickname—Bulldogs	Soccer	Tennis
Athletic Director—		
(423) 745-7504 ext. 5253		

TREVECCA NAZARENE UNIVERSITY

	Men	Women
333 Murfreesboro Road	Baseball	Basketball
Nashville, TN 37210-2834	Basketball	Cheerleading
Affiliation—NAIA I		Softball
Nickname—Trojans		Volleyball
Athletic Director—		
(615) 248-1274		

TUSCULUM COLLEGE

PO Box 5021,	**Men**	**Women**
2299 Tusculum Boulevard	Baseball	Basketball
Greeneville, TN 37743	Basketball	Cross Country
Affiliation—NAIA II, NCAA II	Cross Country	Golf
Nickname—Pioneers	Football	Soccer
Athletic Director—	Golf	Softball
(423) 636-7323	Soccer	Tennis
	Tennis	Volleyball
	Volleyball	

UNION UNIVERSITY

1050 Union University Drive	**Men**	**Women**
Jackson, TN 38305-3656	Baseball	Basketball
Affiliation—NAIA	Basketball	Softball
Nickname—Bulldogs	Golf	Volleyball
Athletic Director—	Soccer	
(901) 661-5277	Tennis	

VANDERBILT UNIVERSITY

2601 Jess Neely Drive,	**Men**	**Women**
PO Box 120158	Baseball	Basketball
Nashville, TN 37212-0158	Basketball	Cross Country
Affiliation—NCAA I	Cross Country	Golf
(I-A Football)	Football	Lacrosse
Nickname—Commodores	Golf	Soccer
Athletic Director—	Soccer	Tennis
(615) 322-4831	Tennis	Track

TEXAS

ABILENE CHRISTIAN UNIVERSITY

ACU Station, Box 27916	**Men**	**Women**
Abilene, TX 79699	Baseball	Basketball
Affiliation—NCAA II	Basketball	Cross Country
Nickname—Wildcats	Cross Country	Softball
Athletic Director—	Football	Tennis
(915) 674-2400	Tennis	Track
	Track	Volleyball

ANGELO STATE UNIVERSITY

2601 W. Avenue N, Box 10884,	**Men**	**Women**
ASU Station	Basketball	Basketball
San Angelo, TX 76909	Cross Country	Cross Country
Affiliation—NCAA II	Football	Soccer
Nickname—Rams	Track	Track
Athletic Director—Men		Volleyball
(915) 942-2091		
Athletic Director—Women		
(915) 942-2264		

AUSTIN COLLEGE

900 N. Grand Avenue, Suite 6A	**Men**	**Women**
Sherman, TX 75090-4440	Baseball	Basketball
Affiliation—NCAA III	Basketball	Diving
Nickname—Kangaroos	Golf	Soccer
Athletic Director—	Soccer	Swimming
(903) 813-2228	Swimming	Tennis
	Tennis	Track
	Track	Volleyball

BAYLOR UNIVERSITY

150 Bear Run	**Men**	**Women**
Waco, TX 76711-1267	Baseball	Basketball
Affiliation—NCAA I	Basketball	Cross Country
(I-A Football)	Cross Country	Golf
Nickname—Bears	Football	Soccer
Athletic Director—	Golf	Tennis
(254) 710-1222	Tennis	Track
	Track	Volleyball

CONCORDIA UNIVERSITY AT AUSTIN

IH 35 North	**Men**	**Women**
Austin, TX 78705	Baseball	Basketball
Affiliation—NAIA I, NCAA II	Basketball	Golf
Nickname—Tornados	Golf	Soccer
Athletic Director—	Soccer	Softball
(512) 452-7662 ext. 1164	Tennis	Tennis
		Volleyball

DALLAS, UNIVERSITY OF

	Men	Women
1845 S. Northgate Drive	Baseball	Basketball
Irving, TX 75062-4736	Basketball	Cross Country
Affiliation—NCAA III	Cross Country	Golf
Nickname—Crusaders	Golf	Soccer
Athletic Director—	Soccer	Tennis
(972) 721-5207	Tennis	Track
	Track	Volleyball

DALLAS BAPTIST UNIVERSITY

	Men	Women
3000 Mountain Creel Parkway	Baseball	Cross Country
Dallas, TX 75211-9209	Cross Country	Soccer
Affiliation—NAIA I, NCAA II	Soccer	Tennis
(NCAA I—Baseball)	Tennis	Track
Nickname—Patriots	Track	Volleyball
Athletic Director—	Volleyball	
(214) 333-5324		

DALLAS CHRISTIAN COLLEGE

	Men	Women
2700 Christian Parkway	Basketball	Basketball
Dallas, TX 75234-7229	Soccer	Volleyball
Affiliation—NCCAA		
Nickname—Crusaders		
Athletic Director—		
(972) 241-3371		

EAST TEXAS BAPTIST UNIVERSITY

	Men	Women
1209 N. Grove Street	Baseball	Basketball
Marshall, TX 75670-1423	Basketball	Softball
Affiliation—NAIA I, NCAA II	Soccer	Volleyball
Nickname—Tigers		
Athletic Director—		
(903) 935-7963 ext. 271		

HARDIN-SIMMONS UNIVERSITY

	Men	Women
PO Box 16185	Baseball	Basketball
Abilene, TX 79698	Basketball	Golf
Affiliation—NCAA III	Football	Soccer
Nickname—Cowboys	Golf	Tennis
Athletic Director—	Soccer	Volleyball
(915) 670-1273	Tennis	

HOUSTON, UNIVERSITY OF

3100 Cullen Boulevard	**Men**	**Women**
Houston, TX 77204-6742	Baseball	Basketball
*Affiliation—*NCAA *I*	Basketball	Cross Country
(I-A Football)	Cross Country	Soccer
Nickname—Cougars	Football	Swimming
Athletic Director—	Golf	Tennis
(713) 743-9370	Track	Track
		Volleyball

HOUSTON BAPTIST UNIVERSITY

7502 Fondren Road	**Men**	**Women**
Houston, TX 77074-3204	Baseball	Softball
*Affiliation—*NAIA *I*	Basketball	Volleyball
Nickname—Huskies		
Athletic Director—		
(281) 649-3450		

HOWARD PAYNE UNIVERSITY

508 2nd Street	**Men**	**Women**
Brownwood, TX 76801-3441	Baseball	Basketball
*Affiliation—*NCAA *III*	Basketball	Cross Country
Nickname—Yellow Jackets	Cross Country	Golf
Athletic Director—	Football	Softball
(915) 649-8813	Golf	Tennis
	Tennis	Track
	Track	Volleyball
	Volleyball	

HUSTON-TILLOTSON COLLEGE

1820 E. 8th Street	**Men**	**Women**
Austin, TX 78702-2762	Baseball	Basketball
*Affiliation—*NAIA *I*	Basketball	Track
Nickname—Rams	Golf	Volleyball
Athletic Director—	Tennis	
(512) 505-3052	Track	

INCARNATE WORD, UNIVERSITY OF THE

	Men	Women
4301 Broadway Street	Baseball	Basketball
San Antonio, TX 78209-6318	Basketball	Cross Country
Affiliation—NAIA	Cross Country	Golf
Nickname—Crusaders	Golf	Soccer
Athletic Director—	Soccer	Softball
(210) 829-6053	Tennis	Tennis
		Volleyball

JARVIS CHRISTIAN COLLEGE

	Men	Women
PO Box G	Baseball	Basketball
Hawkins, TX 75765	Basketball	Cheerleading
Affiliation—NCAA II	Soccer	Track
Nickname—Bulldogs	Track	Volleyball
Athletic Director—		
(903) 769-5763		

LAMAR UNIVERSITY

	Men	Women
PO Box 10066,	Baseball	Basketball
211 Red Bird Lane	Basketball	Cross Country
Beaumont, TX 77710-0066	Cross Country	Golf
Affiliation—NCAA I	Golf	Tennis
Nickname—Cardinals	Tennis	Track
Athletic Director—	Track	Volleyball
(409) 880-8323		

LE TOURNEAU UNIVERSITY

	Men	Women
PO Box 7001,	Baseball	Basketball
2001 S. Mobberly	Basketball	Cross Country
Longview, TX 75607-7001	Cross Country	Soccer
Affiliation—NCAA III, NCCAA I	Soccer	Volleyball
Nickname—Yellow Jackets	Tennis	
Athletic Director—		
(903) 233-3371		

LUBBOCK CHRISTIAN UNIVERSITY

	Men	Women
5601 W. 19th Street	Baseball	Basketball
Lubbock, TX 79407-2031	Basketball	Cross Country
Affiliation—NAIA I	Cross Country	Track
Nickname—Chaparrals	Track	Volleyball
Athletic Director—		
(806) 796-8800 ext. 346		

MARY HARDIN-BAYLOR, UNIVERSITY OF

	Men	Women
9th and College	Baseball	Basketball
Belton, TX 76513	Basketball	Cross Country
*Affiliation—*NAIA *I,* NCAA *II*	Cross Country	Golf
Nickname—Crusaders	Football	Soccer
Athletic Director—	Golf	Softball
(254) 295-4618	Soccer	Tennis
	Tennis	Volleyball

McMURRY UNIVERSITY

	Men	Women
S. 14th and Salyes	Baseball	Basketball
Abilene, TX 79697	Basketball	Cheerleading
*Affiliation—*NCAA *III*	Cross Country	Cross Country
Nickname—Indians	Football	Golf
Athletic Director—	Golf	Tennis
(915) 793-4630	Tennis	Track
	Track	Volleyball

MIDWESTERN STATE UNIVERSITY

	Men	Women
3410 Taft Boulevard	Basketball	Basketball
Wichita Falls, TX 76308-2095	Football	Soccer
*Affiliation—*NCAA *II*	Soccer	Tennis
Nickname—Indians	Tennis	Volleyball
Athletic Director—		
(940) 397-4774		

NORTH TEXAS, UNIVERSITY OF

	Men	Women
PO Box 311397	Basketball	Basketball
Denton, TX 76203-1397	Cross Country	Cross Country
*Affiliation—*NCAA *I*	Football	Diving
(I-A Football)	Golf	Golf
Nickname—Eagles/Mean Green	Track	Soccer
Athletic Director—		Swimming
(940) 565-3646		Tennis
		Track
		Volleyball

NORTHWOOD UNIVERSITY

	Men	Women
PO Box 58	**Men**	**Women**
Cedar Hill, TX 75104	Basketball	Cross Country
Affiliation—NAIA *I*	Cross Country	Golf
Nickname—Knights	Golf	Soccer
Athletic Director—	Soccer	Softball
(972) 243-5439	Track	Track

PAUL QUINN COLLEGE

	Men	Women
3837 Simpson Stuart Road	**Men**	**Women**
Dallas, TX 75241-4331	Basketball	Basketball
Affiliation—NSCAA *I*	Track	Volleyball
Nickname—Tigers		
Athletic Director—		
(214) 302-3567		

PRAIRIE VIEW A&M UNIVERSITY

	Men	Women
Administration Building,	**Men**	**Women**
Room 003	Baseball	Basketball
Prairie View, TX 77446	Basketball	Cross Country
Affiliation—NCAA *I*	Cross Country	Golf
(I-AA Football), NAIA	Football	Softball
Nickname—Panthers	Golf	Tennis
Athletic Director—	Tennis	Track
(409) 857-4398	Track	Volleyball

RICE UNIVERSITY

	Men	Women
PO Box 1892, MS548	**Men**	**Women**
Houston, TX 77251-1892	Baseball	Basketball
Affiliation—NCAA *I*	Basketball	Cross Country
(I-A Football)	Cross Country	Swimming
Nickname—Owls	Football	Tennis
Athletic Director—	Golf	Track
(713) 527-9851	Swimming	Volleyball
	Tennis	
	Track	

SAINT EDWARDS UNIVERSITY

3001 S. Congress Avenue	**Men**	**Women**
Austin, TX 78704-6425	Baseball	Basketball
Affiliation—NAIA I, NCAA II	Basketball	Soccer
Nickname—Hilltoppers	Golf	Softball
Athletic Director—	Soccer	Tennis
(512) 448-8450	Tennis	Volleyball

SAINT MARY'S UNIVERSITY

1 Camino Santa Maria Street	**Men**	**Women**
San Antonio, TX 78228-5433	Baseball	Basketball
Affiliation—NAIA I, NCAA II	Basketball	Cheerleading
Nickname—Rattlers	Golf	Soccer
Athletic Director—	Soccer	Softball
(210) 436-3528 ext. 1387	Tennis	Tennis
		Volleyball

SAINT THOMAS, UNIVERSITY OF

3800 Montose Boulevard	**Men**	**Women**
Houston, TX 77006-4626	Basketball	Basketball
Nickname—Fightin' Celts	Rugby	Soccer
Athletic Director—	Soccer	Volleyball
(713) 525-3512		

SAM HOUSTON STATE UNIVERSITY

PO Box 2268	**Men**	**Women**
Huntsville, TX 77341-2268	Baseball	Basketball
Affiliation—NCAA I	Basketball	Cross Country
(I-AA Football)	Cross Country	Golf
Nickname—Bearkats	Football	Softball
Athletic Director—	Golf	Tennis
(409) 294-1980	Track	Track
		Volleyball

SCHREINER COLLEGE

2100 Memorial Boulevard	**Men**	**Women**
Kerrville, TX 78028-5611	Baseball	Basketball
Affiliation—NAIA I, NCAA III	Basketball	Soccer
Nickname—Mountaineers	Soccer	Softball
Athletic Director—	Tennis	Tennis
(830) 792-7289		Volleyball

SOUTHERN METHODIST UNIVERSITY

	Men	Women
PO Box 650216,	Basketball	Basketball
6024 Airline Road	Cross Country	Cross Country
Dallas, TX 75275-0216	Diving	Diving
*Affiliation—*NCAA *I*	Football	Golf
(I-A Football)	Golf	Soccer
Nickname—Mustangs	Soccer	Swimming
Athletic Director—	Swimming	Tennis
(214) 768-4301	Tennis	Track
	Track	Volleyball

SOUTHWEST TEXAS STATE UNIVERSITY

	Men	Women
Jowers Center	Baseball	Basketball
San Marcos, TX 78666	Basketball	Cross Country
*Affiliation—*NCAA *I*	Cross Country	Soccer
(I-AA Football)	Golf	Softball
Nickname—Bobcats	Track	Tennis
Athletic Director—		Track
(512) 245-2114		Volleyball

SOUTHWESTERN ADVENTIST UNIVERSITY

	Men	Women
PO Box 567	Baseball	Basketball
Keene, TX 76059-0567	Basketball	Cross Country
*Affiliation—*NAIA *I*	Soccer	Track
Nickname—Knights		Volleyball
Athletic Director—		
(817) 645-3921 ext. 528		

SOUTHWESTERN ASSEMBLIES OF GOD UNIVERSITY

	Men	Women
1200 Sycamore Street	Basketball	Basketball
Waxahachie, TX 75165-2397		
*Affiliation—*NBCAA *I*		
Nickname—Lions		
Athletic Director—		
(972) 937-4010		

SOUTHWESTERN UNIVERSITY

PO Box 6272	Men	Women
Georgetown, TX 78626	Baseball	Basketball
Affiliation—NCAA III	Basketball	Cross Country
Nickname—Pirates	Cross Country	Diving
Athletic Director—	Diving	Golf
(512) 863-1618	Golf	Soccer
	Soccer	Swimming
	Swimming	Tennis
	Tennis	Track
	Track	Volleyball

STEPHEN F. AUSTIN STATE UNIVERSITY

PO Box 13010	Men	Women
Nacogdoches, TX 75962	Basketball	Basketball
Affiliation—NCAA I	Cross Country	Cross Country
(I-AA Football)	Football	Soccer
Nickname—Lumberjacks	Golf	Softball
Athletic Director—	Track	Track
(409) 468-4540		Volleyball

SUL ROSS STATE UNIVERSITY

East Highway 90	Men	Women
Alpine, TX 79832	Baseball	Basketball
Affiliation—NCAA III	Basketball	Softball
Nickname—Lobos	Football	Tennis
Athletic Director—	Tennis	Track
(915) 837-8226	Track	Volleyball

TARLETON STATE UNIVERSITY

Box T-80	Men	Women
Stephenville, TX 76402	Baseball	Basketball
Affiliation—NCAA II	Basketball	Cross Country
Nickname—Texans	Cross Country	Golf
Athletic Director—	Football	Softball
(254) 968-9178	Track	Tennis
		Track
		Volleyball

TEXAS, UNIVERSITY OF

PO Box 7399	Men	Women
Austin, TX 78713-7399	Baseball	Basketball
Affiliation—NCAA I	Basketball	Cross Country
(I-A Football)	Cross Country	Diving
Nickname—Longhorns	Diving	Golf
Athletic Director—Men	Football	Rowing
(512) 471-5757	Golf	Soccer
Athletic Director—Women	Swimming	Softball
(512) 471-7693	Tennis	Swimming
	Track	Tennis
		Track
		Volleyball

TEXAS, UNIVERSITY OF, ARLINGTON

Box 19079	Men	Women
Arlington, TX 76019	Baseball	Basketball
Affiliation—NCAA I	Basketball	Cross Country
Nickname—Mavericks	Cross Country	Softball
Athletic Director—	Golf	Tennis
(817) 272-5039	Tennis	Track
	Track	Volleyball

TEXAS, UNIVERSITY OF, DALLAS

Box 830688 SU 23	Men	Women
Richardson, TX 75083	Basketball	Basketball
Affiliation—NCAA	Golf	Golf
Nickname—Comets	Soccer	Soccer
Athletic Director—		
(972) 883-2094		

TEXAS, UNIVERSITY OF, EL PASO

201 E. Baltimore Drive	Men	Women
El Paso, TX 79902-2543	Basketball	Basketball
Affiliation—NCAA I	Cross Country	Cheerleading
(I-A Football)	Football	Cross Country
Nickname—Miners	Golf	Golf
Athletic Director—	Tennis	Rifle
(915) 747-6831	Track	Soccer
		Tennis
		Track
		Volleyball

TEXAS, UNIVERSITY OF, PAN AMERICAN

	Men	Women
1201 W. University Drive	Baseball	Basketball
Edinburg, TX 78539-2909	Basketball	Cheerleading
Affiliation—NCAA I	Cross Country	Cross Country
Nickname—Broncs	Golf	Golf
Athletic Director—	Tennis	Tennis
(956) 381-2222	Track	Track
		Volleyball

TEXAS, UNIVERSITY OF, PERMIAN BASIN

	Men	Women
4901 E. University Boulevard	Soccer	Softball
Odessa, TX 79762-8122		Volleyball
Affiliation—NAIA		
Nickname—Falcons		
Athletic Director—		
(915) 552-2675		

TEXAS, UNIVERSITY OF, SAN ANTONIO

	Men	Women
6900 N. Loop 1604 W	Baseball	Basketball
San Antonio, TX 78249-1130	Basketball	Cross Country
Affiliation—NCAA I	Cross Country	Softball
Nickname—Roadrunners	Golf	Tennis
Athletic Director—	Tennis	Track
(210) 458-4444	Track	Volleyball

TEXAS A&M UNIVERSITY

	Men	Women
PO Box 30017	Baseball	Basketball
College Station, TX 77842-3017	Basketball	Cross Country
Affiliation—NCAA I	Cross Country	Diving
(I-A Football)	Diving	Golf
Nickname—Aggies	Football	Soccer
Athletic Director—	Golf	Softball
(409) 845-5129	Rifle	Swimming
	Swimming	Tennis
	Tennis	Track
	Track	Volleyball

TEXAS A&M UNIVERSITY, COMMERCE

Athletic Department	**Men**	**Women**
Commerce, TX 75429	Basketball	Basketball
Affiliation—NCAA II	Cross Country	Cheerleading
Nickname—Lions	Football	Cross Country
Athletic Director—	Golf	Golf
(903) 886-5100	Track	Soccer
		Track
		Volleyball

TEXAS A&M UNIVERSITY, CORPUS CHRISTI

7300 Ocean Drive	**Men**	**Women**
Corpus Christi, TX 78412-5503	Baseball	Basketball
Affiliation—NCAA I	Basketball	Cross Country
Nickname—Islanders	Cross Country	Golf
Athletic Director—	Tennis	Soccer
(512) 980-5541	Track	Softball
		Tennis
		Track
		Volleyball

TEXAS A&M UNIVERSITY, KINGSVILLE

Campus Box 202	**Men**	**Women**
Kingsville, TX 78363	Baseball	Basketball
Affiliation—NCAA II	Basketball	Cross Country
Nickname—Javelinas	Cross Country	Softball
Athletic Director—	Football	Track
(512) 593-2411	Track	Volleyball

TEXAS CHRISTIAN UNIVERSITY

TCU Box 297600,	**Men**	**Women**
2800 Stadium Drive	Baseball	Basketball
Fort Worth, TX 76129	Basketball	Golf
Affiliation—NCAA I	Football	Rifle
(I-A Football)	Golf	Soccer
Nickname—Horned Frogs	Soccer	Swimming
Athletic Director—	Swimming	Tennis
(257) 921-7965	Tennis	Track
	Track	Volleyball

TEXAS COLLEGE

2404 N. *Grand Avenue*	**Men**	**Women**
Tyler, TX 75702-1962	Baseball	Basketball
Affiliation—NAIA I, NSCAA	Basketball	Volleyball
Nickname—*Steers*	Track	
Athletic Director—	Volleyball	
(903) 593-8311		

TEXAS LUTHERAN UNIVERSITY

1000 W. *Court Street*	**Men**	**Women**
Sequin, TX 78155-5978	Baseball	Basketball
Affiliation—NAIA I, NCAA II	Basketball	Cross Country
Nickname—*Bulldogs*	Football	Golf
Athletic Director—	Golf	Soccer
(830) 372-8120	Soccer	Softball
	Tennis	Tennis
		Track
		Volleyball

TEXAS SOUTHERN UNIVERSITY

3100 *Cleburne Street*	**Men**	**Women**
Houston, TX 77004-4501	Baseball	Basketball
Affiliation—NCAA I	Basketball	Bowling
(I-AA Football)	Cross Country	Cheerleading
Nickname—*Tigers*	Football	Cross Country
Athletic Director—	Golf	Golf
(713) 313-7271	Tennis	Tennis
	Track	Track
		Volleyball

TEXAS TECH UNIVERSITY

Box 43021, 6th and Boston	**Men**	**Women**
Lubbock, TX 79409-3201	Baseball	Basketball
Affiliation—NCAA I	Basketball	Cross Country
(I-A Football)	Cross Country	Golf
Nickname—*Red Raiders*	Football	Soccer
Athletic Director—	Golf	Softball
(806) 742-3355	Tennis	Tennis
	Track	Track
		Volleyball

TEXAS WESLEYAN UNIVERSITY

1201 Wesleyan Street	**Men**	**Women**
Fort Worth, TX 76105-1536	Baseball	Basketball
Affiliation—NAIA I, NCAA II	Basketball	Soccer
Nickname—Rams	Golf	Softball
Athletic Director—	Soccer	Tennis
(817) 531-4224	Tennis	Volleyball

TEXAS WOMEN'S UNIVERSITY

PO Box 425349	**Women**	
Denton, TX 76204-5349	Basketball	Tennis
Affiliation—NCAA II	Gymnastics	Volleyball
Nickname—Pioneers	Softball	
Athletic Director—		
(940) 898-2378		

TRINITY UNIVERSITY

715 Stadium Drive	**Men**	**Women**
San Antonio, TX 78212-3104	Baseball	Basketball
Affiliation—NCAA III	Basketball	Cross Country
Nickname—Tigers	Cross Country	Golf
Athletic Director—	Football	Skeet
(210) 736-8222	Golf	Soccer
	Soccer	Softball
	Swimming	Swimming
	Tennis	Tennis
	Track	Track
		Volleyball

WAYLAND BAPTIST UNIVERSITY

1900 W. 7th Street	**Men**	**Women**
Plainview, TX 79072-6900	Baseball	Basketball
Affiliation—NAIA I	Basketball	Cross Country
Nickname—Pioneers	Cross Country	Track
Athletic Director—	Golf	Volleyball
(806) 296-4527	Track	

WEST TEXAS A&M UNIVERSITY

WTAMU Box 60049	**Men**	**Women**
Canyon, TX 79016	Baseball	Basketball
*Affiliation—*NCAA II	Basketball	Cross Country
Nickname—Buffalos	Cross Country	Golf
Athletic Director—	Football	Soccer
(806) 651-2069	Golf	Tennis
	Soccer	Volleyball
	Tennis	

WILEY COLLEGE

711 Wiley Avenue	**Men**	**Women**
Marshall, TX 75670-5151	Baseball	Basketball
*Affiliation—*NAIA I	Basketball	Softball
Nickname—Wildcats	Soccer	Track
Athletic Director—	Track	Volleyball
(903) 927-3350	Volleyball	

UTAH

BRIGHAM YOUNG UNIVERSITY

PO Box 22241	**Men**	**Women**
106 Smith Fieldhouse	Baseball	Basketball
Provo, UT 84602-2241	Basketball	Cross Country
*Affiliation—*NCAA I	Cross Country	Diving
(I-A Football)	Diving	Golf
Nickname—Cougars	Football	Gymnastics
Athletic Director—Men	Golf	Soccer
(801) 378-8704	Gymnastics	Swimming
Athletic Director—Women	Swimming	Tennis
(801) 378-4225	Tennis	Track
	Track	Volleyball
	Volleyball	
	Wrestling	

SOUTHERN UTAH UNIVERSITY

351 W. Center Street	**Men**	**Women**
Cedar City, UT 84720-2470	Baseball	Basketball
*Affiliation—*NCAA I	Basketball	Cheerleading
(I-AA Football)	Cross Country	Cross Country
Nickname—Thunderbirds	Football	Gymnastics
Athletic Director—	Golf	Softball
(435) 586-5469	Track	Tennis
		Track

UTAH, UNIVERSITY OF

	Men	Women
Department of Athletics,	Baseball	Basketball
1825 South Campus	Basketball	Cross Country
Salt Lake City, UT 84112	Cross Country	Diving
Affiliation—NCAA I	Diving	Gymnastics
(I-A Football)	Football	Skiing
Nickname—Utes	Golf	Soccer
Athletic Director—	Skiing	Softball
(801) 581-5605	Swimming	Swimming
	Tennis	Tennis
	Track	Track
		Volleyball

UTAH STATE UNIVERSITY

	Men	Women
Athletic Department,	Basketball	Cheerleading
7400 Old Main Hill	Cross Country	Cross Country
Logan, UT 84322-7400	Football	Gymnastics
Affiliation—NCAA I	Golf	Soccer
(I-A Football)	Tennis	Softball
Nickname—Aggies	Track	Tennis
Athletic Director—		Track
(435) 797-2060		Volleyball

WEBER STATE UNIVERSITY

	Men	Women
Department of Intercollegiate	Basketball	Basketball
Athletics	Cross Country	Cross Country
Ogden, UT 84408-2701	Football	Golf
Affiliation—NCAA I	Golf	Soccer
(I-AA Football)	Tennis	Tennis
Nickname—Wildcats	Track	Track
Athletic Director—		Volleyball
(801) 626-6817		

WESTMINSTER COLLEGE

	Men	Women
1840 S. 1300 E	Lacrosse	Volleyball
Salt Lake City, UT 84105-3617	Soccer	
Affiliation—NAIA		
Nickname—Parsons		
Athletic Director—		
(801) 488-4211		

VERMONT

CASTLETON STATE COLLEGE

Glennbrook Road	**Men**	**Women**
Castleton, VT 05735	Baseball	Basketball
Affiliation—NCAA III, NAIA II	Basketball	Cross Country
Nickname—Spartans	Cross Country	Lacrosse
Athletic Director—	Lacrosse	Soccer
(802) 468-1365	Soccer	Softball
	Tennis	Tennis

GREEN MOUNTAIN COLLEGE

1 College Circle	**Men**	**Women**
Poultney, VT 05764	Basketball	Basketball
Affiliation—NAIA II	Lacrosse	Skiing
Nickname—Eagles	Skiing	Soccer
Athletic Director—	Soccer	Softball
(802) 287-8238	Tennis	Tennis
		Volleyball

JOHNSON STATE COLLEGE

College Road	**Men**	**Women**
Johnson, VT 05656	Basketball	Basketball
Affiliation—NCAA III	Cross Country	Cross Country
Nickname—Badgers	Lacrosse	Soccer
Athletic Director—	Skiing	Softball
(802) 635-1486	Soccer	Tennis
	Tennis	

LYNDON STATE COLLEGE

Vail Hill	**Men**	**Women**
Lyndonville, VT 05851	Baseball	Basketball
Affiliation—NAIA II	Basketball	Cross Country
Nickname—Hornets	Cross Country	Soccer
Athletic Director—	Soccer	Softball
(802) 626-6477	Tennis	Tennis

MIDDLEBURY COLLEGE

Memorial Fieldhouse	**Men**	**Women**
Middlebury, VT 05753	Baseball	Basketball
Affiliation—NCAA *III*	Basketball	Cross Country
Nickname—*Panthers*	Cross Country	Field Hockey
Athletic Director—	Football	Ice Hockey
(802) 443-5253	Golf	Lacrosse
	Ice Hockey	Skiing—Alpine/
	Lacrosse	Nordic
	Skiing—Alpine/	Soccer
	Nordic	Softball
	Soccer	Swimming
	Swimming	Tennis
	Tennis	Track
	Track	Volleyball

NORWICH UNIVERSITY

Main Street	**Men**	**Women**
Northfield, VT 05663	Baseball	Basketball
Affiliation—NCAA *III*	Basketball	Cross Country
Nickname—*Cadets*	Cross Country	Diving
Athletic Director—	Diving	Rifle
(802) 485-8238	Football	Soccer
	Golf	Softball
	Ice Hockey	Swimming
	Lacrosse	Track
	Rifle	
	Soccer	
	Swimming	
	Tennis	
	Track	
	Wrestling	

SAINT JOSEPH, COLLEGE OF

Clement Road	**Men**	**Women**
Rutland, VT 05701	Basketball	Basketball
Affiliation—NAIA *II*	Cross Country	Cross Country
Nickname—*Fighting Saints*	Soccer	Soccer
Athletic Director—		Softball
(802) 773-5900 ext. 247		

SAINT MICHAEL'S COLLEGE

Winooski Park	Men	Women
Colchester, VT 05439	Baseball	Basketball
Affiliation—NCAA II	Basketball	Cross Country
Nickname—Purple Knights	Cross Country	Field Hockey
Athletic Director—	Golf	Lacrosse
(802) 654-2200	Ice Hockey	Skiing
	Lacrosse	Soccer
	Rifle	Softball
	Skiing	Swimming
	Soccer	Tennis
	Swimming	Volleyball
	Tennis	

SOUTHERN VERMONT COLLEGE

982 Mansion Drive	Men	Women
Bennington, VT 05201-9983	Baseball	Basketball
Affiliation—NCAA III	Basketball	Cross Country
Nickname—Mountaineers	Cross Country	Soccer
Athletic Director—	Soccer	Softball
(802) 442-5427		

TRINITY COLLEGE OF VERMONT

208 Colchester Avenue	Women	
Burlington, VT 05401	Basketball	Softball
Affiliation—NSCAA	Soccer	
Nickname—Crusaders		
Athletic Director—		
(802) 658-0337 ext. 536		

VERMONT, UNIVERSITY OF

Patrick Gym	Men	Women
Burlington, VT 05405	Baseball	Basketball
Affiliation—NCAA I	Basketball	Cross Country
Nickname—Catamounts	Cross Country	Field Hockey
Athletic Director—	Golf	Gymnastics
(802) 656-3074	Gymnastics	Ice Hockey
	Ice Hockey	Lacrosse
	Lacrosse	Skiing
	Skiing	Soccer
	Soccer	Softball
	Swimming	Swimming
	Tennis	Tennis
	Track	Track
		Volleyball

VIRGINIA

APPRENTICE SCHOOL

4101 Washington Avenue	**Men**	**Women**
Newport News, VA 23607-2704	Baseball	Basketball
Nickname—Builders	Basketball	
Athletic Director—	Football	
(757) 380-7961	Golf	
	Wrestling	

AVERETT COLLEGE

420 West Main Street	**Men**	**Women**
Danville, VA 24541-1110	Baseball	Basketball
Affiliation—NCAA III	Basketball	Cross Country
Nickname—Cougars	Cross Country	Soccer
Athletic Director—	Golf	Softball
(804) 791-5700	Soccer	Tennis
	Tennis	Volleyball

BLUEFIELD COLLEGE

3000 College Drive	**Men**	**Women**
Bluefield, VA 24605-1737	Baseball	Basketball
Affiliation—NAIA II	Basketball	Cheerleading
Nickname—Ramblin' Rams	Golf	Softball
Athletic Director—	Soccer	Tennis
(540) 326-4349	Tennis	Volleyball

BRIDGEWATER COLLEGE

E. College Street	**Men**	**Women**
Bridgewater, VA 22812	Baseball	Basketball
Affiliation—NCAA III	Basketball	Cross Country
Nickname—Eagles	Cross Country	Field Hockey
Athletic Director—	Football	Lacrosse
(540) 828-5401	Golf	Softball
	Soccer	Tennis
	Tennis	Track
	Track	Volleyball

CHRISTOPHER NEWPORT UNIVERSITY

50 Shoe Lane	Men	Women
Newport News, VA 23606-2949	Baseball	Basketball
Affiliation—NCAA III	Basketball	Cheerleading
Nickname—Captains	Cross Country	Cross Country
Athletic Director—	Golf	Sailing
(757) 594-7217	Sailing	Soccer
	Soccer	Softball
	Tennis	Tennis
	Track	Track
		Volleyball

CLINCH VALLEY COLLEGE

College Avenue	Men	Women
Wise, VA 24293	Baseball	Basketball
Affiliation—NAIA II	Basketball	Cross Country
Nickname—Highland Cavaliers	Cross Country	Golf
Athletic Director—	Football	Soccer
(540) 328-0259	Golf	Tennis
	Tennis	Track
	Track	Volleyball

EASTERN MENNONITE UNIVERSITY

1200 Park Road	Men	Women
Harrisonburg, VA 22802-2402	Baseball	Basketball
Affiliation—NCAA III	Basketball	Cross Country
Nickname—Royals	Cross Country	Field Hockey
Athletic Director—	Soccer	Softball
(540) 432-4439	Tennis	Tennis
	Track	Track
		Volleyball

EMORY & HENRY COLLEGE

King Athletic Center	Men	Women
Emory, VA 24327	Baseball	Basketball
Affiliation—NCAA III	Basketball	Cheerleading
Nickname—Wasps	Football	Cross Country
Athletic Director—	Golf	Soccer
(540) 944-6234	Soccer	Softball
	Tennis	Tennis
		Volleyball

FERRUM COLLEGE

PO Box 1000, Route 40 West	Men	Women
Ferrum, VA 24088	Baseball	Basketball
Affiliation—NCAA *III*	Basketball	Cheerleading
Nickname—Panthers	Cross Country	Cross Country
Athletic Director—	Football	Field Hockey
(540) 365-4493	Golf	Lacrosse
	Riding	Riding
	Soccer	Soccer
	Tennis	Softball
		Tennis
		Volleyball

GEORGE MASON UNIVERSITY

MS 3A5, 4400 University Drive	Men	Women
Fairfax, VA 22030	Baseball	Basketball
Affiliation—NCAA *I*	Basketball	Cheerleading
Nickname—Patriots	Cross Country	Crew
Athletic Director—	Golf	Cross Country
(703) 993-3210	Soccer	Lacrosse
	Tennis	Soccer
	Track	Softball
	Volleyball	Tennis
	Wrestling	Track
		Volleyball

HAMPDEN-SYDNEY COLLEGE

Kirby Field House	Men	
Hampden-Sydney, VA 23943	Baseball	Golf
Affiliation—NCAA *III*	Basketball	Lacrosse
Nickname—Tigers	Cross Country	Soccer
Athletic Director—	Football	Tennis
(804) 223-6153		

HAMPTON UNIVERSITY

Holland Hall	Men	Women
Hampton, VA 23668	Basketball	Basketball
Affiliation—NCAA *I*	Cross Country	Cheerleading
(I-AA Football)	Football	Cross Country
Nickname—Pirates	Golf	Golf
Athletic Director—	Tennis	Softball
(757) 727-5641	Track	Tennis
		Track
		Volleyball

HOLLINS UNIVERSITY

8124 Forest of Arden Lane
Hollins College, VA 24020
Affiliation—NCAA
Athletic Director—
(540) 362-6435

Women
Basketball
Fencing
Field Hockey
Golf
Lacrosse

Riding
Soccer
Swimming
Tennis
Volleyball

JAMES MADISON UNIVERSITY

Athletics, MSC 2301
Harrisonburg, VA 22807
Affiliation—NCAA I
(I-AA Football)
Nickname—Dukes
Athletic Director—
(540) 568-3742

Men
Archery
Baseball
Basketball
Cross Country
Diving
Football
Golf
Gymnastics
Soccer
Swimming
Tennis
Track
Wrestling

Women
Archery
Basketball
Cross Country
Diving
Fencing
Field Hockey
Golf
Gymnastics
Lacrosse
Soccer
Swimming
Tennis
Track
Volleyball

LIBERTY UNIVERSITY

1971 University Boulevard
Lynchburg, VA 24502-2269
Affiliation—NCAA I
(I-AA Football)
Nickname—Flames
Athletic Director—
(804) 582-2100

Men
Baseball
Basketball
Cross Country
Football
Golf
Soccer
Tennis
Track

Women
Basketball
Cross Country
Soccer
Softball
Track
Volleyball

LONGWOOD COLLEGE

201 High Street	Men	Women
Farmville, VA 23909-1800	Baseball	Basketball
Affiliation—NCAA II	Basketball	Field Hockey
Nickname—Lancers	Golf	Golf
Athletic Director—	Soccer	Lacrosse
(804) 395-2057	Tennis	Soccer
	Wrestling	Softball
		Tennis

LYNCHBURG COLLEGE

1501 Lakeside Drive	Men	Women
Lynchburg, VA 24501-3113	Baseball	Basketball
Affiliation—NCAA III	Basketball	Cross Country
Nickname—Hornets	Cross Country	Equestrian
Athletic Director—	Equestrian	Field Hockey
(804) 544-8498	Soccer	Lacrosse
	Tennis	Soccer
	Track	Softball
		Tennis
		Track
		Volleyball

MARY BALDWIN COLLEGE

Frederick Street	Women	
Staunton, VA 24401	Basketball	Softball
Affiliation—NCAA III	Fencing	Swimming
Nickname—Squirrels	Field Hockey	Tennis
Athletic Director—	Lacrosse	Volleyball
(540) 887-7217	Soccer	

MARY WASHINGTON COLLEGE

Goodrich Gymnasium,	Men	Women
1301 College Avenue	Baseball	Basketball
Fredericksburg, VA 22401	Basketball	Crew
Affiliation—NCAA III	Crew	Cross Country
Nickname—Eagles	Cross Country	Field Hockey
Athletic Director—	Lacrosse	Lacrosse
(540) 654-1876	Soccer	Riding
	Swimming	Soccer
	Tennis	Softball
	Track	Swimming
		Tennis
		Track
		Volleyball

MARYMOUNT UNIVERSITY

2807 N. Glebe Road	Men	Women
Arlington, VA 22207-4224	Basketball	Basketball
Affiliation—NCAA III	Golf	Lacrosse
Nickname—Saints	Lacrosse	Soccer
Athletic Director—	Soccer	Swimming
(703) 284-1619	Swimming	Volleyball

NORFOLK STATE UNIVERSITY

2401 Corprew Avenue	Men	Women
Norfolk, VA 23504-3907	Baseball	Basketball
Affiliation—NCAA I	Basketball	Cross Country
(I-AA Football)	Cross Country	Softball
Nickname—Spartans	Football	Tennis
Athletic Director—	Tennis	Track
(757) 683-8152	Track	Volleyball
	Wrestling	

OLD DOMINION UNIVERSITY

Athletic Administration Building	Men	Women
Norfolk, VA 23529	Baseball	Basketball
Affiliation—NCAA I	Basketball	Cheerleading
Nickname—Monarchs	Cross Country	Cross Country
Athletic Director—	Diving	Diving
(757) 683-3369	Golf	Field Hockey
	Soccer	Lacrosse
	Swimming	Sailing
	Tennis	Soccer
	Wrestling	Swimming
		Tennis

RADFORD UNIVERSITY

PO Box 6913	Men	Women
Radford, VA 24142-6913	Baseball	Basketball
Affiliation—NCAA I	Basketball	Cross Country
Nickname—Highlanders	Cross Country	Field Hockey
Athletic Director—	Golf	Golf
(540) 831-5228	Lacrosse	Gymnastics
	Soccer	Soccer
	Tennis	Softball
	Track	Tennis
		Track
		Volleyball

RANDOLPH-MACON COLLEGE

PO Box 5005	Men	Women
Ashland, VA 23005-5505	Baseball	Basketball
Affiliation—NCAA III	Basketball	Field Hockey
Nickname—Yellow Jackets	Football	Lacrosse
Athletic Director—	Golf	Soccer
(804) 752-7303	Lacrosse	Softball
	Soccer	Tennis
	Tennis	Volleyball

RICHMOND, UNIVERSITY OF

College Road	Men	Women
Richmond, VA 23173	Baseball	Basketball
Affiliation—NCAA I	Basketball	Cross Country
(I-AA Football)	Cross Country	Field Hockey
Nickname—Spiders	Football	Lacrosse
Athletic Director—	Golf	Soccer
(804) 289-8371	Soccer	Synchronized
	Swimming	Swimming
	Tennis	Swimming
	Track	Tennis
	Water Polo	Track

ROANOKE COLLEGE

221 College Lane	Men	Women
Salem, VA 24153-3747	Basketball	Basketball
Affiliation—NCAA III	Cross Country	Cross Country
Nickname—Maroons	Golf	Field Hockey
Athletic Director—	Lacrosse	Lacrosse
(540) 375-2337	Soccer	Soccer
	Tennis	Softball
	Track	Tennis
		Track
		Volleyball

SAINT PAUL'S COLLEGE

115 College Drive	Men	Women
Lawrenceville, VA 23868-1200	Baseball	Basketball
Affiliation—NCAA II	Basketball	Cheerleading
Nickname—Tigers	Cross Country	Cross Country
Athletic Director—	Golf	Softball
(804) 848-2001	Tennis	Track
	Track	Volleyball

SHENANDOAH UNIVERSITY

	Men	Women
1460 University Drive	Baseball	Basketball
Winchester, VA 22601-5100	Basketball	Cross Country
Affiliation—NCAA III	Cross Country	Lacrosse
Nickname—Hornets	Golf	Soccer
Athletic Director—	Lacrosse	Softball
(540) 665-4566	Soccer	Tennis
	Tennis	Volleyball

SOUTHERN VIRGINIA COLLEGE

	Men	Women
1 College Hill Drive	Basketball	Basketball
Buena Vista, VA 24416-3038	Cross Country	Cross Country
Affiliation—NAIA	Soccer	Soccer
Nickname—Knights		Softball
Athletic Director—		Volleyball
(540) 261-8418		

SWEET BRAIR COLLEGE

	Women	
Williams Gym	Fencing	Swimming
Sweet Brair, VA 24595	Field Hockey	Tennis
Affiliation—NCAA III	Lacrosse	Volleyball
Nickname—Vixens	Soccer	
Athletic Director—		
(804) 381-6336		

UNITED STATES MARINE CORPS ACADEMY

	Men	
Marine Corps Development and	Basketball	Tennis
Education Command	Boxing	Track
Quantico, VA 22143	Cross Country	Volleyball
Nickname—Marines	Football	Wrestling
Athletic Director—	Soccer	
(703) 640-2014		

VIRGINIA, UNIVERSITY OF

PO Box 3785, University Hall	**Men**	**Women**
Charlottesville, VA 22903-0785	Baseball	Basketball
Affiliation—NCAA *I*	Basketball	Cheerleading
(I-A Football)	Cross Country	Crew
Nickname—*Cavaliers, Wahoos*	Football	Cross Country
Athletic Director—	Golf	Field Hockey
(804) 982-5000	Lacrosse	Lacrosse
	Soccer	Soccer
	Swimming	Softball
	Tennis	Swimming
	Track	Tennis
	Wrestling	Track
		Volleyball

VIRGINIA COMMONWEALTH UNIVERSITY

819 W. Franklin Street, #842003	**Men**	**Women**
Richmond, VA 23284-2003	Baseball	Basketball
Affiliation—NCAA *I*	Basketball	Cross Country
Nickname—*Rams*	Cross Country	Field Hockey
Athletic Director—	Golf	Soccer
(804) 828-1200	Soccer	Tennis
	Tennis	Track
	Track	Volleyball

VIRGINIA INTERMONT COLLEGE

PO Box 199, Moore Street	**Men**	**Women**
Bristol, VA 24203-0199	Baseball	Softball
Affiliation—NAIA *II*	Basketball	Tennis
Nickname—*Cobras*	Tennis	
Athletic Director—		
(540) 466-7910		

VIRGINIA MILITARY INSTITUTE

Main Street, Cameron Hall	Men	Women
Lexington, VA 24450	Baseball	Cross Country
Affiliation—NCAA I	Basketball	Rifle
(I-AA Football)	Cross Country	Track
Nickname—Keydets	Diving	
Athletic Director—	Fencing	
(540) 464-7251	Football	
	Golf	
	Lacrosse	
	Rifle	
	Soccer	
	Swimming	
	Tennis	
	Track	
	Wrestling	

VIRGINIA POLYTECHNIC INSTITUTE AND STATE UNIVERSITY

Jamerson Athletic Center	Men	Women
Blacksburg, VA 24061	Baseball	Basketball
Affiliation—NCAA I	Basketball	Cheerleading
(I-A Football)	Cross Country	Cross Country
Nickname—Hokies	Diving	Diving
Athletic Director—	Football	Lacrosse
(540) 231-3977	Golf	Soccer
	Soccer	Softball
	Swimming	Swimming
	Tennis	Tennis
	Track	Track
	Wrestling	Volleyball

VIRGINIA STATE UNIVERSITY

PO Box 9058	Men	Women
Petersburg, VA 23806	Baseball	Basketball
Affiliation—NCAA II	Basketball	Cheerleading
Nickname—Trojans	Cross Country	Cross Country
Athletic Director—	Football	Softball
(804) 524-6817	Golf	Tennis
	Tennis	Volleyball
	Track	

VIRGINIA UNION UNIVERSITY

1500 N. Lombardy Street	**Men**	**Women**
Richmond, VA 23220-1711	Basketball	Basketball
Affiliation—NCAA II	Cross Country	Cross Country
Nickname—Panthers	Football	Golf
Athletic Director—	Golf	Softball
(804) 321-1874	Tennis	Track
	Track	Volleyball

VIRGINIA WESLEYAN COLLEGE

Wesleyan Drive	**Men**	**Women**
Norfolk, VA 23502	Baseball	Basketball
Affiliation—NCAA III	Basketball	Cross Country
Nickname—Blue Marlins	Cross Country	Field Hockey
Athletic Director—	Golf	Lacrosse
(757) 455-3302	Lacrosse	Soccer
	Soccer	Softball
	Tennis	Tennis

WASHINGTON AND LEE UNIVERSITY

PO Box 928	**Men**	**Women**
Lexington, VA 24450-0928	Baseball	Basketball
Affiliation—NCAA III	Basketball	Cross Country
Nickname—Generals	Cross Country	Lacrosse
Athletic Director—	Football	Soccer
(540) 463-8671	Golf	Swimming
	Lacrosse	Tennis
	Soccer	Track
	Swimming	Volleyball
	Tennis	
	Track	
	Wrestling	

WILLIAM AND MARY, COLLEGE OF

	Men	Women
PO Box 399	Baseball	Basketball
Williamsburg, VA 23187-0399	Basketball	Cross Country
Affiliation—NCAA I	Cross Country	Field Hockey
(I-AA Football)	Football	Golf
Nickname—Tribe	Golf	Gymnastics
Athletic Director—	Gymnastics	Lacrosse
(757) 221-3330	Soccer	Soccer
	Swimming	Swimming
	Tennis	Tennis
	Track	Track
		Volleyball

WASHINGTON

CENTRAL WASHINGTON UNIVERSITY

	Men	Women
400 E. 8th Avenue	Baseball	Basketball
Ellensburg, WA 98926-7502	Basketball	Cheerleading
Affiliation—NAIA I, NCAA II	Cross Country	Cross Country
Nickname—Wildcats	Football	Soccer
Athletic Director—	Swimming	Softball
(509) 963-1914	Track	Swimming
	Wrestling	Track
		Volleyball

EASTERN WASHINGTON UNIVERSITY

	Men	Women
526 5th Street, Stop 66	Basketball	Basketball
Cheney, WA 99004-1619	Cross Country	Cross Country
Affiliation—NCAA I	Football	Golf
(I-AA Football)	Golf	Soccer
Nickname—Eagles	Tennis	Tennis
Athletic Director—	Track	Track
(509) 359-2461		Volleyball

EVERGREEN STATE COLLEGE

	Men	Women
College Recreation Center 210	Basketball	Soccer
Olympia, WA 98505	Soccer	Swimming
Affiliation—NAIA I, NCAA III	Swimming	Tennis
Nickname—Geoducks	Tennis	
Athletic Director—		
(360) 866-6000 ext. 6770		

GONZAGA UNIVERSITY

	Men	Women
502 E. Boone Avenue	Baseball	Basketball
Spokane, WA 99358-1774	Basketball	Cheerleading
Affiliation—NCAA *I*	Crew	Crew
Nickname—Bulldogs, Zags	Cross Country	Cross Country
Athletic Director—	Golf	Golf
(509) 323-3519	Soccer	Soccer
	Tennis	Tennis
	Track	Track

NORTHWEST COLLEGE OF THE ASSEMBLIES

	Men	Women
5520 108th Avenue NE,	Basketball	Basketball
PO Box 579	Cross Country	Cross Country
Kirkland, WA 98033-7523	Soccer	Track
Affiliation—NCCAA *I*, NAIA	Track	Volleyball
Nickname—Eagles		
Athletic Director—		
(425) 889-5275		

PACIFIC LUTHERAN UNIVERSITY

	Men	Women
12180 Park Avenue S	Baseball	Basketball
Tacoma, WA 98447	Basketball	Crew
Affiliation—NAIA, NCAA *III*	Crew	Cross Country
Nickname—Lutes	Cross Country	Golf
Athletic Director—	Football	Skiing
(253) 535-7353	Golf	Soccer
	Skiing	Softball
	Soccer	Swimming
	Swimming	Tennis
	Tennis	Track
	Track	Volleyball
	Wrestling	

PUGET SOUND, UNIVERSITY OF

1500 N. Warner Street	Men	Women
Tacoma, WA 98416	Baseball	Basketball
Affiliation—NAIA II, NCAA III	Basketball	Cheerleading
Nickname—Loggers	Crew	Crew
Athletic Director—	Cross Country	Cross Country
(253) 756-3426	Football	Golf
	Golf	Lacrosse
	Skiing	Skiing
	Soccer	Soccer
	Swimming	Softball
	Tennis	Swimming
	Track	Tennis
		Track
		Volleyball

PUGET SOUND CHRISTIAN COLLEGE

410 4th Avenue N	Men	Women
Edmonds, WA 98020-3119	Basketball	Basketball
Nickname—Anchormen	Volleyball	
Athletic Director—		
(206) 775-8686		

SAINT MARTIN'S COLLEGE

5300 Pacific Avenue SE	Men	Women
Lacey, WA 98503-7500	Baseball	Basketball
Affiliation—NCAA II, NAIA I	Basketball	Cross Country
Nickname—Saints	Cross Country	Golf
Athletic Director—	Golf	Softball
(360) 438-4372		Volleyball

SEATTLE PACIFIC UNIVERSITY

3307 3rd Avenue W	Men	Women
Seattle, WA 98119-1940	Basketball	Basketball
Affiliation—NCAA II	Crew	Crew
Nickname—Falcons	Cross Country	Cross Country
Athletic Director—	Soccer	Gymnastics
(206) 281-2175	Track	Track
		Volleyball

SEATTLE UNIVERSITY

900 Broadway,	**Men**	**Women**
Broadway and Madison	Basketball	Basketball
Seattle, WA 98122	Crew	Crew
Affiliation—NAIA II, NCAA III	Cross Country	Cross Country
Nickname—Chieftains	Golf	Skiing
Athletic Director—	Skiing	Soccer
(206) 296-5451	Soccer	Softball
	Swimming	Swimming
	Tennis	Tennis

WASHINGTON, UNIVERSITY OF

Graves Building, Box 354070	**Men**	**Women**
Seattle, WA 98195	Baseball	Basketball
Affiliation—NCAA I	Basketball	Cheerleading
(I-A Football)	Crew	Crew
Nickname—Huskies	Cross Country	Cross Country
Athletic Director—	Football	Golf
(206) 543-2210	Golf	Gymnastics
	Soccer	Soccer
	Swimming	Softball
	Tennis	Swimming
	Track	Tennis
		Track
		Volleyball

WASHINGTON STATE UNIVERSITY

PO Box 641610	**Men**	**Women**
Pullman, WA 99164-6416	Baseball	Basketball
Affiliation—NCAA I	Basketball	Cheerleading
(I-A Football)	Cross Country	Crew
Nickname—Cougars	Football	Cross Country
Athletic Director—	Golf	Golf
(509) 335-2241	Track	Soccer
		Swimming
		Tennis
		Track
		Volleyball

WESTERN WASHINGTON UNIVERSITY

516 High Street	**Men**	**Women**
Bellingham, WA 98225-5946	Basketball	Basketball
Affiliation—NCAA II	Crew	Crew
Nickname—Vikings	Cross Country	Cross Country
Athletic Director—	Football	Golf
(360) 650-3109	Golf	Soccer
	Soccer	Softball
	Track	Track
		Volleyball

WHITMAN COLLEGE

345 Boyer Avenue	**Men**	**Women**
Walla Walla, WA 99362	Baseball	Basketball
Affiliation—NAIA II, NCAA III	Basketball	Cross Country
Nickname—Missionaries	Cross Country	Golf
Athletic Director—	Golf	Lacrosse
(509) 527-5288	Lacrosse	Skiing
	Skiing	Soccer
	Soccer	Swimming
	Swimming	Tennis
	Tennis	Track
	Track	Volleyball

WHITWORTH COLLEGE

300 W. Hawthorne Road	**Men**	**Women**
Spokane, WA 99251-2515	Baseball	Basketball
Affiliation—NCAA III	Basketball	Cross Country
Nickname—Pirates, Bucs	Cross Country	Soccer
Athletic Director—	Football	Softball
(509) 777-4392	Soccer	Swimming
	Swimming	Tennis
	Tennis	Track
	Track	Volleyball

WEST VIRGINIA

ALDERSON-BROADDUS COLLEGE

Campus Box 306	**Men**	**Women**
Philippi, WV 25416	Baseball	Basketball
Affiliation—NCAA II	Basketball	Cross Country
Nickname—Battlers	Cross Country	Softball
Athletic Director—	Soccer	Volleyball
(304) 457-6266		

BETHANY COLLEGE

Hummel Fieldhouse	**Men**	**Women**
Bethany, WV 26032	Baseball	Basketball
Affiliation—NCAA III	Basketball	Cross Country
Nickname—Bison	Cross Country	Golf
Athletic Director—	Football	Soccer
(304) 829-7251	Golf	Softball
	Soccer	Swimming
	Swimming	Tennis
	Tennis	Track
	Track	Volleyball

BLUEFIELD STATE COLLEGE

219 Rock Street	**Men**	**Women**
Bluefield, WV 24701-2100	Baseball	Basketball
Affiliation—NCAA II	Basketball	Cheerleading
Nickname—Big Blues	Cross Country	Cross Country
Athletic Director—	Golf	Softball
(304) 327-4208	Tennis	Tennis

CHARLESTON, UNIVERSITY OF

2300 MacCorkle Avenue SE	**Men**	**Women**
Charleston, WV 25304-1045	Baseball	Basketball
Affiliation—NCAA II	Basketball	Crew
Nickname—Golden Eagles	Crew	Soccer
Athletic Director—	Golf	Softball
(304) 357-4823	Soccer	Swimming
	Swimming	Tennis
	Tennis	Volleyball

CONCORD COLLEGE

	Men	Women
Vermillion Street	Baseball	Basketball
Athens, WV 24712	Basketball	Cheerleading
Affiliation—NAIA, NCAA II	Cross Country	Cross Country
Nickname—Mountain Lions	Football	Golf
Athletic Director—	Golf	Softball
(304) 384-5347	Tennis	Swimming
	Track	Tennis
		Volleyball

DAVID & ELKINS COLLEGE

	Men	Women
100 Campus Drive	Baseball	Basketball
Elkins, WV 26241-3971	Basketball	Cross Country
Affiliation—NCAA II	Cross Country	Field Hockey
Nickname—Senators	Golf	Softball
Athletic Director—	Soccer	Tennis
(304) 637-1251	Tennis	

FAIRMONT STATE COLLEGE

	Men	Women
1201 Locust Avenue	Baseball	Basketball
Fairmont, WV 26554-2451	Basketball	Golf
Affiliation—NCAA II	Football	Softball
Nickname—Falcons	Golf	Swimming
Athletic Director—	Swimming	Tennis
(304) 367-4220	Tennis	Volleyball

GLENVILLE STATE COLLEGE

	Men	Women
200 High Street	Basketball	Basketball
Glenville, WV 26351-1200	Cross Country	Cross Country
Affiliation—NCAA II	Football	Track
Nickname—Pioneers	Golf	Volleyball
Athletic Director—	Track	
(304) 462-4102		

MARSHALL UNIVERSITY

	Men	Women
PO Box 1360	Baseball	Basketball
Huntington, WV 25715-1360	Basketball	Cheerleading
Affiliation—NCAA I	Cross Country	Cross Country
Nickname—Thundering Herd	Football	Soccer
Athletic Director—	Golf	Softball
(304) 696-2300	Soccer	Tennis
	Track	Track
		Volleyball

OHIO VALLEY COLLEGE

	Men	Women
4501 College Parkway	Baseball	Basketball
Parkersburg, WV 26101-9459	Basketball	Cross Country
Affiliation—NAIA I, NCAA II	Cross Country	Softball
Nickname—Fighting Scots	Golf	Volleyball
Athletic Director—	Soccer	
(304) 485-7384 c 148		

SALEM-TEIKYO UNIVERSITY

	Men	Women
Main Street	Baseball	Basketball
Salem, WV 26426	Basketball	Cheerleading
Affiliation—NCAA II	Golf	Soccer
Nickname—Tigers	Soccer	Softball
Athletic Director—	Swimming	Swimming
(304) 782-5271	Tennis	Tennis
	Water Polo	Volleyball

SHEPHERD COLLEGE

	Men	Women
James Butcher Center	Baseball	Basketball
Shepherdstown, WV 25443	Basketball	Cheerleading
Affiliation—NCAA II	Cross Country	Cross Country
Nickname—Rams	Football	Softball
Athletic Director—	Golf	Tennis
(304) 876-5481	Soccer	Volleyball
	Tennis	

WEST LIBERTY STATE COLLEGE

Bartell Field House	**Men**	**Women**
West Liberty, WV 26074	Baseball	Basketball
Affiliation—NCAA II	Basketball	Cross Country
Nickname—Hilltoppers	Cross Country	Golf
Athletic Director—	Football	Softball
(304) 336-8200	Golf	Tennis
	Tennis	Track
	Track	Volleyball
	Wrestling	

WEST VIRGINIA STATE COLLEGE

Campus Box 181	**Men**	**Women**
Institute, WV 25112	Baseball	Basketball
Affiliation—NCAA II	Basketball	Cheerleading
Nickname—Yellow Jackets	Football	Softball
Athletic Director—	Tennis	Tennis
(304) 766-3165	Track	Track
		Volleyball

WEST VIRGINIA UNIVERSITY

PO Box 0877	**Men**	**Women**
Morgantown, WV 26507-0877	Baseball	Basketball
Affiliation—NCAA I	Basketball	Cheerleading
(I-A Football)	Cross Country	Crew
Nickname—Mountaineers	Football	Cross Country
Athletic Director—	Rifle	Gymnastics
(304) 293-5621	Soccer	Rifle
	Swimming	Swimming
	Tennis	Tennis
	Track	Track
	Wrestling	Volleyball

WEST VIRGINIA UNIVERSITY INSTITUTE OF TECHNOLOGY

Route 61	**Men**	**Women**
Montgomery, WV 25136	Baseball	Basketball
Affiliation—NCAA II	Basketball	Softball
Nickname—Golden Bears	Football	Tennis
Athletic Director—	Golf	Volleyball
(304) 442-3121	Tennis	

WEST VIRGINIA WESLEYAN COLLEGE

College Avenue	**Men**	**Women**
Buckhannon, WV 26201	Baseball	Basketball
Affiliation—NCAA *II*	Basketball	Cross Country
Nickname—Bobcats	Cross Country	Soccer
Athletic Director—	Football	Softball
(304) 473-8098	Golf	Swimming
	Lacrosse	Tennis
	Soccer	Track
	Swimming	Volleyball
	Tennis	
	Track	

WHEELING JESUIT UNIVERSITY

315 Washington Avenue	**Men**	**Women**
Wheeling, WV 26003-5232	Basketball	Basketball
Affiliation—NCAA *II*	Cross Country	Cheerleading
Nickname—Cardinals	Golf	Cross Country
Athletic Director—	Soccer	Soccer
(304) 243-2365	Swimming	Swimming
	Track	Track
	Volleyball	Volleyball

WISCONSIN

BELOIT COLLEGE

700 College Street	**Men**	**Women**
Beloit, WI 53511-5509	Baseball	Basketball
Affiliation—NCAA *III*	Basketball	Cross Country
Nickname—Buccaneers	Cross Country	Golf
Athletic Director—	Football	Soccer
(608) 363-2234	Golf	Softball
	Soccer	Swimming
	Swimming	Tennis
	Tennis	Track
	Track	Volleyball

CARDINAL STRITCH UNIVERSITY

6801 N. Yates Road	**Men**	**Women**
Milwaukee, WI 53217-3945	Baseball	Basketball
Affiliation—NAIA II	Basketball	Cross Country
Nickname—Crusaders	Cross Country	Soccer
Athletic Director—	Soccer	Softball
(414) 410-4121		Volleyball

CARROLL COLLEGE

100 N. East Avenue	**Men**	**Women**
Waukesha, WI 53186-3103	Baseball	Basketball
Affiliation—NCAA III	Basketball	Cross Country
Nickname—Pioneers	Cross Country	Golf
Athletic Director—	Football	Soccer
(414) 524-7246	Golf	Softball
	Soccer	Swimming
	Swimming	Tennis
	Tennis	Track
	Track	Volleyball
	Wrestling	

CARTHAGE COLLEGE

2001 Alford Park Drive	**Men**	**Women**
Kenosha, WI 53140-1929	Baseball	Basketball
Affiliation—NCAA II	Basketball	Cross Country
Nickname—Redmen	Cross Country	Golf
Athletic Director—	Football	Soccer
(414) 551-5942	Golf	Softball
	Soccer	Swimming
	Swimming	Tennis
	Tennis	Track
	Track	Volleyball

CONCORDIA UNIVERSITY

12800 N. Lake Shore Drive	**Men**	**Women**
Mequon, WI 53097-2418	Baseball	Basketball
Affiliation—NCAA III	Basketball	Cheerleading
Nickname—Falcons	Cross Country	Cross Country
Athletic Director—	Football	Golf
(414) 243-4385	Golf	Soccer
	Soccer	Softball
	Tennis	Tennis
	Track	Track
	Wrestling	Volleyball

EDGEWOOD COLLEGE

	Men	Women
855 Woodrow Street	Baseball	Basketball
Madison, WI 53711-1958	Basketball	Cheerleading
Affiliation—NCAA III	Cheerleading	Cross Country
Nickname—Eagles	Golf	Golf
Athletic Director—	Soccer	Soccer
(608) 663-3249	Tennis	Softball
		Tennis
		Volleyball

IMMANUEL LUTHERAN COLLEGE

	Men	Women
W. Grover Road	Basketball	Basketball
Eau Claire, WI 54701		
Nickname—Knights		
Athletic Director—		
(715) 836-6625		

LAKELAND COLLEGE

	Men	Women
PO Box 359	Baseball	Basketball
Sheboygan, WI 53082-0359	Basketball	Cheerleading
Affiliation—NCAA III	Cross Country	Cross Country
Nickname—Muskies	Football	Golf
Athletic Director—	Golf	Soccer
(920) 565-1240	Ice Hockey	Softball
	Soccer	Tennis
	Tennis	Volleyball
	Volleyball	
	Wrestling	

LAWRENCE UNIVERSITY

	Men	Women
PO Box 599	Baseball	Basketball
Appleton, WI 54912-0599	Basketball	Cross Country
Affiliation—NCAA III	Cross Country	Fencing
Nickname—Vikings	Fencing	Soccer
Athletic Director—	Football	Softball
(920) 832-6513	Golf	Swimming
	Ice Hockey	Tennis
	Soccer	Track
	Swimming	Volleyball
	Tennis	
	Track	
	Wrestling	

MADISON COLLEGE

31 S. Henry Street	**Men**	**Women**
Madison, WI 53703-3110	Baseball	Basketball
Nickname—Storm	Basketball	Softball
Athletic Director—	Football	Volleyball
(608) 251-6220		

MARANATHA BAPTIST BIBLE

745 W. Main Street	**Men**	**Women**
Watertown, WI 53094-7638	Baseball	Basketball
Affiliation—NCCAA II, NCAA III	Basketball	Cross Country
Nickname—Crusaders	Football	Soccer
Athletic Director—	Soccer	Softball
(920) 261-9300 ext. 350	Wrestling	Volleyball

MARIAN COLLEGE OF FOND DU LAC

45 S. National Avenue	**Men**	**Women**
Fond du Lac, WI 54935-4621	Baseball	Basketball
Affiliation—NCAA III	Basketball	Golf
Nickname—Sabres	Golf	Soccer
Athletic Director—	Ice Hockey	Softball
(920) 923-7625	Soccer	Tennis
	Tennis	Volleyball

MARQUETTE UNIVERSITY

1212 W. Wisconsin Avenue,	**Men**	**Women**
PO Box 1881	Basketball	Basketball
Milwaukee, WI 53233-2225	Cross Country	Cross Country
Affiliation—NCAA I	Golf	Soccer
Nickname—Golden Eagles	Soccer	Tennis
Athletic Director—	Tennis	Track
(414) 288-5249	Track	Volleyball
	Wrestling	

MILWAUKEE SCHOOL OF ENGINEERING

1025 N. Broadway	**Men**	**Women**
Milwaukee, WI 53202-3109	Baseball	Basketball
Affiliation—NCAA III	Basketball	Cross Country
Nickname—Raiders	Cross County	Soccer
Athletic Director—	Golf	Softball
(414) 277-7230	Ice Hockey	Tennis
	Soccer	Volleyball
	Tennis	
	Wrestling	

MOUNT MARY COLLEGE

2900 N. Menomonee River	**Women**	
Parkway	Soccer	Volleyball
Milwaukee, WI 53222	Tennis	
Affiliation—Independent		
Nickname—Crusaders		
Athletic Director—		
(414) 256-1211		

MOUNT SENARIO COLLEGE

1500 College Avenue W	**Men**	**Women**
Ladysmith, WI 54848-2128	Baseball	Basketball
Affiliation—NAIA II	Basketball	Cross Country
Nickname—Fighting Saints	Football	Soccer
Athletic Director—	Soccer	Softball
(715) 532-5511	Track	Track
		Volleyball

NORTHLAND BAPTIST BIBLE

W10085 Pike Plains Road	**Men**	**Women**
Dunbar, WI 54119-9285	Basketball	Basketball
Affiliation—NCCAA II	Cross Country	Cross Country
Nickname—Pioneers	Golf	Volleyball
Athletic Director—	Ice Hockey	
(715) 324-5245 ext. 6999	Soccer	
	Volleyball	

NORTHLAND COLLEGE

1411 Ellis Avenue	**Men**	**Women**
Ashland, WI 54806-3925	Basketball	Basketball
Affiliation—NAIA II	Ice Hockey	Soccer
Nickname—Lumberjacks	Soccer	Volleyball
Athletic Director—		
(715) 682-1245		

RIPON COLLEGE

| *300 Seward Street*
Ripon, WI 54971
Affiliation—NCAA III
Nickname—Red Hawks
Athletic Director—
(920) 748-8774 | **Men**
Baseball
Basketball
Cross Country
Football
Golf
Soccer
Swimming
Tennis
Track | **Women**
Basketball
Cross Country
Golf
Soccer
Softball
Swimming
Tennis
Track
Volleyball |

SAINT NORBERT COLLEGE

| *100 Grant Street*
De Pere, WI 54115-2002
Affiliation—NCAA III
Nickname—Green Knights
Athletic Director—
(920) 403-3530 | **Men**
Baseball
Basketball
Cross Country
Golf
Ice Hockey
Soccer
Tennis
Track | **Women**
Basketball
Cross Country
Golf
Soccer
Softball
Tennis
Track
Volleyball |

VITERBO COLLEGE

| *815 9th Street S*
La Crosse, WI 54601-8802
Affiliation—NAIA II
Nickname—V-Hawks
Athletic Director—
(608) 796-3811 | **Men**
Baseball
Basketball
Soccer | **Women**
Basketball
Soccer
Softball
Volleyball |

WISCONSIN, UNIVERSITY OF, EAU CLAIRE

McPhee PE Center	**Men**	**Women**
Eau Claire, WI 54702	Basketball	Basketball
Affiliation—NCAA III	Cross Country	Cross Country
Nickname—Bluegolds	Diving	Diving
Athletic Director—	Football	Golf
(715) 836-3159	Golf	Gymnastics
	Ice Hockey	Soccer
	Swimming	Softball
	Tennis	Swimming
	Track	Tennis
	Wrestling	Track
		Volleyball

WISCONSIN, UNIVERSITY OF, GREEN BAY

2420 Nicolet Drive,	**Men**	**Women**
Phoenix Sports Center	Basketball	Basketball
Green Bay, WI 54311-7003	Cross Country	Cheerleading
Affiliation—NCAA I	Diving	Cross Country
Nickname—Phoenix	Golf	Diving
Athletic Director—	Skiing	Skiing
(920) 469-2049	Soccer	Soccer
	Swimming	Softball
	Tennis	Swimming
		Tennis
		Volleyball

WISCONSIN, UNIVERSITY OF, LA CROSSE

Mitchell Hall	**Men**	**Women**
La Crosse, WI 54601	Baseball	Basketball
Affiliation—NCAA III	Basketball	Cross Country
Nickname—Eagles	Cross Country	Diving
Athletic Director—	Diving	Gymnastics
(608) 785-8616	Football	Soccer
	Swimming	Softball
	Tennis	Swimming
	Track	Tennis
	Wrestling	Track
		Volleyball

WISCONSIN, UNIVERSITY OF, MADISON

1440 Monroe Street	Men	Women
Madison, WI 53711-2051	Basketball	Basketball
Affiliation—NCAA I	Crew	Crew
(I-A Football)	Cross Country	Cross Country
Nickname—Badgers	Diving	Diving
Athletic Director—	Football	Golf
(608) 262-5068	Golf	Soccer
	Ice Hockey	Softball
	Soccer	Swimming
	Swimming	Tennis
	Tennis	Track
	Track	Volleyball
	Wrestling	

WISCONSIN, UNIVERSITY OF, MILWAUKEE

PO Box 413,	Men	Women
3415 N. Downer Avenue	Baseball	Basketball
Milwaukee, WI 53201-0413	Basketball	Cheerleading
Affiliation—NCAA I	Cross Country	Cross Country
Nickname—Panthers	Soccer	Soccer
Athletic Director—	Swimming	Swimming
(414) 229-5669	Track	Tennis
		Track
		Volleyball

WISCONSIN, UNIVERSITY OF, OSHKOSH

800 Algoma Boulevard	Men	Women
Oshkosh, WI 54901-3551	Baseball	Basketball
Affiliation—NCAA III	Basketball	Cross Country
Nickname—Titans	Cross Country	Golf
Athletic Director—	Football	Gymnastics
(920) 424-1034	Soccer	Soccer
	Swimming	Softball
	Tennis	Swimming
	Track	Tennis
		Track
		Volleyball

WISCONSIN, UNIVERSITY OF, PARKSIDE

PO Box 2000, 900 Wood Road	**Men**	**Women**
Kenosha, WI 53141-2000	Baseball	Basketball
*Affiliation—*NCAA *II*	Basketball	Cross Country
Nickname—Rangers	Cross Country	Soccer
Athletic Director—	Golf	Softball
(414) 595-2591	Soccer	Track
	Track	Volleyball
	Wrestling	

WISCONSIN, UNIVERSITY OF, PLATTEVILLE

1 University Plaza	**Men**	**Women**
Platteville, WI 53818-3001	Baseball	Basketball
*Affiliation—*NCAA *III*	Basketball	Cross Country
Nickname—Pioneers	Cross Country	Soccer
Athletic Director—	Football	Softball
(608) 342-1567	Soccer	Track
	Track	Volleyball
	Wrestling	

WISCONSIN, UNIVERSITY OF, RIVER FALLS

410 S. 3rd Street	**Men**	**Women**
River Falls, WI 54002-5013	Baseball	Basketball
*Affiliation—*NCAA *III*	Basketball	Cross Country
Nickname—Falcons	Cross Country	Gymnastics
Athletic Director—	Football	Soccer
(715) 425-3705	Ice Hockey	Softball
	Swimming	Swimming
	Wrestling	Tennis
		Track
		Volleyball

WISCONSIN, UNIVERSITY OF, STEVENS POINT

4th Avenue	**Men**	**Women**
Stevens Point, WI 54481	Baseball	Basketball
*Affiliation—*NCAA *III*	Basketball	Cross Country
Nickname—Pointers	Cross Country	Golf
Athletic Director—	Football	Soccer
(715) 346-3888	Ice Hockey	Softball
	Swimming	Swimming
	Track	Tennis
	Wrestling	Track
		Volleyball

WISCONSIN, UNIVERSITY OF, STOUT

Johnson Fieldhouse	**Men**	**Women**
Menomonie, WI 54751	Baseball	Basketball
Affiliation—NCAA III	Basketball	Cross Country
Nickname—Blue Devils	Cross Country	Gymnastics
Athletic Director—	Football	Soccer
(715) 232-2161	Ice Hockey	Softball
	Track	Tennis
		Track
		Volleyball

WISCONSIN, UNIVERSITY OF, SUPERIOR

1800 Grand Avenue	**Men**	**Women**
Superior, WI 54880-2873	Baseball	Basketball
Affiliation—NCAA III	Basketball	Cheerleading
Nickname—Yellowjackets	Cross Country	Cross Country
Athletic Director—	Ice Hockey	Golf
(715) 394-8193	Soccer	Ice Hockey
	Track	Soccer
		Softball

WISCONSIN, UNIVERSITY OF, WHITEWATER

800 W. Main Street	**Men**	**Women**
Whitewater, WI 53190-1705	Baseball	Basketball
Affiliation—NCAA III	Basketball	Cross Country
Nickname—Warhawks	Cross Country	Golf
Athletic Director—Men	Football	Gymnastics
(414) 472-1867	Soccer	Soccer
Athletic Director—Women	Swimming	Softball
(414) 472-1649	Tennis	Swimming
	Track	Tennis
	Wrestling	Track
		Volleyball

WISCONSIN LUTHERAN COLLEGE

8800 W. *Bluemound Road*	**Men**	**Women**
Milwaukee, WI 53226-4626	Baseball	Basketball
Affiliation—NCAA III	Basketball	Cross Country
Nickname—*Warriors*	Cross Country	Fencing
	Football	Golf
	Golf	Soccer
	Soccer	Softball
	Track	Tennis
		Track
		Volleyball

WYOMING

WYOMING, UNIVERSITY OF

PO Box 3414,	**Men**	**Women**
University Station	Basketball	Basketball
Laramie, WY 82071-3414	Cross Country	Cross Country
Affiliation—NCAA I	Football	Golf
(I-A Football)	Golf	Soccer
Nickname—*Cowboys*	Swimming	Swimming
Athletic Director—	Track	Tennis
(307) 766-2292	Wrestling	Track
		Volleyball

PUERTO RICO

CATHOLIC UNIVERSITY

Ave Las America	**Men**	
Ponce, PR 00731-8400	Basketball	Tennis
Nickname—*Pioneers*	Cross Country	Track
Athletic Director—	Soccer	Volleyball
(787) 844-4150 ext. 195	Swimming	

INTER-AMERICAN UNIVERSITY OF PUERTO RICO, SAN GERMAN

Luna, San German, PR 00683	**Men**	**Women**
*Affiliation—*NCAA *III*	Baseball	Basketball
Nickname—Tigers	Basketball	Cross Country
Athletic Director—	Cross Country	Track
(787) 892-5700	Soccer	Tennis
	Softball	Volleyball
	Tennis	
	Track	
	Wrestling	

PUERTO RICO, UNIVERSITY OF, MAYAGUEZ

Rafael Mangual Coliseum	**Men**	**Women**
Mayaguez, PR 00680	Baseball	Basketball
Nickname—Bulldogs	Basketball	Cross Country
Athletic Director—	Cross Country	Judo
(787) 265-3866	Judo	Softball
	Soccer	Swimming
	Swimming	Tennis
	Tennis	Track
	Track	Volleyball
	Volleyball	
	Wrestling	

PUERTO RICO, UNIVERSITY OF

PO Box 23311,	**Men**	**Women**
University Station	Basketball	Basketball
Rio Piedras, PR 00931-3311	Cross Country	Cross Country
*Affiliation—*NCAA	Judo	Judo
Nickname—Gallitos	Soccer	Softball
Athletic Director—	Swimming	Swimming
(787) 763-3985	Tennis	Tennis
	Track	Track
	Volleyball	Volleyball
	Water Polo	
	Wrestling	

COMM. LOG
Pg. 37 'THANKYOU'
Pg 41
P-48 other # Recruits?
"special talent" PAGE 50
PAGE 52 AWARD Letter D-3
7th. tender D 1/2

Pg 67 D-3
Pg 73/75